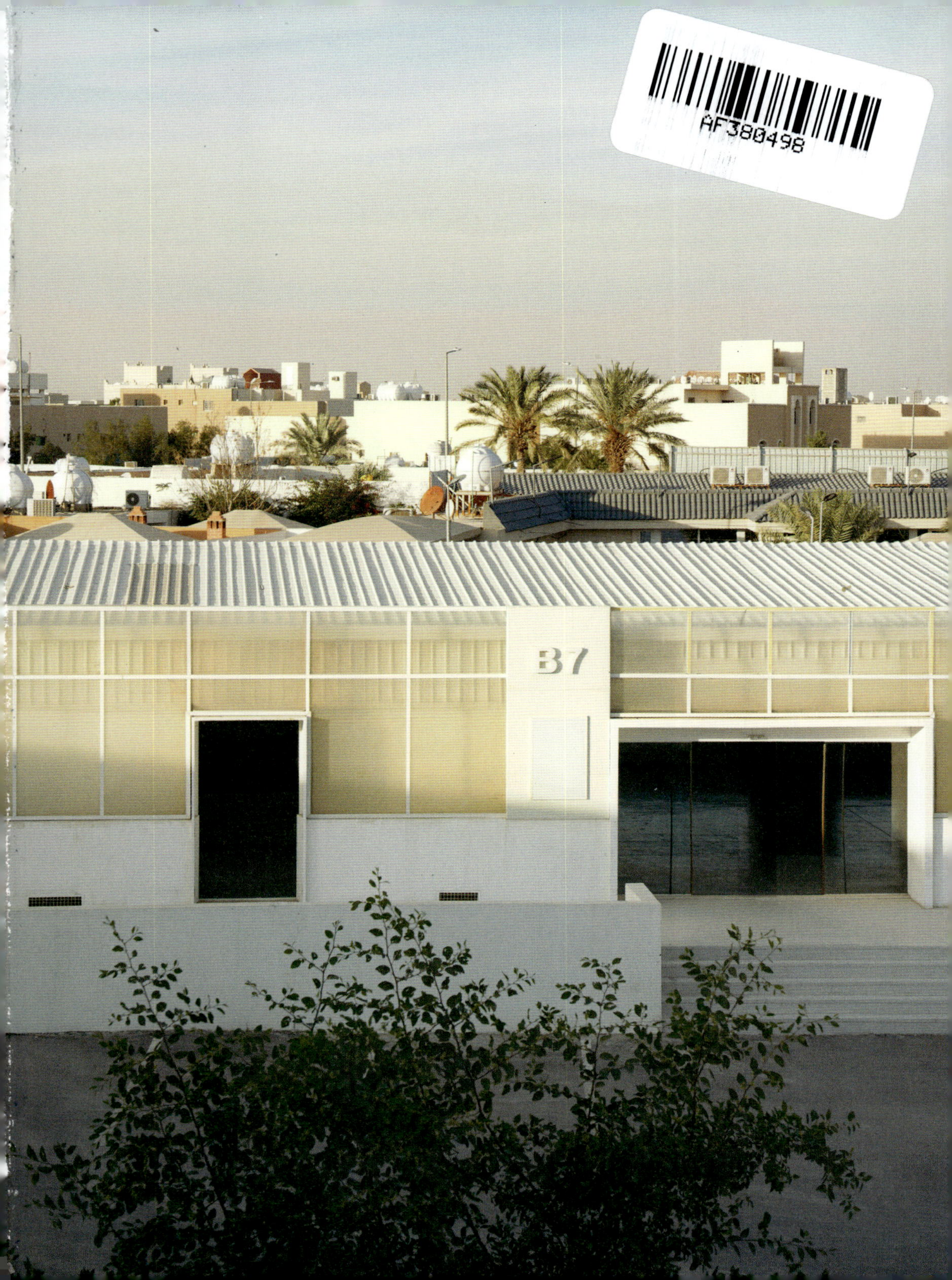

B7

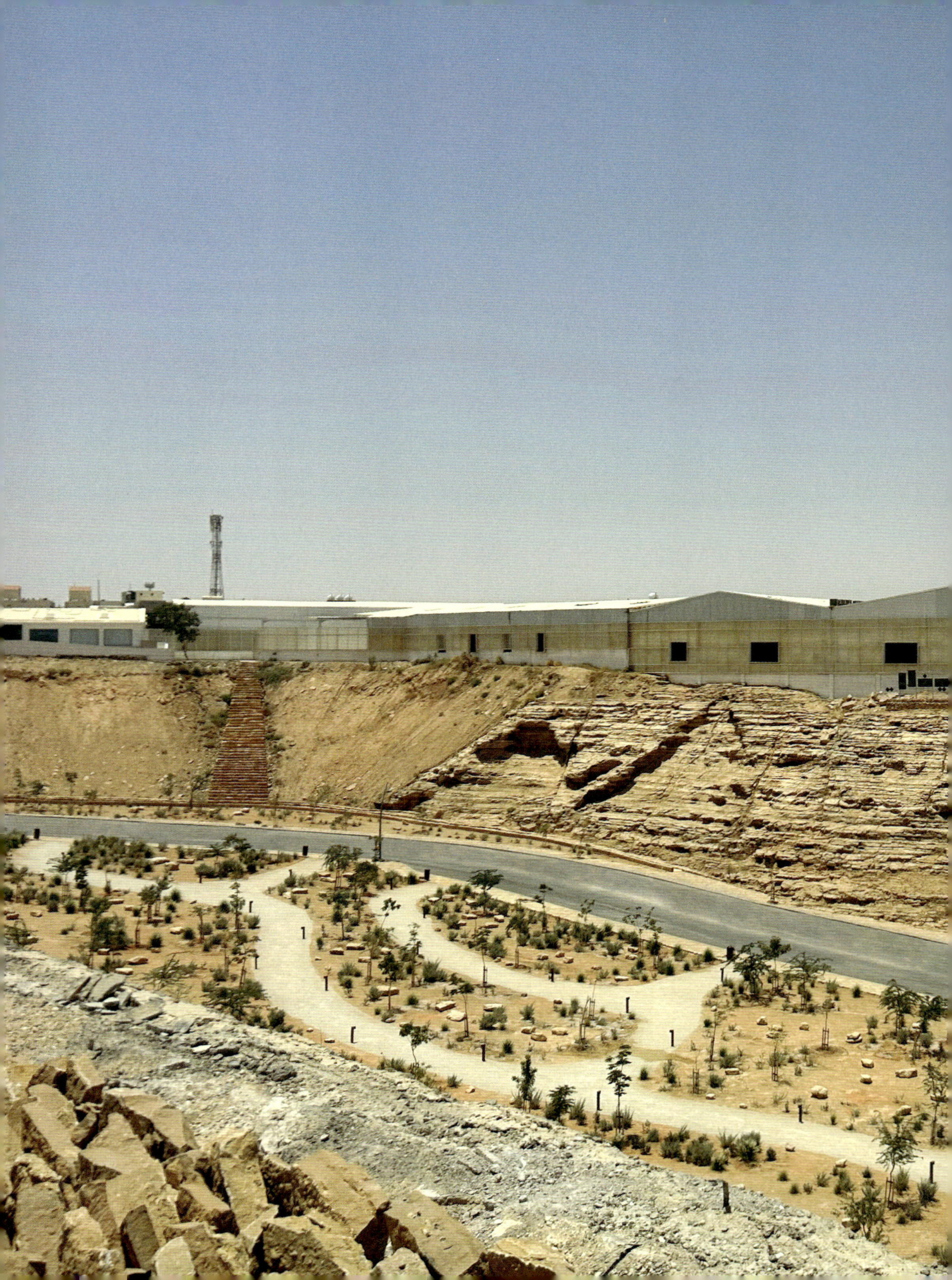

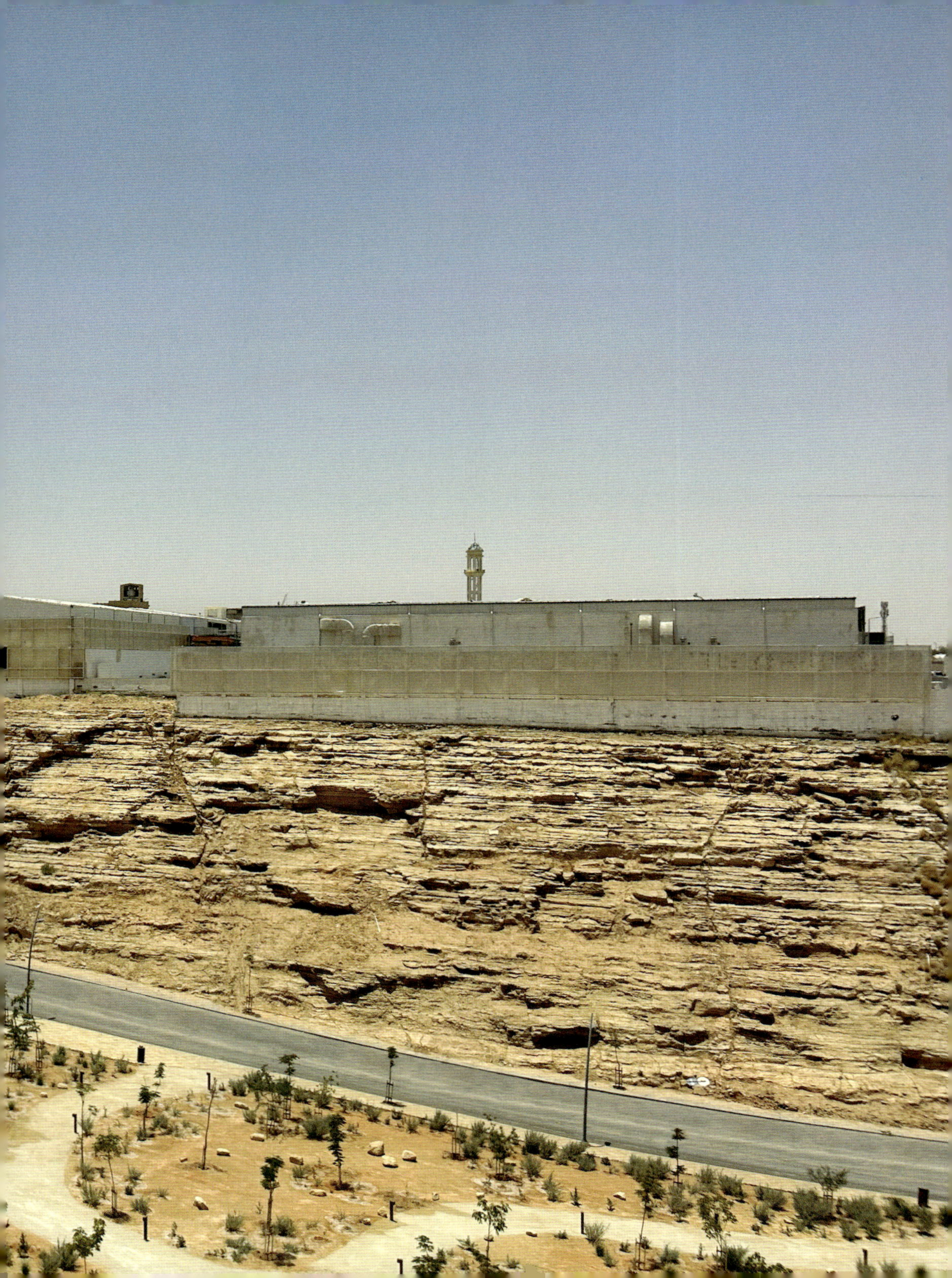

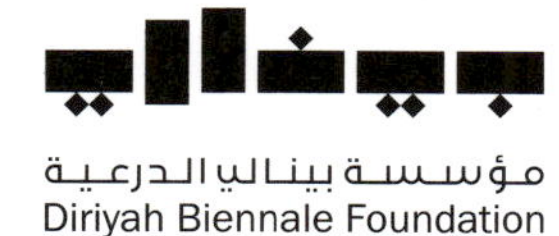

ما بَعد الغيث
AFTER RAIN

Diriyah
Contemporary Art
Biennale 2024

بينالي الدرعية
للفن المعاصر
٢٠٢٤

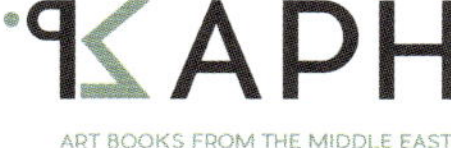

After Rain
Diriyah Contemporary Art Biennale 2024
20 February – 24 May 2024

JAX District
Diriyah, Riyadh
Saudi Arabia

Artistic Director
Ute Meta Bauer

Co-curators
Rose Lejeune
Wejdan Reda
Anca Rujoiu
Ana Salazar Herrera

Adjunct Curator
Rahul Gudipudi

CONTENTS

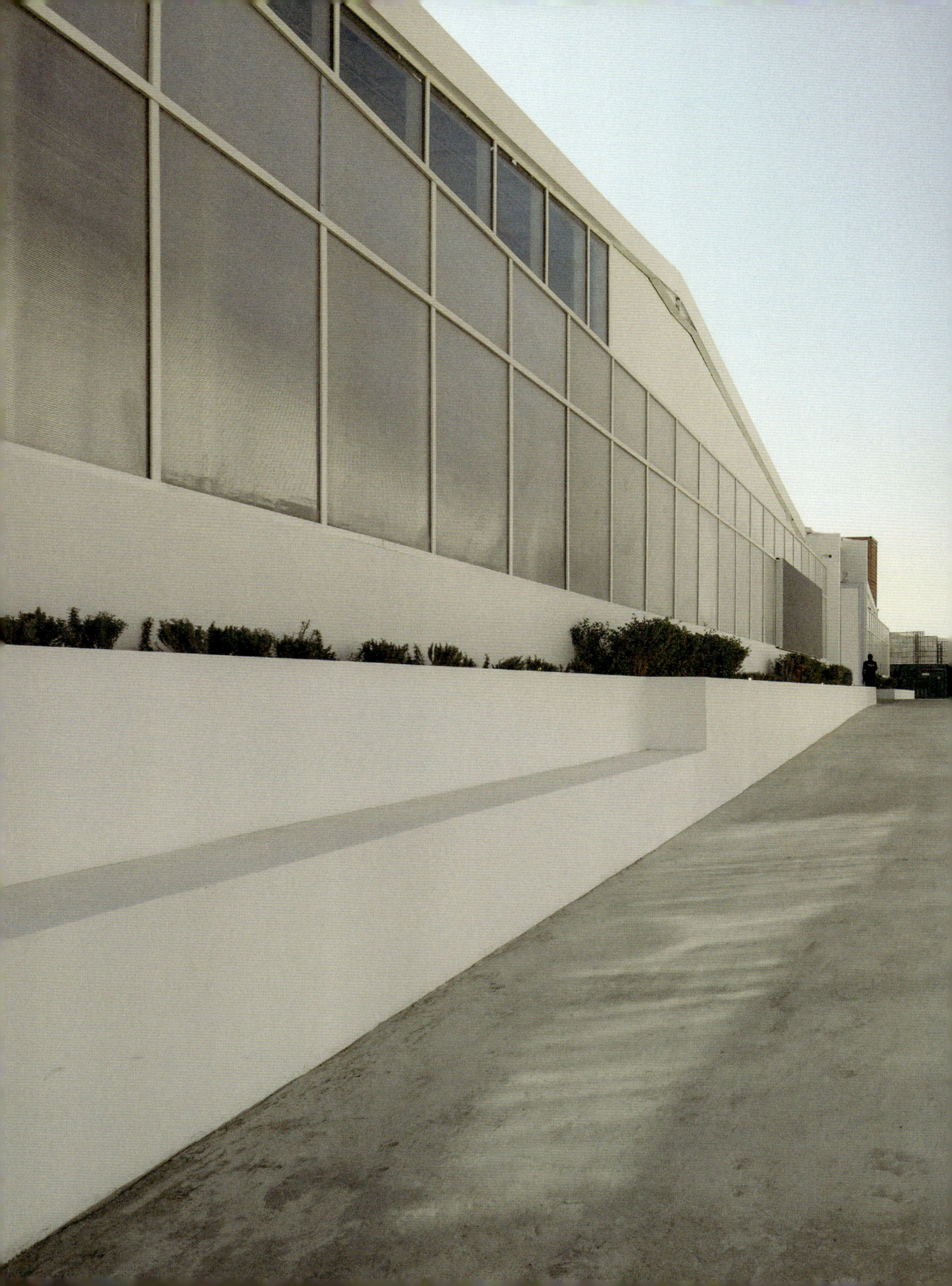

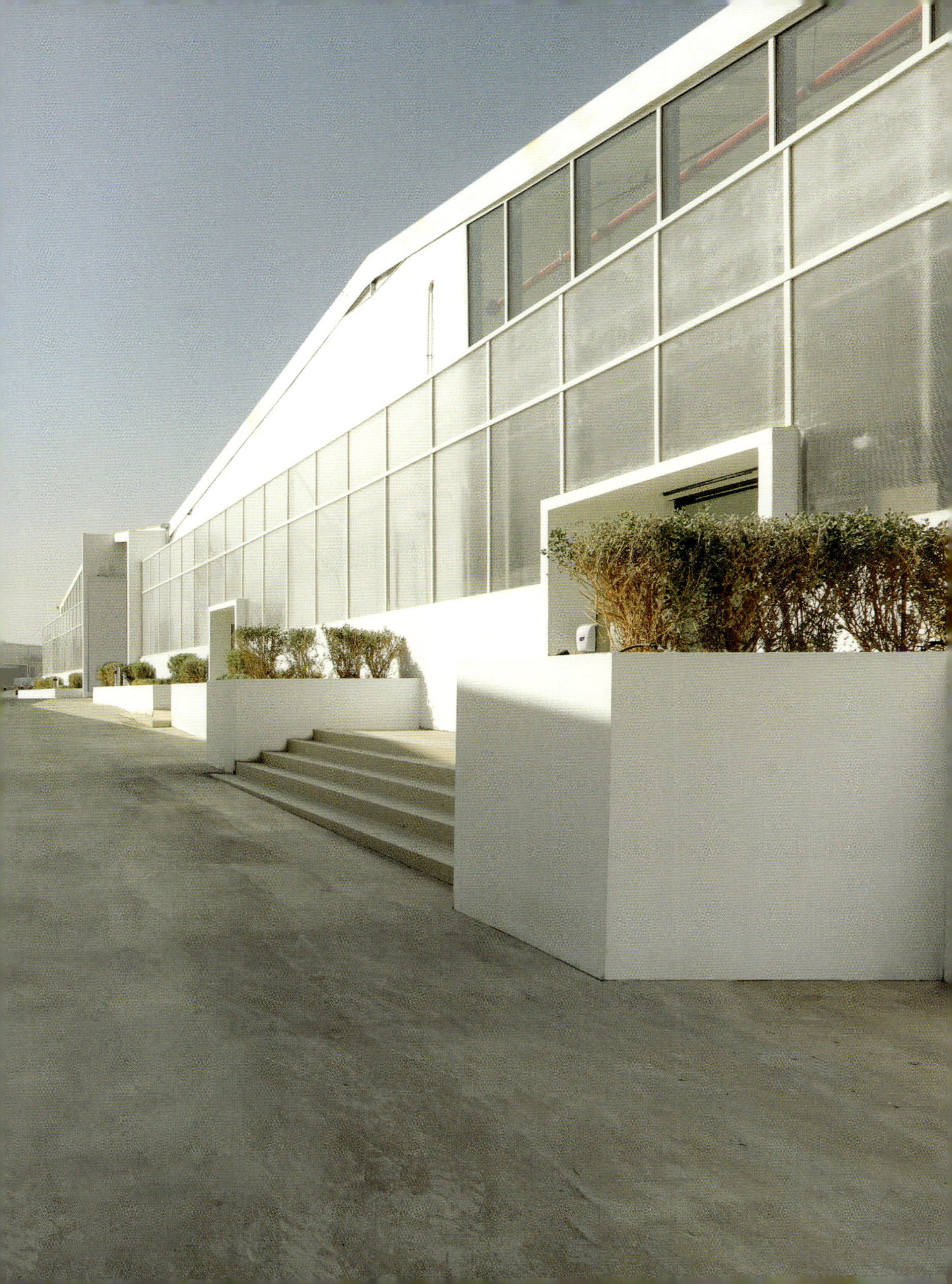

FOREWORD

After Rain, the second edition of the Diriyah Contemporary Art Biennale, is a testament to the energy and vitality that are shaping Saudi Arabia's cultural landscape today. This exhibition brings together a range of voices in a dynamic framework defined by Artistic Director Ute Meta Bauer, and it affirms the crucial role that contemporary art plays in our cultural life.

Organized by the Diriyah Biennale Foundation, under the stewardship of the Ministry of Culture, *After Rain* continues the journey we began with the first edition of the Biennale in 2021, curated by Philip Tinari. It builds on this earlier edition, and it expresses our commitment to fostering dialogue among artists and the public, in Saudi Arabia and beyond. Together with a network of artists, curators, educators, writers, and institutions who share our belief in the power of art to open minds and create connections, we have defined a global platform for exchange that is continuously expanding.

The title of this Biennale, *After Rain*, refers to growth, the flourishing of life, and new beginnings. It encapsulates the exciting period of transformation that we are experiencing in Saudi Arabia. The Biennale makes a major contribution toward defining Saudi Arabia's position in discussions on contemporary art taking place around the world, and it gives Saudi artists a world-class forum for encounters with their peers and with local and global audiences.

The many stories included in this edition of the Biennale unfold in a setting that is itself undergoing an exhilarating transformation: the JAX District in Diriyah, in the historic town just outside Riyadh that is home to the UNESCO World Heritage Site of At-Turaif. Diriyah's combination of heritage and modernity speaks to our work to preserve our rich cultural history while embracing the future.

I extend my gratitude to all the artists, galleries, institutions, and collaborators who have generously contributed their work and shared their knowledge for this Biennale. My deepest thanks go to the Ministry of Culture, led by His Highness Prince Badr bin Abdullah bin Farhan Al Saud, for his unwavering support and leadership of the Diriyah Biennale Foundation's work. I invite you to explore the multiple perspectives included in *After Rain*, and to join us in a conversation on art and culture that will only become more vibrant and inspiring.

H.E. Mr. Rakan Altouq
Assistant Minister of Culture and Vice Chairman of the
Diriyah Biennale Foundation Board of Trustees

FOREWORD

The Diriyah Biennale Foundation was founded in 2020 with a clear mission: to create a platform that would shape the future of the arts in Saudi Arabia, by putting artists at the core of the Kingdom's transformation and by growing our country's voice on the international cultural scene.

We hardly anticipated just how quickly this ambitious idea could become reality.

It fills me with pride to see what we have achieved in only a few years, inspired by the Vision 2030 program of His Royal Highness the Crown Prince, and under the leadership of the Chair of the Board of Trustees of our Foundation, His Highness Prince Badr bin Abdullah bin Farhan Al Saud, Minister of Culture of Saudi Arabia.

With this 2024 edition of the Diriyah Contemporary Art Biennale, we expect to pass a total of 1,000,000 visitors to the events we have produced so far, including the Biennale's inaugural edition in 2022 as well as the first Islamic Arts Biennale in 2023. It is a number that exceeds any targets we could have dreamed of.

The people that have flocked to our events come from all over the world: both young and old, tourists and locals, arts professionals and people who had never visited a biennale before. Almost two-thirds of Saudi Arabia's population is under thirty years old, and it has been incredible to witness the excitement that our program has generated. To date, more than 10,000 children and 30,000 adults have taken part in our talks, classes, workshops, and experiences. I have witnessed firsthand the way the arts can create common ground for people of all ages and backgrounds.

I am delighted that Ute Meta Bauer, Founding Director of the NTU Centre for Contemporary Art Singapore and Professor in the School of Art, Design and Media at Nanyang Technological University, came on board as Artistic Director of the 2024 edition of the Diriyah Contemporary Art Biennale. The world-renowned educator and curator of contemporary art has explored new exhibition formats and helped us build on the success of our inaugural edition.

From February 20 to May 24, 2024, the historic city of Diriyah—located just outside Riyadh and home to the UNESCO World Heritage Site of At-Turaif—once again welcomes the public to an expansive display within the JAX District, a repurposed industrial area. With the input of Co-curators Rose Lejeune, Wejdan Reda, Anca Rujoiu, and Ana Salazar Herrera, Adjunct Curator Rahul Gudipudi, and the wider curatorial team, the Biennale's second edition explores the role of a contemporary art biennale in a country that is undergoing rapid social change.

The Biennale will feature one hundred artists from over forty countries, with a focus on the Middle East. Approximately a third of the artists are from the wider Gulf region. A large share of the artworks has been specifically commissioned for the Biennale and engages with Saudi Arabia's present moment of transformation.

These numbers reflect the Foundation's central mission to push for cultural and creative exchange on both a national and international level.

After visiting our first-ever Biennale in the Kingdom—*Feeling the Stones* curated by Philip Tinari—the team from the Biennale de Lyon in France selected four works we had commissioned by Saudi artists to feature in their 2022 edition and awarded a new commission to a fifth. Works from the first edition also found their way to the Staatliche Kunsthalle in Baden-Baden, Louvre Abu Dhabi, and Art Basel. Our Foundation also commissioned a Saudi artist to produce an artwork for the UAE's Sharjah Biennial.

In 2024 and beyond, our priority is to keep nurturing relationships between our Saudi Arabian artists and institutions across the globe and, in turn, to welcome with open arms contemporary artists from all over the world to exhibit their work in Diriyah.

I would like to extend my gratitude to His Highness Prince Badr bin Abdullah bin Farhan Al Saud, Minister of Culture of Saudi Arabia and the Chairman of the Diriyah Biennale Foundation Board of Trustees, to His Excellency the Assistant Minister of Culture and the Vice Chairman of the Diriyah Biennale Foundation Board of Trustees Mr. Rakan Altouq, and to the members of the Diriyah Biennale Foundation Board of Trustees; to Ute Meta Bauer, our curators, our entire team, advisors, and partners; to the lenders who have so generously offered their works to be included in the show; and to every artist who has so kindly contributed their time and creativity to produce this remarkable exhibition.

I am excited to welcome you to another art-filled spring in Diriyah.

Aya Albakree
CEO, Diriyah Biennale Foundation

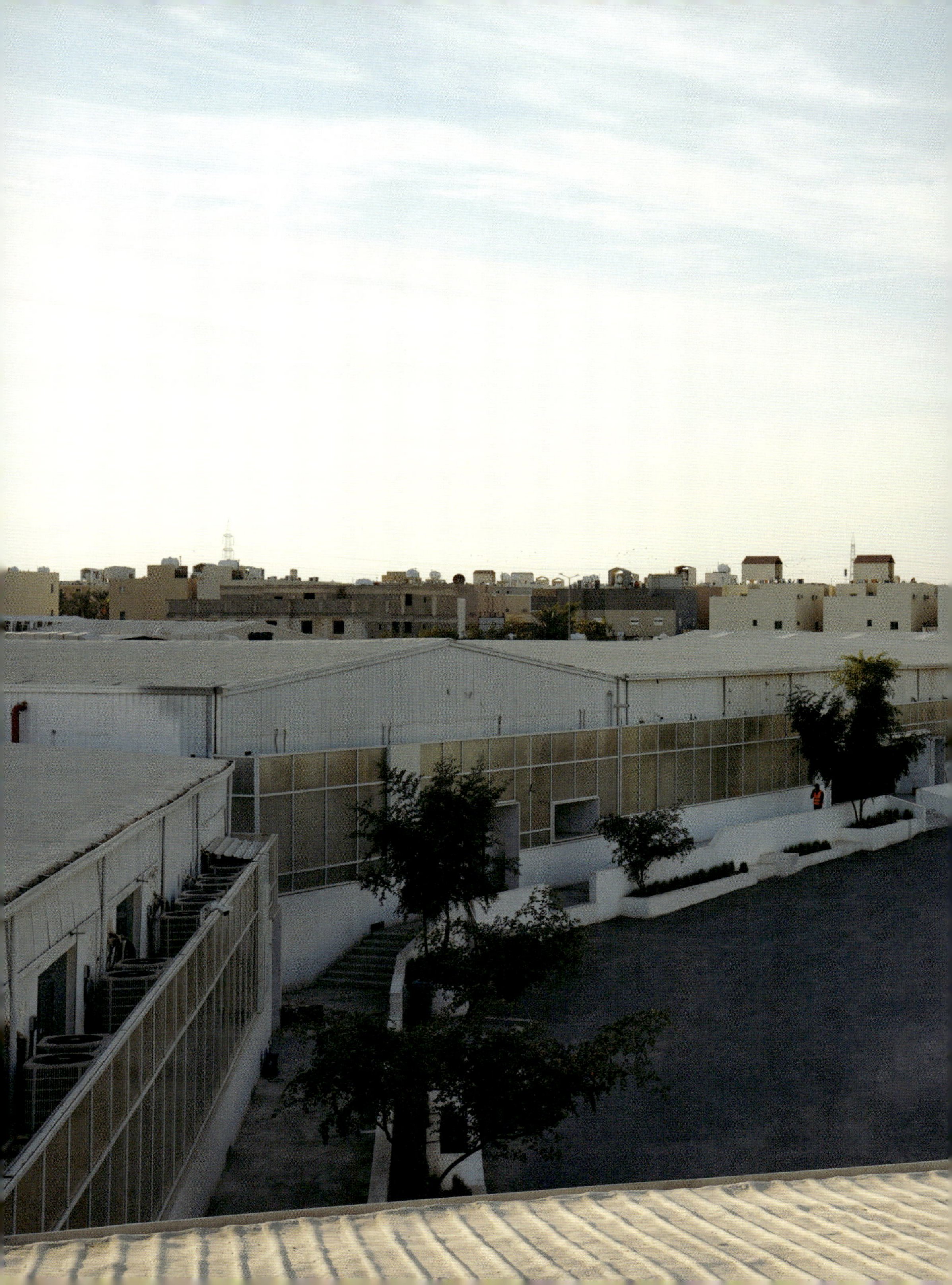

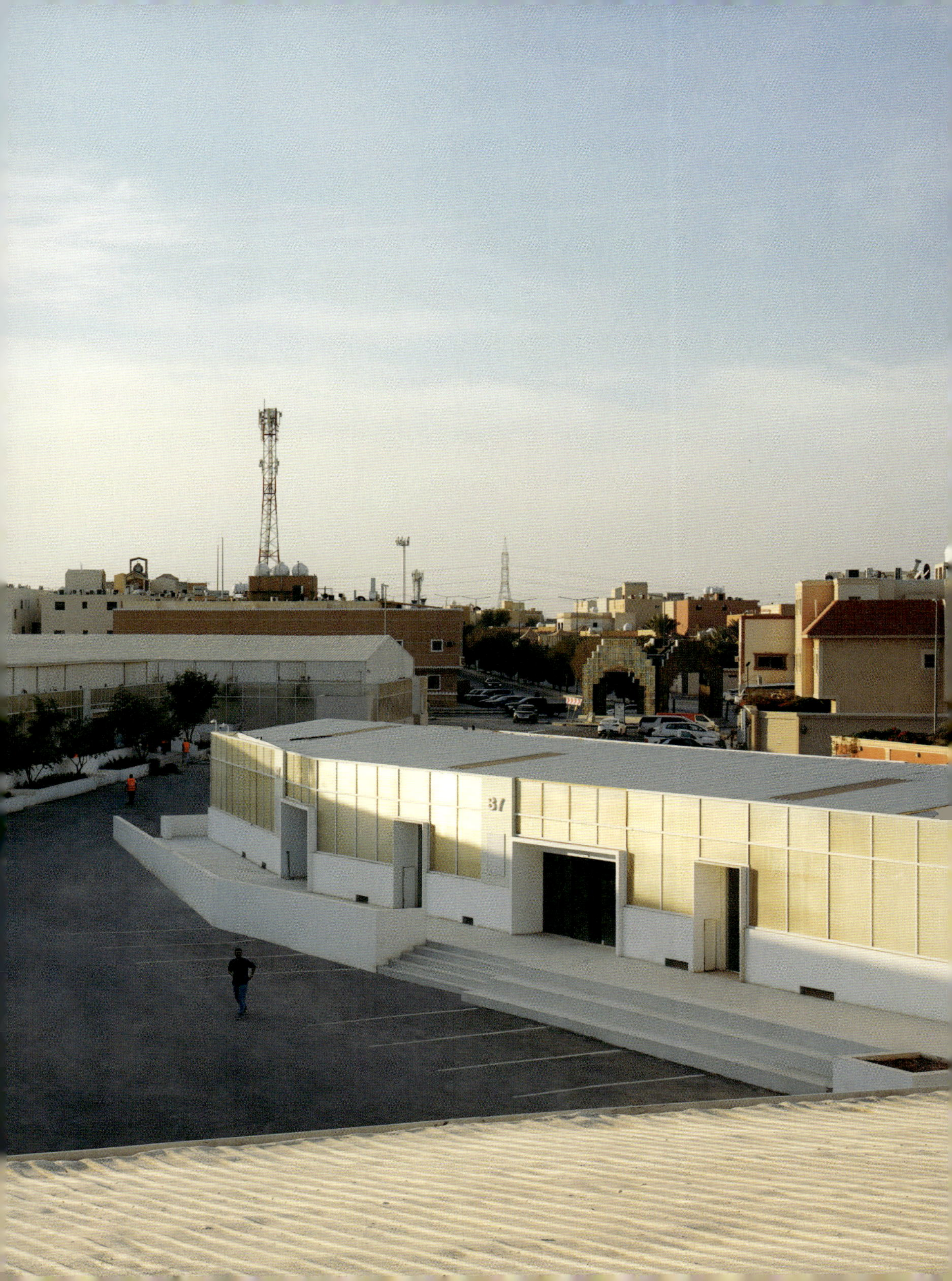

AFTER RAIN

**Notes by the Artistic Director
Ute Meta Bauer**

The second edition of the Diriyah Contemporary Art Biennale, *After Rain*, speaks to a sense of revitalization and renewal, calling to mind the refreshing scent of the air when rain has fallen. The title serves as a metaphor for presenting the Biennale as a nourishing experience filled with life. The reference also acknowledges the importance of water for all living beings and the significance of water for a city like Riyadh, situated in a desert climate. When it rains in an arid landscape, moisture mixes with the natural oils produced by plants and elements in the soil to generate the unforgettable "earthy" and intense smell of rain, scientifically called *petrichor*.

The Biennale site in the JAX District, a repurposed area of former industrial warehouses turned arts hub, is situated between a working-class neighborhood, the seasonal riverbed Wadi Hanifah, and At-Turaif, a UNESCO World Heritage Site that was the royal residence of the House of Saud and the seat of the First Saudi State. This rich topography provides the context for the featured artworks, particularly for those newly commissioned for this occasion. Like in Diriyah, the curatorial framework also expands into different layers of time, engaging with artistic practices that draw from historical, archaeological, architectural, environmental, and ecological concerns.

A biennial is a space for artistic experimentation, while simultaneously providing an opportunity to introduce new audiences to the role that the arts play in society. Such an innovative event, taking place every two years, also bears testimony to the inspiring impact that art can have on people's lives. From a wider perspective, it also frames discussions about how artists are responding to the world we inhabit. Unfolding across six halls and surrounding courtyards and terraces, the Biennale's distinctive location invites conversations on urban transformation, human dwellings, and co-existence with nonhuman habitats. The environmental awareness embedded in many of the presented works defines how the Biennale interacts with the space it occupies, influencing decisions to reduce the carbon footprint and be conscious about sustainability.

Appointed as artistic director of the second edition of this young Biennale, I questioned what my contribution could be as a curator and educator working in a country so unknown to me. At the same time, I was excited about the possibility of exploring and engaging with art and culture from Saudi Arabia in this unique moment of transformation. Naturally, having lived in Singapore for the past decade, the long-existing links between Saudi Arabia and the regions of South and Southeast Asia—beginning with the Silk Route and its spice trade and extending to the centuries of pilgrimage to Makkah and Madinah—emerged as a focus of exchange.

In the development and realization of *After Rain*, I have been joined by co-curators Rose Lejeune, Wejdan Reda, Anca Rujoiu, Ana Salazar Herrera, and adjunct curator Rahul Gudipudi. As a seasoned curator, I have found this work with a younger generation of professionals highly valuable. It expanded the horizons of the project, as everyone brought with them not only their different geographical experiences and backgrounds but also different curatorial approaches to the various areas each oversaw.

The creation of this Biennale has been an intense and rewarding journey. Informed by several curatorial research trips across Saudi Arabia and neighboring countries, at times accompanied by local artists and those visiting from abroad, we had many insightful conversations about artistic processes and ways of working, which have been essential in the emergence of new commissions. We were met with wonderful hospitality in the Saudi capital Riyadh and throughout the country, as well as across the wider Gulf region, not only during our visits to institutions, but also in our outreach to many individuals, who generously supported us. These travels and the carefully planned artist research trips resulted in ongoing exchanges and collaborations between both local artists and those from elsewhere as well as between practitioners from diverse disciplines. Our curatorial team and the participating artists and architects have met over the past year with craftspeople, herbal specialists, and farmers as well as biologists and other scientists. These unconventional gatherings inspired many of the newly developed projects, and we are certain these conversations will continue into the future. This is more than I could have anticipated during my first exchanges with His Excellency Mr. Rakan Altouq, the Assistant Minister of Culture and the Vice Chairman of the Diriyah Biennale Foundation Board of Trustees, and Aya Albakree, CEO of the Diriyah Biennale Foundation, in early 2022.

After Rain brings together diverse formats and languages used by artists, ranging from drawings and paintings to sculptures, installations and photography as well as time-based media practices such as performance and film. Some of the artists focus on the cultural histories of natural resources and materials in their practices, such as smell, earth, and edible and medicinal plants, while others discuss urban conditions, including access to water, food, and shelter. Convening several generations of artists engaged with these complex histories, *After Rain* offers multisensorial experiences, pointing out the interconnectedness of local and global issues.

The exhibition itself spans 12,900 square meters within a former warehouse complex. A stunning 177 works of art are assembled, which speak to ecological concerns and basic necessities for all life forms and ask questions about cultural heritage and its conservation. Central is also how the materiality of certain artworks make complex circumstances more tangible. Due to the long tradition of storytelling, poetry, and the performative in Arab cultures, the Biennale deliberately introduces a purpose-built cinema specifically for a rotating program of films by artists. These alternate with a series of performances that take place over the three months of the exhibition, offering a novel and collective way of seeing. Another area, the Re/Search section, is dedicated to research-based works and the investigative process behind selected exhibited artworks. It has also been important to us to celebrate the legacies of senior artists from the region.

A year-long series of artist talks and workshops, presentations of sound and performance art, as well as storytelling, titled Biennale Encounters, marked the beginning of the Biennale in April 2023. Our aim was to provide access to artists and researchers early on, offering behind-the-scenes insights and sharing the core concerns that this edition of the Biennale raises. Inviting international curators further connected the Saudi artistic scene with institutions from abroad. We are glad that these encounters have been a nourishing contribution to a local community of artists and art professionals as well as to other stakeholders. We tasked ourselves with inspiring those who only recently learned about the varied opportunities that the field of art is offering. The Learning Garden, another extension of this Biennale, is rooted in the digital realm and will continue after the exhibition closes its physical doors in Diriyah.

I am thankful to the Diriyah Biennale Foundation that through the exhibition, the film program, Re/Search, Biennale Encounters, and The Learning Garden we have been able to introduce one hundred artists and collective art projects from over forty countries to a curious and committed audience in Saudi Arabia. The forty-seven newly commissioned artworks and reproductions reflect this Biennale's conscious effort to ground itself in the local context, highlighting regional cultural practices and acknowledging the livelihood that natural resources provide to a community.

The ambition of this Biennale is to become a public space, to serve as a destination for family and friends and as a place to gather, to share experiences, to listen, to discuss, to agree, and to disagree. Artists and architects were invited to create communal spaces to cook or to experience locally produced food. There are artworks and workshops that inspire dreams and play. Together with the artists, we would like to reciprocate the warm welcome we received by sharing *After Rain*. We hope that the featured works of art and the stories they tell inspire us to ask questions and awaken our curiosity for the new and unknown.

It has been a privilege to be entrusted with the artistic direction of this Biennale and to spend extended periods of time in Saudi Arabia. I would like to express my sincere gratitude to His Highness Prince Badr bin Abdullah bin Farhan Al Saud, Saudi Minister of Culture and Chairman of the Diriyah Biennale Foundation Board of Trustees; His Excellency Mr. Rakan Altouq, Saudi Assistant Minister of Culture and Vice Chairman of the Diriyah Biennale Foundation Board of Trustees; and board members: Abdullah K. Al-Turki, Jumanah Alrashid, Firas Al-Turki, and Asim Al Tuwaijri, Secretary of the Board; to Aya Albakree, CEO of the Diriyah Biennale Foundation; and to the Diriyah Contemporary Art Biennale Curatorial Advisory Committee, headed by Rafal Niemojewski and consisting of Sara Binladen, Antonia Carver, Raneem Farsi, and Akram Zaatari.

I would also like to thank the many institutions in Saudi Arabia that so generously opened their doors for our artists more than once, in particular the Museums Commission and the Visual Arts and Music Commissions at the Ministry of Culture, the Royal Institute of Traditional Arts and King Abdullah University of Science and Technology, and the Diriyah Gate Development Authority. I also would like to thank the artists Maha Malluh, Ahmed Mater, and Muhannad Shono, who never got tired of hosting us, the visiting artists, and our other guests in their studios.

The making of this Biennale has been the effort of many. I'm grateful for everyone's individual contributions. Turning this complex curatorial endeavor into reality would have been impossible without the commitment of the co-curators, as well as Snejana Krasteva, Head of Curatorial Programs; Amina Diab, Assistant Curator; and our Curatorial Assistants Dian Arumningtyas and Alanood Al-Sudairi. I thank Yaser Musleh for his reliable presence during all my stays.

To turn this vision into a spatial parcour, I am indebted to the exhibition architects, Laura Miotto and Savina Nicolini, who created scenography in sync with this Biennale's sustainable approach. mono.studio/Kai von Rabenau and bytwo had the challenging task of creating a graphic identity that functions in two entirely different language systems, which they mastered with bravura. Without the endurance of managing editor Laura Schleussner and Ebrahim Hasan, her Arabic-speaking counterpart, our bilingual publications would have never seen the light of day. My thanks also go to Send/Receive, who took care of the Biennale's regional and international communication, and to the agency Pomelo, which continuously feeds our social media platforms. Thanks also to the hardworking Partnerships team of Nada Sheikh-Yasin, Ali Alshammary, Reema Alanzi, and the team at Zenith who made the impossible possible. A myriad of teams ranging from production to implementation, outreach, and hospitality are working tirelessly behind the scenes to make all aspects of such a large-scale endeavor possible. I would like to express my deepest thanks to all of them.

We tested the patience of the Diriyah Biennale Foundation core team more than once. I owe my deepest gratitude to Directors Lina Saleh and Will Glendinning. All members of the Foundation's committed team deserve recognition, although it is impossible to acknowledge everyone here. Not least, I would like to thank: Senior Advisors Arwa Al Ali, Donya Abdulhadi, and Alia Al-Senussi; the Foundation's Production Director Aden Wessels and supporting staff member Sara Black; Registrars Reem Alireza and Louise Rambaud; Rasim Alhussaini, Marketing and Communications Manager; Omar Diab, Events and Production Director; Muath Alhusayni, CEO Office Head; Sultan Alessa, Logistics Coordinator; Dalia Al Akki, Creative and Social Media Lead; and Dalia Alireza, International VIP Outreach Manager; and last, but not least, for helping extend the reach of the Biennale to wider audiences, I would like thank the Director of Public Programs Sybel Vazquez, Public Program Lead, Rayanne Zaim, and their team.

I would like to thank the entire Black Engineering team for their reliability and smooth overall production. My thanks also go to Simple Solutions for the precise fabrication and installation of the scenography; Hasenkamp for the art handling; Plowden & Smith for the conservation; and Imagination for taking great care of the artists and guests logistics and hospitality.

I am grateful to the NTU Centre for Contemporary Art Singapore and its team and the College of Humanities, Art, and Social Sciences at Nanyang Technological University, my academic home, who generously gave me the time to curate this biennial.

Last but not least, I would like to thank all the participating artists and their studios, as well as the lenders, who enthusiastically entrusted their works to us. Together with the curators, our various teams, and alongside the participating artists, we believe that visiting this Biennale will not only bring moments of thoughtfulness and joy, but also provide solace and hope during a time of immense suffering around the globe.

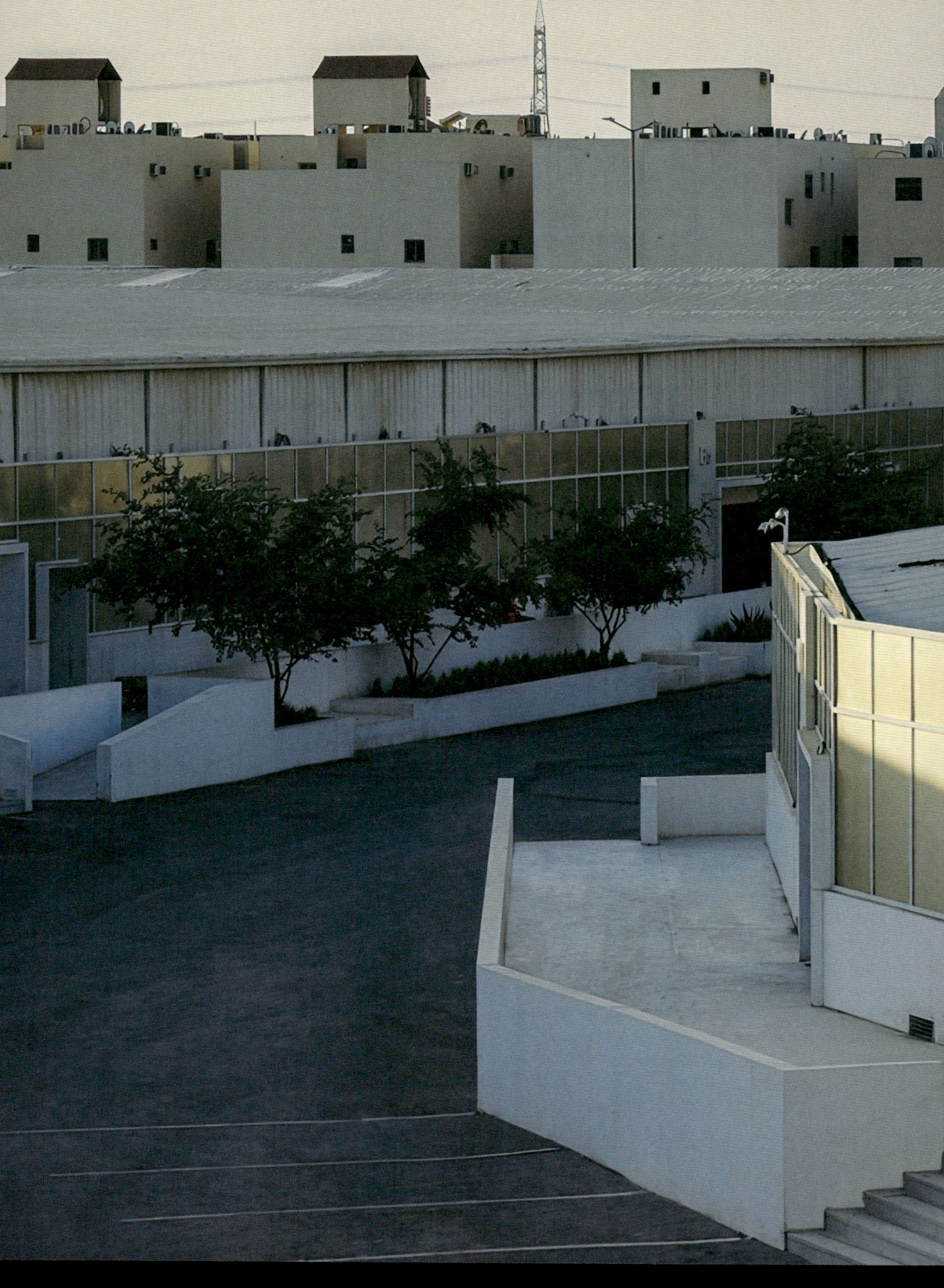

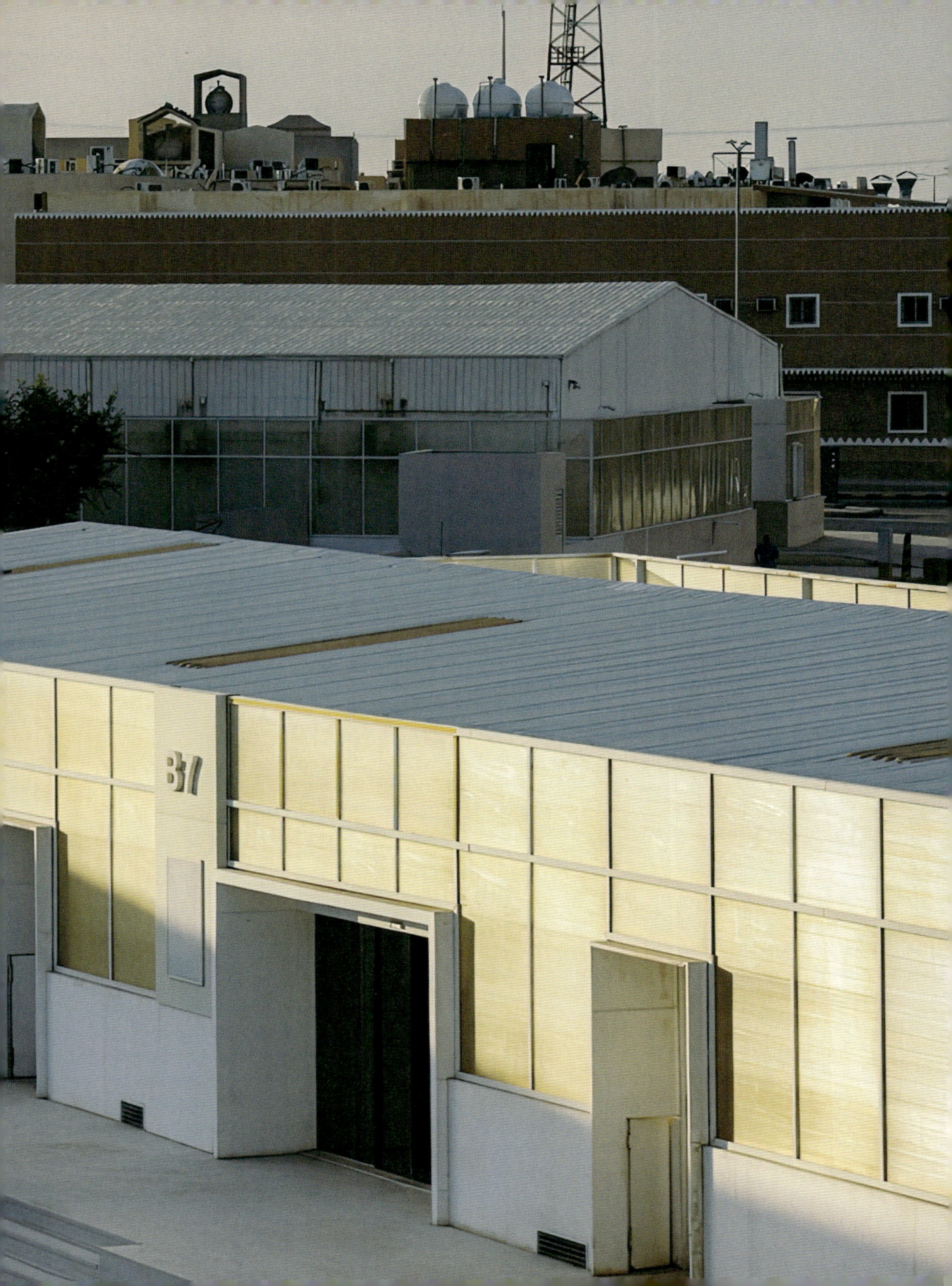
337

PLATFORMS

The works included in the Diriyah Contemporary Art Biennale 2024 span different forms of presentation, from works shown in the exhibition halls or on view in the dedicated Re/Search area or cinema in B1, to the live events of Biennale Encounters and the digital space of The Learning Garden. Some artists have multiple contributions or aspects of their work that are shown across several platforms.

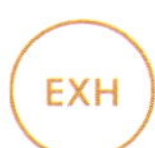 ## EXHIBITION

The Biennale exhibition is located at the Diriyah Biennale Foundation site and spans six repurposed former industrial warehouses, numerous courtyards, terraces, and off-site locations. It introduces diverse artistic formats and languages, ranging from drawings and paintings to sculptures, installations, and photography, as well as time-based media such as performances and film. The featured works are grouped around various issues, from theatricality and storytelling to broader ecological concerns, with a focus on the legacies of senior artists from the region, the essential role of water for life, questions of heritage and conservation, and multisensory experience.

 ## RE/SEARCH

Many of the artists participating in the Biennale pursue intensive research that flows into the different types of work they create. The B1 Mezzanine area is dedicated to highlighting these processes of investigation and presenting this form of artistic practice to Saudi audiences.

 ## FILM PROGRAM

During the opening hours of the exhibition, a rotating sequence of films is presented in a black box cinema in Exhibition Hall B1. Scheduled screenings also take place at this location.

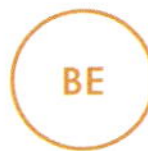

BIENNALE ENCOUNTERS

Biennale Encounters was launched in April 2023 as a yearlong event series of talks, conversations, workshops, performances, and readings. Throughout the 2024 exhibition, this scheduled program is an ongoing invitation to engage with the artists and guests of the Diriyah Contemporary Art Biennale 2024. These events take place at the Diriyah Biennale Foundation Auditorium in the JAX District, within the exhibition venues, and at several off-site locations.

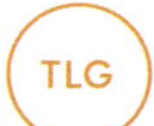

THE LEARNING GARDEN

The online platform The Learning Garden acts as a companion to the Biennale. Exploring the ideas and questions running throughout the Diriyah Contemporary Art Biennale 2024, the digital space includes commissions by artists specifically invited to contribute to this format as well as research-based works by artists participating in the physical exhibition. Visitors to the exhibition can access The Learning Garden on their phones or at a dedicated station in the B1 Mezzanine section of the exhibition.

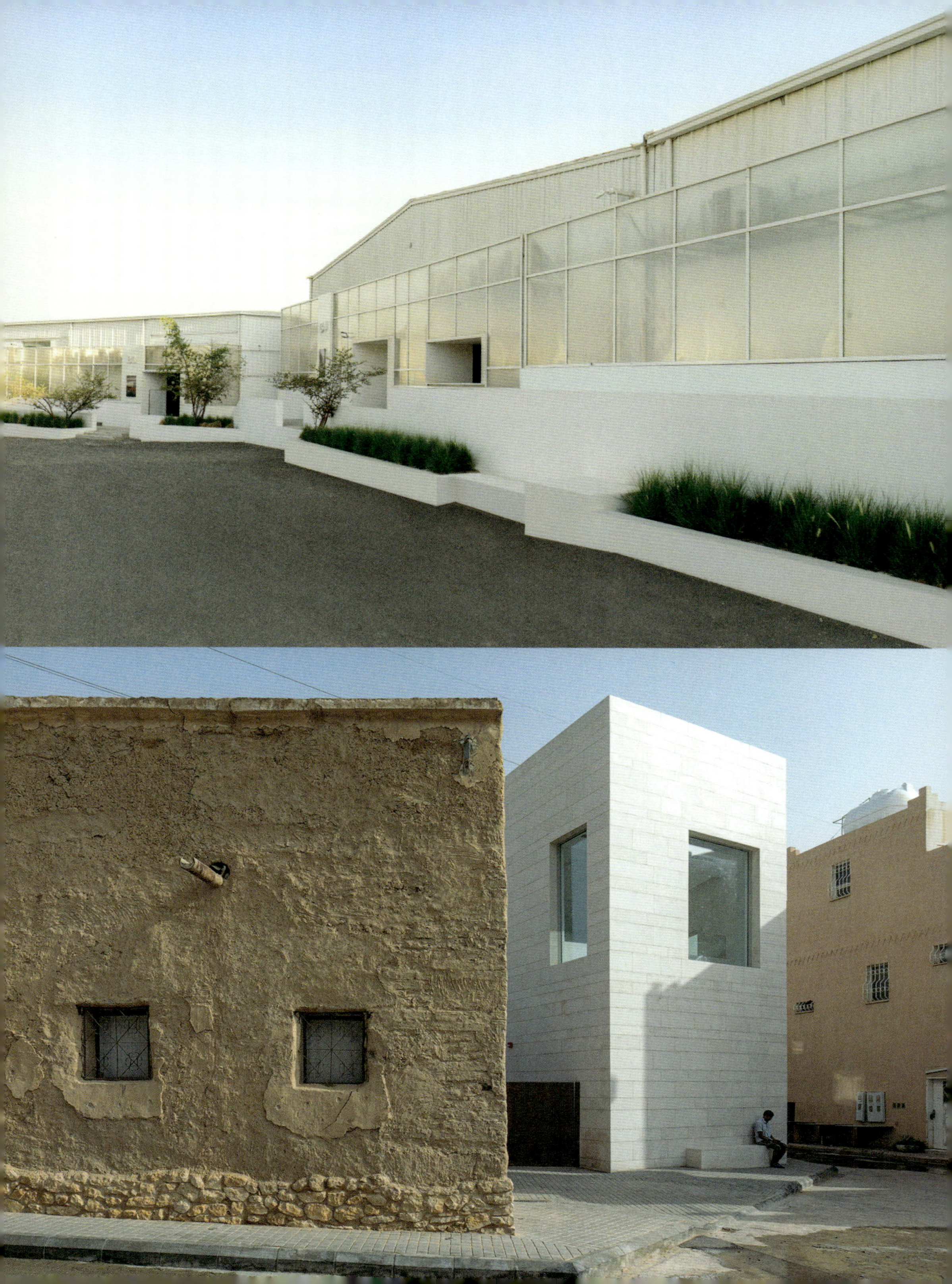

VENUES

DIRIYAH BIENNALE FOUNDATION (DBF)

JAX District, 7120 Muhammad Ibn Rashid Al Uraini Diriyah, Riyadh 13732

The Diriyah Biennale Foundation is a not-for-profit organization established by the Saudi Arabian Ministry of Culture in 2020. It produces two biennials in different cities in alternating years: the Diriyah Biennale of Contemporary Art in Riyadh and the Islamic Arts Biennale in Jeddah. Its offices and exhibition spaces in Riyadh are situated in the JAX District in Diriyah. Its exhibition space encompasses six repurposed exhibition halls (former industrial spaces) with courtyards and terraces, a venue for its ongoing public program, a bookshop, and numerous food and beverage outlets.

SHAMALAT

Shamalat, 4102, 6089 King Faisal Rd, Al Diriyah, Riyadh 13713

Shamalat is a cultural space initiated and developed by Maha Malluh, one of Saudi Arabia's eminent visual artists. This long-term project aligns with Malluh's core interest in generating a dialogue between the past, present, and future. Shamalat is a continuation of this line of inquiry. Embarking on this project in early 2013, the artist purchased a mud house at the periphery of Old Diriyah, which she reimagined in collaboration with a young architectural duo, syn architects.

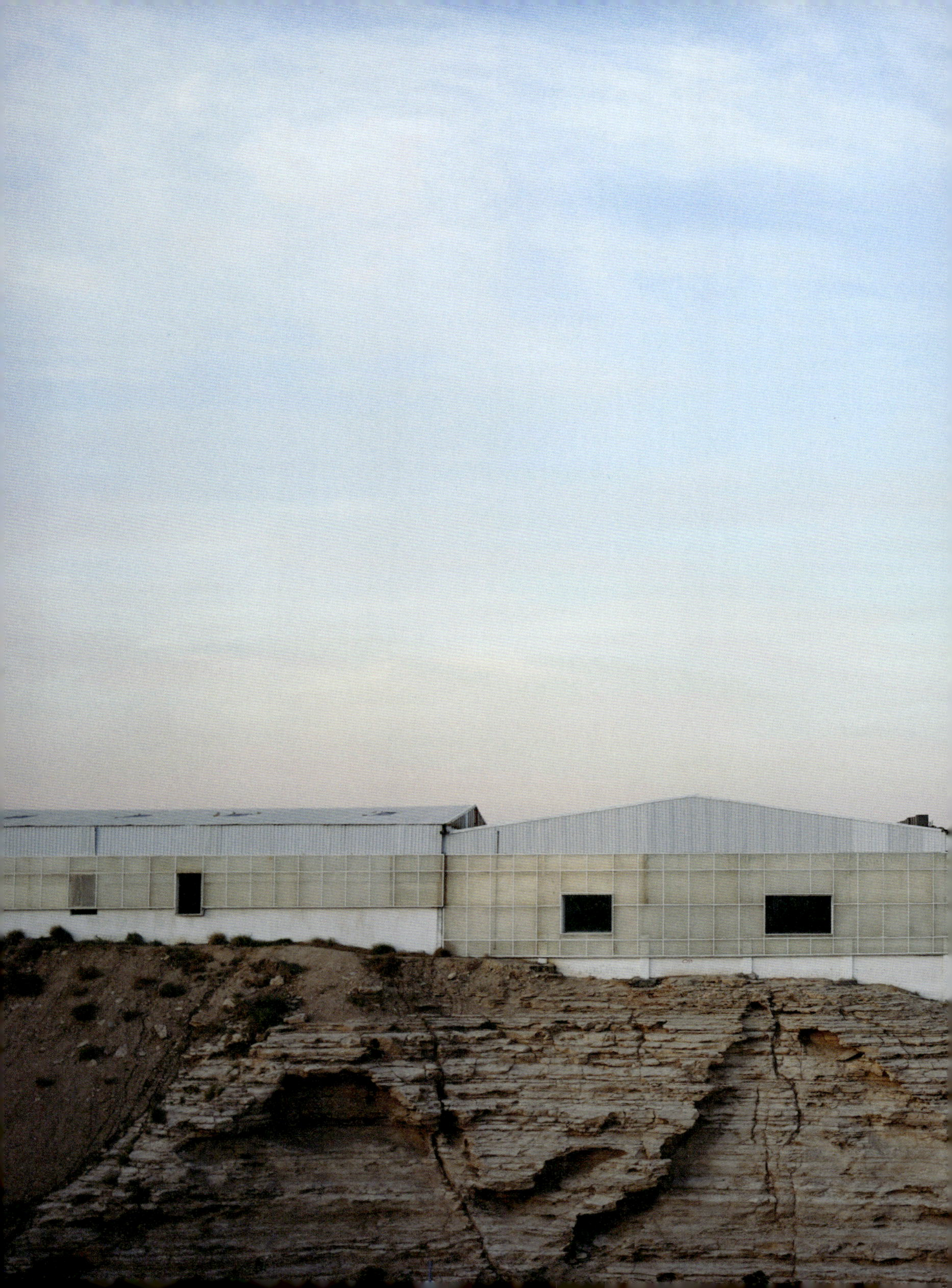

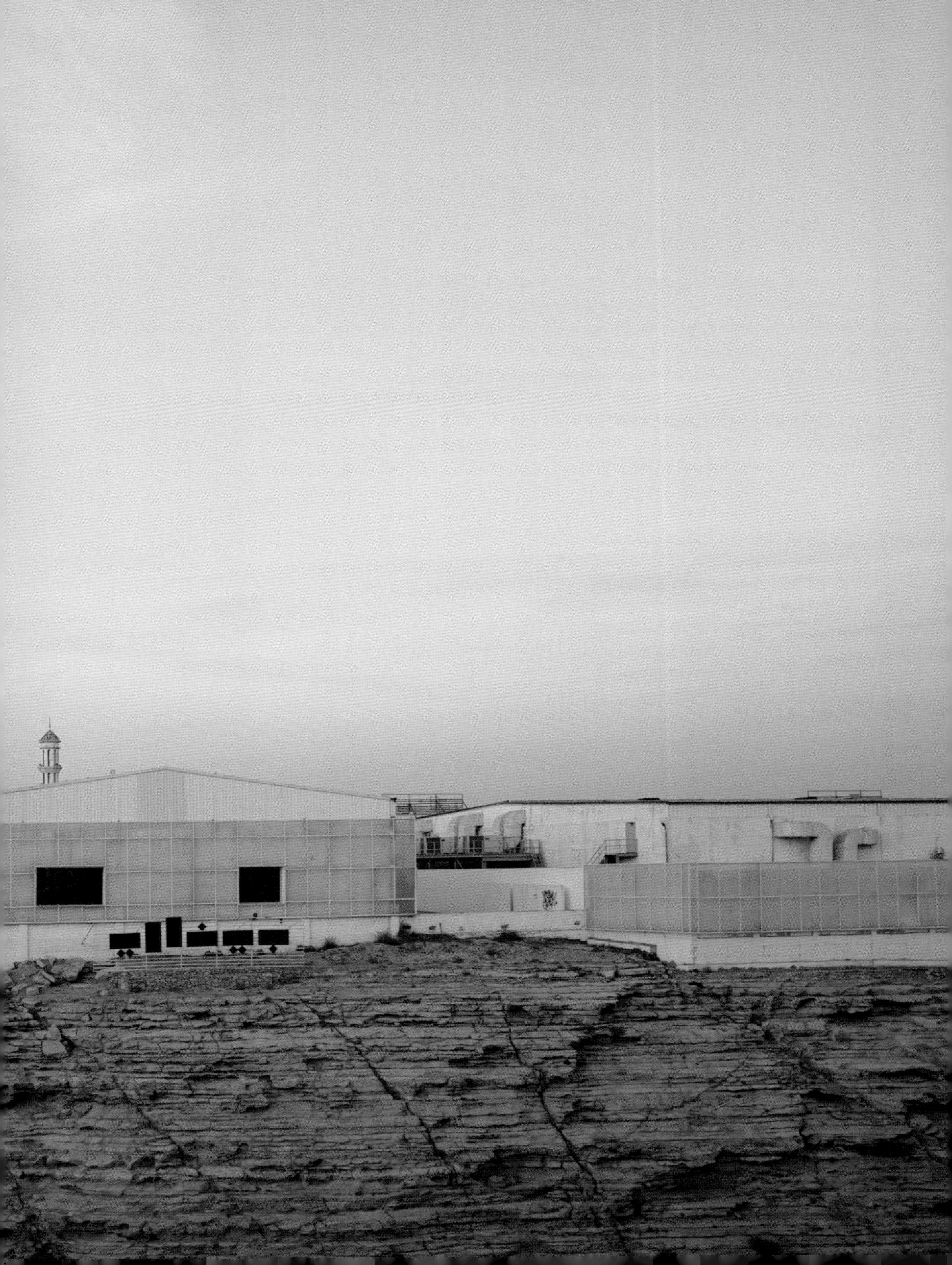

AFTER RAIN
20 February – 24 May 2024

The exhibition *After Rain* spans six halls totaling 12,900 square meters and expands into the surrounding courtyards and terraces of the JAX District. This multisensorial parcour invites viewers to discover the richness of artistic languages, ranging from traditional formats to contemporary experimental approaches. The featured works reflect on ecological concerns and the essential requirements for life: water, food, and shelter. Through an open-space concept, the scenography is designed to facilitate a dialogue between different artworks and the various topics addressed in this edition of the Biennale, and also taking into consideration the carbon footprint created by such large-scale exhibitions.

The Biennale's first hall, B1, is dedicated to performativity and time-based art, interweaving narratives grounded in historic moments that unfold through animated installations, moving images, and performances commissioned for the Biennale. A purpose-built Black Box houses a rotating program of single-screen films and scheduled performances, while the mezzanine is a space dedicated to artistic research and research-based art practices. This presentation provides viewers with an idea of what takes place in artist studios, offering a look at the extended processes underlying many of the works in *After Rain*.

Exhibition Halls B2, B4, B5, and B6 include artists from across three generations, whose work engages with the complexity of local realities and global constellations and the interconnectedness of the two, in the past and present. While some halls address the environmental crisis and the aftermath of colonialism and extractivism, others pose questions about heritage and conservation through multiformat installations. Highlighting the sophistication of craft traditions, various artists use natural materials, revealing the unique knowledge intrinsic to organic matter. Exhibition Hall B3 features a senior generation of artists, many of whom have had an immense influence on the younger artists who followed, despite practicing under challenging conditions.

The commissioned outdoor projects also serve as gathering spaces, taking the form of a communal kitchen, an herbal garden, or a juice bar, while architecturally inspired projects—material experiments, pavilions, and tent structures—offer shelter from the sun and rain. In addition, there are multiple settings conceived as invitations for visitors to linger and experience the exhibition with all their senses—providing tastes, textures, sights, and sounds. Situated in the mesmerizing environment of historic Wadi Hanifah, these multi-functional artworks are intended as spaces to congregate and converse.

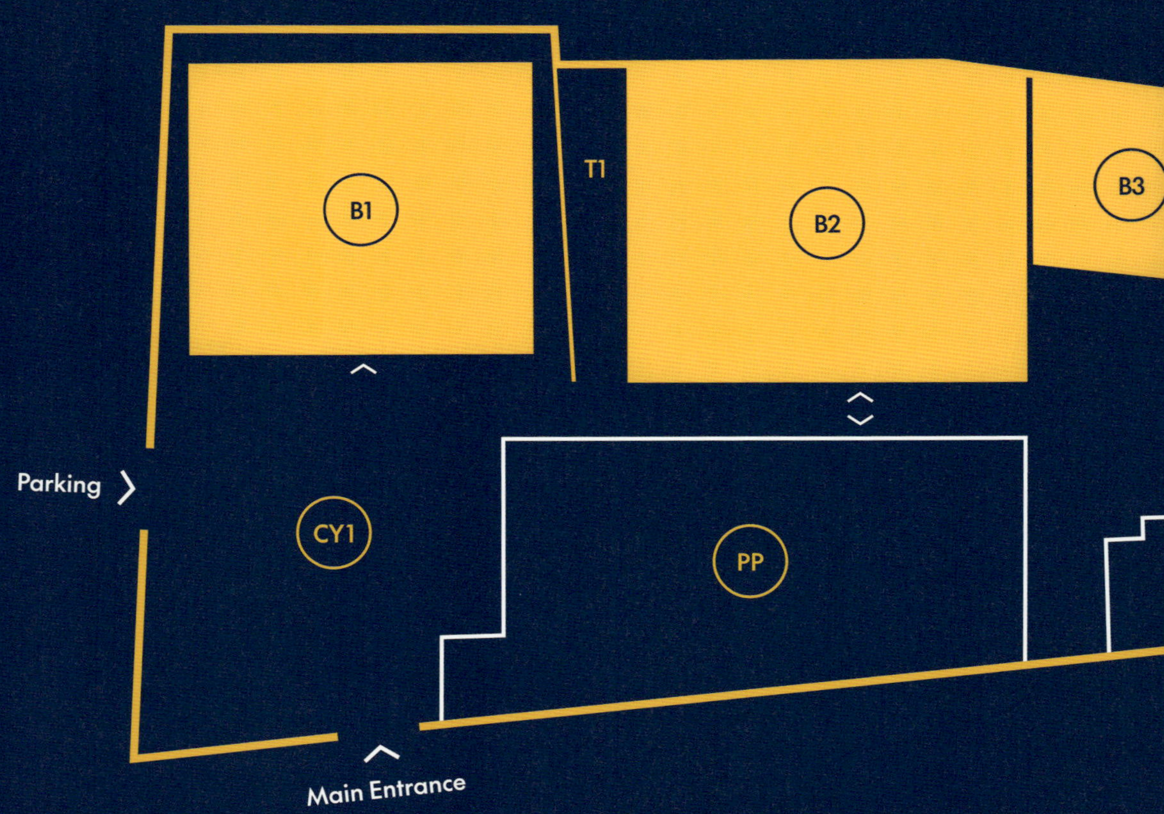

B1–B6 Exhibition Halls
CY1–CY2 Courtyards
T1–T2 Terraces
PP Public Programs

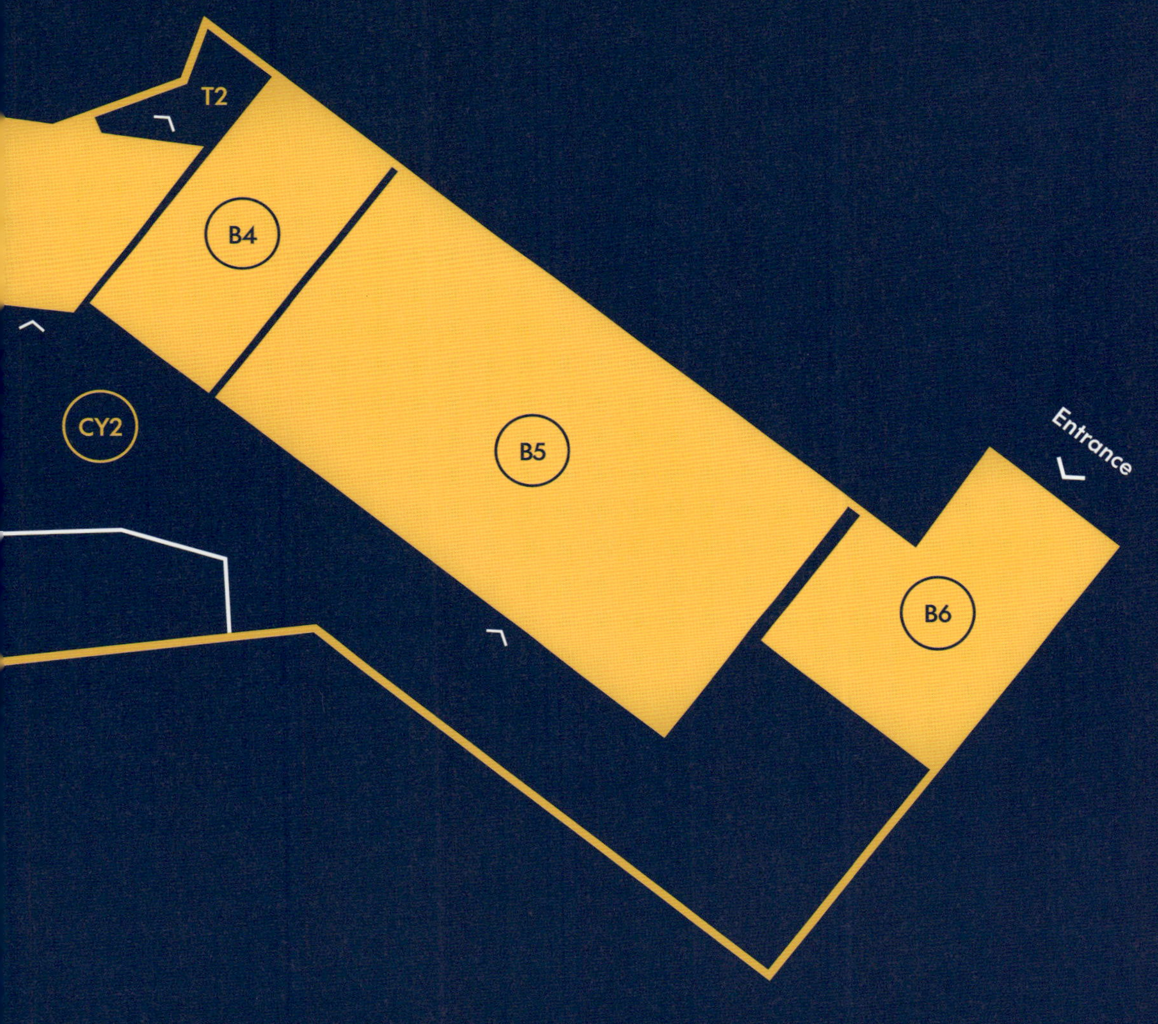

T2
B4
CY2
B5
Entrance
B6

EXHIBITION HALL B1

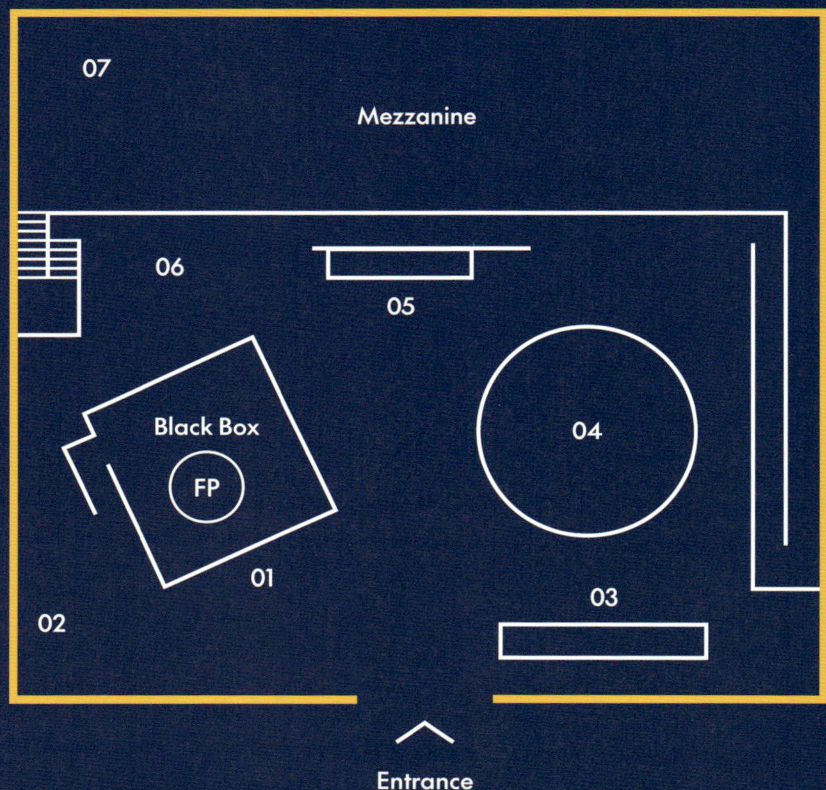

01   El Anatsui / p. 42
02   Liam Young / p. 66
03   Dhali Al Mamoon / p. 40
04   Taus Makhacheva / p. 46
05   María Magdalena Campos-Pons / p. 44
06   Tarek Atoui / p. 236
07   Ines Weizman / p. 48

STORIES AND HISTORIES

The entry to the Biennale is dedicated to performative works and time-based practices, including cinematic works of art. This hall welcomes viewers with a reminder that life is a continuous performance. Theatricality is embedded in all societal and political interactions. The act of staging is central to the selection of the featured works that occupy the space as storytellers, vibrant protagonists, and acteurs.

A playful tension is created between a black box and a white circle. The Black Box houses films by artists alternating with performances that occur throughout the duration of the Biennale exhibition. Arranged on and around a large white circle are works dedicated to the stage, the circus, the burlesque, and the spiritual. This hall highlights the importance of the viewer as an active contributor in unlocking the stories contained within a work of art.

DHALI AL MAMOON

Born 1958 in Chandpur, Bangladesh, lives and works in Chittagong, Bangladesh

Kather Nripati (Wooden Lord)
2021

Dhali Al Mamoon is an artist and educator whose prolific output in diverse media engages with the history of Bengal and the persistence of colonialism as a historical trauma. In his practice, he excavates memory and meaning, disavowing literal narration in favor of nuanced visual and corporeal experiences. Al Mamoon holds an MFA from the University of Chittagong, where he also teaches, and was a DAAD fellow at the University of the Arts Berlin in 1993–94. He is inspired by the diversity of life, landscapes, and everyday objects that he encounters as an inhabitant of one of the world's oldest and most historically significant port cities.

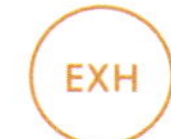

Al Mamoon's series of kinetic sculptures that comprise *Kather Nripati (Wooden Lord)* (2021) derives from the palm-leaf puppets he often played with at carnivals as a child. Traditional objects of folk art, the *Taal-patar Sepai* of West Bengal made fun of the sepoys, the Indian soldiers hired by the British East India Company, with the twirling, flailing movements of their jointed limbs. The name for these children's toys also came to describe a weak person with a swaggering attitude. Originating around the time of the Sepoy Mutiny (1857–59) against colonial rule, the dolls, now outdated, were a subtle form of resistance, shared by the makers of the puppets and those who used them. Thus, the hierarchical social order was temporarily subverted in a playful act meant to elicit laughter and relief. With these puppets, the artist reconstructs and reconsiders a period of unfreedom—a wound still present many generations later.

Al Mamoon has delved into this chapter of collective trauma via his own childhood memories, creating life-sized, wooden versions of the toy mounted on plinths that rotate periodically. The knocking about of the puppets' arms and legs add a sonic element to the installation. Immaculately costumed in the ceremonial regalia of the colonizers, Al Mamoon's mostly headless figures attempt to exert a menacing presence, in all directions, but are continually thwarted by their own captivity.

Number 1 of five figures from *Kather Nripati (Wooden Lord)*, 2021

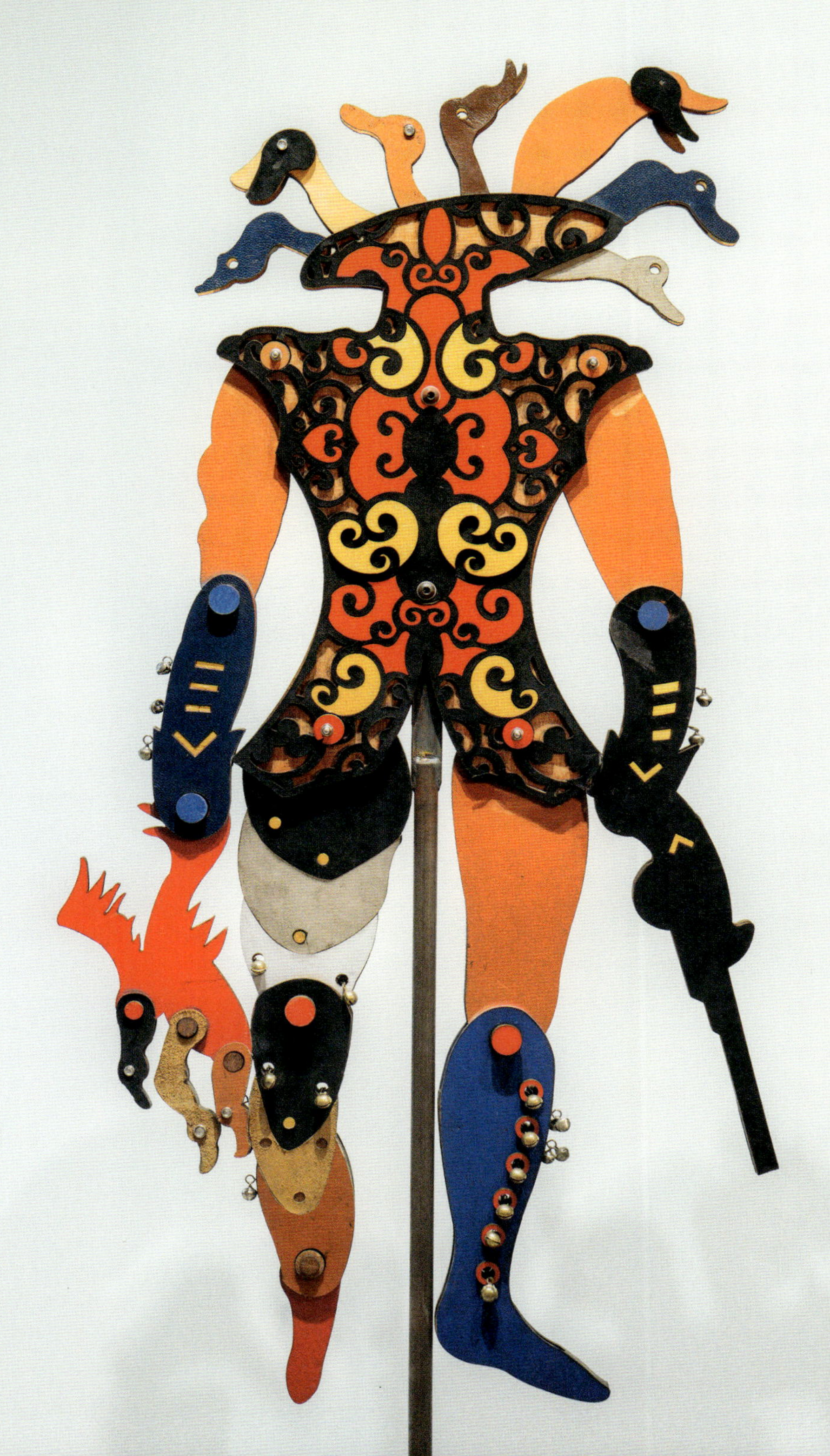

EL ANATSUI

Born 1944 in Anyako, Ghana, lives and works in Nsukka, Nigeria,
and Tema, Ghana

Detsi

2008–21

El Anatsui works with found objects and everyday materials to create
imposing installations that interrogate colonial imports, consumption,
and waste. Trained in art at the Kwame Nkrumah University of Science
& Technology in Ghana, he rose to acclaim with his large-scale works
made of bottle tops. He received the Golden Lion award for Lifetime
Achievement at the 56th Venice Biennale (2015). While his work repurposes discarded resources such as bottle caps and cassava graters, it is
his meticulous transformation of these scraps into precisely composed,
tapestry-like sculptures that underscore the formal brilliance of his visual
language. Anatsui spent four decades teaching sculpture at the Fine
and Applied Art department at the University of Nigeria, Nsukka. He
is a member of the Nsukka Group artist collective, which incorporates
and adapts the traditional, abstracted designs of the Igbo people into
contemporary practices.

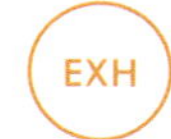

Detsi (2008–21) exemplifies the labor-intensive work needed to create
these installations, which are typically carried out by local workers
and studio assistants. Spanning eight meters in length, the work took
thirteen years to complete; it involved flattening, cutting, and twisting
bottle caps and stitching them together, with copper wires, into a
cohesive fabric. In keeping with Anatsui's pursuit of artistic freedom
and versatility, his sculptures mutate as they move from one location
to another and are hung differently. This adaptability embodies his
preoccupation with context and how African aesthetic traditions can
be resituated within the global canon of abstraction.

Installation view of *Detsi*, from the exhibition *Shard Son* at Efie Gallery, Dubai, United Arab Emirates, 2022

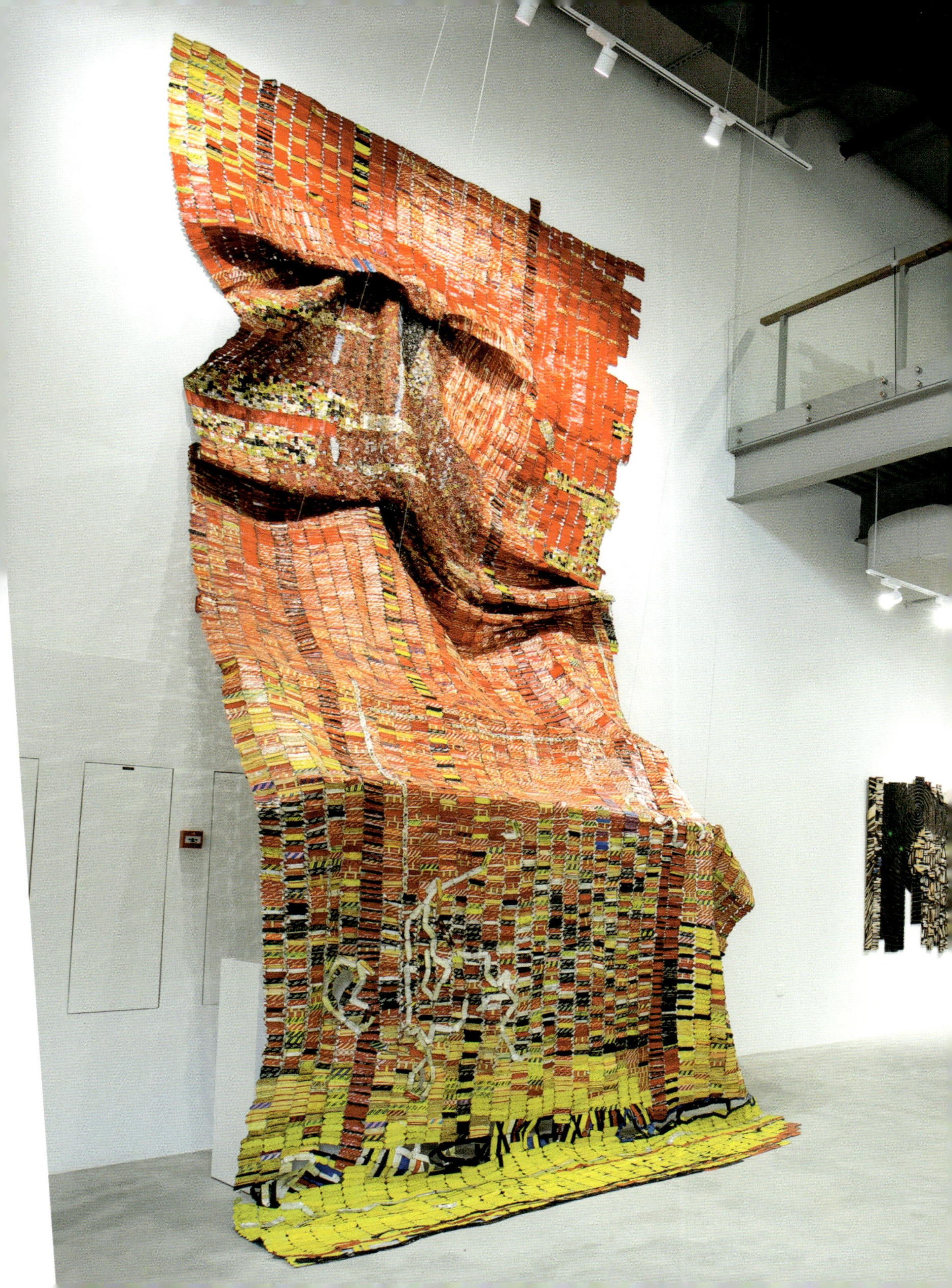

MARÍA MAGDALENA CAMPOS-PONS

Born 1959 in Matanzas, Cuba, lives and works in Nashville, TN,
United States

Liminal Circularity

2021–23

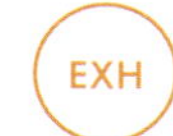

Afro-Cuban artist María Magdalena Campos-Pons addresses the
African diaspora, spirituality, collective resistance, and healing in her
multidisciplinary practice. Studying in Havana, she received degrees
from the Escuela Nacional de Arte in 1980 and the Instituto Superior
de Arte in 1985, gaining international recognition as part of the New
Cuban Art movement. Moving to the US, she received an MFA from
Massachusetts College of Art and Design in 1988. Campos-Pons is
currently the Cornelius Vanderbilt Endowed Chair Professor of Fine
Arts at Vanderbilt University in Nashville. Her work has been exhibited
at documenta 14 (2017) and the 55th Venice Biennale (2013). She is a
2023 recipient of the Macarthur Fellowship.

With African, Cuban, and Chinese descent, Campos-Pons describes
her work as a "merging of ideas, merging of ethnicities, merging
of traditions." Family history and autobiography become a means
of unpacking and commenting on the political. *Liminal Circularity*
(2021–23) consists of two large painted portraits, each divided into
multiple vertical panels, which represent a female and a male figure. They are part of a series of portraits that pay homage to family
members, particularly women, who endured the Middle Passage—the
Atlantic slave trade route from West Africa to the Americas. Each
painting merges the traits of the portrayed person with symbolic
elements attributed to a specific *orisha*, one of the many deities that
make up the Yoruba pantheon of the Santería religion.

The paintings are accompanied by two translucent stools, cast in glass
from a wooden original passed down in Campos-Pons's family from
generation to generation. One of the glass stools is yellow, representing Oshun, the manifestation of divine femininity, fertility, love, and
fate; the other is purple, standing for Babalú-Ayé, a manifestation of
the supreme creator and a spirit of the earth associated with healing.
The stools are part of a set that the artist displays on rectangular
lightboxes, often arranged in triangles or circles. They reflect a twofold sentiment of absence and presence, representing the myriad
human lives lost to slavery and exploitation, while simultaneously
symbolizing ancestral legacies, the divine force of the *orishas*, and
the collective memory of diasporic narratives. The arrangement thus
becomes a site of remembrance, return, and healing.

Bench 7 and *Portrait #2* from the series *Liminal Circularity*, 2023

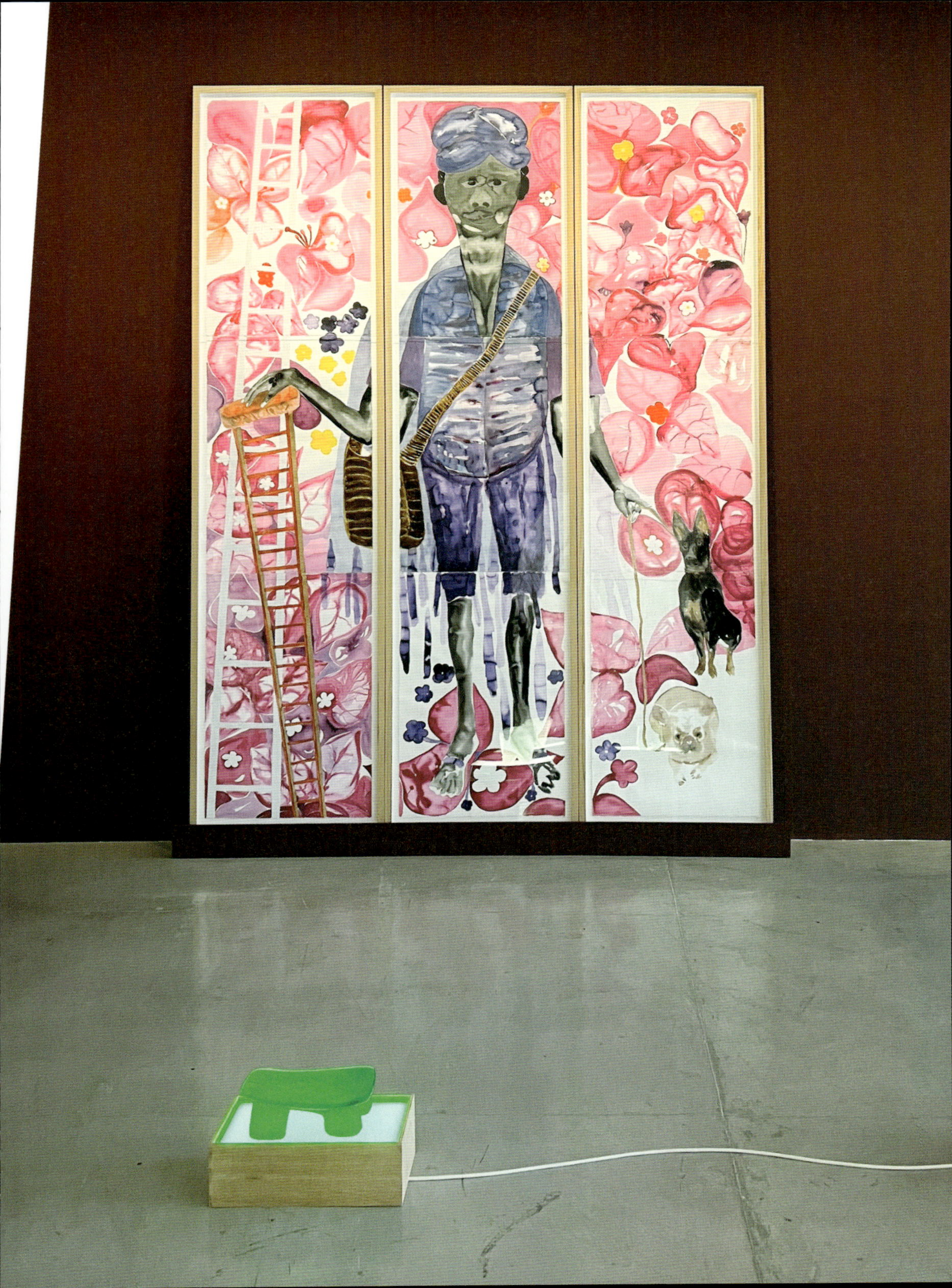

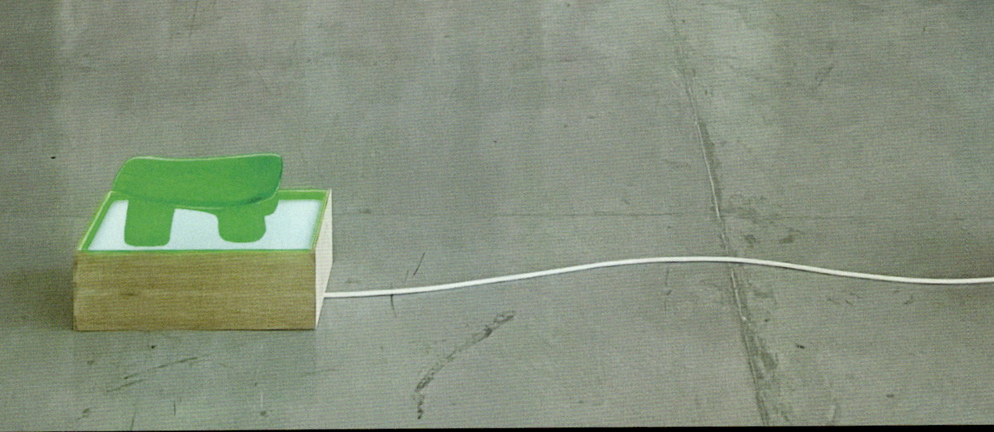

TAUS MAKHACHEVA

Born 1983 in Moscow, Russian Federation, lives and works in Dubai,
United Arab Emirates

Charivari

2019

Growing up in Moscow, Taus Makhacheva was raised in a family with origins in the Republic of Dagestan, a mountainous area in the North Caucasus, which has served as both the stage and protagonist in several of her works. These are inhabited by a pantheon of unruly characters—including her alter ego Super Taus—who negotiate complex histories, social norms, and myths through humor and imagination. Makhacheva studied art in London at the Royal College of Art and Goldsmiths, University of London.

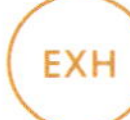

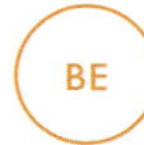

Charivari (2019) takes a flying leap into the Soviet circus tradition in a performative installation infused with the combination of irony and irreverence typical of Makhacheva's work. In circus speak, *charivari* is the traditional name for a collective act of tumultuous gymnastic feats performed by acrobats and clowns. Makhacheva revisits the Soviet history of the Baku State Circus in the Republic of Azerbaijan, while drawing on the traditions of the avant-garde and its taste for the experimental and absurd in defiance of social norms. In collaboration with the architect Maria Serova, the artist translates the circus setting into an abstract drawing in space. Hoops, ladders, swings, and pyramids synthesize the modernist ideal of a disciplined body with the sophisticated artistry and skillfulness of the circus school.

Similarly two-dimensional are the surreal costumes designed by Panika Derevya: a fanfare musician whose body takes the shape of an open accordion; the "magician's assistant" whose robe is also a staircase; a convoluted snake; a half-horse, half-elephant animal made in macramé; and so on. The flatness of the scenery is contrasted by the visceral absurdity of the audio stories written by Alexander Snegirev, based on archival research and oral interviews in Baku. These tales feature characters including synthetic bears, a talking horse, a lion ventriloquist, and a strongwoman accountant. As philosopher Mikhail Bakhtin proposes, the carnival traditions allow for a suspension of official norms and deviations from the everyday. That is how the circus, suggests the artist, operated in Soviet times, crafting a space of freedom within a society controlled by ideology and state narratives. Snegirev's wry commentary on the post-Soviet era suggests that this fundamental role of the circus persists. Visitors are called to approach the podium: "Circus, circus, circus—it's a fabulous sparkling tent."

Installation view of *Charivari* at YARAT Contemporary Art Space, Baku, Azerbaijan, 2019

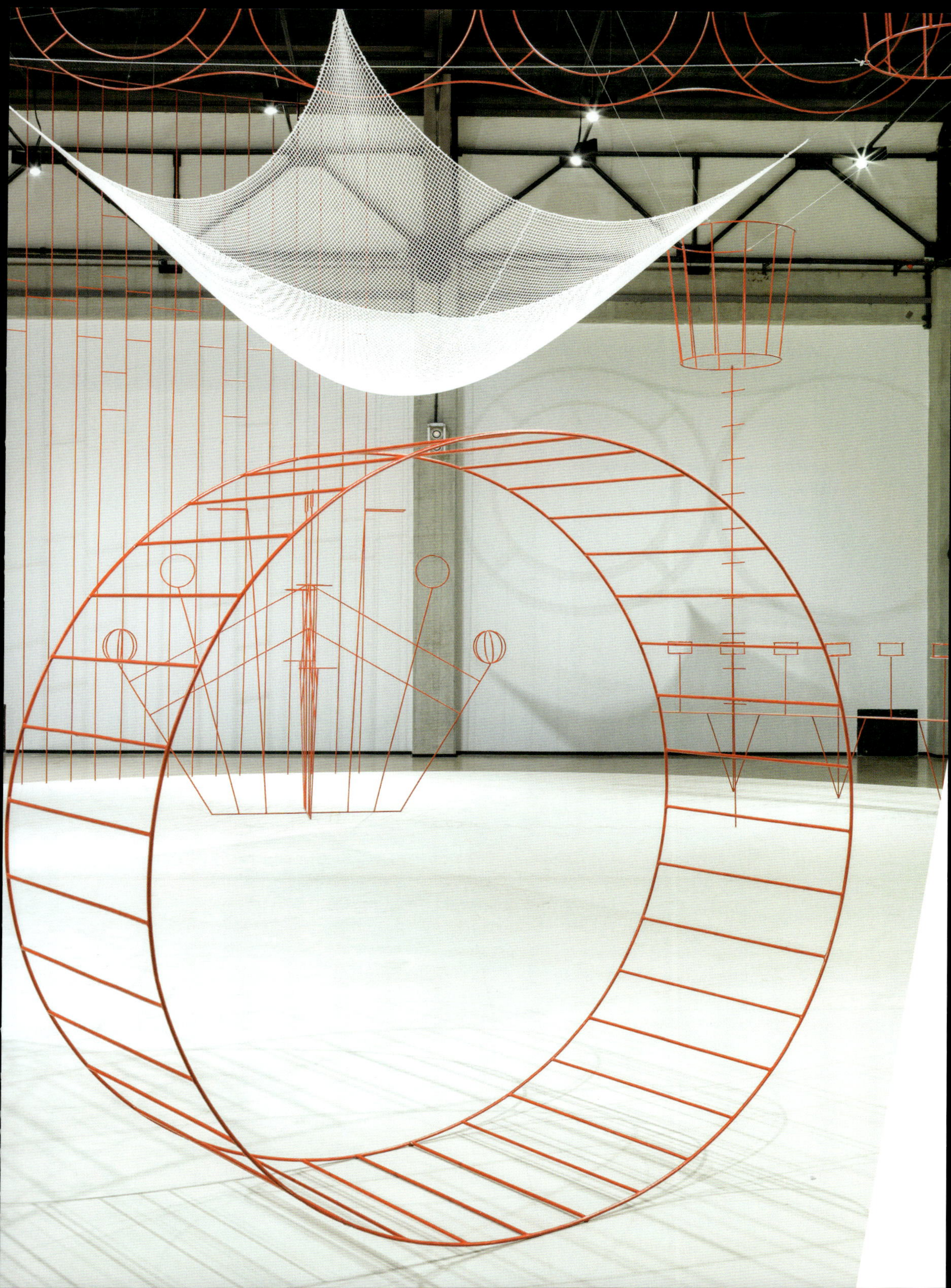

INES WEIZMAN

Born 1973 in Leipzig, Germany, lives and works in London,
United Kingdom, and Vienna, Austria

"Of all the gin joints in all the towns in all the world…"
2023

Ines Weizman is an architect, architectural historian, theorist, and curator. Through her investigative and interdisciplinary practice, she studies international modernism and colonialism, the politics of architecture, the history of the Bauhaus, and Cold War planning. She is the founding director of the Centre for Documentary Architecture and professor of architectural theory and design at the Academy of Fine Arts, Vienna. At the Royal College of Art, London, she directs the Architecture PhD Program. In 2023 she was both a contributor to the 18th Venice Architecture Biennale and the commissioner of the Lithuanian pavilion.

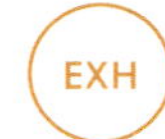

"To write about a building is to map the world in which it is located," writes Ines Weizman, a statement that resonates in her video work *"Of all the gin joints in all the towns in all the world…"* (2023). A compilation of archival images of architecture and fragmentary histories, the film traces the itinerary of Josephine Baker (1906–1975), the renowned African-American and French performer, who crisscrossed the Arab world during World War II, from Algiers to Casablanca, Tunis, Cairo, Damascus, Beirut, and British Mandate Palestine. Enlisted by the Free French Army as a spy, she traveled throughout the region in 1941–43, taking to the stage in hotel bars and private clubs, gathering points for officers, refugees, journalists, and agents. Fame gave Baker access to information, as her enemies tended to underestimate her.

Although no photographic record of these performances remains, Weizman has unearthed an immense amount of archival material evocative of this period and the places through which Baker traveled: street scenes in Algiers, bomb-damaged archaeological sites and museums in Tunisia, military bands, US troops in Casablanca—and, most evocatively, the exteriors, ballrooms, and lobbies of early twentieth-century grand hotels. These modernist structures served as markers and meeting points in the colonial world of the Middle East, which Baker navigated. As evidenced by a fading French tricolor painted on the wall of a Haifa casino, these spaces were the backdrop for her fight against fascism, part of her larger struggle against racism and xenophobia that did not end with the war.

Video stills from *"Of all the gin joints, in all the towns, in all the world…"*, 2023
Above: Woman in Tangier (1935) / Below: Interior of the Orient Palace Hotel, Damascus (2022)

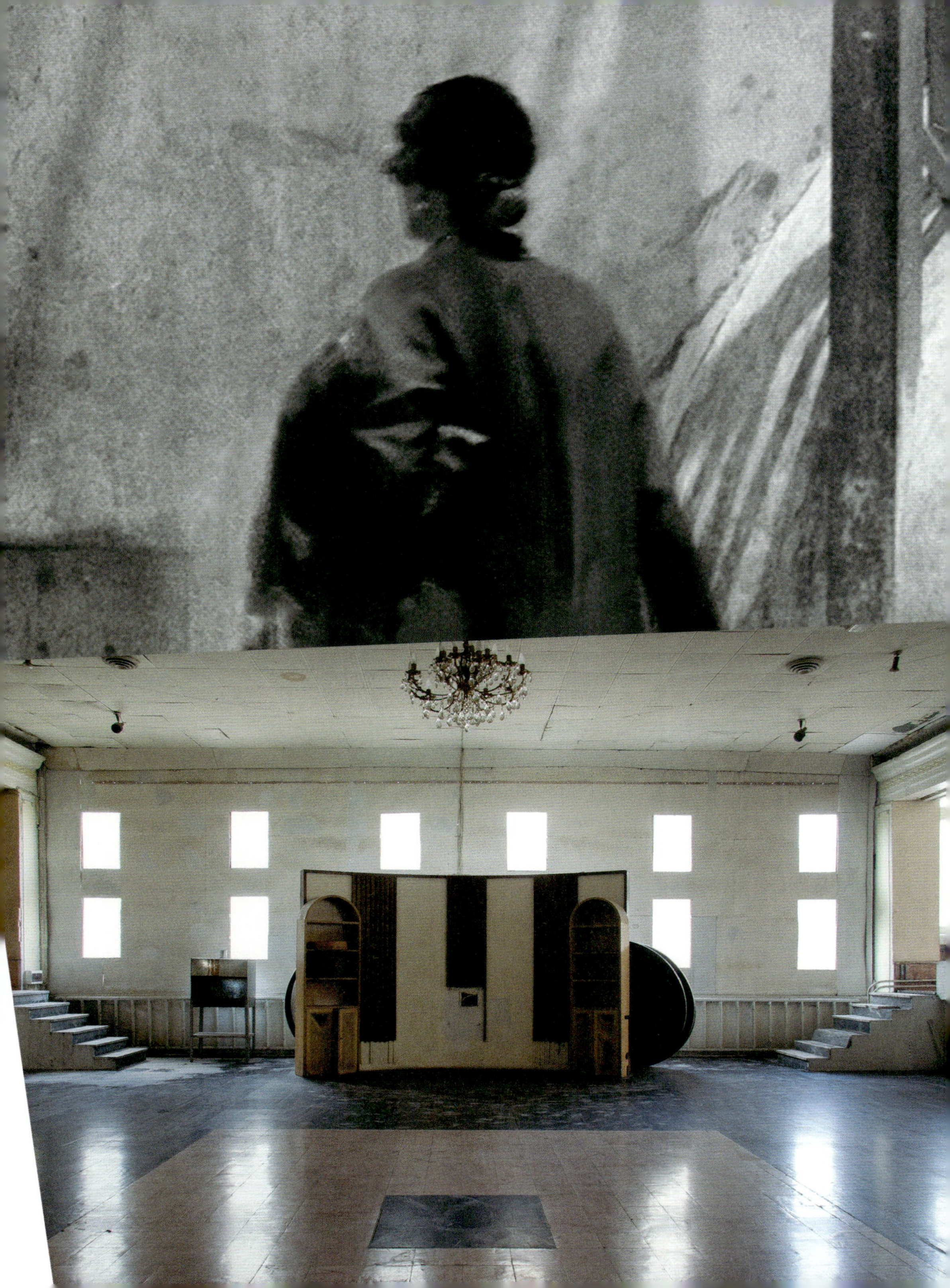

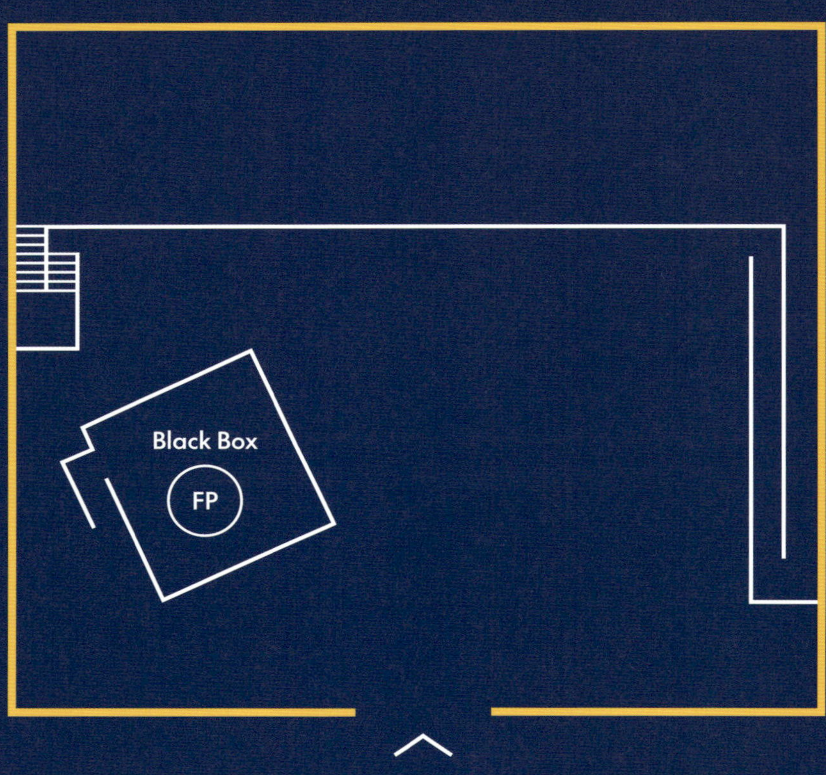

Dana Awartani / p. 160
Sammy Baloji / p. 52
Ursula Biemann / p. 54
Saodat Ismailova / p. 56
Liu Chuang / p. 58
The Migrant Ecologies Project / p. 60

Nguyễn Trinh Thi / p. 62
Tomás Saraceno / p. 182
Munem Wasif / p. 108
Yeo Siew Hua / p. 64
Liam Young / p. 66

THE DOCUMENTED AND THE FICTIONALIZED FILM PROGRAM

Presented in a black box cinema, the film program includes a sequence of cinematic works by artists screened continuously throughout the opening hours of the exhibition. This selection probes the boundaries between the documentary and the fictional. While a number of films use poetic language or mythical characters to excavate the past and unfold the stories embedded in places and histories, others draw from science fiction to speculate about future realities or address the social impact of new technologies. The presented films share the same concern that unfold throughout *After Rain*, addressing the global environmental crisis and the long-term impact of colonialism and new forms of extractivism. From ancient Arabic poetry to the science of the Amazonian Forest, the migration of birds, plantations, and crypto mining—the lines of inquiry pursued in each film contextualize the impact of hegemonic structures within a range of geographies, while offering windows into alternate imaginaries.

SAMMY BALOJI

Born 1978 in Lubumbashi, Democratic Republic of the Congo,
lives and works in Lubumbashi and Brussels, Belgium

Aequare: the Future that Never Was

2023 / Video, 20 min

Sammy Baloji is a photographer and filmmaker who documents the long shadow of extractive colonialism. The Democratic Republic of the Congo officially gained its independence from Belgium in 1960, but in many ways the linked exploitation of its people and the environment never ended. Through diptychs, collage, and other juxtaposition techniques, he highlights how the brutalities of direct rule morphed seamlessly into economic imperialism. These effects are particularly felt in the mineral-rich mining stronghold of Katanga, Baloji's native region, whose cultural, industrial, and architectural inheritance is at the heart of his practice. In 2008, he co-founded the Lubumbashi Biennale.

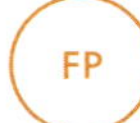

Blending Belgian newsreels from the 1940s and 1950s with present-day footage, Baloji's video *Aequare: the Future that Never Was* (2023) depicts an agricultural research center in colonial and post-colonial times and makes clear just how much has remained the same over the decades. The National Institute for Agronomic Study of the Belgian Congo was established in 1933 to leverage scientific research in modernizing Indigenous agrarian practices. The colonizers wanted to make Congolese land, already showing signs of soil depletion from overcultivation, even more productive, profitable. They wanted, as a voice-over near the end of the film suggests, to tame and civilize the land, along with its people—and simultaneously frame this as a humanitarian service.

Since then, the center has been nationalized and changed its name, but land, like people, bears witness to the ravages of empire. The European scientists and their families are gone; now local children play in the same pools, presently empty and overgrown, while laboratories sit unused. The evidence of decline is everywhere: vehicles and once meticulously maintained archives are rusty and musty—one can smell the dust through the screen—but every new frame feels like a perfect match cut, so strong is the sense of continuity. Despite the colonizers' best attempts to clear the rainforest for cash crops, it has grown back. All the life that remained out of frame in the propaganda reels is now in view, from teeming insects to river fish and local residents. Everything remains calm and lush and beautiful.

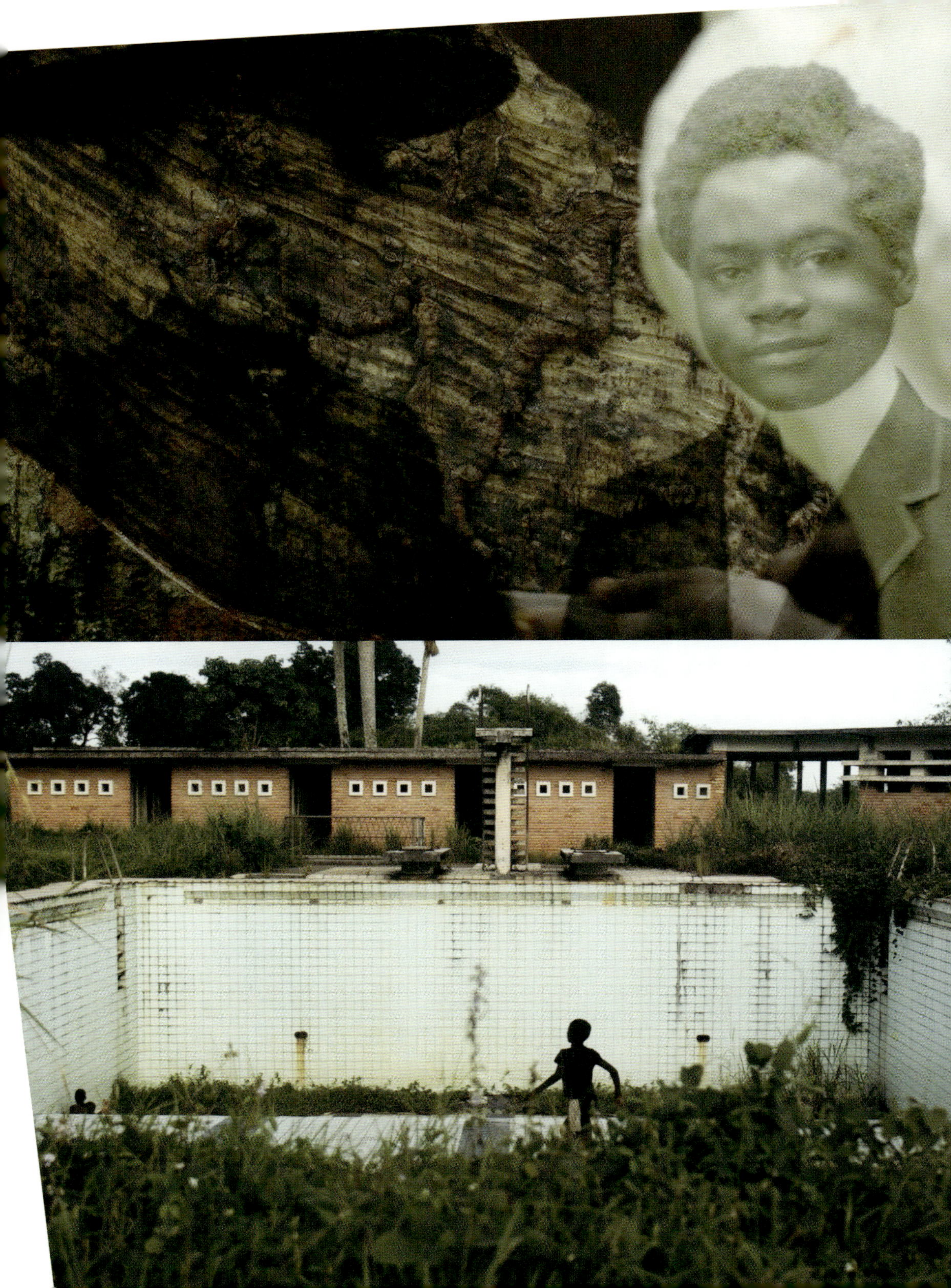

URSULA BIEMANN

Born 1955 in Zurich, Switzerland, where she lives and works

Forest Mind

2021 / Video, 31 min 45 sec

Ursula Biemann is an artist, video essayist, and writer. Her research-oriented practice is based on extensive fieldwork in remote landscapes, from icy Greenlandic waters to Amazonian rainforests, where she investigates the geopolitics of climate change and the human impact on natural ecologies, questioning the role of modern science in decolonial knowledge production. Biemann's artistic training began in Mexico City. She then studied at New York's School of Visual Arts and later at the Whitney Museum of American Art's prestigious Independent Study Program. She was awarded the Swiss Grand Award for Art / Prix Meret Oppenheim in 2009. Biemann's intellectual and incisive video essays intricately interweave cinematic vistas with documentary footage, science fiction speculations, and academic scholarship, forming rich tapestries of knowledge in which the boundaries of epistemological realities are tested, stretched, and expanded.

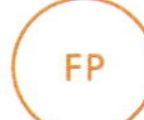

Filmed in Piamonte in southern Colombia, one home of the Inga people, Biemann's video *Forest Mind* (2021) builds on a previous work, *Forest Law* (2014), and blends together the alchemical and biochemical, the scientific and shamanic. It opens with a mesmerizing visualization: the digital code of rainforest sound recordings, a still image, and a biopsy of a seed from the endangered forest are transcoded into an eternal DNA sequence. Interspersed with performances by and interviews with the artist's longtime Indigenous collaborators, the video becomes a medium through which audiences encounter the mind-altering plant (and teacher) ayahuasca; they come to *know*—as opposed to simply learn—the cosmological depth and breadth of ancient wisdom. Here, advances of modern science, including in plant neurobiology, quantum biology, ethnobotany, and the anthropology of science itself, are brought into a common paradigm with decentralized vegetal intelligences and cellular states of consciousness familiar to traditional medics of the Amazonian rainforests.

Forest Mind was created in the wider context of Devenir Universidad, a long-term, Inga-led artistic and research collaboration from 2018, whose goal is to establish an Indigenous institute of higher learning in the community. Devenir Universidad, whose name means "becoming university," marks a shift in Biemann's critical practice to embrace alternative forms of cultural and pedagogical co-production of knowledge, while buttressing her commitment to using artistic action to positively impact lived realities and engage in crucial reparative exchanges.

Video stills from *Forest Mind*, 2021

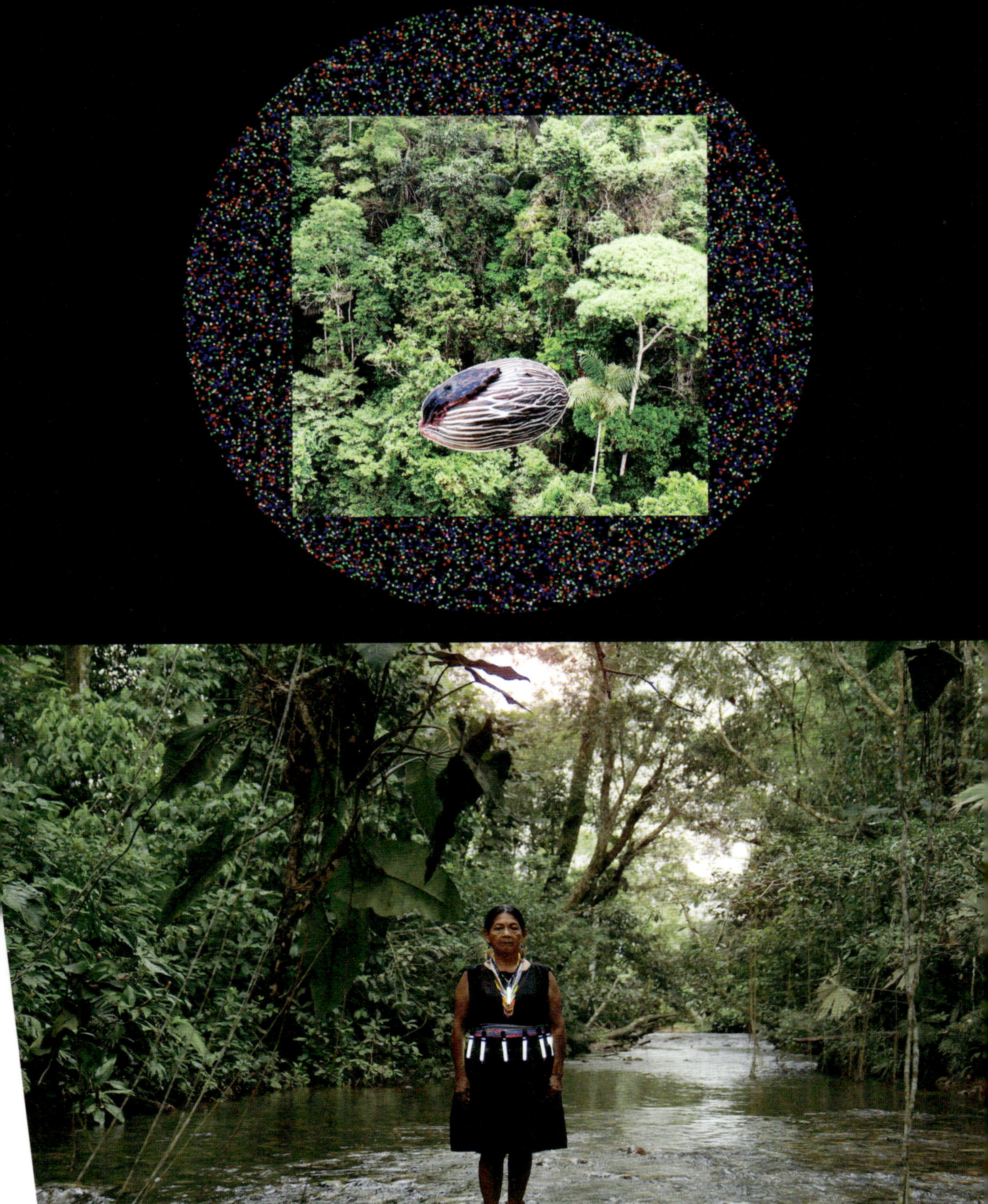

SAODAT ISMAILOVA

Born 1981 in Tashkent, Uzbekistan, lives and works in Tashkent
and Paris, France

18 000 Worlds

2023 / Video, 31 min

Saodat Ismailova's films unspool the landscapes and traditions of
post-Soviet Central Asia, in particular her homeland of Uzbekistan.
Weaving a rich tapestry of ritual, folklore, and a timeless atmosphere
that envelops her predominantly female protagonists, Ismailova's
cinematography is slow and meditative, employing long, dreamy
takes. The daughter of a cinematographer, she graduated in filmmaking in Uzbekistan, then moved to Treviso and Berlin, respectively,
for residencies with the research center Fabrica in Treviso and the
DAAD program in Berlin. Her documentary and fiction films have won
awards at major film festivals and international exhibitions. In 2021,
she set up DAVRA, a film collective dedicated to documenting Central
Asian cinematic heritage.

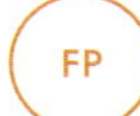

Sufi traditions suffuse Uzbeki life, among them the belief that our world
is one of 18,000 that comprise the universe. Shihab al-Din Suhrawardi,
the twelfth-century mystic and founder of Illuminationism, a school
of Islamic philosophy, proposes that reality is structured not by existence, but by these worlds, featuring varying intensities of divine light
and darkness. Ismailova's film *18 000 Worlds* (2023) casts light as a
main protagonist. It glances off futuristic atomic-era monuments and
burnishes tiled turquoise domes and piles of stones, glowing red in the
golden hour. It appears as a shy moon, as resplendent sunrises and
sunsets, as a lime-green aurora, and streams in from a cave ceiling.
There are people, too: wizened and smiling, weaving silk, or plucked
from the annals of Soviet military history and Western anthropology
through archival black-and-white footage. As the camera meditatively
pans across steppes and cities alike, interspersed with sequences of
flashing images, a manifold and refracted sense of time and place
slowly emerges. Afterimages from several alternate temporalities dance
like sunspots.

At various points in the film, a woman in a sunny studio—an archae-
ologist or maybe a conservationist—sifts through hand-drawn maps
and excavation photographs, then carefully brushes caked dirt off an
unidentified surface. Ismailova engages in a similar autoethnographic
process in this work, which incorporates unused fragments from her
own shoots alongside historical material from the Eye Filmmuseum.
18 000 Worlds suggests that a world is a multitude of realities; perhaps
a single reality can also inhabit thousands of worlds.

Video stills from 18 000 Worlds, 2023

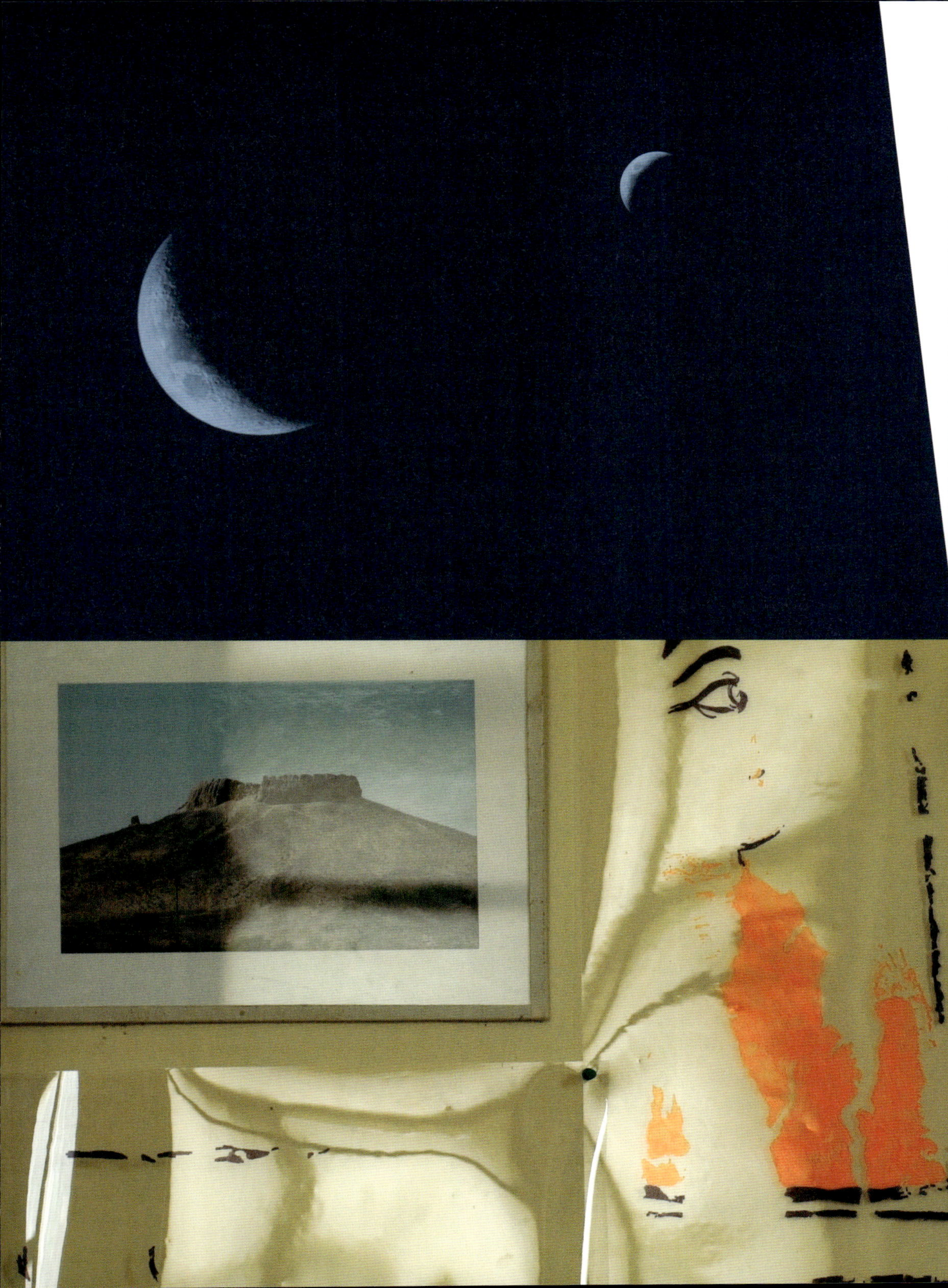

LIU CHUANG

Born 1978 in Hubei, China, lives and works in Shanghai, China

Bitcoin Mining and Field Recordings of Ethnic Minorities

2018 / Video, 40 min

Liu Chuang's films and installations elliptically analyze the various systems underpinning everyday life in our contemporary era. While his earlier works considered the relationship between individual autonomy and rapid, large-scale modernization in China, his recent projects are extensively researched explorations of how global capital flows and social technologies affect marginalized communities and transform natural landscapes. Liu's work has been shown in film festivals and exhibitions throughout the world, including at the Dhaka Art Summit (2020); the Centre Pompidou, Paris (2019); and the Asian Art Biennial, Taichung, Taiwan (2019).

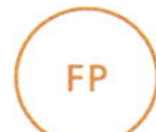

Liu's monumental three-channel video *Bitcoin Mining and Field Recordings of Ethnic Minorities* (2018) is a cinematic essay that connects ethnographic, economic, military, and visual histories with theoretical references. Narrated in Muya, a Sino-Tibetan language spoken in southwestern China, it identifies the physical effects that the seemingly invisible, placeless forces of modernization—such as electricity, the digital cloud, and cryptocurrency—have on bodies and landscapes. Territories traditionally occupied by ethnic minorities in China are disproportionately taken over by national infrastructure projects such as massive hydroelectric dams. Abandoned dams, in turn, are occupied by opportunistic actors to operate electricity-guzzling bitcoin mines that primarily benefit remote owners as they create virtual currencies used in international markets. Liu observes that these sites are frequently located in what Willem van Schendel calls *Zomia*, a term demarcating the highland regions that extend across East and Southeast Asia. It is a space of contradictions: rich with the cultural and linguistic diversity of its minority occupants yet sparsely populated and resourced, fiercely anti-assimilationist and often politically and economically isolated. The work draws a parallel between the deliberate statelessness of the region's occupants and the original intent behind bitcoin's creation, which was to enable peer-to-peer transactions outside the control of centralized authorities. Even though revolutionary technological inventions might claim to counter the concentration of power, they frequently perpetuate other forms of control.

The final third of the video takes a speculative turn as it progresses from the title's "field recordings" of Indigenous peoples in the Sichuan highlands to the otherworldly encounters portrayed in two iconic 1970s science fiction films. By juxtaposing realities with the fictive imaginary of cinema, Liu suggests that the sources of enlightenment and humanity extend beyond the limited perceptual bounds of dominant discourses.

Video stills from *Bitcoin Mining and Field Recordings of Ethnic Minorities*, 2018

DIRIYAH CONTEMPORARY ART BIENNALE 2024

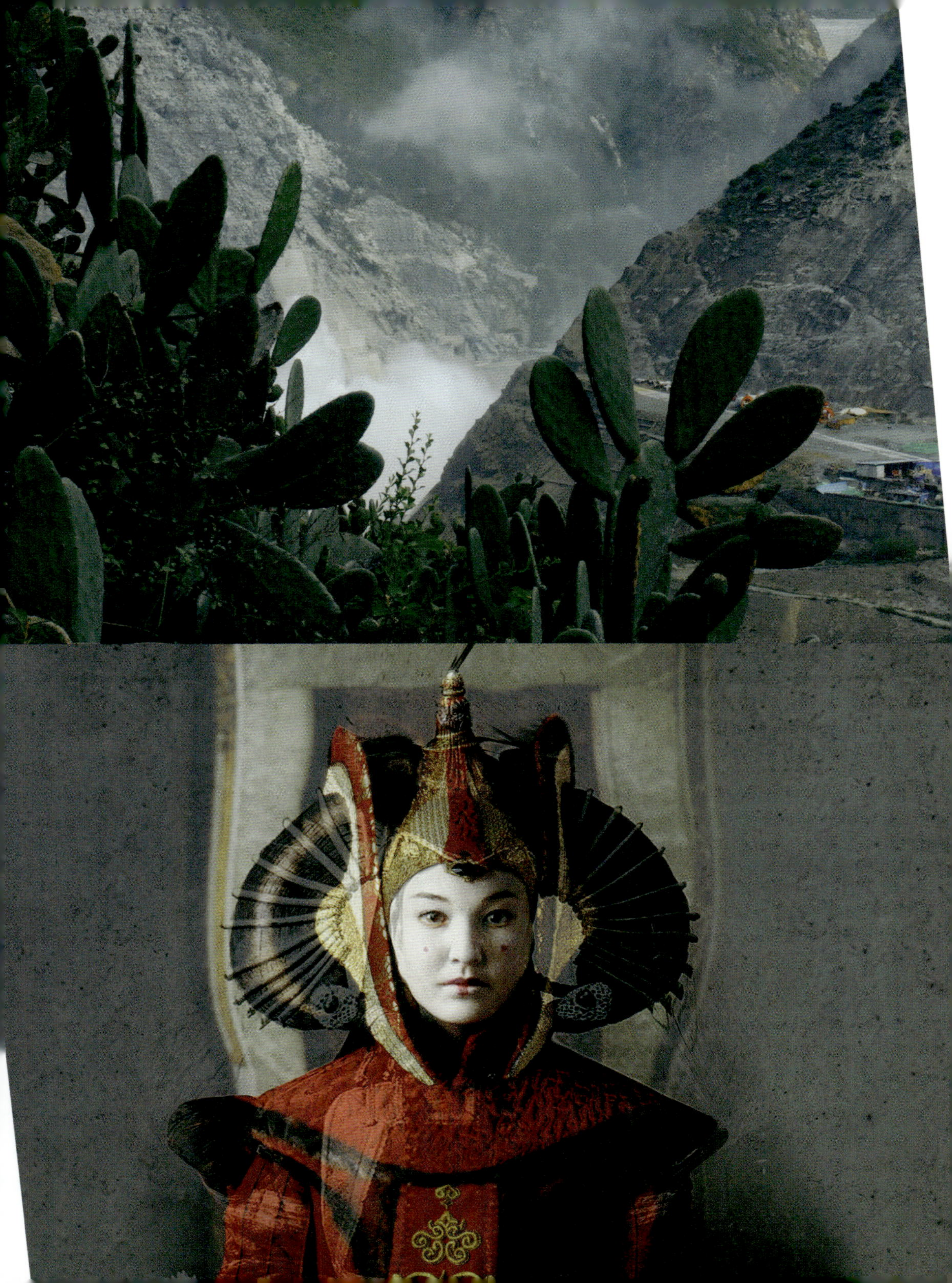

THE MIGRANT ECOLOGIES PROJECT

Established in 2009, Singapore
Lucy Davis, born 1970 in Singapore, lives and works in Helsinki, Finland
Zachary Chan, born 1990 in Singapore, where he lives and works
Kee Ya Ting, born 1988 in Singapore, where she lives and works
Zai Tang, born 1984 in London, United Kingdom, lives and works in Singapore

{if your bait can sing the wild one will come} Like Shadows Through Leaves

2021 / Video, 28 min

The Migrant Ecologies Project was founded in 2009 by artist, art writer, and academic Lucy Davis as an umbrella for informal, durational, transdisciplinary collaborations in and around art and ecology, primarily in Southeast Asia. Davis is an associate professor in Visual Cultures at Aalto University, Finland. Between 2005 and 2016, Davis was a founding member of the School of Art, Design and Media at Nanyang Technological University (NTU), Singapore. Her collaborators on the project, Zachary Chan, Kee Ya Ting, and Zai Tang are artists with backgrounds, respectively, in the fields of sonic arts and graphic design, photography and video production, and sound design. In 2021 *{if your bait can sing the wild one will come} Like Shadows Through Leaves* was awarded the FIPRESCI International Federation of Film Critics Award at the 67th International Short Film Festival Oberhausen.

The Migrant Ecologies Project's film is part of the artists' long-term engagement with Tanglin Halt, one of Singapore's oldest public housing estates. Built alongside a railway track that ran through the heart of Singapore but is no longer in operation, these once pioneering modern housing blocks are now empty and slated for demolition. The ten-meter-wide strip of railway land, formerly owned by the Malaysian state and now a zone of indeterminate governance, hosted a wealth of human and animal activities. Ornithologists observed 105 different species of birds in the property. Now the low-income residents who called Tanglin Halt home have been relocated elsewhere. Tree shrines, community vegetable gardens, and gathering places that had grown up on the former railroad tracks have been removed, while bird life has drastically declined.

The artists returned to this site in transition and traced the remaining echoes, shadows, and memories defining this piece of land. Using online images sourced from birdwatcher groups, they projected the shadows of birds at dawn with overhead projector transparencies. In addition, they recreated the birds' presence using paper cut-outs. The fragmentary voices and bird calls of the film's soundtrack are drawn from field recordings of birds in the area, interviews with former residents and nature activists, and a selection of bird-specific Malay *pantuns* (four-line poems), compiled by writer Alfian Sa'at.

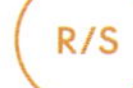
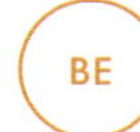

Above: Staart! Detail: Bird People Series 3/8 Dedicated to Alan Owyong, Ow Yong Sue Lin and a Burung Kunyit Besaror Black-naped oriole, 2020 / Below: Video still from {if your bait can sing the wild one will come} Like Shadows Through Leaves, 2021

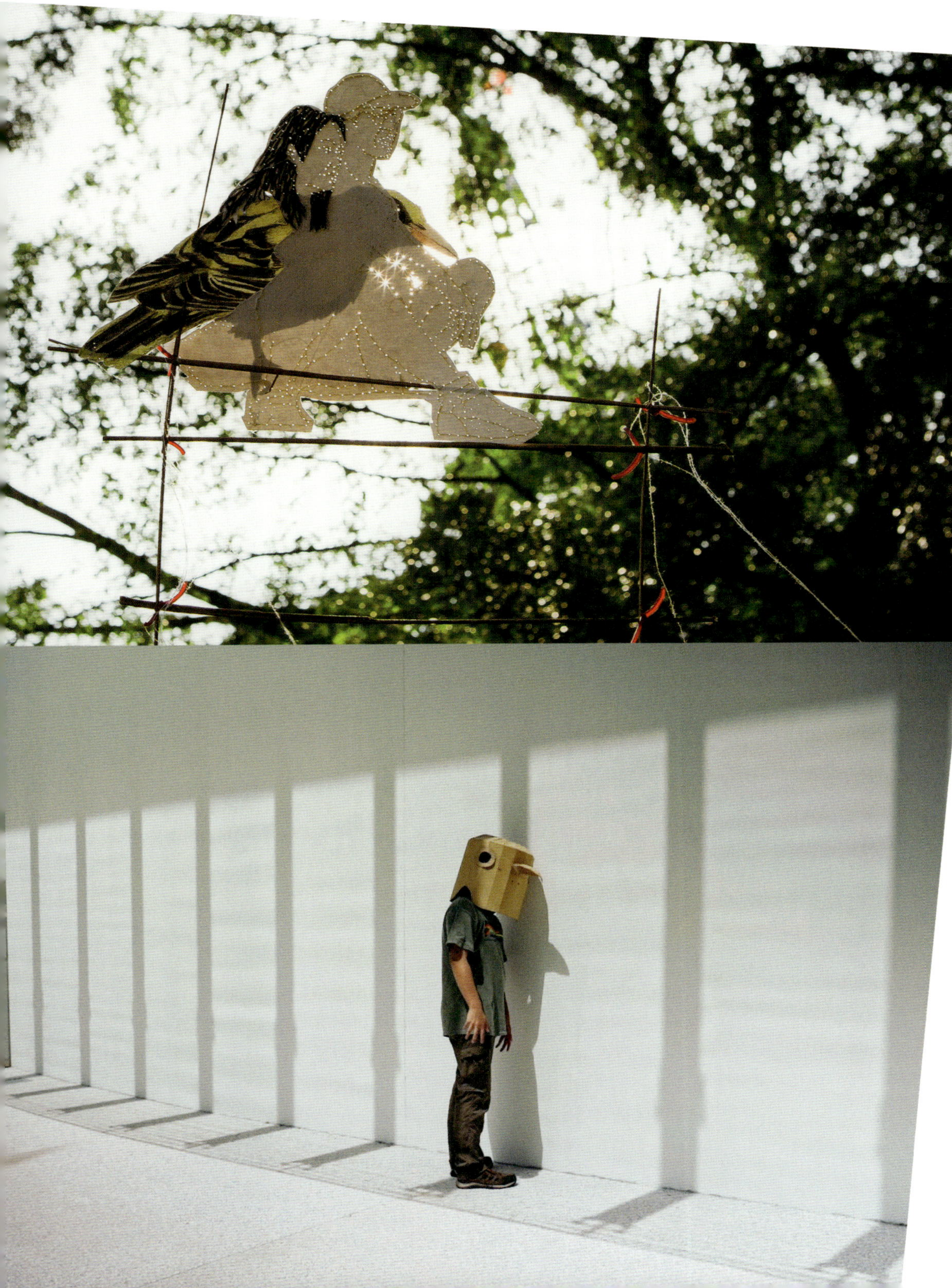

NGUYỄN TRINH THI

Born 1973 in Hanoi, Vietnam, where she lives and works

How to Improve the World / Cải tiến Thế giới
2021 / Video, 46 min

Nguyễn Trinh Thi is an experimental filmmaker and media artist, whose poetic films are deep reflections on the role of the observer and the subtle relationship between images, sound, and text. Countering what she calls "displaced or misinterpreted" constructions of history and culture, her works on Vietnam explore the shadows of its past, often foregrounding overlooked landscapes and cultural figures. Nguyễn's training—in journalism, photography, international relations, and ethnographic film, all in the United States—is aligned with her practice of working in the field; she researches, archives, and redeploys current and historical materials to construct alternative records and aesthetic taxonomies. From 2009 to 2015 she was the co-founder and co-director of Hanoi DocLab, which through workshops, discussions, and screenings served as a focal point for the development of independent filmmaking and video practice in Vietnam.

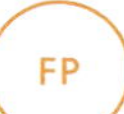

Set in Vietnam's Central Highlands, *How to Improve the World / Cải tiến Thế giới* (2021) concludes a trilogy that explores Indigenous culture. The film highlights the role of sound in the cultural practices and spiritual beliefs of the Jarai people, for whom the gong plays a central role in rituals commemorating the dead and rites of protection and fertility. Their animistic religion has waned in the face of war and Christian missionizing, but they continue to sing folk songs accompanied by bamboo instruments such as the *k'ni* (one-stringed mouth fiddle) and *ting ning*, whose strings are plucked to imitate the gong.

In the film, Nguyễn asks Ksor Sep, a Jarai shaman, and her own teenage daughter, An Nguyễn Maxtone-Graham, various questions about the role that sound plays for them. Her daughter's matter-of-fact responses show the dominance of the image in contemporary society. In contrast, listening is paramount in every aspect of Jarai life: from the ear-blowing ritual practiced on newborns to the oral transmission of *khan* (epic tales). The testimony of Ksor Sep—who performs, ventriloquizes, recollects, and forgets—underscores the costs of privileging the visual over the auditory in the hierarchy of senses. Simultaneously, the film's mix of Jarai, Vietnamese, and English—at times selectively or belatedly translated—creates spaces for nonverbal sonic expressions, including silence. Through her montage, Nguyễn valorizes these alternate pathways of perception and creation, while depicting their inevitable disappearance.

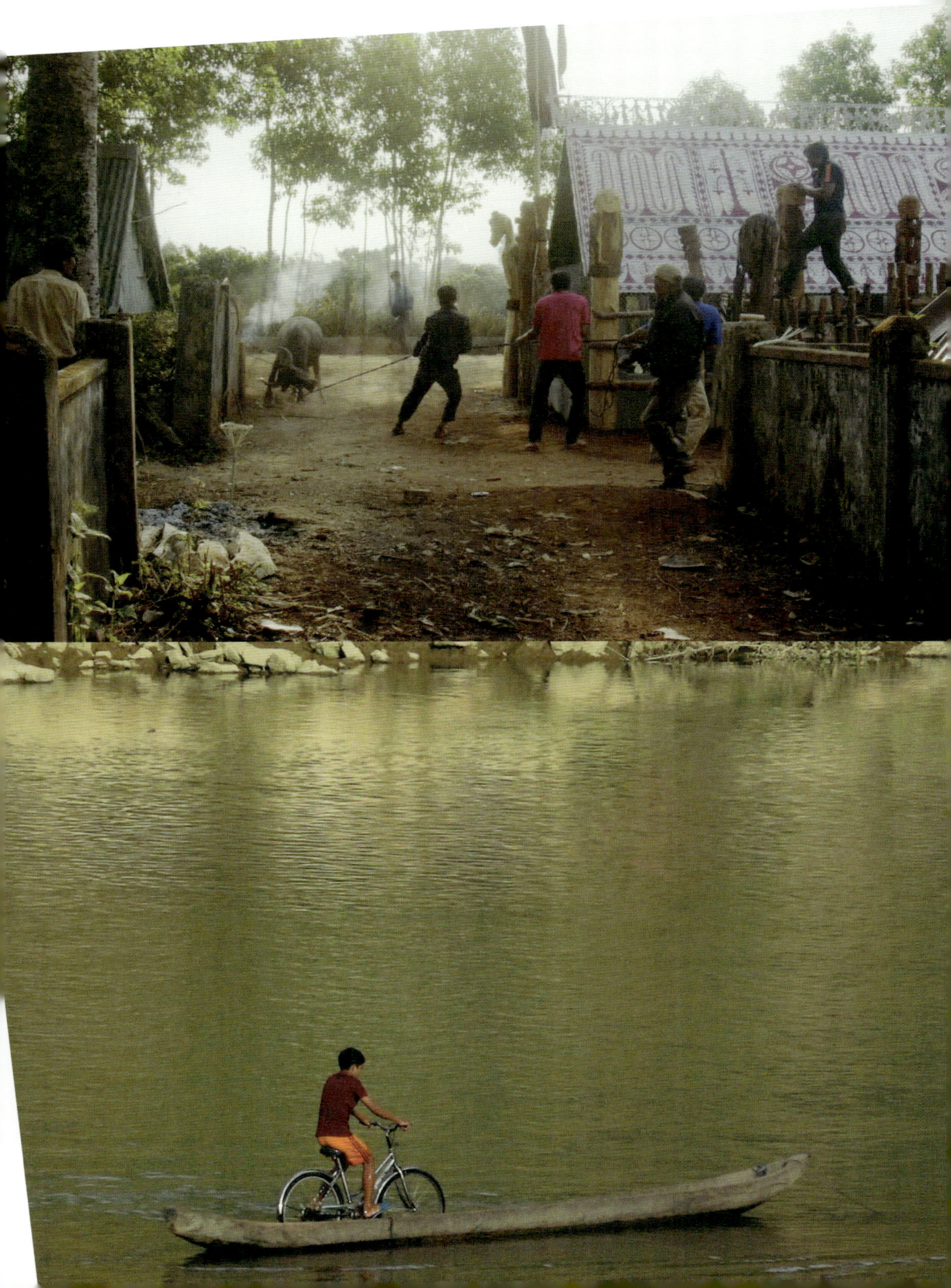

YEO SIEW HUA

Born 1985 in Singapore, lives and works in Singapore and
Buenos Aires, Argentina

An Invocation to the Earth
2020 / Video, 16 min 10 sec

Filmmaker and visual artist Yeo Siew Hua harnesses the moving image
in imaginative and empathetic ways to speculate upon possibilities
of human transformation. Graduating with a film and media studies
diploma, he then studied philosophy at the National University of
Singapore. In his ambitious films and videos Yeo navigates subjects
as diverse as the migrant experience in Singapore; the ancient, animistic beliefs of Southeast Asia; and industrial animal husbandry in
his adoptive country of Argentina. Celebrated for his bold cinematic
explorations, Yeo was awarded the Locarno Film Festival's Golden
Leopard in 2018 for his film *A Land Imagined* (2018).

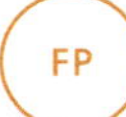

In *An Invocation to the Earth* (2020), Yeo revives and inverts the
Malay folktale of Sang Kancil, a wily mouse-deer who deftly outsmarts its foes, and intertwines this underdog fable with the region's
environmental politics. In the film, Kancil appears in human form.
Wearing an animal mask, she carries her mortal enemy Buaya (crocodile) through the rainforest on her back. In contrast to the traditional narrative, Buaya then takes long-overdue, fatal revenge upon
Kancil. Next, a forest fire reanimates the mouse-deer and unites the
two protagonists as they face this existential threat. They remove
their masks and embrace. It is now Buaya's turn to carry her adver-
sary. As they retreat, the blackened forest slowly lights up with the
facial-recognition grids of surveillance technology, like stars in the
night. Each constellation, however, represents the faces, names, and
years of death of fallen ecological defenders from the Philippines,
where such activists are murdered with impunity.

Yeo's video was shot during the Hungry Ghost Festival, when people of
Chinese origin traditionally pay homage to their ancestors and burn
paper effigies of money and material goods. The inferno in the film
also references another kind of fire: Southeast Asia's transboundary
haze, caused by the large-scale burning of peatland in Sumatra
and Borneo to clear and, it is believed, fertilize the soil. The tension
between old and new practices and between mythical and scientific
worldviews permeate Yeo's practice. *An Invocation to the Earth* is a
portal into a dimension where time, space, and individual identities
collapse, transporting viewers toward a collective humanity.

Video stills from *An Invocation to the Earth*, 2020

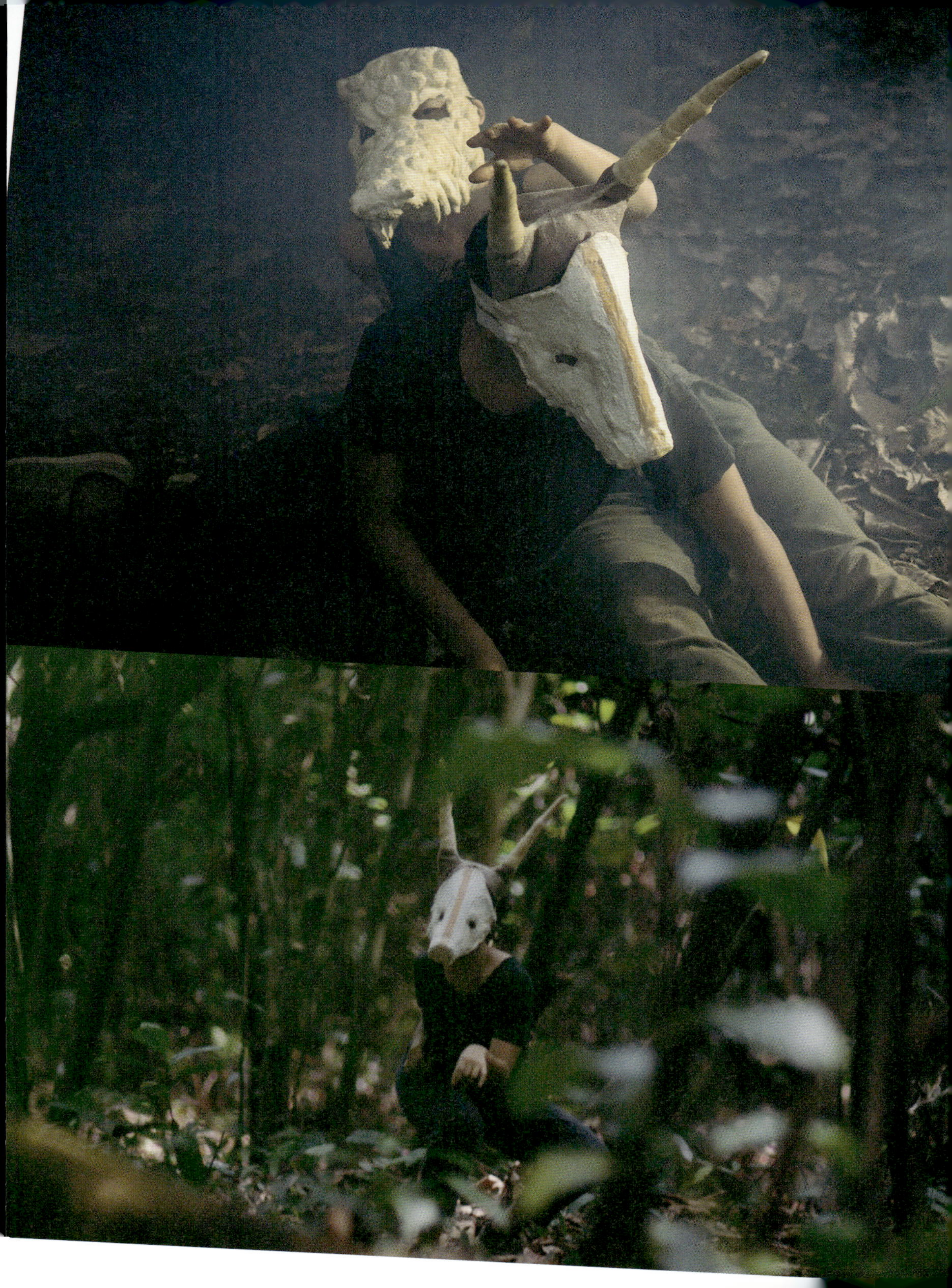

LIAM YOUNG

Born 1979 in Brisbane, Australia, lives and works in Los Angeles, CA,
United States, and London, United Kingdom

The Great Endeavor
2023 / Video, 9 min

Speculative architect, production designer, and director Liam Young thinks on a planetary scale. A visual consultant for television and film, he also creates his own immersive films and installations, which transport us to possible worlds of the near future. The imagery and footage for his propositional earthscapes build upon the research of his nomadic studio, Unknown Fields, which documents the impact extractive processes have on far-flung lands—from Madagascar sapphire pits to Amazonian oil fields—often with the help of autonomous drones or remote sensing technology. Young is an educator and author as well, and currently directs the master's in fiction and entertainment at SCI-Arc in Los Angeles.

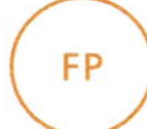

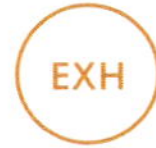

In *The Great Endeavor* (2023), Young presents a stubbornly optimistic proposition to terraform our collapsing planet. Beyond curbing or reducing carbon emissions, environmental scientist Holly Jean Buck, the short film's science consultant, advocates we "decolonize the atmosphere" by removing greenhouse gases entirely. What if an enormous carbon-capturing infrastructure were built to mineralize carbon dioxide into desert rock, or inject it beneath the seabed? What if this were the largest engineering project ever, matching the scale of the international fossil fuel industry, but wholly powered by renewable energy?

With sweeping pans and long takes, Young highlights a giant, machine-like edifice being towed by ships to rise, like a leviathan robot savior, from the crashing waves. The hyperrealistic, coldly gray steel structure, outlined by blinking red lights, ironically resembles an oil rig, except ecological rescue is in action here. Across the endless ocean, constellations of tidal turbines spin; in dusty deserts, solar panel fields glimmer like dragon skin. Young's "new technological sublime" hums along to "a new planetary workers' song": the pulsing, increasingly loud chorus of multi-tracked voices underscores new labor's invisibility—human presence is only implied here, presumably operating the massive machineries that save us from ourselves. (Workwear imagined for these unseen inhabitants is on view in Exhibition Hall B1.) Young is no romantic dreamer: in its very title, *The Great Endeavor* acknowledges the unprecedented degree of global collaboration needed for this undertaking. In his visual materialization of solutions, currently being researched, he challenges us to make the seemingly impossible an urgent reality.

Video stills from *The Great Endeavor*, 2023

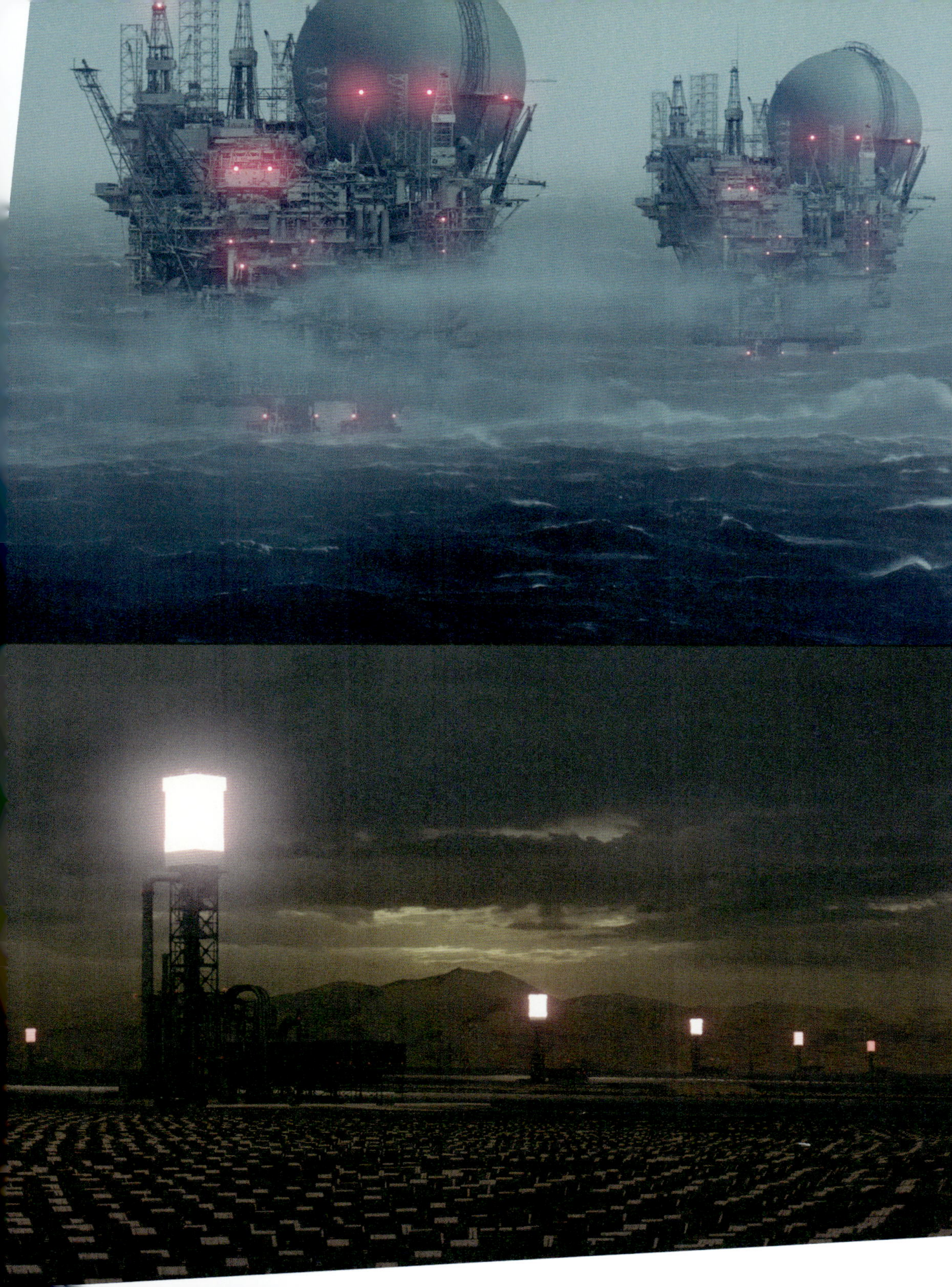

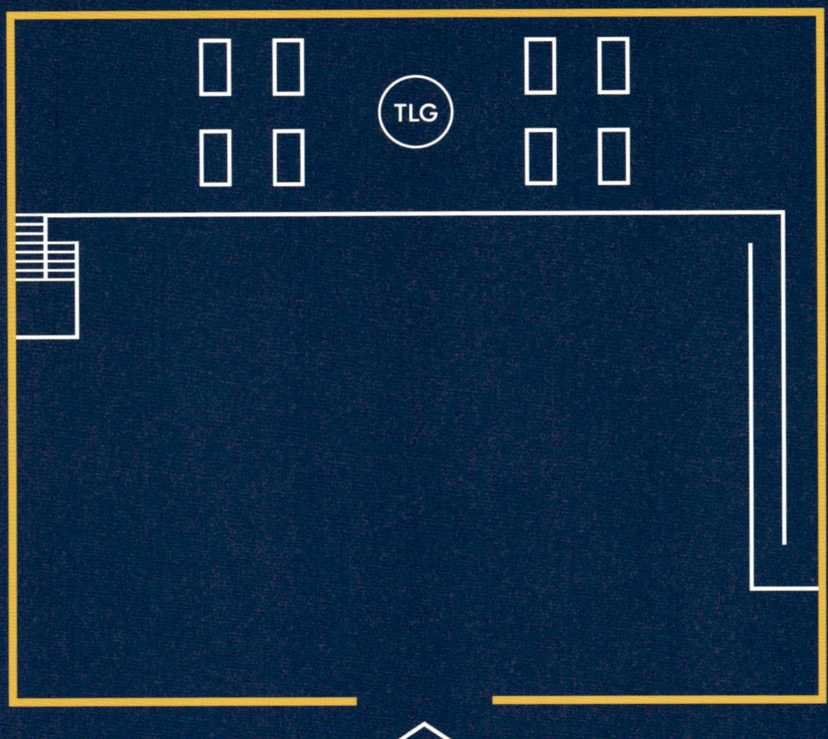

TLG
Entrance

RESEARCH AND SEARCH

Artistic research translates into a discursive and multidisciplinary approach to art-making, as artists often engage with their subjects of interest over the longterm. The arranged materials offer viewers a close look into artists' diverse areas of inquiry. These range from environmental to archaeological, from architectural to community-building topics. This section also introduces different artistic languages and methods used across *After Rain*, such as approaches to photographic representation, interviews, archival research, and mapping. It also presents studies of materials, forms, and typologies. In addition, on several screens an opportunity is provided to view the projects specifically commissioned for The Learning Garden, the online platform of the Biennale.

DANIAH ALSALEH

Born 1970 in Riyadh, Saudi Arabia, lives and works between Jeddah
and Riyadh, Saudi Arabia

A Stone's Palette

2023–24

Daniah Alsaleh is a Saudi artist whose artworks explore the intersections of social discourse, identity, and digital space. Her practice uses physical materials in combination with computational methodologies and aims to enable art as a critical mediator in human relationships. The multidisciplinary nature of her work is derived from her education background and exploratory practice; Alsaleh holds an undergraduate degree in computer applications from King Saud University in Riyadh (1993). She subsequently took selected courses at art academies in London, including Central Saint Martins, Slade School of Art, and The Prince's Foundation School of Traditional Arts, and began producing art and exhibiting in 2013. In 2019 Al Saleh won the second edition of the Ithra Art Prize with an audiovisual installation titled *Sawtam* (2019), an audio track with pronunciations of all twenty-eight Arabic phonemes accompanied by a generative visual representation of the sounds made in speech. The artwork acted as a visual representation of women's voices in a new era for female empowerment in Saudi Arabia. She completed an MFA with distinction in computational art at Goldsmiths, University of London (2020), and has since continued to exhibit and take part in residencies regionally and internationally.

Her 2023 residency with the Goethe-Institut Riyadh made it possible for the artist to explore archaeological sites AlUla and Tayma alongside a Saudi-German team of archaeologists headed by the German Archaeological Institute (DAI). Encountering the archaeological finds from this region, she became interested in carnelian stone beads as objects with an embodied history and cultural significance. Carnelian beads were produced in Tayma and served as important social artifacts. These beads, once central to rituals and identity, continue to resonate in modern times, echoing the unbroken thread of human expression. Bridging the ancient and the contemporary, she reflects on the role of these beads and their ongoing usage in a series of mixed-media artworks conceived as abstractions of the archaeological sites. Using sketches, photo transfer, oil paint, and carnelian powder, the works use the materiality of these sites to offer a view of history—and continuity.

Above: Indian carnelian semiprecious stones to be ground into powdered pigment, Jeddah, Saudi Arabia, 2023
Below: Studio view during the artist's residency at Hayy Jameel, Jeddah, Saudi Arabia, 2023

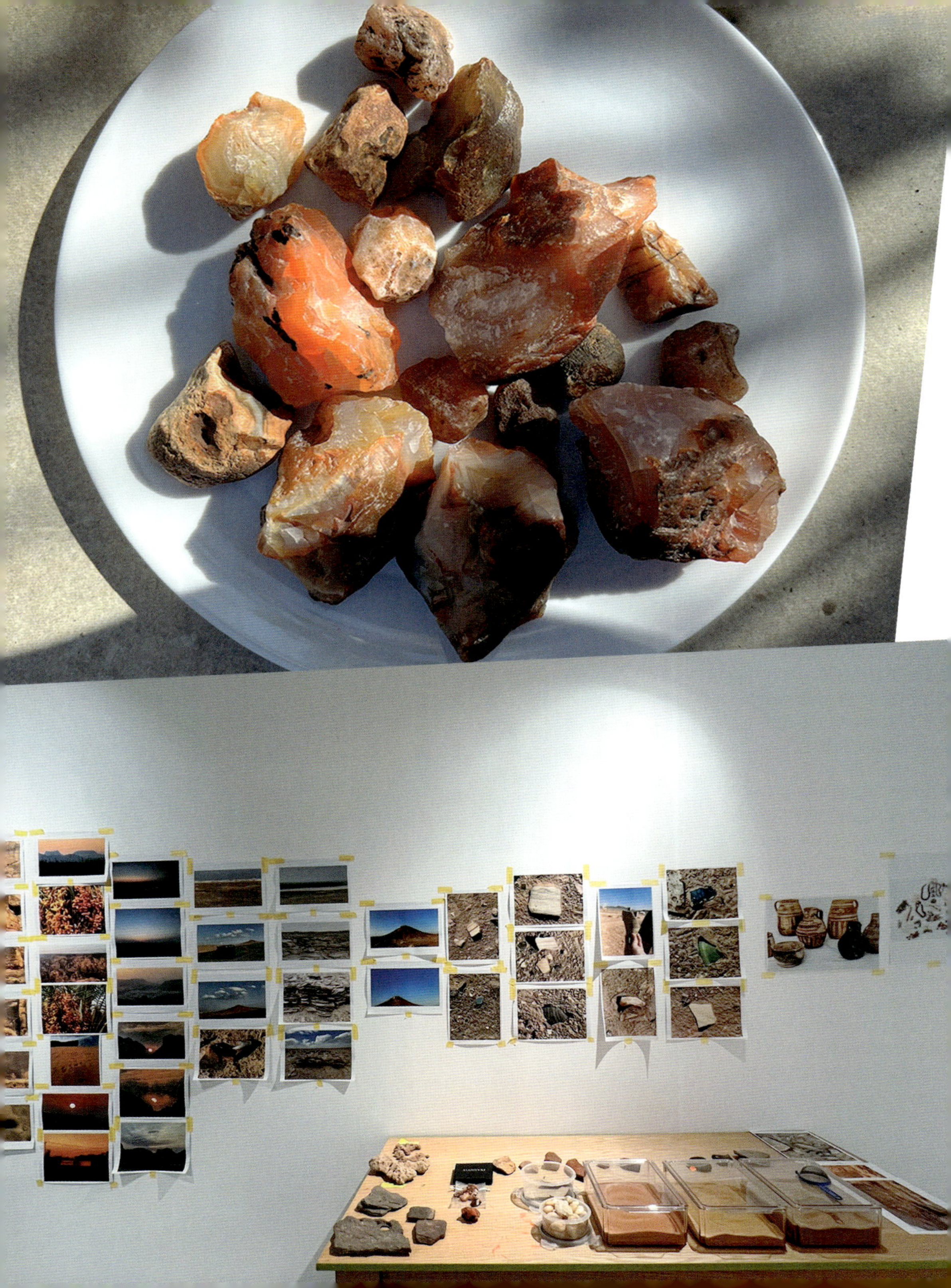

ASEEL ALYAQOUB

Born 1986 in Kuwait City, Kuwait, where she lives and works

The Secret Lake
2024

Desert as Method /
Art Practice as Research
Workshop / Artist Talk, September 16, 2023

Aseel AlYaqoub is an artist, curator, and author whose inquiries into the past and present of Kuwait span the fields of architecture, history, and cultural studies. Through her archival research and interdisciplinary artistic practice, she deconstructs symbols and narratives surrounding emerging Kuwaiti nationhood and Arab identity from the postcolonial era into the present; she also explores imaginaries of the region's natural landscapes. After studying architecture at the AA School of Architecture in London and working in the field, she received an MFA from the Pratt Institute in New York in 2015. She is the founder of Safat Studios, an artist-run initiative in Kuwait City. In 2021 she co-curated the Kuwait Pavilion at the 17th Venice Architecture Biennale with the project *Space Wars*, which revisited the conflict and military occupation of the Gulf War thirty years later, interrogating the environmental implications of the military conflict and occupation.

As a backdrop for modernization and development, the desert has featured prominently in AlYaqoub's investigations. As part of Biennale Encounters, she conducted a workshop, titled "Desert as Method," for participants residing in Saudi Arabia and coming from diverse backgrounds and regions, which addressed different representations of the desert across fictional and colonial accounts, from cinema and history to art and architecture. Challenging the view of the desert as barren land, AlYaqoub traced the colonial and orientalist history of "emptiness" as a notion that has legitimized exploitation and military expansion. Drawing on her research for *Space Wars* and the work of historians such as Samia Henni (*Deserts Are Not Empty*, 2022), AlYaqoub examined the deployment of the hinterlands—remote spaces outside of densely populated, urban areas—as sites of military infrastructure and oil extraction. In her presentation for the research section of the Biennale, she builds on the insights gained in her workshop to examine a site on the periphery of Riyadh in Al Uyaynah commonly known as the Secret Lake. Through utilizing mapping technologies and satellite imagery, AlYaqoub traces and analyzes the site's ecological history, its current uses for purposes ranging from camel farms to resource industries, and its prospective transformations.

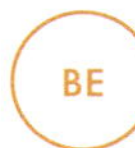

Above: Wara Hill in Al Ahmadi, Kuwait, 1966 / Below: An aerial photograph of the old port town of Kuwait showing the interplay between land and sea, while the desert extends on the horizon, 1927

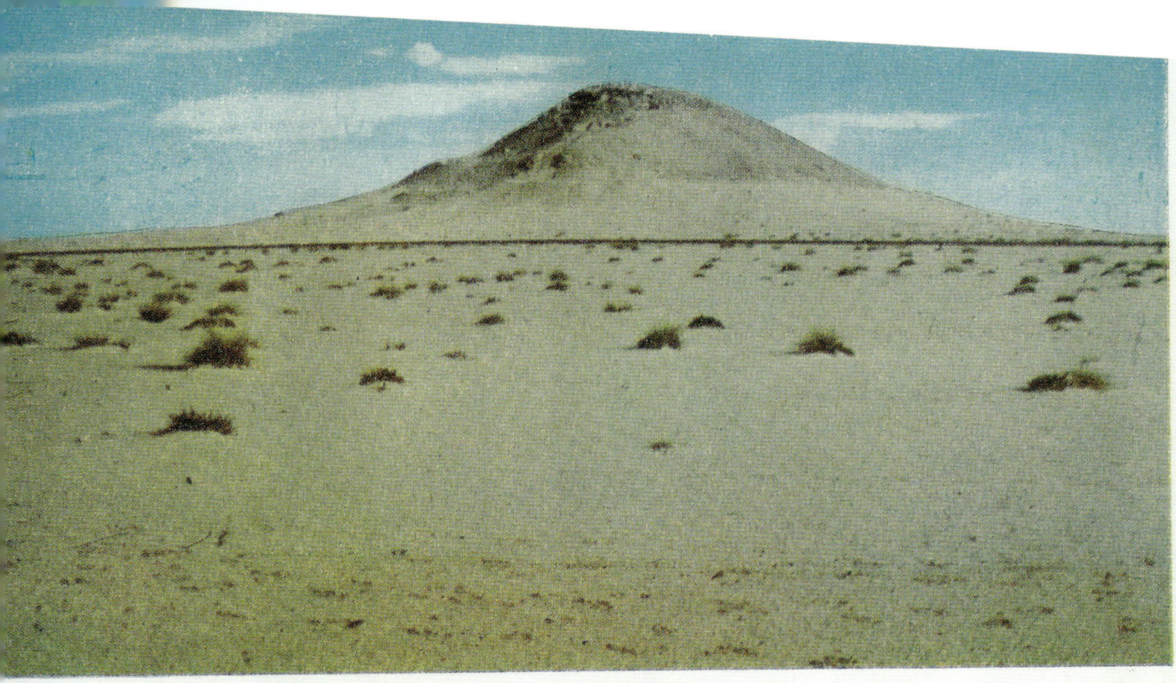

جبل وارة (أواره) بالأحمدى بالكويت من تصوير المؤلف في شهر
نوفمبر ١٩٦٦ .

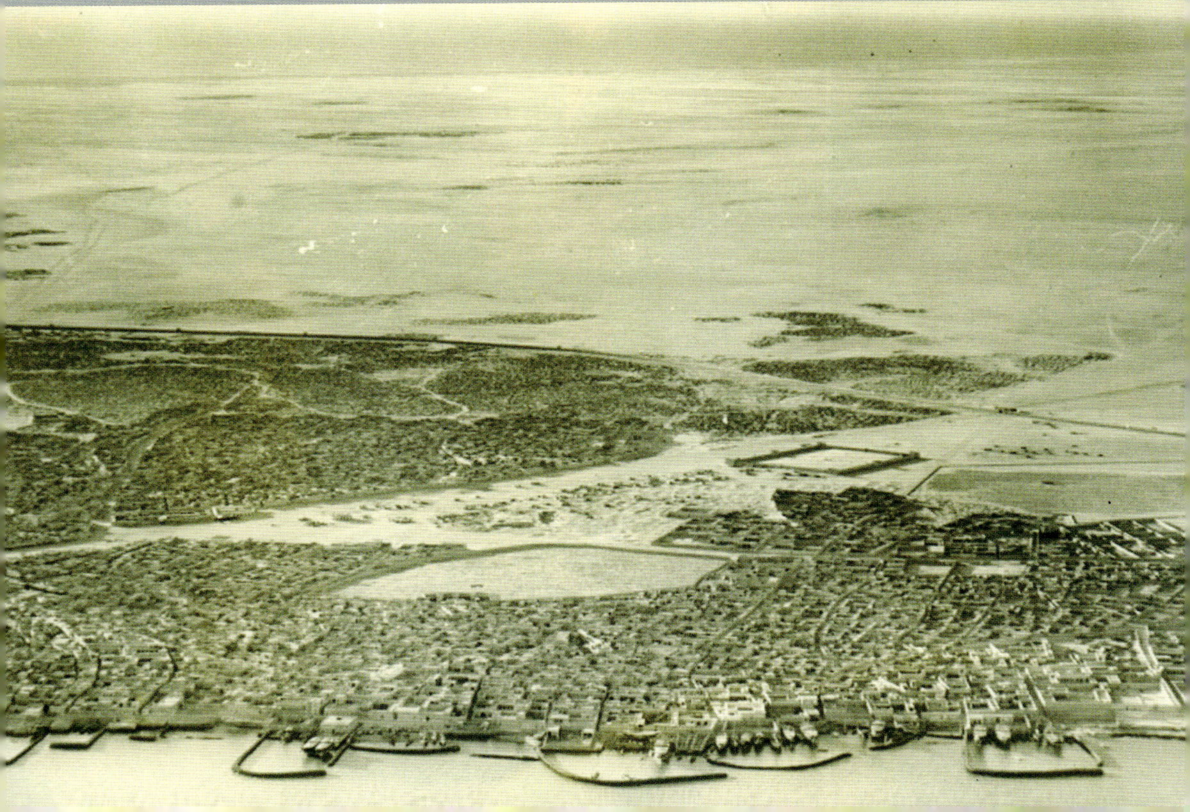

BAHRAINI—DANISH

Studio established 2016 in Manama, Bahrain
Christian Vennerstrøm Jensen lives and works in Copenhagen, Denmark
Maitham Almubarak and Batool Alshaikh live and work in Manama, Bahrain

Surface Finds

2024

bahraini—danish studio and art collective uses cross-cultural references and dialogue as the basis of a practice that borrows and bridges new forms for furniture, objects, and installations. Founded by the architects Christian Vennerstrøm Jensen, Maitham Almubarak, and Batool Alshaikh, the practice's dual-country name reflects not only the origins of its constituents, but also critical histories in the relations between the two states. In 1953 a Danish archaeological expedition made groundbreaking discoveries of almost 12,000 Dilmun burial mounds dating from 2050–1750 BCE near Qal'at Al-Bahrain (the Bahrain Fort), earning it UNESCO World Heritage Site status. The group's work references this history. Its practice is based on the principle that dialogue can yield solutions to long-standing design challenges and evolutions of form. The studio's transnational approach also includes exchange and debate with artisans and craftspeople in different locations, with creative decision-making and consensus drawn from different cultural perspectives.

In *Surface Finds* (2024), a project conceived specifically for the Biennale, the collective examines the Saudi Arabian archeological hobby of "pot-picking," in which Aramco oil field engineers would take their families out into the desert on weekend mornings to sift through the sand in search of potsherds and other objects. On professional digs, such excavations are vertical, systematic, and findings are recorded by layer, creating a timeline of culture, history, and change. After the archaeologists have gone, what remains on such sites are piles of sand mixed with excavated and discarded "evidence"—a cataloguing of cultural history. *Surface Finds* takes these discarded piles found at archaeological sites including Qal'at Al-Bahrain as its subject matter, surveying the evidence (clay shards) into a classification system centered around color, texture, and composition. Using color-scanning devices and microscopic cameras to photograph the shards in detail, bahraini—danish undertakes a comparative study with the clay currently used in Bahrain and presents this in an installation format. In this way, *Surface Finds* offers a continuum of dialogue between the potters of the Dilmun civilization, Danish archaeologists, and ceramicists, excavators, and artists of today.

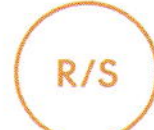

Pottery sherds, A'Ali, Bahrain, 2023

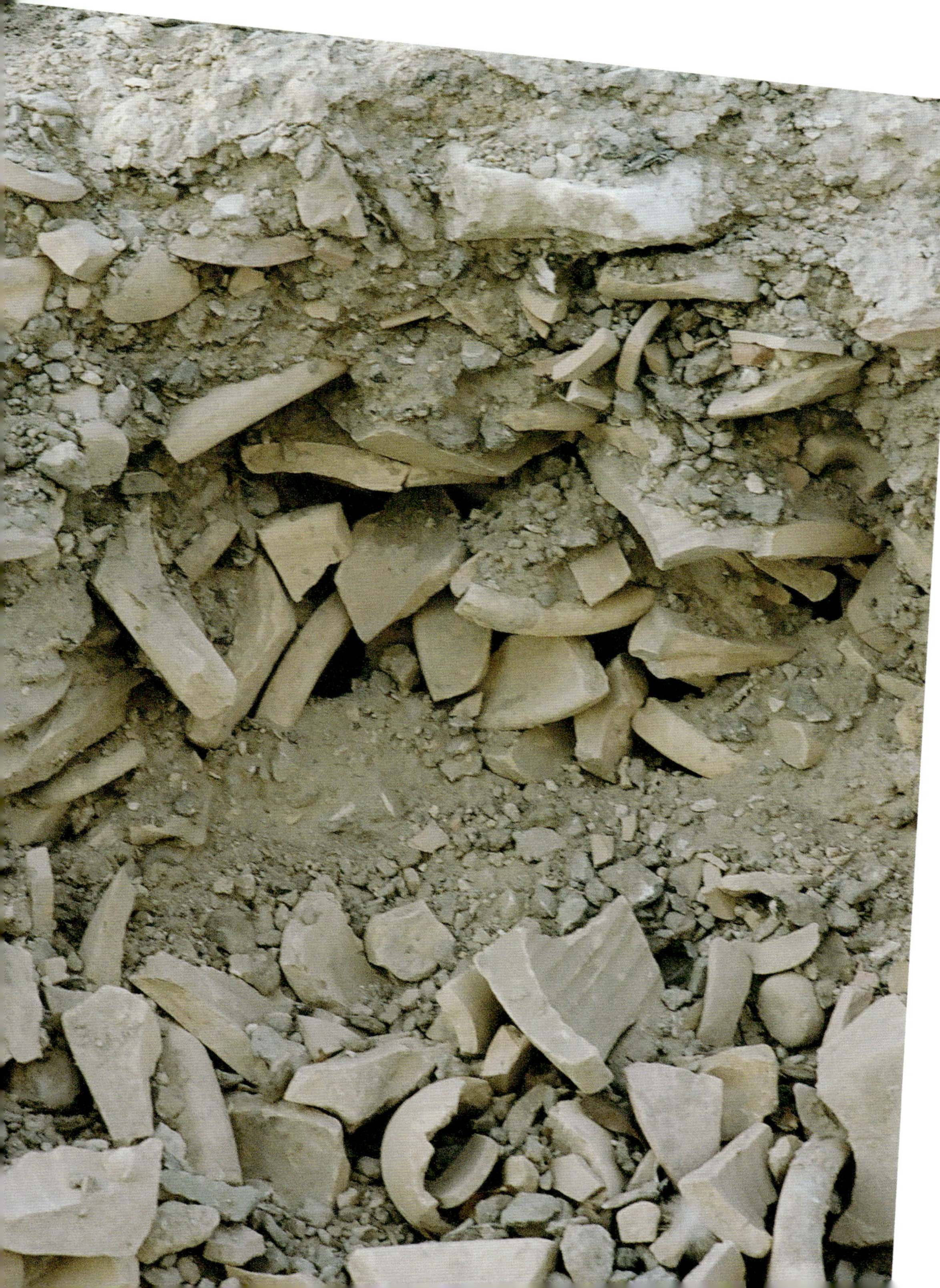

BRICKLAB

Studio established in 2015 in Jeddah, Saudi Arabia
Abdulrahman Gazzaz, born 1985 in Jeddah, Saudi Arabia, where he lives and works
Turki Gazzaz, born 1988 in Jeddah, Saudi Arabia, where he lives and works

Diriyah Biennale Foundation Building / Saudi Modern
2024

Bricklab is a studio for architecture, design and experimental research based in Jeddah, Saudi Arabia. The Gazzaz brothers Abdulrahman and Turki are architects who situate their practice around innovative approaches to research, space-making, and materiality. After studying at the University of the West of England in Bristol, and McGill University in Montreal, respectively, the brothers returned to Jeddah and established Bricklab with like-minded architects. For almost ten years, their practice has been associated with a revived interest in architecture, design, art, and history in Saudi Arabia. Their work has aimed to advance design as a discipline bridging multiple fields and practices. It also investigates how design shapes social and community structures. Bricklab were the designers of the Saudi Pavilion *Spaces in Between* at the 16th Venice Architecture Biennale in 2018, where they produced a scenography of cast resin and sand walls. In 2019 the practice won the competition to design the Hayy Cinema at Hayy Jameel in Jeddah, a landmark cultural commission. More recently, they have compiled and exhibited the first edition of a long-term body of research on modern architecture in Saudi Arabia, titled *Saudi Modern* (2021), which traces recent architectural histories and urbanism in Jeddah from 1939–64. Bricklab are the architects for the Diriyah Biennale Foundation venue and offices in addition to multiple projects in the JAX District. They were also participants in the inaugural Diriyah Contemporary Art Biennale in 2021–22 and the Islamic Arts Biennale in 2023. In addition to their practice's design work and research, the Gazzaz brothers initiated Rawdah Print, a publishing house and store for printed matter and design.

For this edition of the Biennale, Bricklab has been invited to show the development and research behind various projects within the studio's wide range of intellectual explorations. Their presentation highlights two core aspects of the studio's work. The first, *Diriyah Biennale Foundation Building*, introduces their architectural practice with a focus on the development of the JAX District and the refurbishment of the industrial site where the Biennale takes place. It displays the floor plans, models, and sketches that guided their design process. The second, *Saudi Modern*, presents archival materials, incorporating drawings, photographs, casts, and historical artifacts that have informed their ongoing research on this topic.

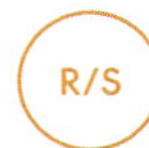

On-site 1:1 model of Diriyah Biennale Foundation façade, JAX District, Riyadh, Saudi Arabia, 2021

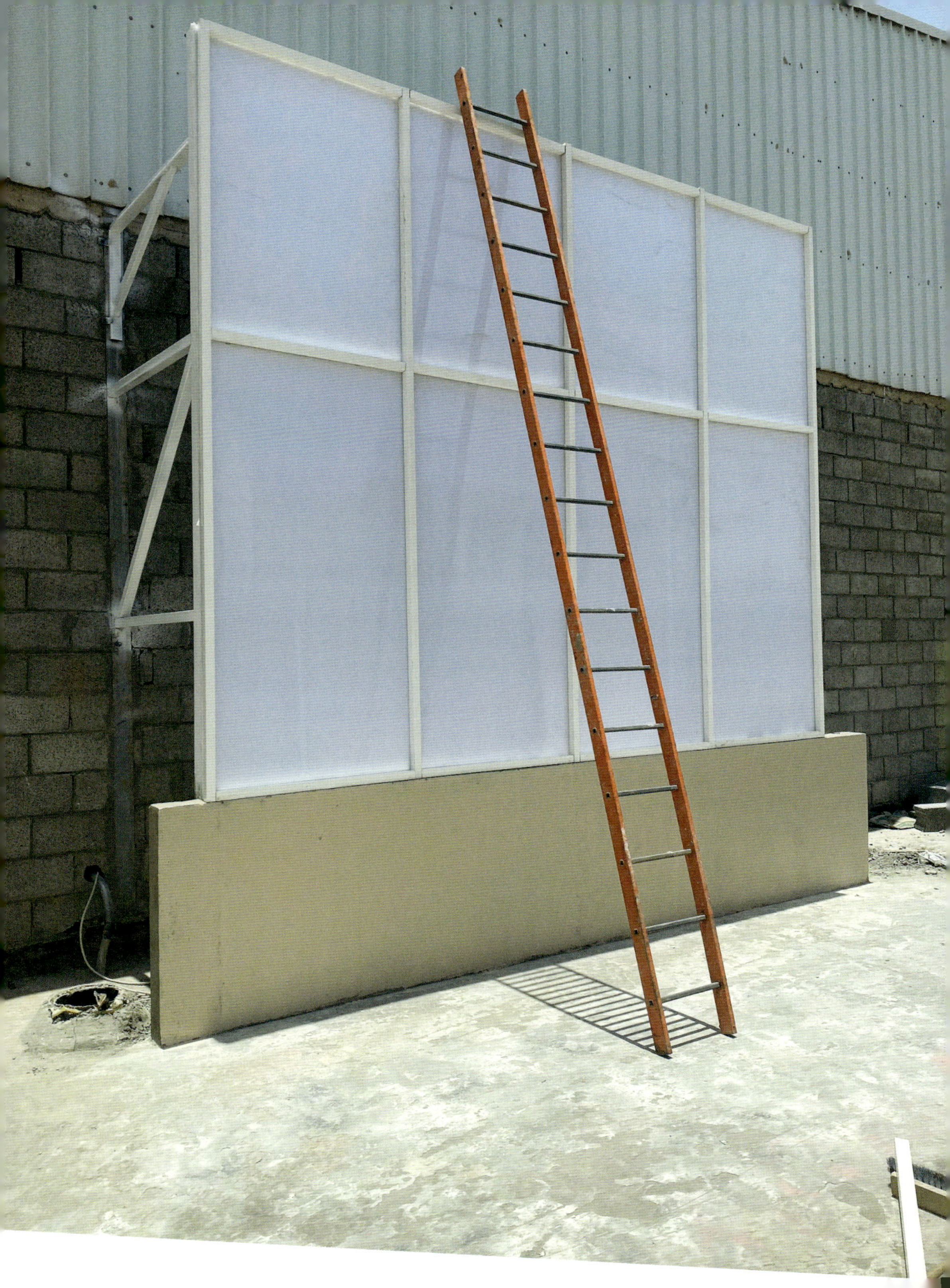

ALEXANDER ERIKSSON FURUNES & SUDAR KHADKA

Alexander Eriksson Furunes born 1988 in Trondheim, Norway, where he lives and works
Sudharshan V. Khadka Jr. born 1986 in Manila, Philippines, where he lives and works

To Lift Together: Mutual Support and Collective Action

2024

Architects Alexander Eriksson Furunes and Sudarshan V. Khadka Jr. have been working together since 2014, when the two first collaborated on *Streetlight Tagpuro*, a post-disaster rebuilding project in the City of Tacloban, Philippines, after Super Typhoon Haiyan. The project won awards in the Civic and Community and Small Project of the Year categories at the World Architecture Festival in 2017. Aligned through a deep commitment to the concept of mutual support, Furunes and Khadka have realized multiple projects since. Founded on participatory planning and construction, often in rural contexts, the communal structures that they facilitate are enabled by the traditions of communal work specific to each respective cultural context: from the Filipino *bayanihan* to the Norwegian *dugnad*, the Vietnamese *đổi công*, the Brazilian *mutirão*, and the Arabic *majlis*.

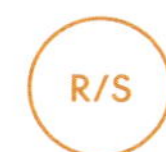

Mutual support, in the words of Furunes and Khadka, "is a mode of self-organization and collaboration for communities to build resilience and support each other through adversity, crisis, conflict, or natural disaster." Furunes and Khadka use a dialogical method, a six-step process of learning, questioning, making, conceptualizing, designing, and building to help distil different communities' needs for private spaces for conflict resolution and alternative learning. Activating and accompanying such collective decision-making in different cultural contexts forms the core of the architects' practice as much as the contingencies of actual construction. Frictions that can arise in such processes are accepted as elements of creative practices that foster reciprocity and cohesion.

Invited to curate the Philippine pavilion of the 17th Venice Architecture Biennale (2021), the pair presented *Structures of Mutual Support* as an example of architecture as process. The project was initially developed as a collective effort undertaken in collaboration with the Gawad Kalinga (GK) Enchanted Farm community in Angat, Bulacan, in the Philippines. The dialogic method used in developing community building created a democratic space in which different perspectives were heard and considered together, while demystifying the blueprints of architectural design into exercises through which the community and the architects could embed values and meanings into the built object. The pavilion was awarded a special mention in the Golden Lion Award for the Best National Participation.

On view is documentation of the architects' various projects and research dedicated to the theme of communal spaces, mutual support, and community building.

Above: Documentation of the project library and conflict resolution space, Angat, Philippines, 2019
Below: Research catalogue, Philippine Pavilion, 17th Venice Architecture Biennale, 2021

DIRIYAH CONTEMPORARY ART BIENNALE 2024

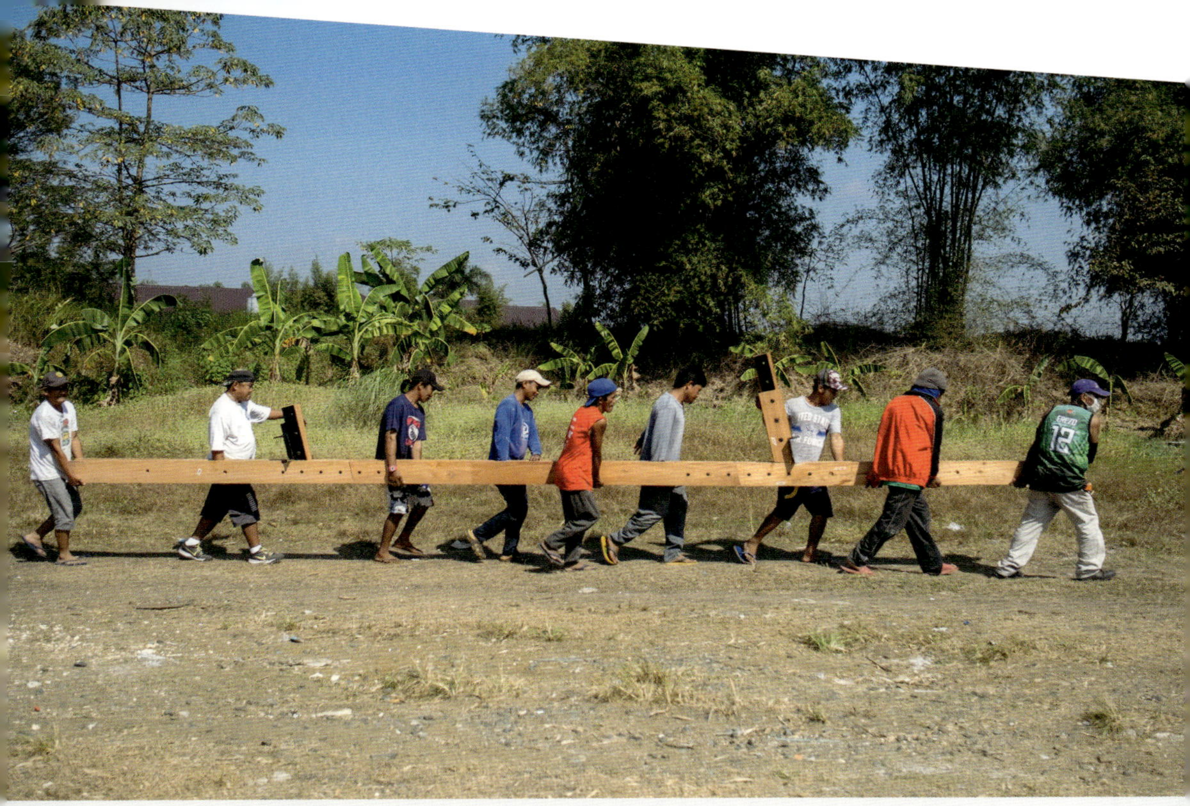

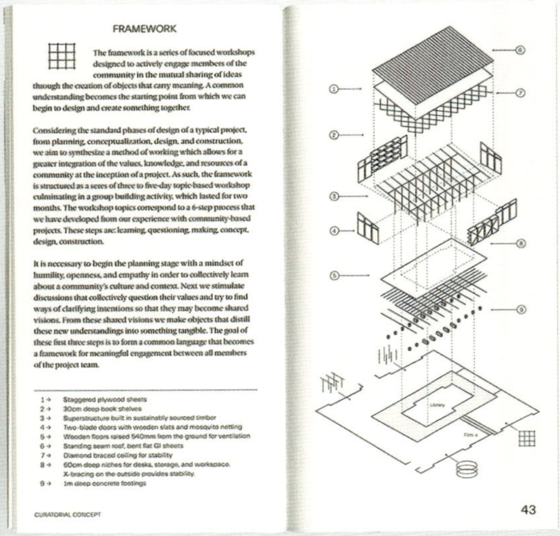

FRAMEWORK

The framework is a series of focused workshops designed to actively engage members of the community in the mutual sharing of ideas through the creation of objects that carry meaning. A common understanding becomes the starting point from which we can begin to design and create something together.

Considering the standard phases of design of a typical project, from planning, conceptualization, design, and construction, we aim to synthesize a method of working which allows for a greater integration of the values, knowledge, and resources of a community at the inception of a project. As such, the framework is structured as a seres of three to five-day topic-based workshop culminating in a group building activity, which lasted for two months. The workshop topics correspond to a 6-step process that we have developed from our experience with community-based projects. These steps are: learning, questioning, making, concept, design, construction.

It is necessary to begin the planning stage with a mindset of humility, openness, and empathy in order to collectively learn about a community's culture and context. Next we stimulate discussions that collectively question their values and try to find ways of clarifying intentions so that they may become shared visions. From these shared visions we make objects that distill these new understandings into something tangible. The goal of these first three steps is to form a common language that becomes a framework for meaningful engagement between all members of the project team.

1 → Staggered plywood sheets
2 → 30cm deep book shelves
3 → Superstructure built in sustainably sourced timber
4 → Two-blade doors with wooden slats and mosquito netting
5 → Wooden floors raised 540mm from the ground for ventilation
6 → Standing seam roof, bent flat GI sheets
7 → Diamond braced ceiling for stability
8 → 60cm deep niches for desks, storage, and workspace.
     X-bracing on the outside provides stability.
9 → 1m deep concrete footings

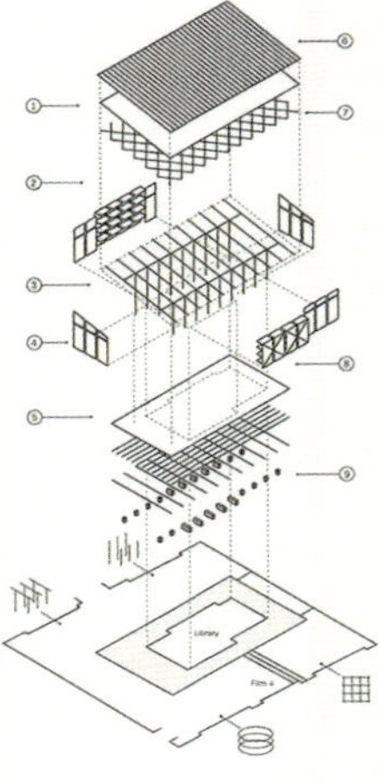

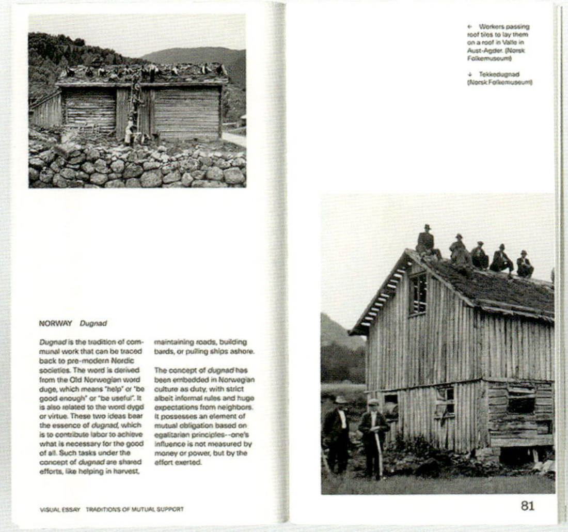

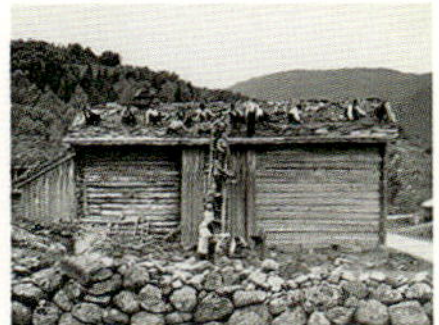

NORWAY *Dugnad*

Dugnad is the tradition of communal work that can be traced back to pre-modern Nordic societies. The word is derived from the Old Norwegian word duge, which means "help" or "be good enough" or "be useful". It is also related to the word dygd or virtue. These two ideas bear the essence of *dugnad*, which is to contribute labor to achieve what is necessary for the good of all. Such tasks under the concept of *dugnad* are shared efforts, like helping in harvest, maintaining roads, building bards, or pulling ships ashore.

The concept of *dugnad* has been embedded in Norwegian culture as duty, with strict albeit informal rules and huge expectations from neighbors. It possesses an element of mutual obligation based on egalitarian principles—one's influence is not measured by money or power, but by the effort exerted.

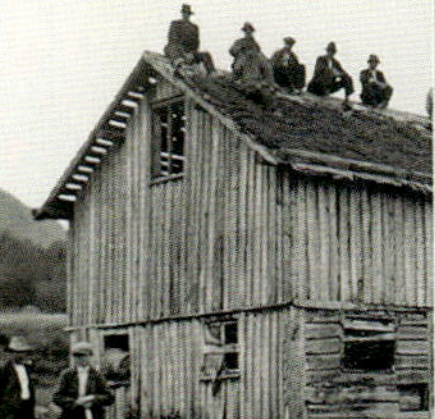

← Workers passing roof tiles to lay them on a roof in Valle in Aust-Agder. (Norsk Folkemuseum)

↓ Tekkedugnad (Norsk Folkemuseum)

SUSANNE KRIEMANN

Born 1972 in Erlangen, Germany, lives and works
in Berlin, Germany

Datadust skin of sand

2024

Susanne Kriemann is an artist whose complex installations and research-based works are grounded in photographic processes. Her interest in photography is deeply linked with the notion of the ruin, both historical and ecological. Recent exhibitions at international institutions include the Centre for Canadian Architecture, Montreal; C/O Berlin; and Kunst Haus Wien, (all in 2023). She currently is artist-in-residence at the Museum für Gegenwartskunst/University of Siegen. In 2019 she had a residency at NTU Centre for Contemporary Art Singapore. Kriemann is a professor at the University of the Arts and Design Karlsruhe (since 2017) and co-founder of the artists-led initiative AiR Berlin Alexanderplatz in Berlin (since 2010).

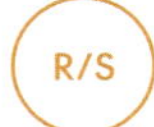

Working from an expanded notion of the photograph, Kriemann uses a range of techniques to produce images that are both visual and material registers of information. Through the use of pigments sourced from sites she is investigating, she reflects on the world itself as an analogue "recording system" of human-driven processes. Mining, radioactivity, and the omnipresence of (micro)plastic waste in different environments are central themes in works involving extended periods of study and documentation. "Material matter is as much a co-author of my works with nature as image-taking, data-storing, and (dis-)appearing. What unfolds occupies the threshold between fact and fiction, science, and poetry."

Datadust skin of sand (2024) explores the convergence of ancient data and contemporary consumer waste found in archaeological research sites of AlUla and Tayma in the northern Arabian desert. The coexistence of high levels of microplastics alongside archaeological contexts forms the starting point of the work in progress. On view are silk-screen prints of contemporary discarded objects that Kriemann collected on site. Printed with date syrup and makeup, which is full of microplastics, and then coated with sand, the images have a compelling tactile quality and seem to be of indeterminate age—as artifacts of recent human presence. Every grain of sand stores information in crystals that can be billions of years old; granules of contemporary plastics will be markers of human activity for hundreds of years to come. The work *Datadust skin of sand* situates itself within the hypersites of data and the desert, questioning our relationship to the seemingly unending stream of plastics production and its afterlives.

Research protocols *Datadust skin of sand*, Tayma archaeological site.
Above: October 30, 2023, textile IX ("pullover"), coordinates: 27.62385° north, 38.54804° east
Below: November 1, 2023, textile I ("bag"), coordinates: 27.60037° north, 38.54271° east

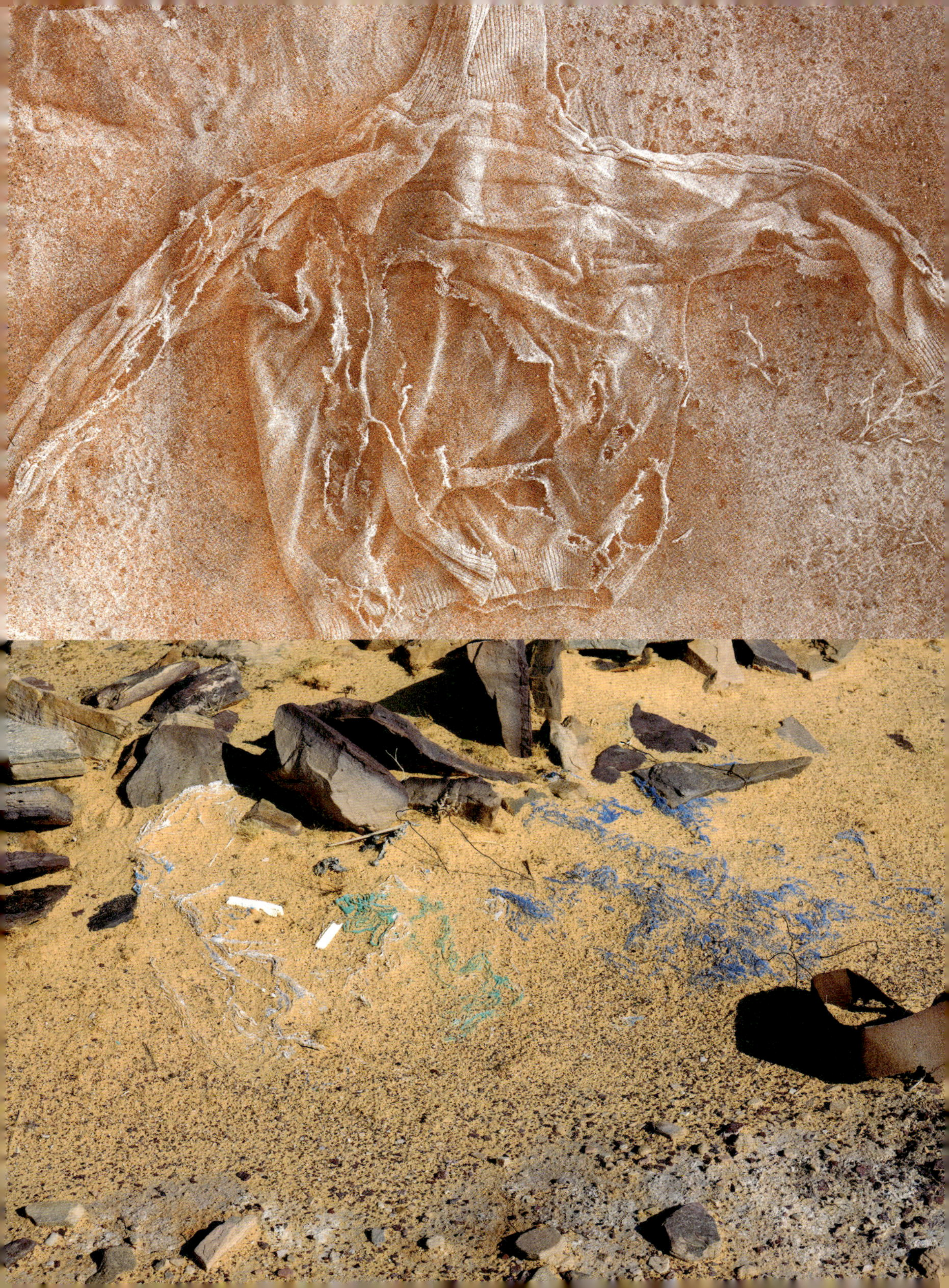

EXHIBITION HALL B2

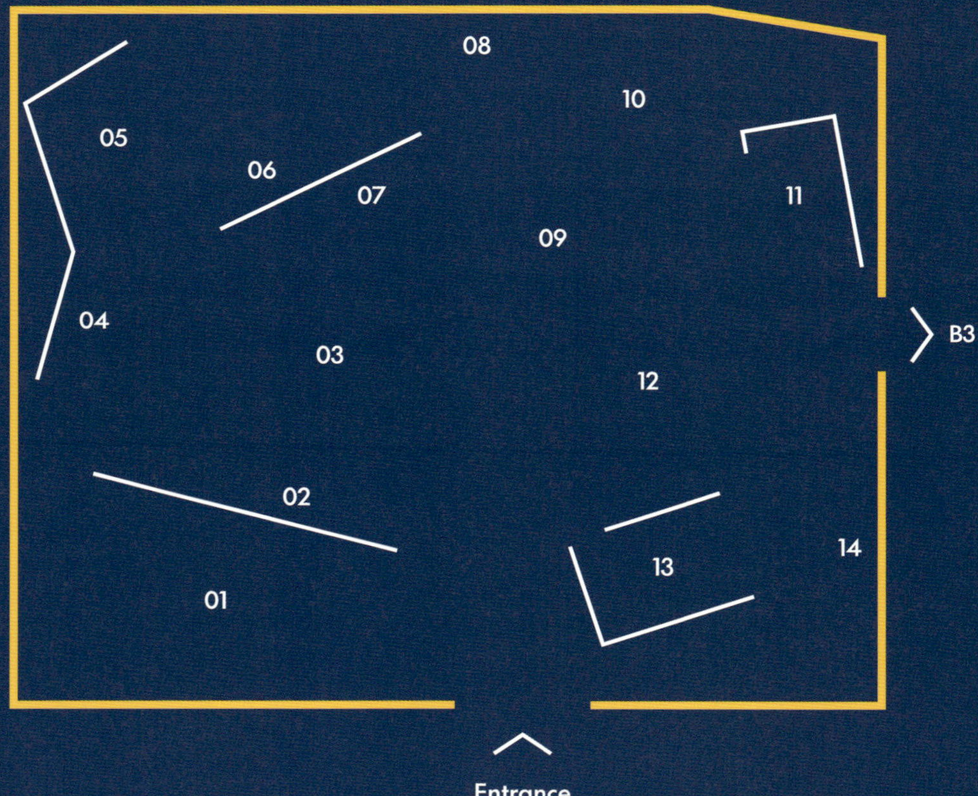

ENVIRONMENTS AND ECOLOGIES

The ongoing climate crisis magnifies shared concerns about access to water, food, and shelter, as this severely impacts the habitats of humans and other life forms. Some of its causes are rooted in extractivism, colonialism, and the pursuit of endless progress and growth. Witnessing the loss of the way we used to live, traditional knowledge and the riches of the planet's biological variety, artists demonstrate an acute understanding of complex interrelations, the risk posed to habitats, ecosystems, and communities, and the rate of their destruction.

Looking out of the hall's large windows, one sees Wadi Hanifah, an important seasonal riverbed that extends across Diriyah, suggesting a dialogue between this unique landscape and the works that engage with themes of infrastructure. Several works address the cultural and architectural heritage of natural environments. Others point to patterns of displacement, forced migration, and the extent of pollution. In a variety of photographic series, artists reflect the richness of cultures resisting standardization and offer a look at futurist developments and urban planning in Saudi Arabia. Multimedia installations offer potential solutions for water purification, show how seeds are being preserved for the protection of biodiversity, or investigate CO2 emissions.

MARTHA ATIENZA

Born 1981 in Manila, Philippines, lives and works in Bantayan Island, Philippiness

Equation of State
2019/2024

In developing her films and video installations, Martha Atienza engages in a process that has a sociological dimension, investigating the potential of contemporary art as a tool for affecting social change and development. Atienza grounds her practice in her home on Bantayan Island in the Philippines, working from within her local community and initiating dialogue on the impact of climate change. Atienza received her bachelor's in fine arts from the Academy of Visual Arts and Design in the Netherlands. She also won the Baloise Art Prize at Art Basel for her seminal work *Our Islands* (2017) and was awarded the Cultural Center of the Philippines Thirteen Artist Award (2015).

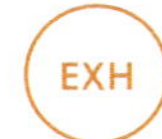

Referring to a thermodynamic equation that calculates the relationship between variables and a given set of physical conditions, *Equation of State* (2019/2024) addresses the questions surrounding the ownership and privatization of Bantayan Island's land and coastline in the context of rising water temperatures and sea levels. Fundamental to the island's ecology are the mangrove plants that populate the brackish, tidal waters of the coast but are threatened by development. Twenty-four such mangrove trees form the centerpiece of the installation and are shown suspended from the ceiling over a long basin of water. The plants are raised and lowered into the water by automated, randomized winches, so that their roots are submerged in a rhythm mimicking the tides. On view in Diriyah is a streamlined version of the initial construction, which was built using found materials and programmed with an Arduino mechanism. Highlighting the function of the mangroves, the work is also a statement on human interference and control of these natural protectors of the shoreline.

Installed nearby, two silent films focus on the human inhabitants of the island. One, shot in black and white, traces the decay of Bantayan's coastal communities, which face both existential and legislative threats to their livelihoods and way of life. The other, shown on three screens, portrays three fishermen, silently submerging and reemerging from the water as they look into the camera—portraits of survival and resilience. *Equation of State* was created in 2019, the same year that Congress of the Philippines voted to withdraw Bantayan Island's Wilderness Status. The question Atienza ultimately asks is: Who has control over the future of the island and its residents?

Finalizing *Equation of State* installation in the studio, Bantayan Island, Philippines, 2019

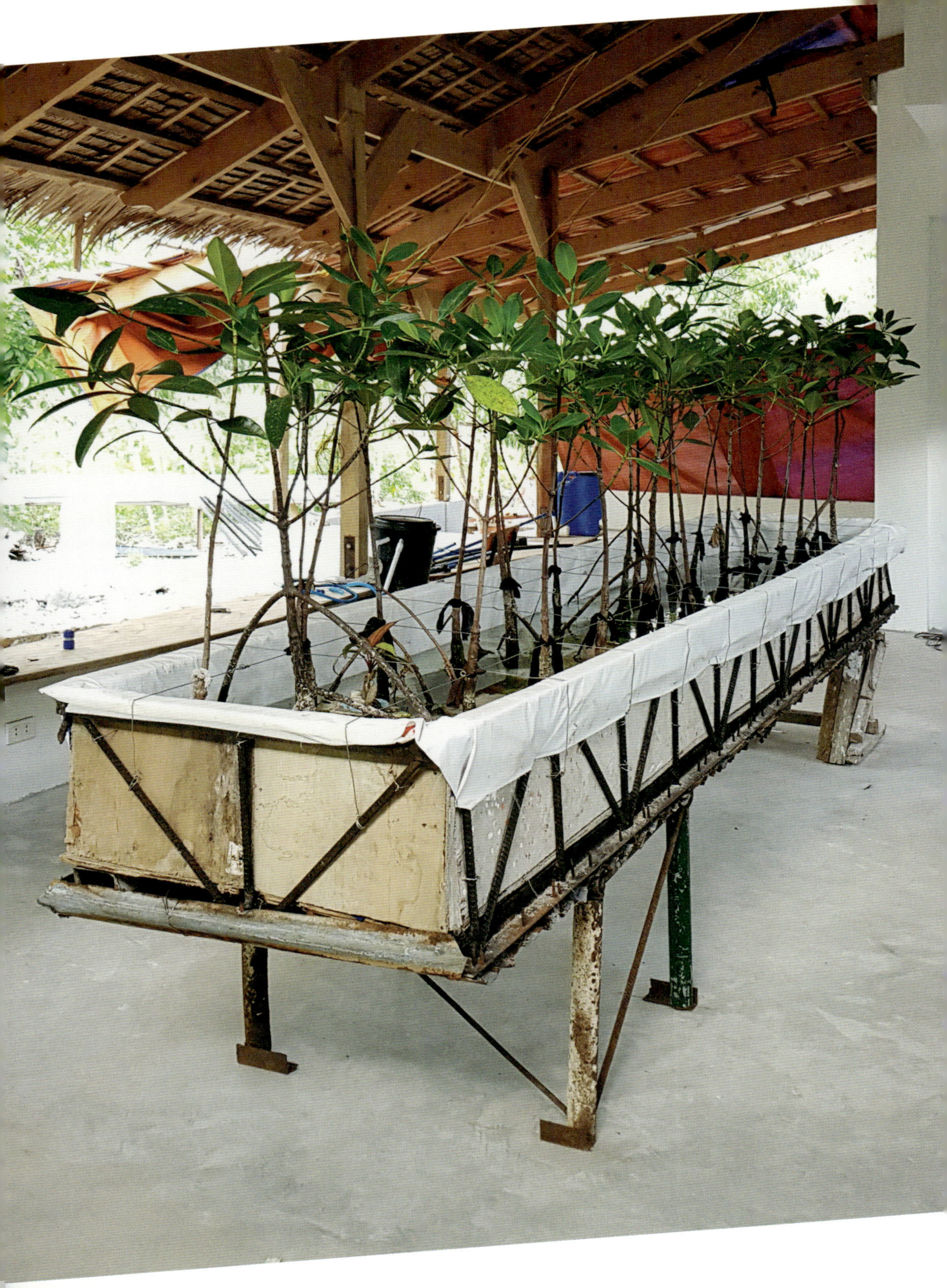

TIFFANY CHUNG

Born 1969 in Da Nang, Vietnam, lives and works in
Houston, TX, United States

Energy Policy vol.166: potential CO2 emissions until 2050 by key fossil fuel and coal extraction projects [each>1 Gt] worldwide
2023

Mapping Global Displacement and Migration: nexus dynamics between conflict & violence and climate disaster [UNHCR, IDMC, EM-DAT: cross-border refugees, asylum-seekers, IDPs and those affected in selected cases >2022<]
2023

Tiffany Chung is a multimedia artist acclaimed for her critical work on geo-political conflict, environmental crisis, and forced migration. Her meticulous research-driven practice transforms the minutiae of data into intricately ornate cartographic works and installations. After earning her MFA from the University of California, Santa Barbara, Chung returned to Saigon, where she co-founded the artist-led platform Sàn Art in 2007 and played a pivotal role in nurturing Vietnam's nascent contemporary art landscape. Her work has been collected by institutions such as the British Museum, Louisiana Museum of Modern Art, M+ Museum, Queensland Art Gallery, and Smithsonian American Art Museum. She was a Mellon Arts & Practitioner Fellow at RITM, Yale University, in 2021.

A child of the Vietnam War, Chung has experienced displacement twofold: first, internally, to *Đồng Tháp Mười* (Plain of Reeds) in Vietnam's Mekong Delta, where the artist and her family survived a historic flood in 1978. The area was one of many agricultural New Economic Zones implemented by Vietnam's recently independent communist government as part of a series of ill-conceived socioeconomic experiments to isolate and resettle urban South Vietnamese populations. Following this first traumatic episode of internal displacement, Chung later sought cross-border asylum in the United States, as part of an epic and perilous refugee exodus of Vietnamese, Lao, and Cambodian communities fleeing the region's new authoritarian regime.

As Chung wrote in an essay "While the World Stands Still: Remembering the Swelling River" (2021) reflecting on these twin displacements, "Climate and economic crises coupled with political and armed conflicts have produced and will continue to produce refugees." For the Biennale she has produced two new embroidered maps explicating these entanglements, based on technical maps produced by software tracking potential carbon dioxide emissions from major fossil fuel and coal extraction projects worldwide from 2019 to 2050, on the one hand, and global displacement emerging out of the complex dynamics found at the nexus of climate, conflict, and migration, on the other. The two works, mounted on construction scaffolds, highlight the tension and inequality between the world's biggest contributors to environmental degradation, and the mass displacement of its most vulnerable populations, who most acutely bear the impact of extreme climate events.

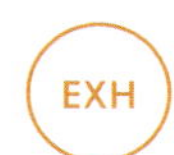

EXH

Above: Detail of global displacement, digital mapping, 2023
Below: Detail of global displacement data synthesizing spreadsheet, 2023

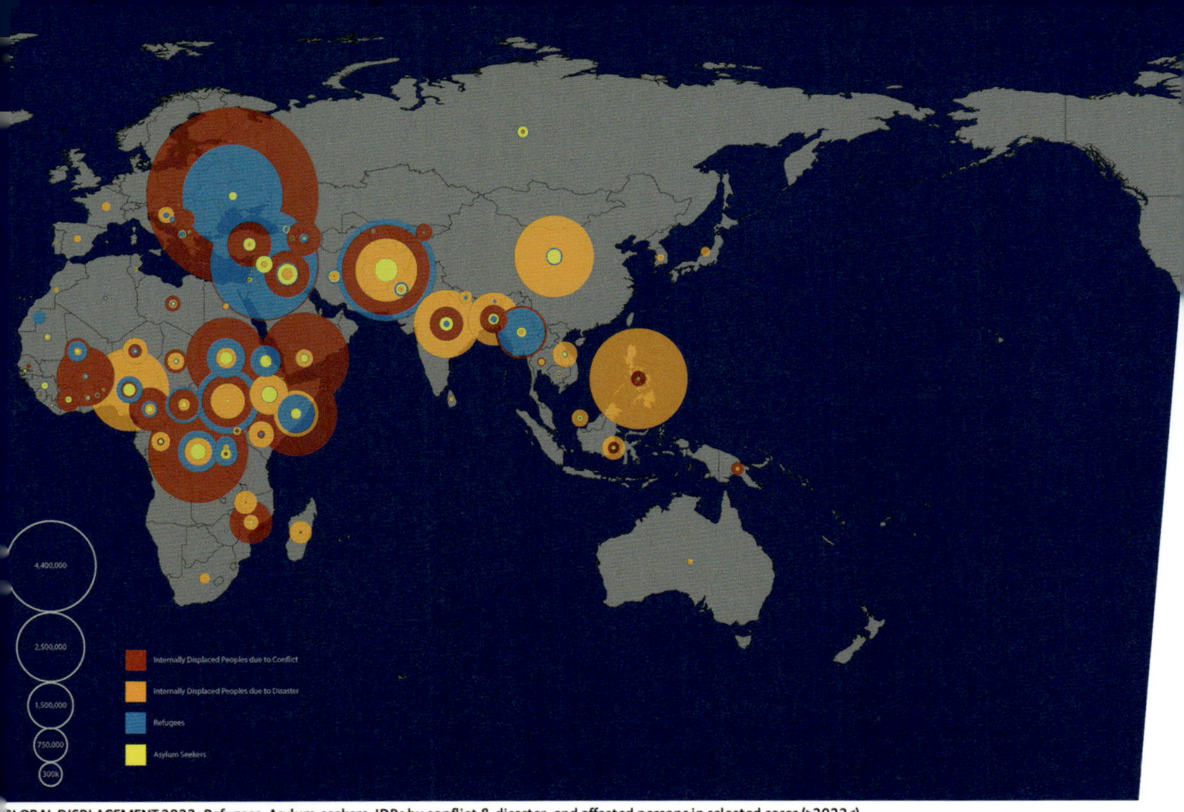

GLOBAL DISPLACEMENT 2022: Refugees, Asylum-seekers, IDPs by conflict & disaster, and affected persons in selected cases (>2022<)

Country	IDs 2022 (diasters)	IDs 2022 (conflict | violence)	Total IDPs at end of 2022 (disasters)	Total IDPs at end of 2022 (conflict | violence)	Refugees-UNHCR's mandate 2022	Asylum-seekers 2022	Notes
Abyei Area SAS	29,000	56,000		56,000			
Afghanistan	220,000	32,000	2,164,000	4,394,000	5,661,675	294,493	
Albania	320				20,847	34,406	
Algeria	2,000		1,500		7,703	8,923	
Angola	1,800				11,751	16,523	
Argentina	730				178	2,271	
Armenia	18,000	7,600	18,000	8,400	14,844	13,474	2023: storm, hail,
Australia	17,000						
Azerbaijan	190			659,000	42,013	5,726	
Bangladesh	1,524,000	560	8,600	427,000	23,927	61,298	
Belize	5,100		820		65	481	
Benin	6,900	1,200	6,900	1,200	816	1,407	
Bolivia	3,000		650		576	2,324	
Bosnia and Herzegovina	78		58	91,000	17,913	1,500	
Brazil	708,000	5,600	44,000	5,600	1,954	26,440	
Bulgaria	900		14				
Burkina Faso	2,400	438,000		1,882,000	20,209	5,585	
Burundi	13,000	600	67,000	8,500	323,635	52,171	
Bhutan	502				6,697	465	2021: earthquake
Cambodia	28,000		3,900		11,689	978	
Cameroon	66,000	139,000	23,000	987,000	147,359	21,927	
Central African Republic	77,000	290,000		516,000	748,327	14,291	
Chad	158,000	80,000		300,000	12,810	7,091	
Chile	1,500		1,500		1,335	11,879	
China	3,632,000		146,000		161,234	116,338	
Colombia	281,000	339,000	41,000	4,766,000	109,135	144,210	
Congo	42,000		201,000	27,000	13,286	9,580	
Costa Rica	1,600		38		275	1,279	
Côte d'Ivoire	2,500			302,000	25,103	22,037	
Croatia (2023; do not used)	6,101		6,101				
Croatia	149,415		149,415				
Cuba							

ADE DARMAWAN

Born 1974 in Jakarta, Indonesia, where he lives and works

Tuban
2019

Ade Darmawan is an artist and curator. Incorporating historical materials and found objects, his object-laden installations, graphic works, and videos are often commentaries on economic and sociopolitical issues relevant to Southeast Asia. Darmawan has been an influential figure in the art scene of Indonesia. A member of the Jakarta Arts Council from 2006 to 2009, he was appointed director of the Jakarta Biennale in 2009 and served as its executive director for the 2013, 2015, and 2017 editions. He is also a co-founder and co-director of the artist collective ruangrupa, a non-profit collective formed in 2000 with a communal structure that seeks to advance critical voices and cross-disciplinary perspectives in the visual arts.

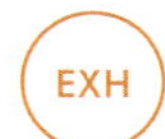

Tuban (2019) takes its name from an Indonesian port town that flourished during the Javanese Majapahit empire of the thirteenth to early sixteenth centuries. The subsequent decline of this one-time center of Islamic culture and government features prominently in the book *Arus Balik* (published 1995) by Indonesian author Pramoedya Ananta Toer (1925–2006). Branded a communist by the Suharto New Order regime, Pramoedya was imprisoned from 1969 to 1979, during which time he wrote the novel. The work, whose title translates as "the turning of the tide," suggests that the shift from independence to colonial rule was partially caused by geopolitical intrigues around the Java Sea. Due to increasing provincialism—and incursions by European traders—weakened Javanese kingdoms gradually turned their backs to the sea, instead of continuing to pursue the rich maritime passages that connected the region.

Darmawan reread this epic with a special focus on the way in which natural resources were referenced and used by different characters. After a field trip to Tuban as well as to Bojonegoro, an oil-rich town, the artist created a distillation laboratory to point at the extractivist greed that has fueled the fights over the control of the archipelago for centuries. Using water from the Java Sea, Darmawan's laboratory distills spices and leaves, such as nutmeg, sandalwood, cinnamon, pepper, candlenut, clover leaf, betel leaf, attap palm, coconut leaf, and the medicinal *tapak liman*, imbuing the air with their scents. The drops from the laboratory tubes fall onto open books about Suharto and his corrupt policies on land and resources, drawing parallels to the Dutch colonial policies demanding that a portion of agricultural production be devoted to export crops, both ruthless models of worker exploitation.

Installation and detail view of *Tuban*, from the exhibition *Arus Balik: From below the wind to above the wind and back again* at NTU Centre for Contemporary Art Singapore, 2019

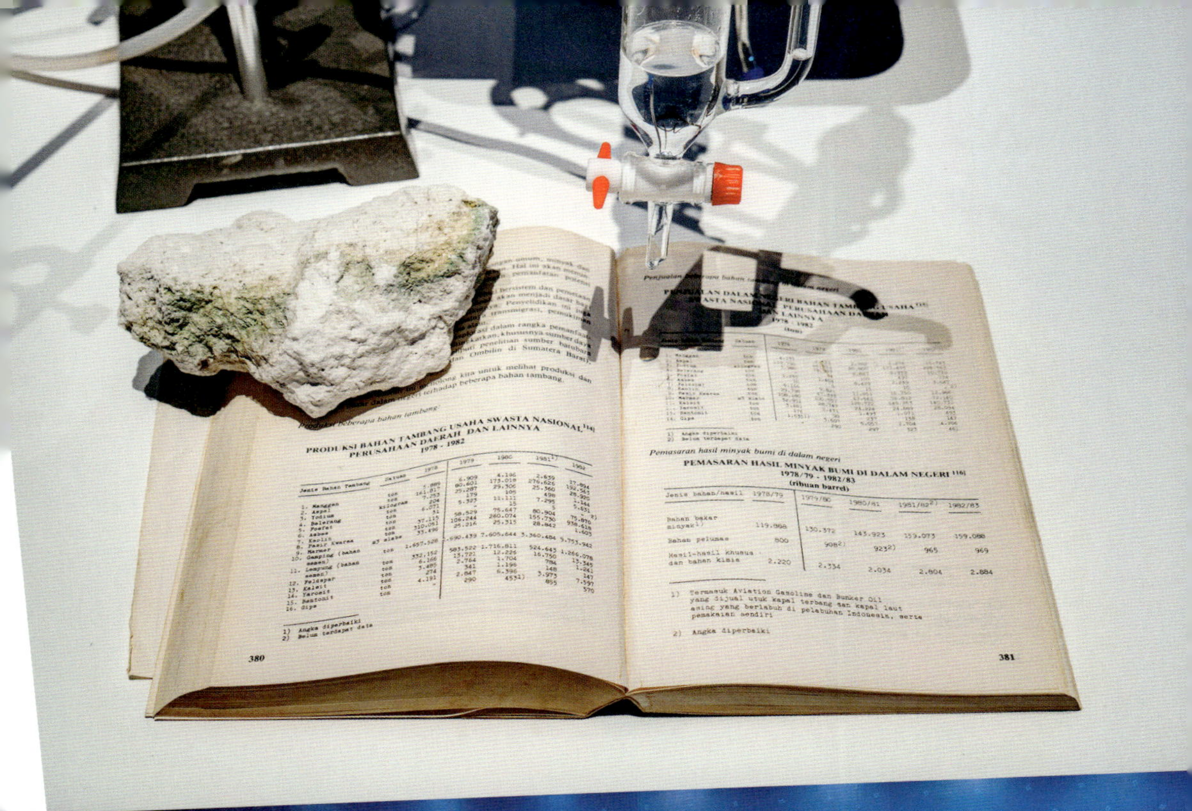

Produksi beberapa bahan tambang

PRODUKSI BAHAN TAMBANG USAHA SWASTA NASIONAL [116]
PERUSAHAAN DAERAH DAN LAINNYA
1978 - 1982

Jenis Bahan Tambang	Satuan	1978	1979	1980	1981 [1]	1982
1. Manggan	ton		6.909	4.196	2.639	37.894
2. Aspal	ton	141.812	80.601	173.018	276.626	192.563
3. Yodium	kilogram	7.753	25.287	29.306	25.360	28.920
4. Belerang	ton	204	179	105	498	1.144
5. Posfat	ton	6.071	5.923	11.111	7.295	5.651
6. Asbes	ton	51		15	5	
7. Kaolin	ton	37.115	58.529	75.647	80.904	75.870 [2]
8. Pasir Kwarsa	m3 slabs	910.051	106.244	260.074	155.730	956.618
9. Marmer		33.490	25.216	25.315	28.842	1.605
10. Gamping (bahan semen)	ton	1.657.528	690.439	7.605.644	3.360.484	5.753.942
11. Lempung (bahan semen)	ton	532.152	583.522	1.716.811	524.643	1.266.078
12. Feldspar	ton	6.166	15.721	12.226	16.750	13.345
13. Kalsit	ton	3.485	2.764	1.704	784	1.241
14. Yarosit	ton	274	341	1.198	148	147
15. Bentonit	ton	4.191	2.847	6.396	3.973	7.597
16. Gips	ton		290	4532 [2]	855	570

1) Angka diperbaiki
2) Belum terdapat data

Pemasaran hasil minyak bumi di dalam negeri

PEMASARAN HASIL MINYAK BUMI DI DALAM NEGERI [116]
1978/79 - 1982/83
(ribuan barrel)

Jenis bahan/hasil	1978/79	1979/80	1980/81	1981/82 [2]	1982/83
Bahan bakar minyak [1]	119.868	130.372	143.923	153.073	159.088
Bahan pelumas	800	908 [2]	923 [2]	965	969
Hasil-hasil khusus dan bahan kimia	2.220	2.334	2.034	2.804	2.884

1) Termasuk Aviation Gasoline dan Bunker Oil yang dijual utuk kapal terbang dan kapal laut asing yang berlabuh di pelabuhan Indonesia, serta pemakaian sendiri

2) Angka diperbaiki

380   381

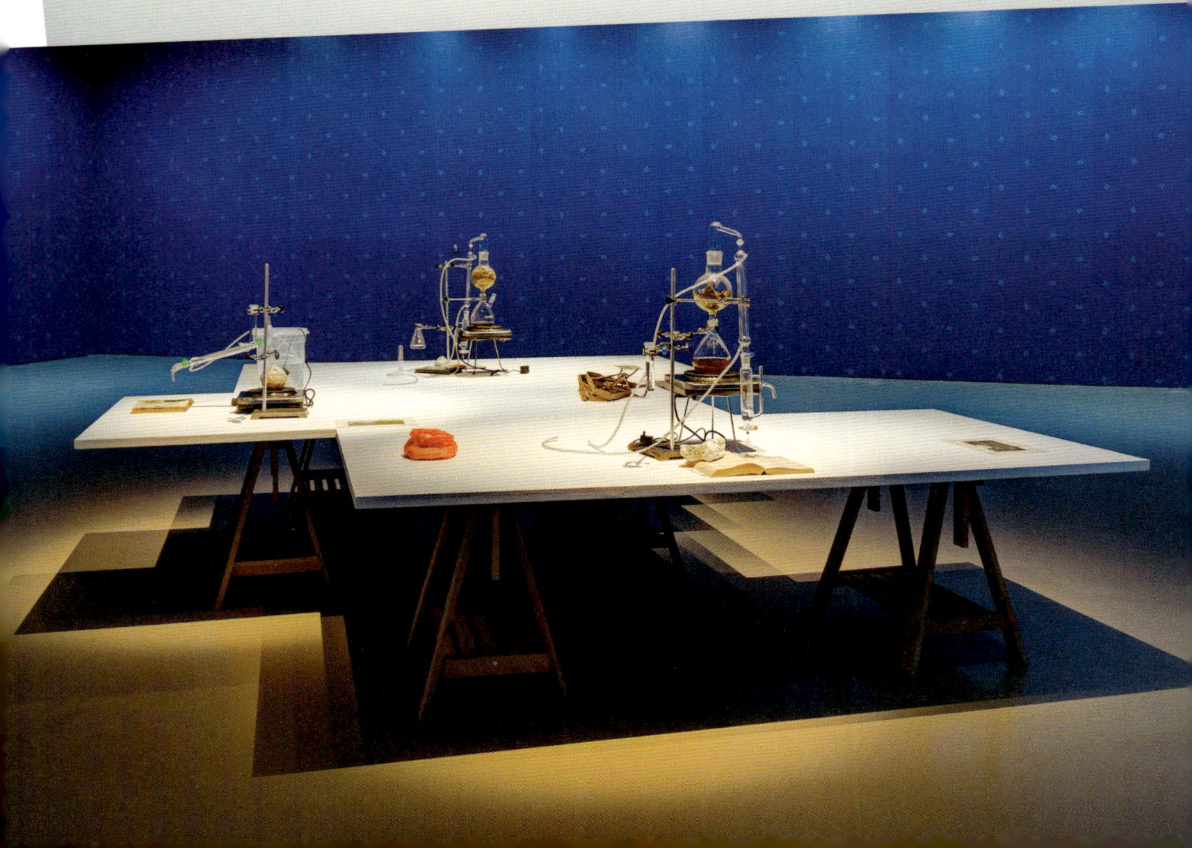

CHRISTINE FENZL

Born 1967 in Munich, Germany, lives and works in Berlin, Germany

Women of Riyadh

2023

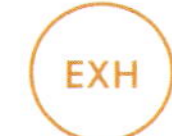

Christine Fenzl is a photographer whose work documents young people in their living environments. Shown in series, her portraits bring together representatives of a generation or group, offering a picture of its unique environment and historical context. After studying photography in Munich, she spent several years in New York, returning to Germany and working as the assistant to American photographer Nan Goldin in Berlin in the early 1990s and subsequently as an independent photographer. Her images have been featured in *ZEITmagazin*, *Liberation*, *New York Times Magazine*, and *Vogue*.

Many of her projects are developed over an extended period, such as her photographs capturing children and teenagers in street football clubs run by NGOs in different continents. Through her photos shot in Lithuania, Poland, Belfast, Berlin, and Shanghai, she has offered a view of people coming of age on different sides of the former Iron Curtain or other lines of conflict. Her work also portrays individuals living on the cusp of major developments and societal shifts, as in her portraits taken in Shanghai during the preparations for EXPO 2009. Lasting over ten years, Fenzl's *Land in Sonne* project on young adults in neighborhoods of former East Berlin was published by Hatje Cantz in 2019, marking the thirtieth anniversary of the fall of the Wall.

Women of Riyadh (2023) was commissioned for the Biennale. Working for two weeks, Fenzl documented women born and living in Riyadh in their homes and neighborhoods. Shown face on and at eye level, they are presented in near-life-size prints. Each image is the result of a collaborative process, in which women chose where and how they wished to be shown. Some decided to be photographed with a partner or parent, for example in a mother-daughter image, others alone or outdoors. Accompanying the portraits is a single photograph, a cityscape that shows a view of Riyadh from the perspective of a pedestrian. Fenzl always includes at least one image that provides a sense of location and the overall setting of her portraits. The variety of clothing and poses of these professional women—including a lawyer, architect, and wellness coach—expresses the confidence and accomplishment of a group of women at a time of transition and social change. For Fenzl, the project was an experience of "sharing moments that did not exist before" and reflecting on a new kind of visibility for women in all aspects of life.

Ghaida, Diriyah, Saudi Arabia, from the series *Women of Riyadh*, 2023

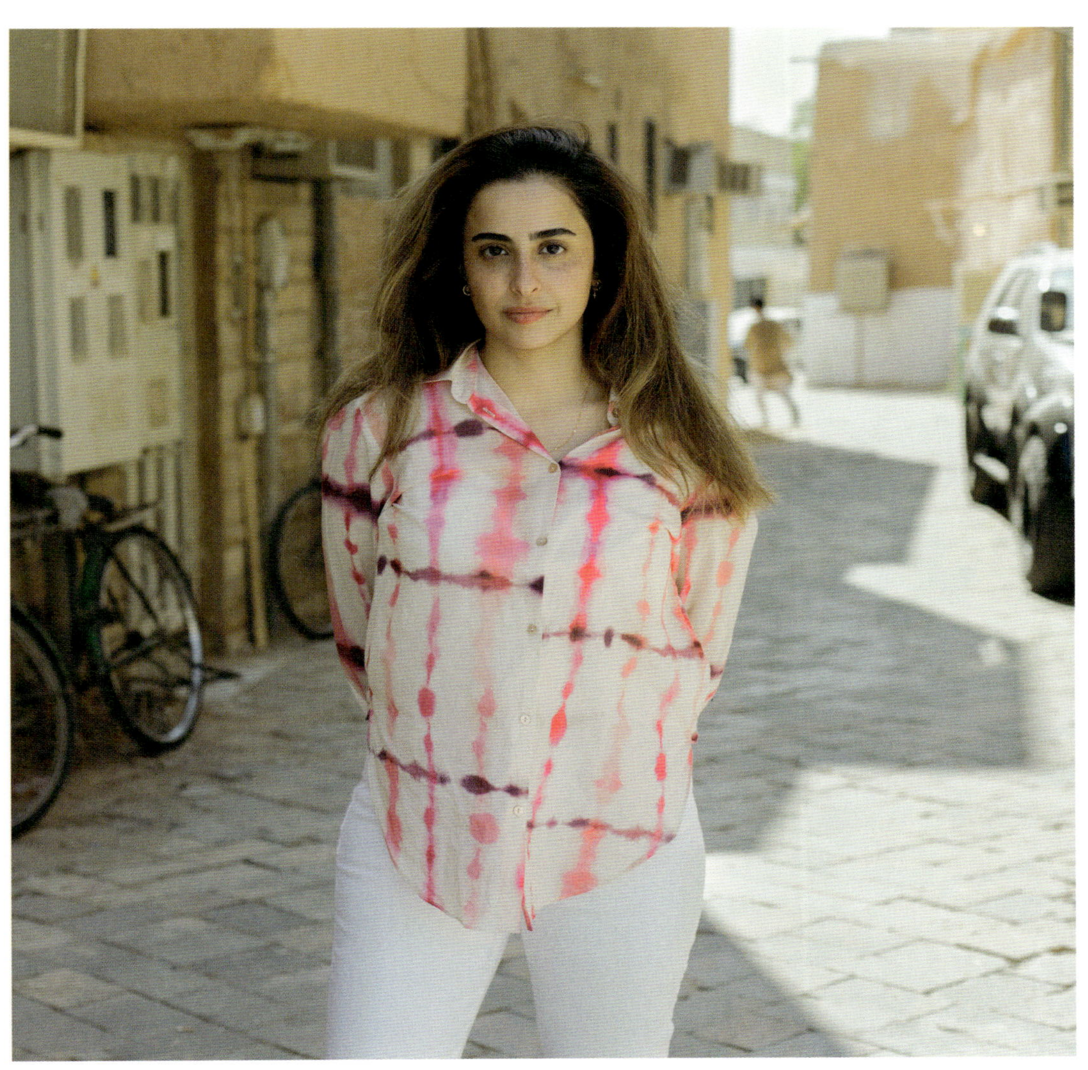

CHRISTINE FENZL

91

SIMRYN GILL

Born 1959 in Singapore, lives and works in Sydney, Australia and
Port Dickson, Malaysia

Dalam

2001

Simryn Gill grew up in Malaysia and moved to Australia in 1996. She works with photography, printmaking, writing, drawing, books, and publishing, attending to our relationships to landscapes and places that formed us. Whether walking through the coastal Port Dickson, Malaysia, or the suburbs of Adelaide and Sydney, Australia, Gill observes, gathers, and collects objects and images of places in transition, always questioning how to bear witness to these moments of transformation.

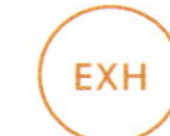

Dalam (2001), which translates as "interior" in Malay, comprises 260 photographs of living rooms taken across West Malaysia over a three-month period. This photograph series chronicles the spaces where identity, home, and a sense of belonging intersect. Unfolding in strong colors, *Dalam* offers a glimpse into the most public domain of the home, which is nonetheless an intimate context where access is privileged. The uniform square format serves as a metaphorical window through which the viewer "peers" into one room after another, revealing a diversity of cultures and ways of living characterizing multiethnic, postcolonial Malaysia. The varied furnishings—with Malay, Indian, and Chinese ethnic specificities and indications of different religious affiliations—hint at a national identity that is still a work in progress and is undergoing constant negotiation. The distinctiveness of each interior captures a complex tapestry of the Malaysian social fabric, in which the whole is downplayed by the diversity of its parts.

A living room is a reflection of its inhabitants, a place where objects and pieces of furniture preserve personal stories, convey desires, and reveal aspirations through the consumption manifested in the domestic realm. The absence of the inhabitants heightens the strong material presence of the spaces that Gill has chronicled. Her images are all a result of a durational approach that defines her artistic process: hours of looking and looking, wandering, and collecting. Gill probes the nature of photographic process: "When does one have enough? For what ... to represent an idea? Does a big group tell you more or less? Does it tell you more truthfully?"

Dalam, 2001, series of 260 photographs

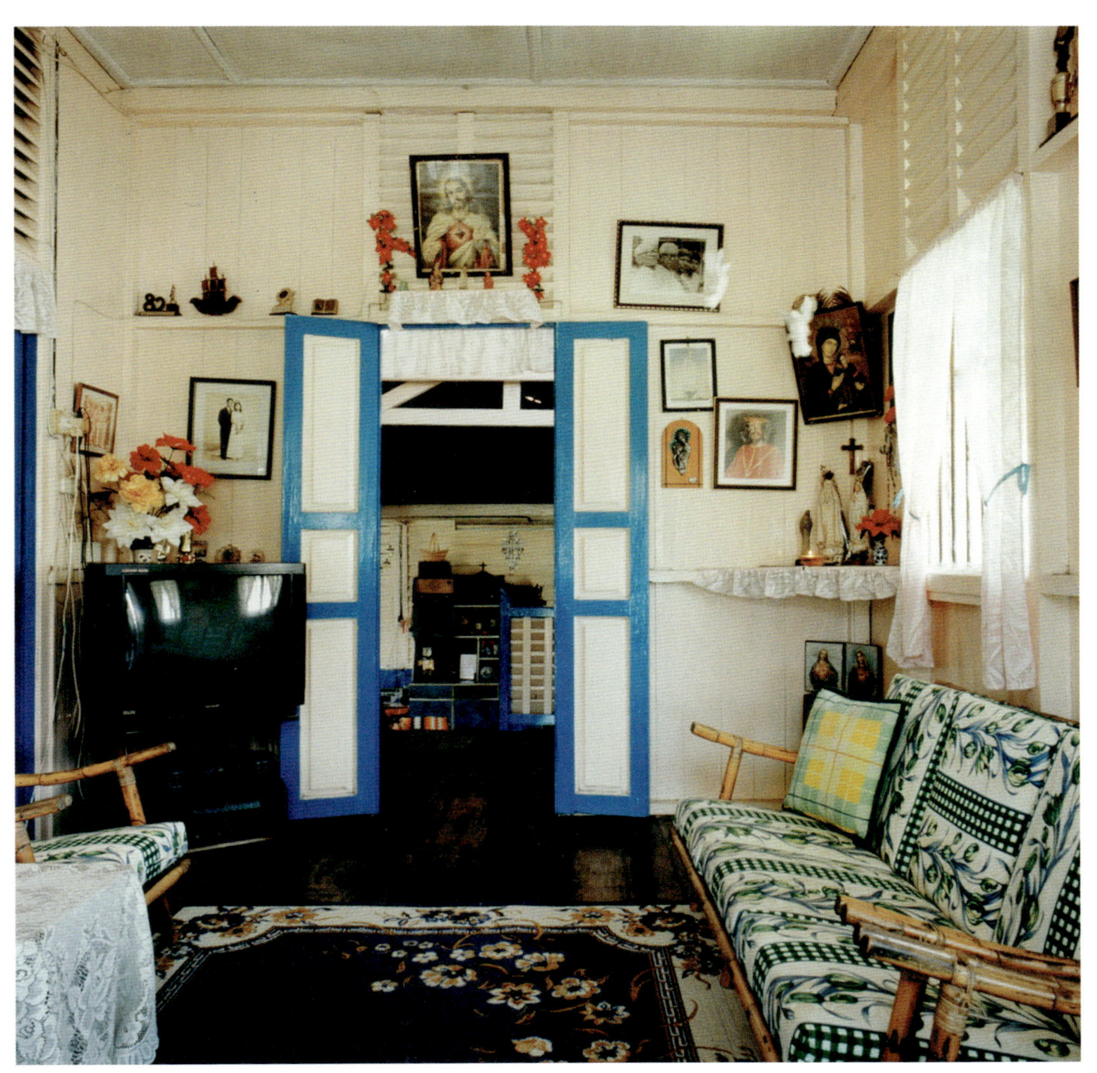

ARMIN LINKE & AHMED MATER

Armin Linke, born 1966 in Milan, Italy, lives and works in Berlin, Germany
Ahmed Mater, born 1979 in Tabuk, Saudi Arabia, lives and works in
Riyadh, Saudi Arabia

Saudi Futurism

2024

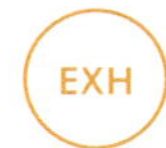

Armin Linke is a photographer and filmmaker who documents the impact of globalization, the built environment, and postindustrial economies while questioning the nature of the photographic medium and its conventions of display. Often working with scientists and other experts, he has explored topics ranging from space mining to a particle physics laboratory, power sources, and his own photographic archive. He has had solo exhibitions recently at Centre Pompidou (2023/2024), the Canadian Centre for Architecture (2023), and the Luxembourg Pavilion at the 18th Venice Architecture Biennale (2023). He is a professor at the Academy of Fine Arts Munich.

Ahmed Mater, trained as a physician, is a multidisciplinary artist known for his photography and conceptual works. In long-term projects such as the historical survey *Prognosis/Saudi Arabia* (2022) and *Desert of Pharan* (2016), a compelling photographic portrait of the holy city of Makkah, he has scrutinized the changing realities and unofficial histories of Saudi Arabia. As a co-founder of Edge of Arabia and founding director of the Misk Art Institute, Riyadh (2017–18), he has also played a key role in cultivating the Saudi contemporary art scene. He has had major solo exhibitions at the Brooklyn Museum (2019), King Abdullah Economic City (2018), Smithsonian Institute, Washington, DC (2016), and has taken part in the Venice Biennale (2009/2011) and the Sharjah Biennial (2007/2013).

Saudi Futurism (2024) is an installation that explores the changing infrastructure of a country in transition and the projected futures of the past and present. For this first-time collaboration, Linke and Mater traveled throughout the country documenting industrial, scientific, and historical sites, from a dairy farm to the Aramco archives, landmark buildings, the Shaheen supercomputer, and the exhibition of the megaproject NEOM. Their photographs are installed in an array of multi-sized prints, a physical set of hyperimages. Viewers make associations between the photographs, editing them into their own sequence of meaning as they walk through the space of the installation. Implementing materials discarded from other exhibitions held at the site and giving them a new context, the presentation structure is also an open cache. Theoretically the images could be switched out or "reloaded" through the sides, a possibility indicating that the visions and technologies of one age become rapidly outdated and are constantly being replaced.

From *Saudi Futurism*, 2024. Above: Ahmed Mater, *Yamama Cement Factory (Old), Riyadh*, 2023. Below: Armin Linke, *Frei Otto, Diplomatic Club Heart Tent, Boutique Group, Riyadh*, 2023

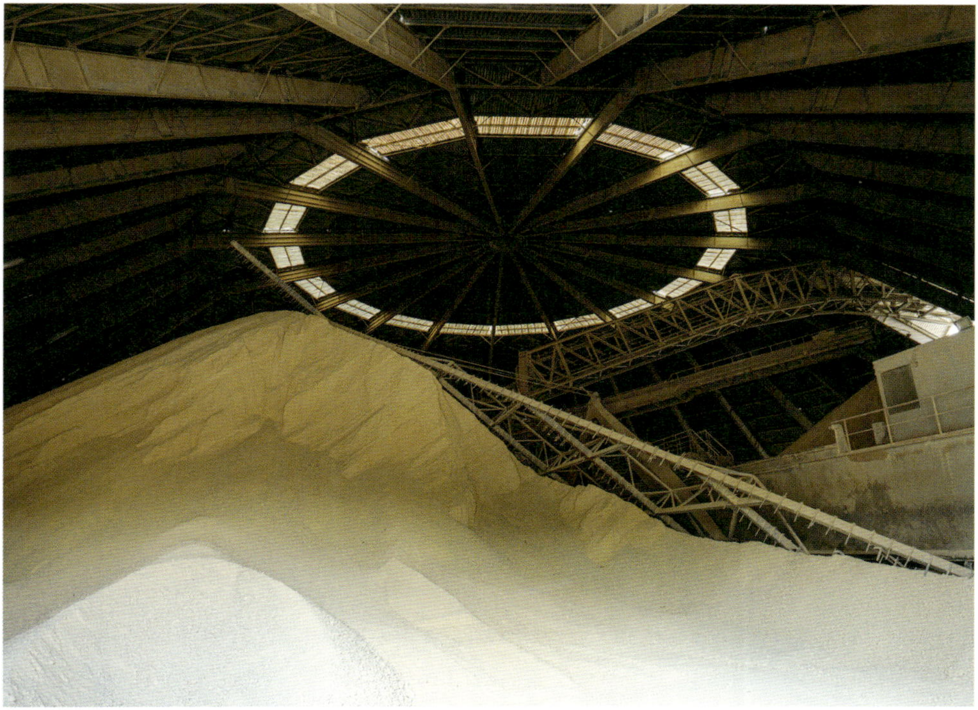

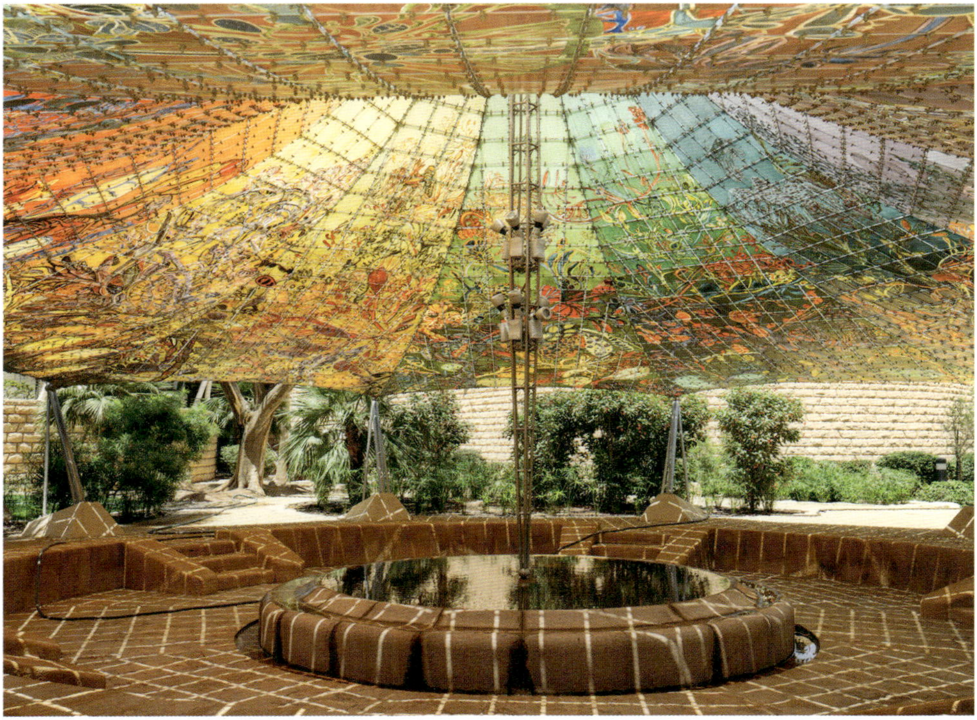

MAŁGORZATA MIRGA-TAS

Born 1978 in Zakopane, Poland, lives and works in Czarna Góra, Poland

Katarzyna Oraczko with her son Leszek, from the series Siukar Manusia
2022

Augustyn Gabor with his daughter Elżbieta, from the series Siukar Manusia
2022

Małgorzata Mirga-Tas is an artist, educator, and activist committed to challenging stereotypical representations of Roma people, Europe's largest ethnic minority. Trained in sculpture at the Academy of Fine Arts in Kraków, Mirga-Tas works in various ways to create resilient and affirming images of Romani culture and identity. In 2011, Mirga-Tas initiated the *Jaw Dikh!* residency in her hometown for Roma artists. That same year she designed a monument to Romani murdered during the Holocaust near Kraków, a work that was vandalized five years later. The artist's studio in the Carpathian Mountains is a meeting point for members of her community, who are protagonists in her work as well as active participants in its production. In 2022 she represented Poland at the 59th Venice Biennale as the first Roma artist to be featured in a national pavilion in the history of the biennial.

In Romani *Siukar Manusia* means "great or wonderful people." This series shows different first-generation Romani inhabitants of Nowa Huta—an eastern district of Kraków developed after World War II as a large-scale, socialist settlement to house working-class populations. Using her characteristic fabric and patchwork technique as a method of image-making, Mirga-Tas celebrates the lives and livelihoods of the Roma in Nowa Huta, who include steelworkers, cooks, activists, and musicians. Each individual is portrayed in life-sized scale, isolated against a vivid blue background to enhance their presence and, importantly for the artist, also their dignity. The bright patterned fabrics of the figures are taken from used garments. Mirga-Tas sees this clothing as an important marker of identity and an expression of a culture that was long suppressed.

Sourced from personal photographs and historical archives, the portrait images are significant carriers of micro-histories: chronicles of personal achievements and stories of survival. Mirga-Tas's work avoids hierarchies. Every person has an important story to tell. On view is a portrait of Katarzyna Oraczko, who came to Nowa Huta in the 1950s together with her husband, Andrzej Oraczko, and worked as a cook in a Kraków restaurant. Augustyn Gabor was a respected violinist of Hungarian origins. Through the transformative power of Mirga-Tas's portrait-making, each protagonist becomes, in the artist's words: "part of something bigger, a fight against racism."

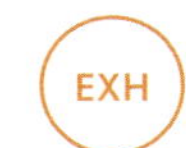

Augustyn Gabor with his daughter Elżbieta, from the series Siukar Manusia, 2022

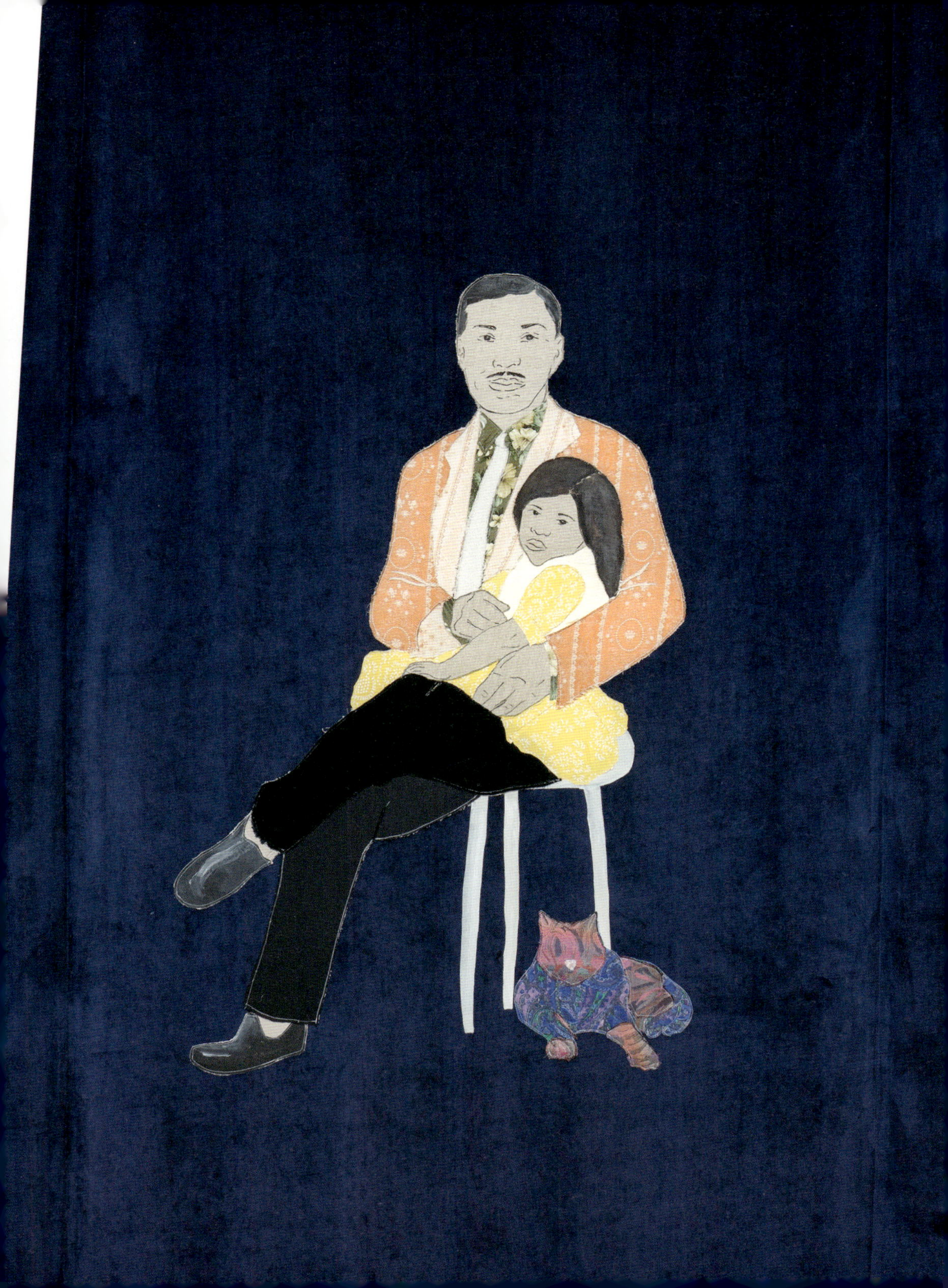

JAMES MORRIS

Born 1963 in Griffithstown, United Kingdom, lives and works
in Bwlchllan and London, United Kingdom

Butabu

1999–2000 / Selected works from the series (see p. 292 for details)
Also in Exhibition Halls B5 and B1 Re/Search

Trained as a historian at University College London, James Morris
originally considered becoming a documentary filmmaker. Through
film he discovered his affinity for the more unencumbered process
of photography as well as the control and aesthetic offered by the
still image. His photographic work is rooted in a fundamental interest
in architecture and built environments, which has taken him to the
Middle East and Africa, including the Sahel region. Many of his projects are pursued over an extended period, during which he explores
the layers of history evident in a landscape, whether that of Egypt,
Mali, London, or Morris's native Wales.

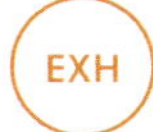

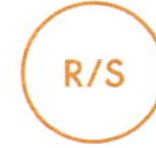

The photo series *Butabu* (1999–2000) stems from the photographer's
travels through multiple countries in West Africa in the years 1999
and 2000, including Mali, Niger, Nigeria, Togo, Benin, Ghana, and
Burkina Faso. Morris explored far-flung villages and towns with the
help of a local guide. His photographs show the richness of forms and
textures in vernacular mud-brick architecture, and its range of applications: from a domestic space to a traditional ruler's audience rooms
and the minarets of mosques. The title *Butabu* stems from a word in
the language of the Batammaliba of Togo and Benin for wetting the
earth before building. Made of dried mud, these structures require
consistent maintenance, and the wooden beams seen protruding
from the façades of some buildings are not only decorative but serve
as scaffolding to facilitate upkeep and repair.

The wealth of this architectural tradition dates back at least to the
period when trading caravans crossed important political and cultural centers of the Sahel, connecting it with the Islamic world further
east, and before these routes were eclipsed by the Portuguese ports
established along the western African coast in the fifteenth century.
Historically the builders of this architecture were neither anonymous,
nor were its influences utterly Indigenous. Guild-like castes of famed
master builders still pass knowledge down across generations, and
Islamic, Berber, and, later, French colonial impetuses can be traced
throughout the region. Today the biggest threat to these magnificent buildings is modernization and the use of industrial building
materials. Simultaneously many contemporary African architects
continue to be inspired by the striking and expressive aesthetic of
this architectural heritage.

Friday Mosque, Djenne, Mali, 2000, from the series Butabu, 1999–2000

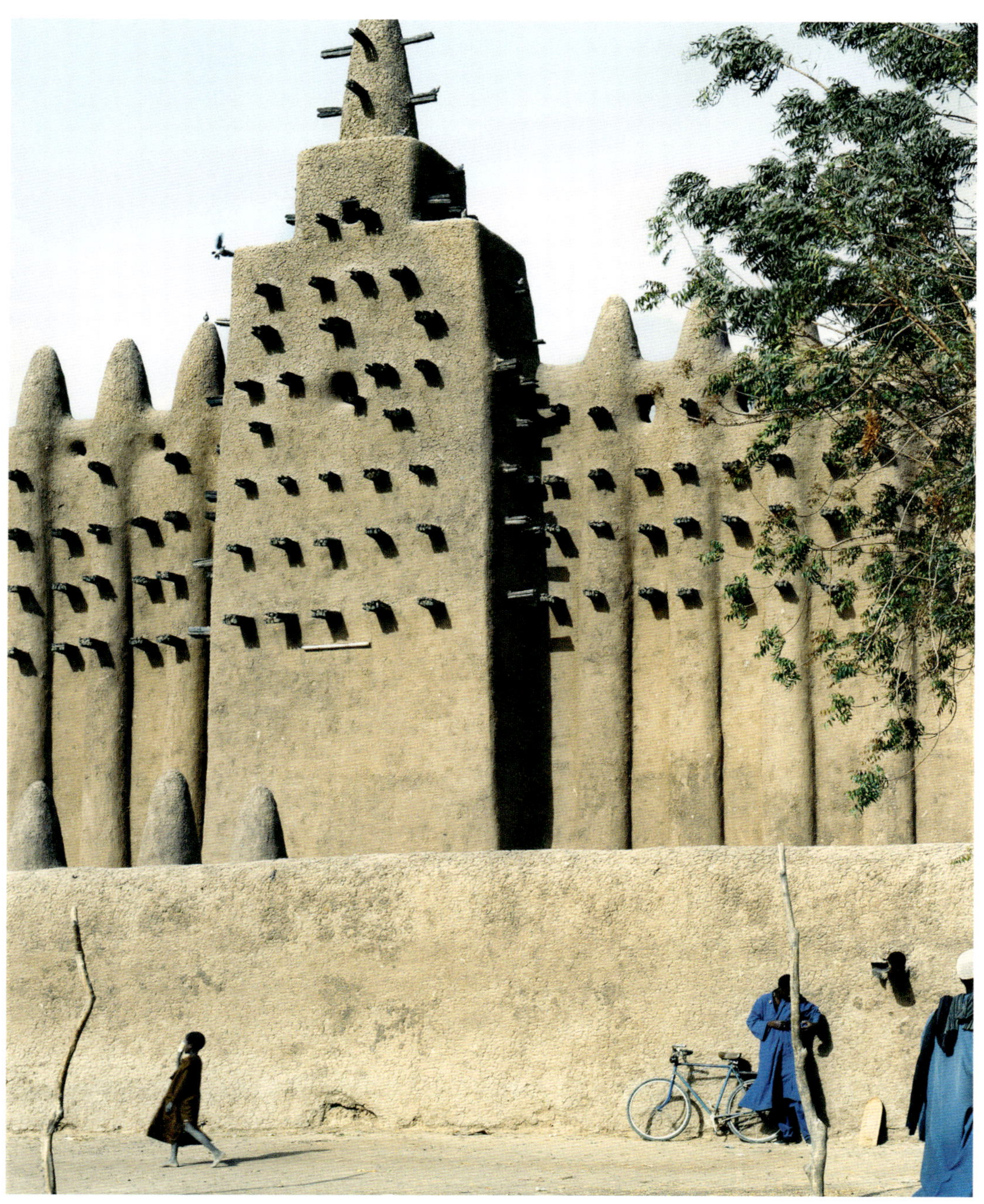

LUCY + JORGE ORTA

Lucy Orta, born 1966 in Sutton Coldfield, United Kingdom
Jorge Orta, born 1953 in Rosario, Argentina
Live and work between Paris, Seine-et-Marne, France, and London, United Kingdom

OrtaWater — Purification Factory

2012

Lucy and Jorge Orta work as a collaborative multimedia visual arts practice to address critical social and ecological challenges such as water scarcity, corporate control of resources, and the impacts of climate change on migration. Taking form in works that include drawing, sculpture, and performance, their installations have investigated the possibilities of portable eco-minimal habitats and alternative models of community building. In recognition of their commitment to sustainability, they received the 2007 Green Leaf Award for Artistic Excellence, presented by the United Nations Environment Program in partnership with the Nobel Peace Center in Oslo and the Natural World Museum. Their collaborative process involves working with artists, architects, designers, craftsmen, and technicians to realize their installations. As an extension of this practice, the duo founded the community-based artistic research and production complex Les Moulins in the French countryside in 2000.

The two-part installation *OrtaWater* (2012)—comprising *Mobile Reservoir* and *Portable Water Fountain*—is designed in conversation with engineers to address the issue of global water scarcity and the possibilities of low-cost, accessible, portable water devices. Made of scrap metals and recycled materials, previous iterations of the project pumped and distilled water from sources including Venice's Canal Grande and the Emmersingel in Rotterdam. It also transformed local urban vehicles, such as Mexican and Chinese tricycles, into customized portable drinking fountains.

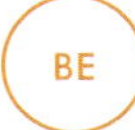

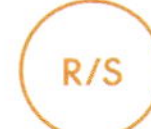

Installation view of *OrtaWater — Purification Factory*, from the 9th Shanghai Biennale, China, 2012–13

DIRIYAH CONTEMPORARY ART BIENNALE 2024

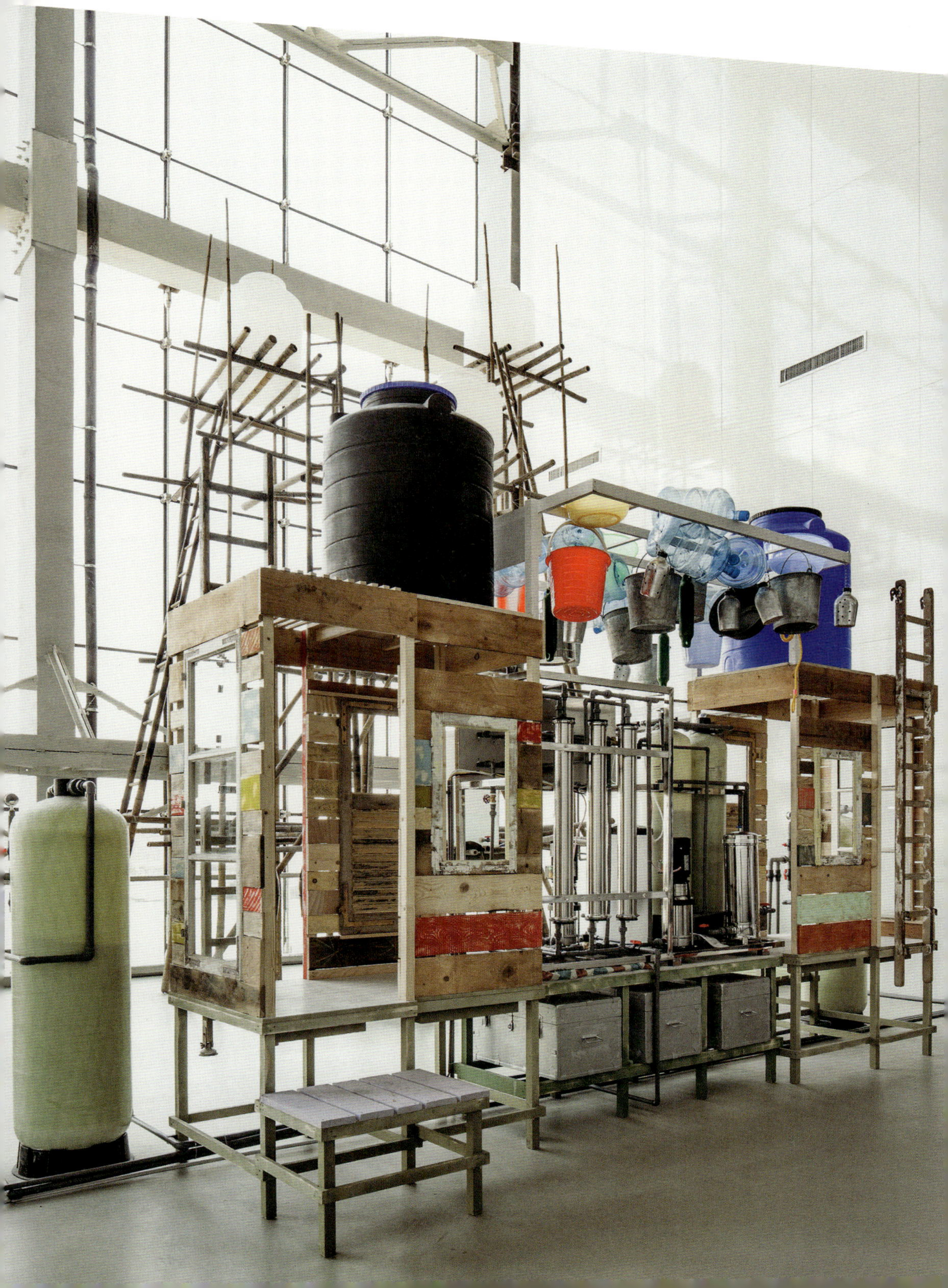

MARJETICA POTRČ

Born 1953 in Ljubljana, Slovenia, where she lives and works

Acre Palafita with Infrastructure
2024

The Time of Humans on the Soča River
2021/2024

Marjetica Potrč is an artist and architect whose participatory and interdisciplinary practice takes the form of architectural case studies, public artworks, diagrammatic drawings, and visual essays. Born before the breakup of the Socialist Federal Republic of Yugoslavia, Potrč completed degrees in architecture and sculpture at the University of Ljubljana amid a tumultuous period of political and economic crisis in the 1970s and 1980s. After spending four years in the United States, she returned to a newly independent Slovenia in 1994. Her socially inflected works have been exhibited in major international exhibitions, including the Venice Biennale (1993, 2003, and 2009), the Bienal de São Paulo (1996 and 2006), and Skulptur: Projekte Münster 1997.

Potrč's practice is a long-term engagement with global conditions of living and coexisting together and issues of sustainability. It is rooted in extensive collaboration with communities that are constantly reinventing themselves and their built environments. Her architectural case studies—large-scale installations of vernacular architectural typologies presented in gallery spaces—have become well-known aspects of her work. These "theatrical objects," as the artist calls them, are reconstructions of real-world dwellings and infrastructure, which highlight the architectural practices of their specific localities and how these respond to the changing environmental, social, economic, and political contexts of their respective inhabitants. In case studies ranging from rooftop houses in her native Balkan region and rural dwellings in Yinchuan, China, to homes and water meters in the Soweto township of Cape Town, South Africa, and informal city houses in Caracas, Venezuela, Potrč always includes a photograph of the original architectural source, reshaping the gallery space into a nexus of historic and geographic exchange.

For the Biennale, the artist has recreated the architectural case study of the *palafita* (stilt house), which is found across South America. A form of Indigenous architecture without walls common in the rainforest of Amazonian Brazil and coastal areas, the *palafita* recreated in Riyadh, with solar panels and a satellite dish, highlights issues of resource infrastructure that connect the two distant places. Also on view is the mural work *The Time of Humans on the Soča River* (2021/2024). Incorporating imagery from Slovenian folk art, it celebrates the caretakers and environmentalists of the Soča River in Slovenia.

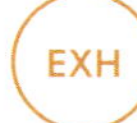

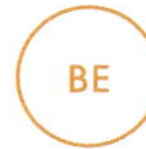

Above: Source image for *Palafita*, the State of Acre, Brazil, 2006
Below: Installation view of *Shelter: Closed and Open* at VISUAL Carlow, Ireland, 2018

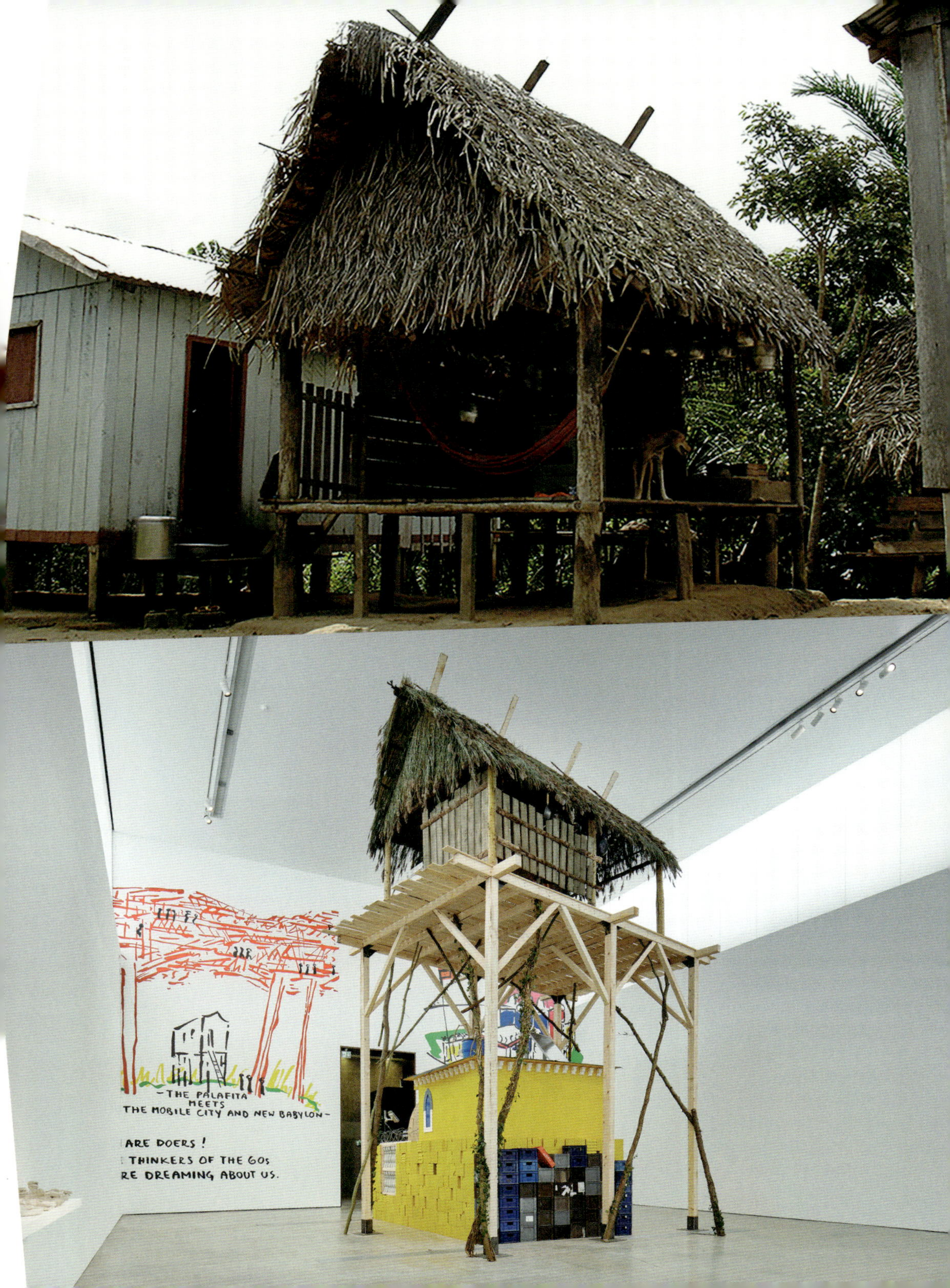

—THE PALAFITA
MEETS
THE MOBILE CITY AND NEW BABYLON—

ARE DOERS !
THINKERS OF THE 60s
RE DREAMING ABOUT US.

SHOOSHIE SULAIMAN

Born 1973 in Muar, Malaysia, lives and works in
Kuala Lumpur, Malaysia, and Onomichi, Japan

Lore of Equator #2

2024

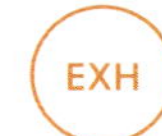

Preoccupied with our subjective relationships to history and the environment, Shooshie Sulaiman works with soil, water, rubber sap, plants, trees, and books—materials that she uses in installations and performances to insert personal memories into the broader narratives and histories of her Malaysian homeland. Sulaiman began making art in the 1990s, a time of accelerated economic transformation in Malaysia, and in 2007 she founded the gallery space Artspace 12, which she still runs. Believing that art is integral to life and health, Sulaiman always creates conditions for her works to be experienced in intimate settings that nourish moments of contemplation and self-reflection.

Lore of Equator #2 (2024) consists of several smaller artworks related to the equator—paintings, video, found objects, earthenware pitchers, woven baskets, altered maps—grouped into a wall composition along an equatorial axis. Addressing concerns around conservation and creativity, the artist explores historic and contemporary legacies of the equator and its associated knowledges through a gesture of arbitrary mythmaking. Sulaiman uses traditional materials and techniques that stem from a part of the world that has been interconnected across national borders since ancient times through the Indigenous technologies of equatorial peoples, who the artist praises as "great seafarers, great forest people, and amazing islanders."

According to traditional wisdom, the equator is an essential energy point in the universe. Living at the equator, the landscape where the artist was born and raised, is a spiritual journey filled with storytelling and mysticism. From this place of learning, it is possible to tap into a wealth of cosmic energy that fosters well-being; it is also a place of finding connection with nature and honoring it, as our ancestors did. Sulaiman advocates for an "Indigenous Attitude" to combat the capitalist mindset of greed and competition that creates a disconnection between the body and the mind, making humans physically and mentally ill. In contrast, Malaysian tradition teaches how to cultivate a deep connection to everything that surrounds us—flora and fauna, the sea and the sky. *Lore of Equator #2* includes woven plants, organic "plastic," tapioca drawings, wood mountains, rubber paintings, and soil maps, through which Sulaiman reminds the viewers that our role is "to be a witness to the universe's greatness."

DIRIYAH CONTEMPORARY ART BIENNALE 2024

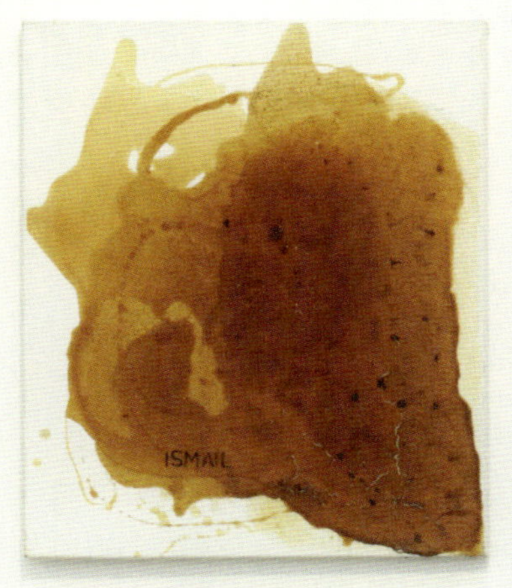

ISMAIL

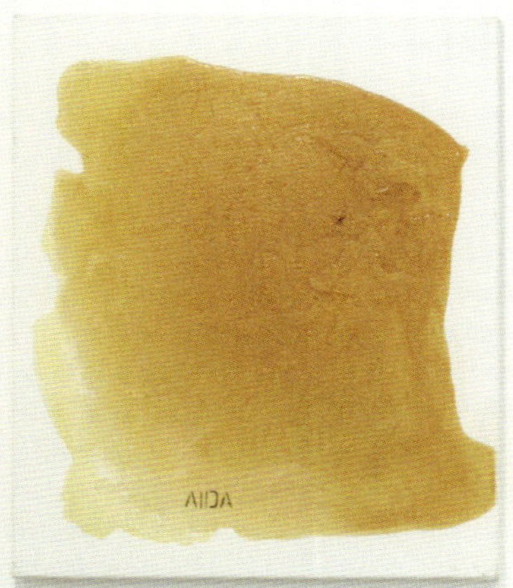

AIDA

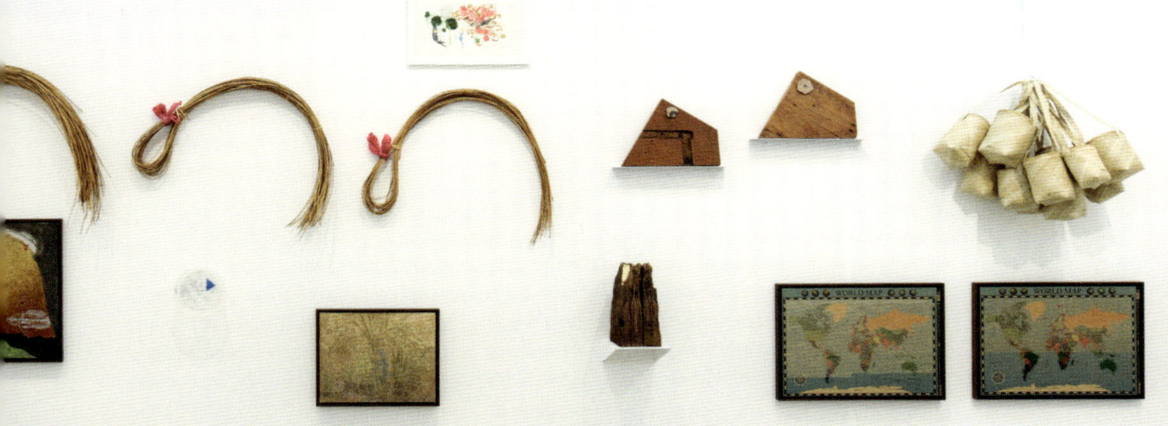

WORLD MAP
WORLD MAP

PAULO TAVARES / AUTONOMA

Born 1980 in Campinas, Brazil, lives in Brasília, Brazil, and works across Latin America

An Architectural Botany
2018–22

Trees, Vines, Palms, and Other Architectural Monuments
2017–22

Paulo Tavares is an architect, educator, and curator whose work questions colonial legacies of modernity in architecture and culture. In 2017 he founded autonoma, an agency dedicated to the practice of architecture as advocacy. Exploring conflicts embedded in space and land, his work has most recently focused on collaborations with communities at the frontlines of land conflicts in the Brazilian Amazonia, to propose strategies for reparations in the face of forced dispossession and rampant modernization. Tavares has collaborated with the research group Forensic Architecture and teaches at Columbia GSAPP and the Universidade de Brasília. In 2023 his project *Terra*, co-curated with Gabriela de Matos, was awarded the Golden Lion award for Best National Participation at the 18th Venice Architecture Biennale.

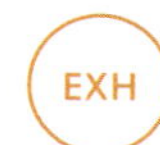

Tavares's installation comprises two interconnected bodies of work. *An Architectural Botany* (2018–22) centers around the lives and knowledge of the Ka'apor of eastern Amazonia. The historical relationship of the community with their forest environment has been extensively documented and archived by American ethnobotanist William Balée, who describes Ka'apor life and culture as deeply interwoven with the mindful use and transformation of their habitat. Tavares draws from Balée's book *Cultural Forests of the Amazon* (2013) and proposes that what is categorized as botanical history be reinscribed within the region's sociocultural and architectural history.

The second work, *Trees, Vines, Palms, and Other Architectural Monuments* (2017–22), brings to the fore the concerns of the A'uwe (Xavante) people of central Brazil who inhabit the contemporary territories of Marãiwatsédé. The Xavante were subjected to violent and brutal displacement from their ancestral lands in the 1960s, under the guise of development and integration into the nation-state of Brazil. Working in collaboration with the Bö'u Xavante Association of Marãiwatsédé, Tavares and members of autonoma use the testimonies of elders, supported by aerial and terrestrial imagery, as evidentiary documents mapping where these ancient settlements once stood. The imagery reveals a multitude of arc-shaped tree and vegetation patterns that mark these sites. These otherwise indiscernible arcs, encoded within the forests, are early examples of "terraformations" designed and planted by the Xavante over many generations. These documents have been gathered in support of a petition to recognize these constructed vegetal forms as architectural heritage and to affirm the Xavante people's right to land and sovereignty.

Above: Video still from An Architectural Botany, 2018–22 / Below: Video still from Landscape Archaeology, from the project Trees, Vines, Palms, and Other Architectural Monuments, 2017–22

DIRIYAH CONTEMPORARY ART BIENNALE 2024

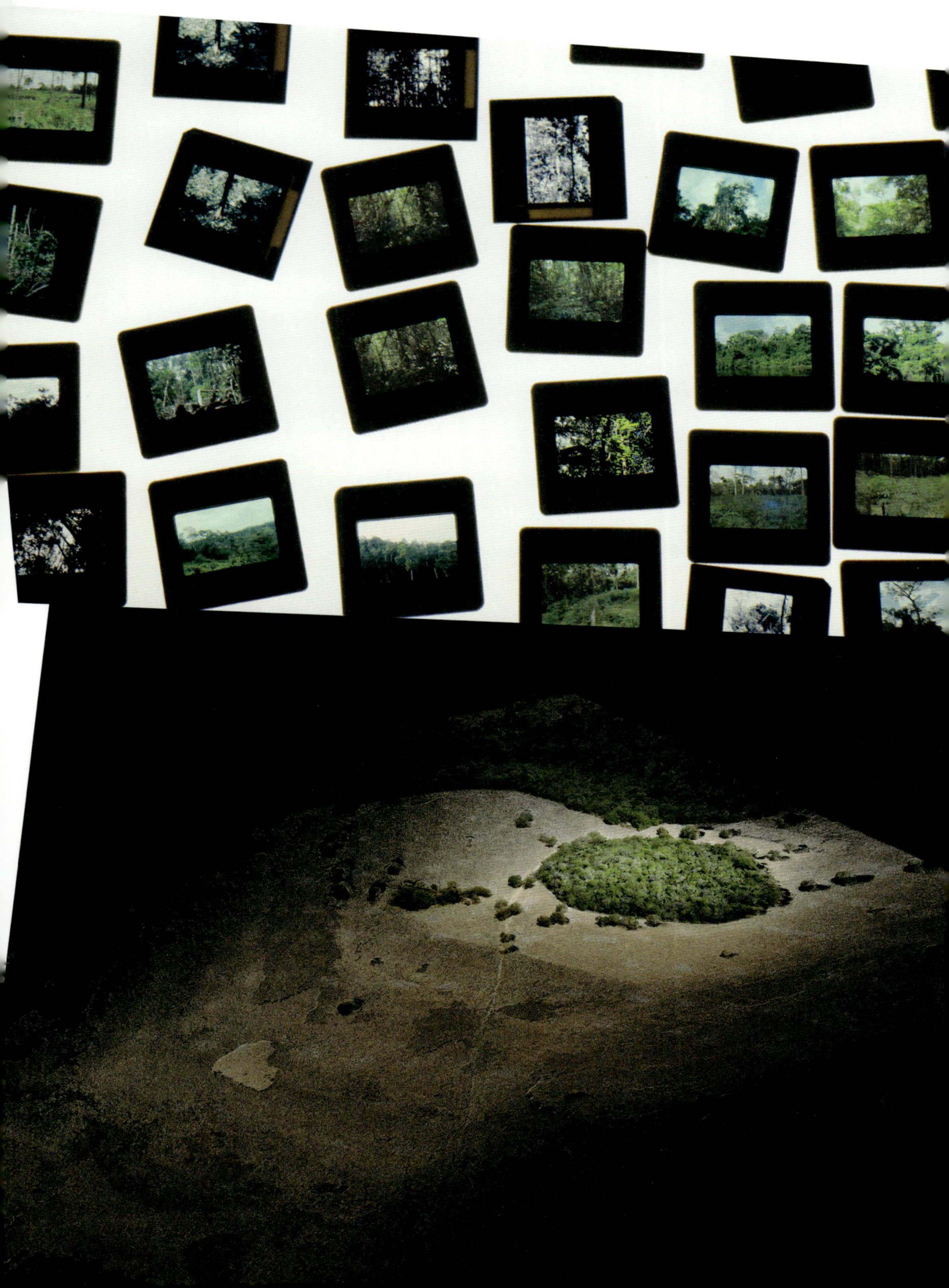

MUNEM WASIF

Born 1984 in Comilla, Bangladesh, lives and works in Dhaka, Bangladesh

Seeds Shall Set Us Free II
2016–19

Kheyal
2015–19 / Video, 23 min 34 sec
Film Program

Munem Wasif works primarily with photography, video, and sound. His works emerge from long-term engagements with specific places and their histories, particularly within the context of Bangladesh. His complex installations often mix photographs with moving images and archival documents, investigating topics that resonate with larger global concerns, such as food sovereignty, labor exploitation, and borders and migration. Having exhibited at the Lyon Contemporary Art Biennale (2022), Dhaka Art Summit (2020), Taipei Biennial (2020), Centre Pompidou (2019), Sharjah Biennial (2019) Gwangju Biennale (2018), Victoria and Albert Museum (2017), and the Singapore Biennale (2016), Wasif was named the 2023 Robert Gardner Fellow in Photography at Harvard University, awarded to support his work on the critical history of the indigo industry in Bengal.

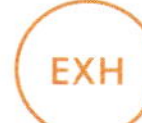

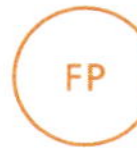

In his long-term project *Seeds Shall Set Us Free II* (2016–19) Wasif investigates the cultural history of grain—a topic closely connected with memories of the Bengal famine of 1943–44 under British colonial rule. In the installation, cyanotypes of rice grains and plants are combined with archival documents and photographs from one of the largest community grain banks in the country, the research center UBINIG (Policy Research for Development Alternative), which works to counter the corporatization of agricultural practices and promote biodiversity. These archival materials include handwritten documents and photographs produced by researchers and farmers and give a sense of locally rooted agricultural stakeholders and their struggle for legitimacy. Probing the impact of ecological colonialism, plantation farming, and cash crops, the work imagines an "ecosophical" type of agriculture, in which other species and beings have equal agency with humans, as reflected in the philosophy of local farmers.

The film *Kheyal* (2015–19) is an intimate portrait of Old Dhaka, a historical quarter of the Bangladeshi capital, and its residents. Following four characters through the neighborhoods of Bangla Bazar and Farashganj, the film is part fiction, part documentary. *Kheyal* (originally derived from the Persian/Arabic word for "fiction" or "imagination") is the name of a major form of Hindustani classical music that offers freedom for musical improvisation and is often linked to poetry about longing. This title bestows a metaphorical meaning to the hovering nature of the characters, while also referencing the artist's relationship with Old Dhaka. The sequences amplify the city's infrastructure and affective textures, pursuing memories sustained by the senses—scents, colors, and the passing of time—while the sounds of *riyaz*, or music practice, guide our ears.

Details of the installation Seeds Shall Set Us Free II, 2016–19

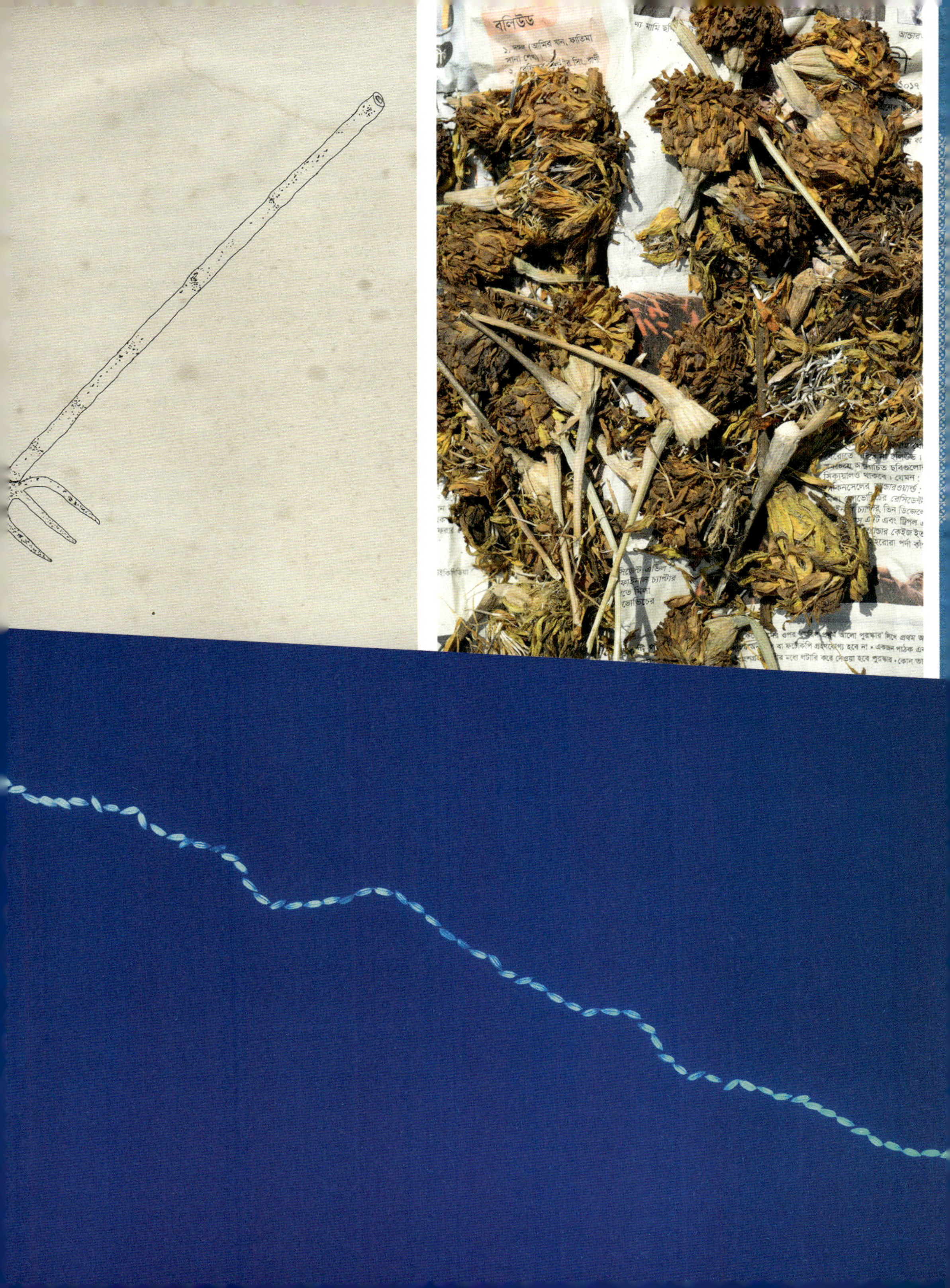

CAMILLE ZAKHARIA

Born 1962 in Tripoli, Lebanon, lives and works in Manama, Bahrain

Al Bar
2010–16

Coastal Promenade
2010

The Mountain My Neighbor
2024

Inspired by urban landscapes and themes of belonging, home, and identity, Camille Zakharia obtained a degree in civil engineering from the American University of Beirut in 1985, at the height of the Civil War. It was during this time that Zakharia acquired his first camera, a Canon AE1, which he used to document his surroundings, the scarred buildings, and random residues of war. Fleeing Lebanon, he lived in various countries, including Canada, where he studied fine art at NSCAD in Halifax, Nova Scotia, and further developed his practice of photography, photomontage, and collage. Since 1999 his home has been the island of Bahrain, which he explores in weekly walks with his medium-format Rolleiflex camera.

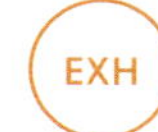

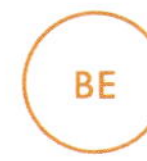

Coastal Promenade (2010) is a series of photographs originally commissioned by Bahrain's Ministry of Culture for its first pavilion at the 18th Venice Architecture Biennale in 2010. Titled *Reclaim*, it was awarded the Golden Lion for best national participation. The project documents fishermen's huts that once dotted the island's coast. Solitary huts of varying constructions stand seemingly abandoned or neglected. As markers of history, these fragile, makeshift structures bear witness to transient cultures and economies—and the changing nature of humankind's relationship to the sea. Development and land rehabilitation projects along the coastline made the huts obsolete; they were demolished shortly after Zakharia took the photographs.

Mirroring the emptiness of the coastal series, *Al Bar* (2010–16) captures the island's interior. The images follow the seasonal transformation of the desert in Bahrain from November to March, when inhabitants take advantage of cooler temperatures to fleetingly reconnect with the land. The photographs show the campsites that they leave behind, along with the vestiges of social gatherings: tents bleached by the sun, burnt wood from bonfires, furniture arranged to form a *majlis* seating arrangement, and dried-out plants. Consumer artifacts such as cars, toys, and electronics feature prominently in an otherwise arid landscape.

Zakharia's *The Mountain My Neighbor* (2024), which was commissioned for the Diriyah Contemporary Art Biennale 2024, documents the expansion of the city into the surrounding landscape. During a several-week stay in Riyadh, the artist was intrigued by the dramatic constellations he discovered between new constructions and the rocky terrain, which he captured in this typological series.

Above: *Al Narjis — Riyadh, Saudi Arabia*, from the series *The Mountain My Neighbor*, 2024
Below: *Al Bar — Sakhir, Bahrain*, from the series *Accidental Landscape*, 2020

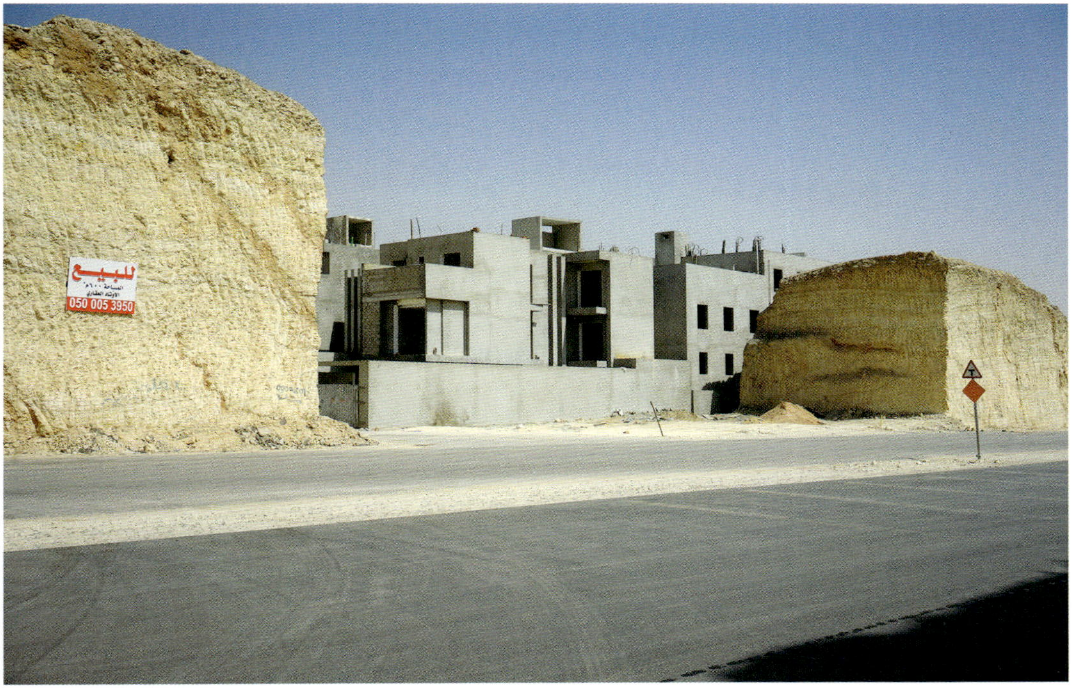

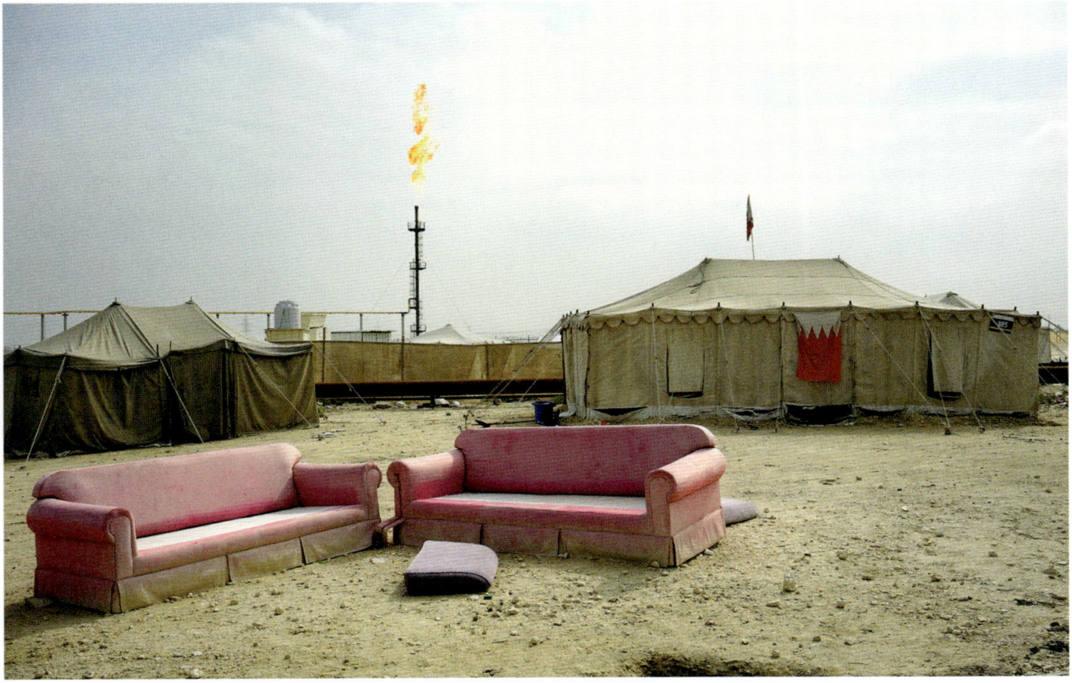

EXHIBITION HALL B3

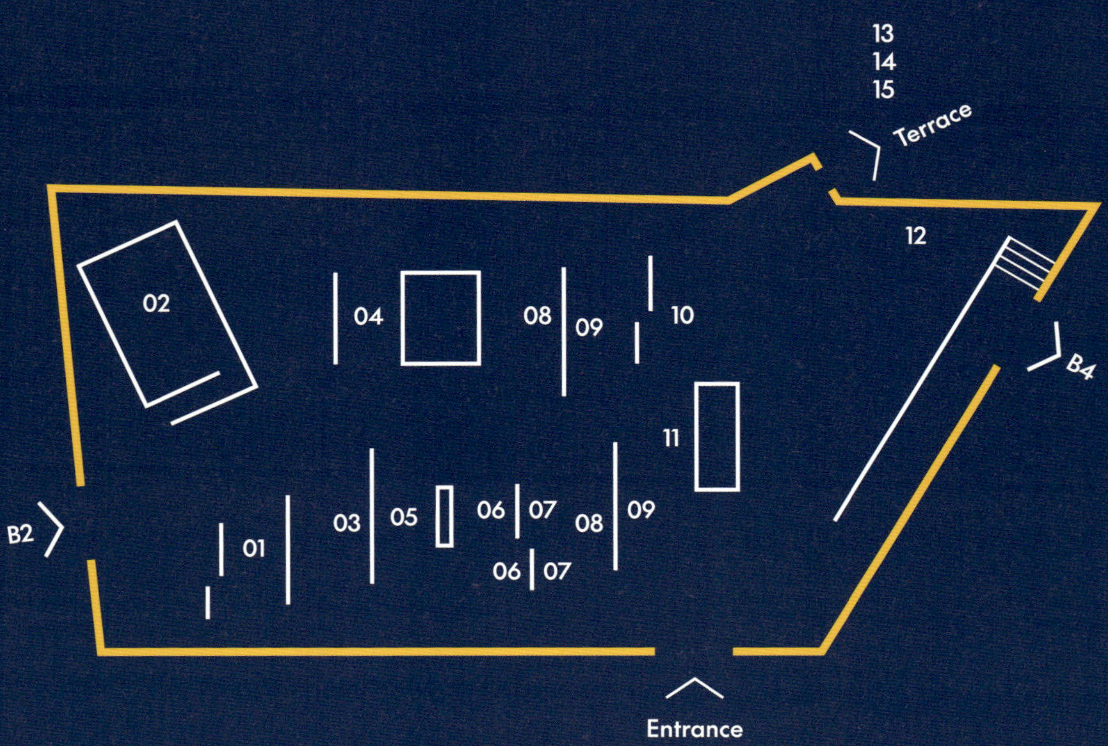

MODERN LEGACIES AND GEOPOETICS

This hall presents a generation of preeminent artists from Asia and the Gulf region, many of whom have pursued their art under politically, socially, and economically challenging conditions. Some only received museum recognition very late in their artistic careers, while others have yet to be discovered by major institutions. A number of works are being presented to the public for the first time. Ranging from ink drawings to watercolors, paintings, and textile works, their work is rooted both in modern traditions and conceptual approaches. Many of these artists have had an immense influence on following generations. They have worked as educators, created works of public art, and founded essential spaces of debate. Also featured is a video work that marks the transition from the colonial period to the era of modern nation states, which formed the postcolonial constellation in which these practices are situated. Positioned at the end of the hall is a large-format painting by a young Saudi artist that exemplifies the concerns of the current generation and a renewed interest in the landscape and natural environment.

ALIA AHMAD

Born 1996 in Riyadh, Saudi Arabia, where she lives and works

Alwasm

2023

Alia Ahmad is a painter who works with the color palettes of Riyadh's urban and desert landscapes to explore how memory and place can be translated into a personal, visual language. Trained in digital culture at King's College London, she recently graduated with a MFA from the Royal College of Art in London and has since gained international attention for her lush, large-scale canvases. Often context-specific, her work reflects the particularities of place, mirroring the tones and shapes of local flora and the land in compositions that build on vibrant color and networks of organic shape and line. The range of her palette extends from the temporalities of night and day, shifts of tone and light, and the slight transformations of color across the day. She considers her paintings "social spaces" or "blueprints," suggesting an open-endedness in her process. She has recently shown at CICA, Vancouver (2023); 21,39 Jeddah Arts (2021); the RCA Research Biennale, London (2020); and the Design Museum, London (2020).

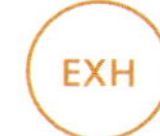

In her new work *Alwasm* (2023), commissioned for the Biennale, Ahmad finds inspiration in historic Wadi Hanifah located in the Najd region of Riyadh, creating a work that probes this specific terrain with its seasonal shifts and traditions. In the period between October and December, known as *alwasm*, relief sets in after the scorching and arid heat of summer. Temperatures drop, a cool breeze blows, and the land suddenly blossoms. People go out, and families take rugs to the waterside for a *kashtah*, an outdoor picnic or camp gathering, enjoying the patches of green that find their way through the sands after the extended warm season. Integrating elements of these scenes—textiles, books, photographs, and even road signs—the painting is a compositional collage of found motifs in warm tones that convey this seasonal bloom. Central to the painting with its gestural strokes and vibrant colors in the interplay of vertical treelike shadows and the composition of the ground are the geometric and linear patches that recall the technique of weaving. The work becomes a visual reading, exploration and celebration, of how nature and humans commune in the Wadi Hanifah. As Ahmad explains: "My intention is to illuminate that there is a lot of life from a land that is perceived as dry."

Studio documentation of *Alwasm*, Riyadh, Saudi Arabia, 2023

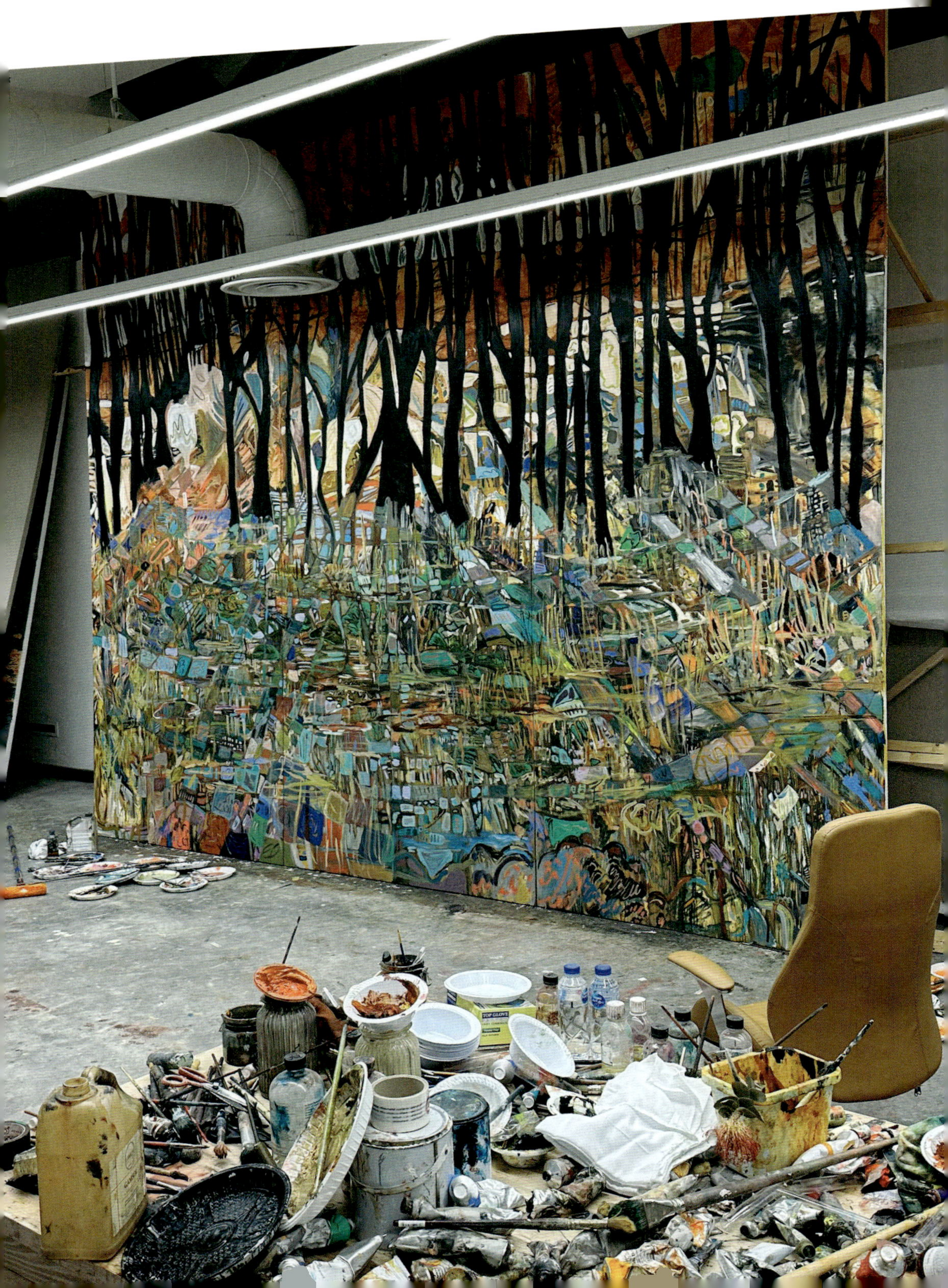

NABILA AL BASSAM

Born Mumbai, India, lives and works in Al Khobar, Saudi Arabia

Selected Works

1993–99
(see p. 282 for details)

Nabila Al Bassam works with mixed-media and traditional textile-making processes to produce multilayered collages on canvas that explore materiality and structure. Trained as an educator and teacher at the American University of Beirut in the late 1960s, she then studied silk-screen printing and drawing in the United States. After returning to Saudi Arabia in 1979, Al Bassam spent years traveling across the Kingdom, conducting extensive research and interviews with crafts-women involved in the production of traditional textiles. Drawing on her deep knowledge of the histories and techniques of fabrics and weaving, Al Bassam uses cut-outs of handmade textiles along with embroidered and antique fabrics, beads, and other decorative elements collected from her travels to form works that celebrate traditional crafts. In 1979 she founded the Arab Heritage Gallery in Al Khobar to serve as an exhibition space for artists as well as an archive and holding for modern and contemporary works inspired by these traditional crafts.

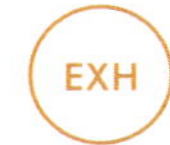

The works on view convey Al Bassam's distinctive interpretation of Saudi Arabian landscapes. Cut and woven fragments of textiles are layered horizontally to create backgrounds giving the illusion of foreground and depth. In two works each with the title *Buildings of Southern Arabia* she uses the characteristic front embroidery from traditional dresses of Aseer to collage and shape the traditional houses of the Aseer and Najd regions of Saudi Arabia within a landscape setting. The iconic indigenous palm trees of the desert punctuate these vistas, as do variations of texture. Vibrant colors and paint applied over the collage of fabrics create emphasis—windows, outlines, figures, shadow, and light. *The Lighthouse of Saudi* (1999) and *The Lighthouse of the South* (1999) show stacked, compact structures suggesting a town or city, sometimes highlighted with beads. The first shows the painted forms of female figures who live within, while an additional untitled work draws on Al Sadu weaving techniques. For Al Bassam, her compositions and use of fabric are both an assertion of the legacy of ancestral art and an homage to the women who have typically produced these works.

Buildings of Southern Arabia, 1993

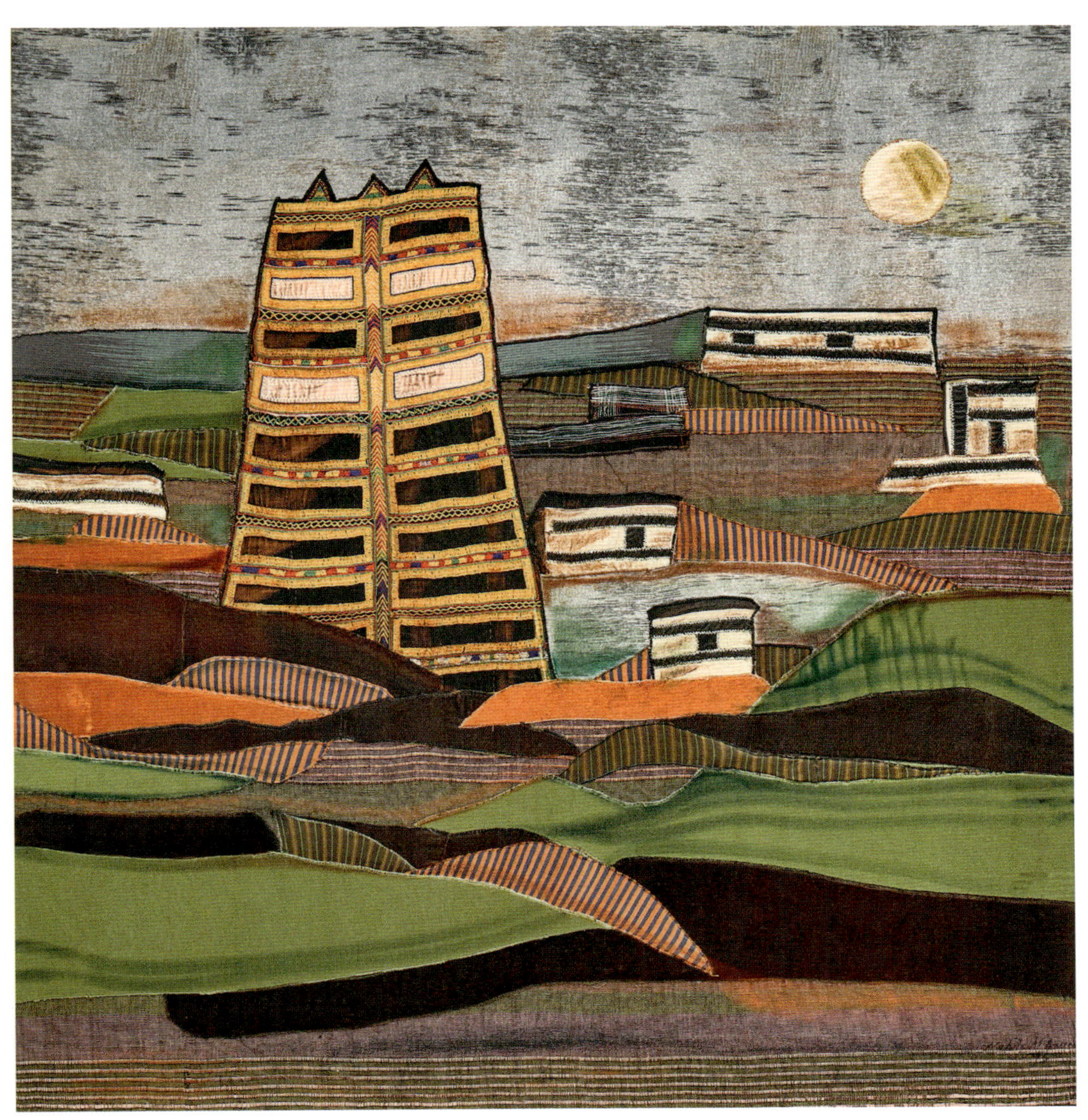

NABILA AL BASSAM

ABDULRAHMAN AL-SOLIMAN

Born 1954 in Al Ahsa, Saudi Arabia, lives and works in Dammam,
Saudi Arabia

Palm, Bow, and Fragments
1990–91

Abdulrahman Al-Soliman belongs to a generation of pioneering Saudi artists who came of age in the 1960s and 1970s and defined the artistic transformations of this era. Like a number of his peers, he not only pursued his own work as a painter but also actively fostered the community of contemporary art. An avid writer, journalist, and researcher, he has been documenting Saudi art practices, in particular those of the Eastern Province, since 1983 as the Fine Arts Editor of the *Al Yaum* newspaper and as the author of books such as *The Journey of the Saudi Fine Arts Movement* (2000). In his own work, over the course of decades, he has distilled a masterful, expressive, yet highly personal visual vocabulary sprung from memories of landscapes and spaces.

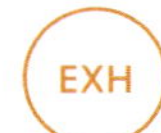

The series of drawings *Palm, Bow, and Fragments* (1990–91) was started during the Gulf War of 1990 and is being shown here for the first time. Often traveling between his hometown Al Ahsa and the city of Dammam, where he currently resides, the artist bore witness to ramifications of the war unfolding in neighboring Kuwait. The haziness of the sky caused by the fires in Kuwait's oil fields settled on Dammam; sparks from distant Patriot missiles lit up the deep darkness of night; and during rainfalls ash residue would run down the trunks of palm trees, coloring the ground. In response, Al-Soliman started creating gestural drawings using Chinese ink sourced from a local crafts store, the perfect medium to mark the time spent waiting for peace amid the chaos of war.

The intensity of the black ink varies slightly from one drawing to another, shifting from bold marks to lighter strokes. The palm tree is referenced throughout, as an important symbol of Al Ahsa, the world's largest oasis and home to over 2.5 million palms. Used to construct the ceilings of traditional mud houses, palms suggest shelter. More importantly for the artist, the palm tree was a symbol of strength, freedom, and perseverance amid all the uncertainty, a standing figure unbothered by the winds of change. In his drawings, a palm tree becomes a bullet, the arches of the houses form an embrace, and dots of ink burst into fragments.

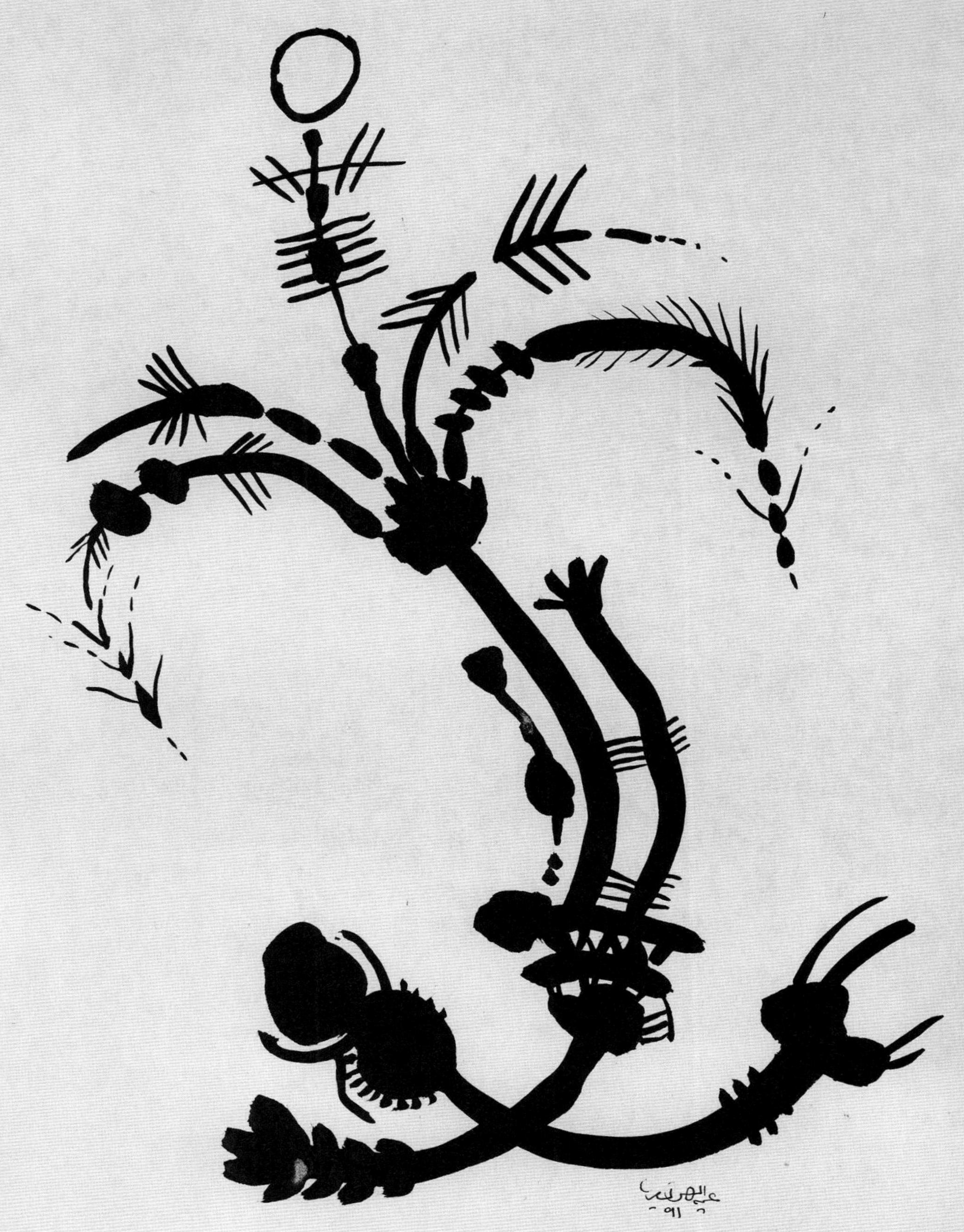

RASHEED ARAEEN

Born 1935 in Karachi, Pakistan, lives and works in London,
United Kingdom

People of Karachi
1955–58

Cube as Sculpture
1966/2020

The One that Could Not Float Away
1970

Based in London since 1964, Rasheed Araeen is a pivotal figure in postcolonial art and art history. Araeen initially trained and worked as a civil engineer, and he incorporated materials and methods used in this context into his early art practice. In parallel to his art, which ranges from Minimalist and geometric sculptures, reliefs, and paintings to participatory installations and performances, Araeen has countered the Eurocentrism of mainstream art institutions and histories through criticism, publishing, and curating exhibitions. He is most widely recognized for founding (and editing) the influential journal *Third Text* in 1987 and for organizing the groundbreaking 1989 exhibition *The Other Story: Afro-Asian Artists in Postwar Britain* at the Hayward Gallery in London, which showcased the unacknowledged contributions of immigrant artists to postwar British art.

Among Araeen's earliest extant works, *People of Karachi* (1955–58) comprises thirty portraits he made during informal drawing and painting sessions in Karachi. Despite their realist style and subject matter, they demonstrate his early interest in line as the basis of form, as later reflected in the Minimalist sculptures he made following his arrival in London. His earliest such works, which he dubbed "Structures," consisted of simple geometric compositions made of steel I-beams, painted blue or red. Araeen's *Cube as Sculpture* (1966/2020) consists of twelve identical, skeletal, and white aluminum cubes arranged in a neat three-by-four grid. Araeen's signature addition of diagonal struts to each of the cube's faces, possibly inspired by the complex geometries found in traditional Islamic art and architecture, introduced a dynamic rhythm into the otherwise static cubic form. These early works form an important and long overlooked contribution to the history of modern sculpture.

By the end of the 1960s, Araeen had begun experimenting with geometric forms as prompts for participation and collective action. *Chakras* (1969–70) involved throwing fluorescent red wooden discs into a waterway close to his studio in St. Katherine Docks, London. It was the first of a series of related works: ephemeral and sometimes participatory actions that he documented in photographs such as *The One That Could Not Float Away* (1970), in which the disc's simple geometry served as a foil for the unpredictability of the environment. This growing openness to contingency and context fed into the more politically charged and confrontational artworks and performances of the decades that followed.

Above: From the series *People of Karachi*, 1955–58
Below: *Cube as Sculpture*, 1966/2020, two of a total of 12 aluminum cubes

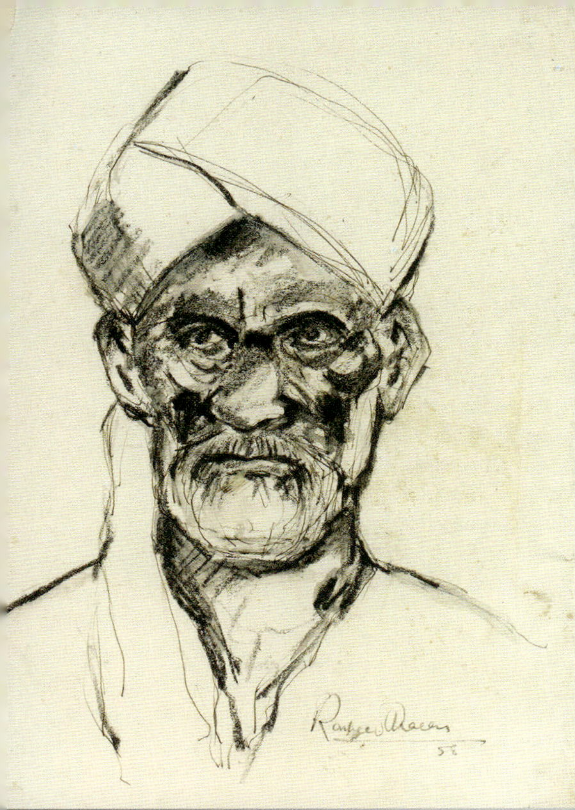

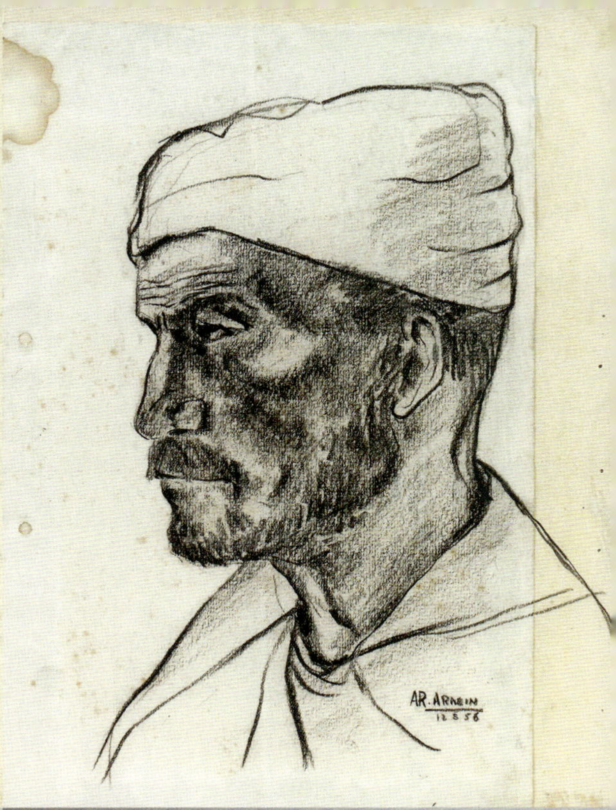

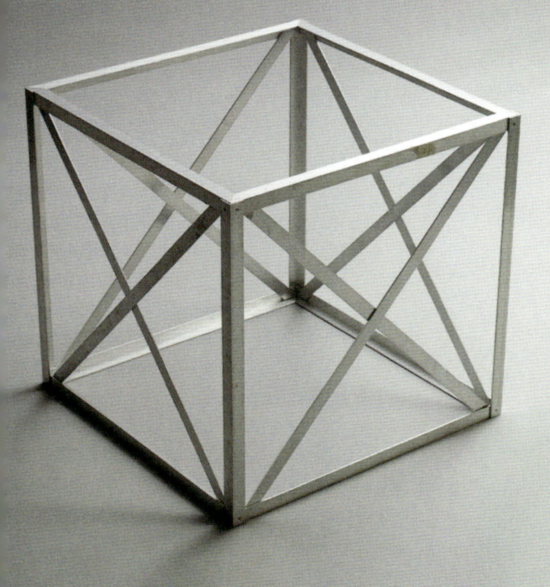

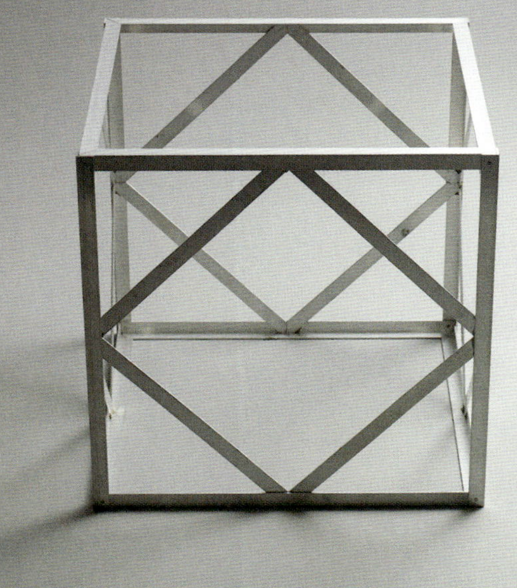

SIAH ARMAJANI

Born 1939 in Lahijan, Iran, died 2020 in Minneapolis, MN, United States

Selected works

1957–2016
(see p. 284 for details)

Iranian-American artist Siah Armajani is best known for public structures—reading rooms, gardens, lounges, and gazebos—that encourage civic assembly, dialogue, reflection, and contemplation. Among his most notable public works are the *Irene Hixon Whitney Bridge* (1988) in Minneapolis, where he lived and worked until his death in 2020, and *Bridge, Tower, Cauldron*, which housed the flame at the 1996 Summer Olympics in Atlanta. Harboring artistic ambitions from a young age, Armajani studied for a time with a master painter and calligrapher. His earliest works, completed while he was still a university student in Tehran, are unruly subversions of traditional Persian book art. In place of measured calligraphic strokes are hasty, improvised scribbles akin to handwriting or graffiti, tricky to read even for those fluent in Farsi. Ghostly echoes of familiar figures haunt the negative spaces, often intruding into and obscuring parts of texts haphazardly scattered across the page, which juxtapose the writings of canonical and modernist Persian poets with slogans, talismans, and other popular written ephemera.

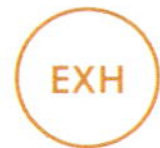

In 1960 Armajani's father sent him to stay with an uncle who taught at Macalester College in Saint Paul. Armajani continued to work with Farsi after his arrival in the US, completely filling shirts and canvases with lines of indecipherable script. In *Poetry* (1965), words and sentences, rather than conveying meaning, function like brushstrokes in a monochrome composition. At Macalester, Armajani studied philosophy and mathematics, the latter possibly instigating a shift in his artistic vocabulary from the calligraphic to the typographic and computational that defines his conceptual works of the late 1960s and early 1970s, which feature programming code and dot-matrix print. This transition is apparent in *Three Pears* (1966–67) where the fruit—an often repeated reference to early still-life exercises also seen in *Dictionary of Numbers* (1957)—is embedded in a neat grid of stamped English letters.

By the late 1960s, Armajani had begun applying his irreverent deconstructive approach to the vernacular wooden architecture that surrounded him in the American Midwest, remixing its language into playful compositions—both as scale models and the public artworks for which he is renowned. Drawn to the simplicity and self-evident construction of such architecture, especially bridges and houses, he continued to reference it for decades to follow. In *House with a Golden Chimney* (1975), a toy house blocks passage across a trussed bridge, its gilded chimney adding a whimsical accent. In *Kansas City Bridge No. 2* (2016), various types of bridges are jumbled together. Forgoing function, the logic of these architectural propositions is always more poetic than semantic.

Above: Songs #1 and #2, 1957 / Below: Kansas City Bridge No. 2, 2016

DIRIYAH CONTEMPORARY ART BIENNALE 2024

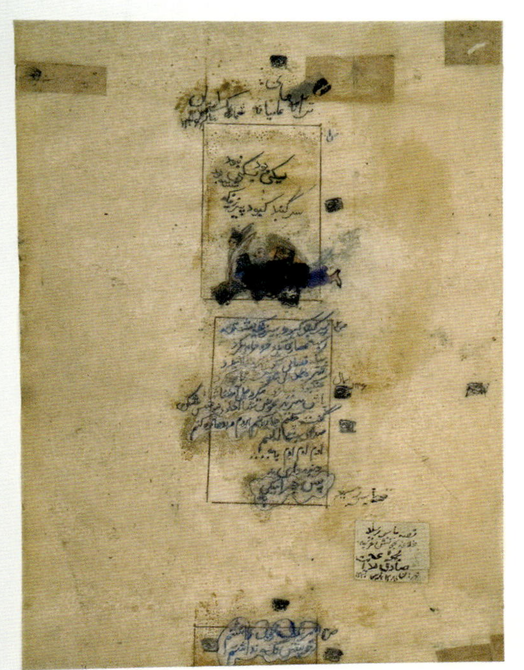
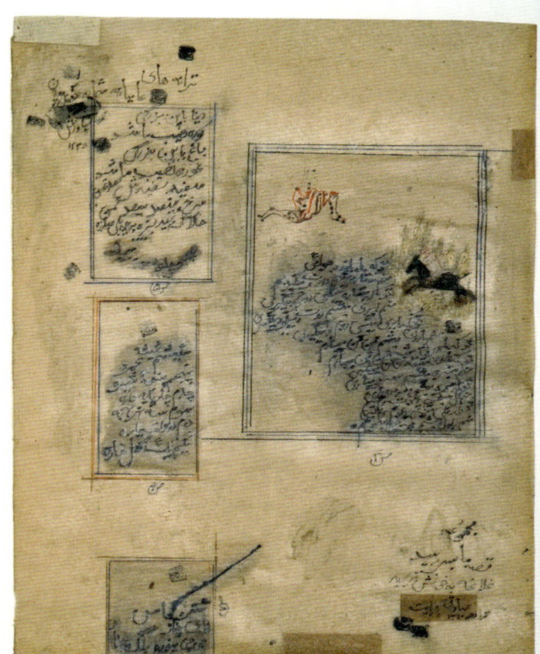
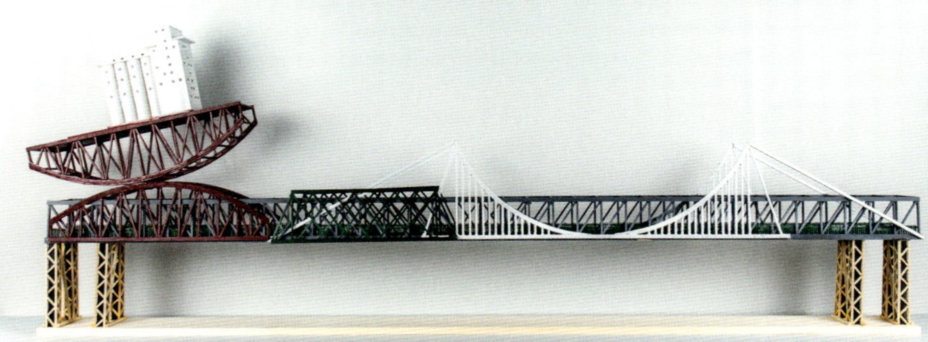

ZARINA BHIMJI

Born 1963 in Mbarara, Uganda, lives and works in London,
United Kingdom

Yellow Patch

2011

Zarina Bhimji works with film, sound, photography, sculpture, and textiles, always distilling politics into poetry and facts into emotions. Trained at Goldsmiths, University of London, and the Slade School of Fine Art, Bhimji was nominated for the Turner Prize in 2007. While Bhimji's works are informed by archival research and extensive fieldwork, her approach to colonial histories is—as a deliberate artistic choice—imbued with aesthetics. Her filmmaking is defined by a distinct formal language: painterly compositions, crafted camera movements, saturated colors, textures, and layered soundtracks. The triangular relationship between East Africa, India, and the United Kingdom traverses her filmic work and carries personal and political implications.

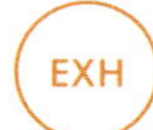

Yellow Patch (2011) is part of a larger project and sequence of films that engages with the residues of colonial history within the landscape and urban structures—"the echo," in the artist's words, that facts and power produce. Shot on 35 mm film, *Yellow Patch* takes as its starting point the history and migration between India and East Africa during the nineteenth century, under the system of British indentured labor. The artist includes filmed material from four main locations across the Indian subcontinent, loosely referencing the migration of Bhimji's father in colonial times: the Victorian-era offices of the Mumbai Port Trust, the desert landscape of the Rann of Kutch, the Indian Ocean near the port of Mandvi, and various structures in western Gujarat.

Yellow Patch is defined by an elusiveness characterizing many of Bhimji's works, situating it within what the art critic T. J. Demos has aptly defined as the genre of "postdocumentary." The film resists any factual information, immersing the viewer into a close and slow observation of derelict buildings, abandoned archives, dusty furniture, a broken candelabra, marks on the walls, and so on. The collapse of the imperial system takes a material form, all these traces marking the disintegration of power. The moving image is correlated with a layered soundtrack, which is produced independently of the film and added during postproduction. Combining atmospheric field recordings with snippets of speeches by Mahatma Gandhi, Lord Mountbatten, Jinnah, and Nehru, and also music performances by Bi Kidude and Abida Parveen, the artist uses sound to produce an additional score in which history is registered.

Film stills from *Yellow Patch*, 2011

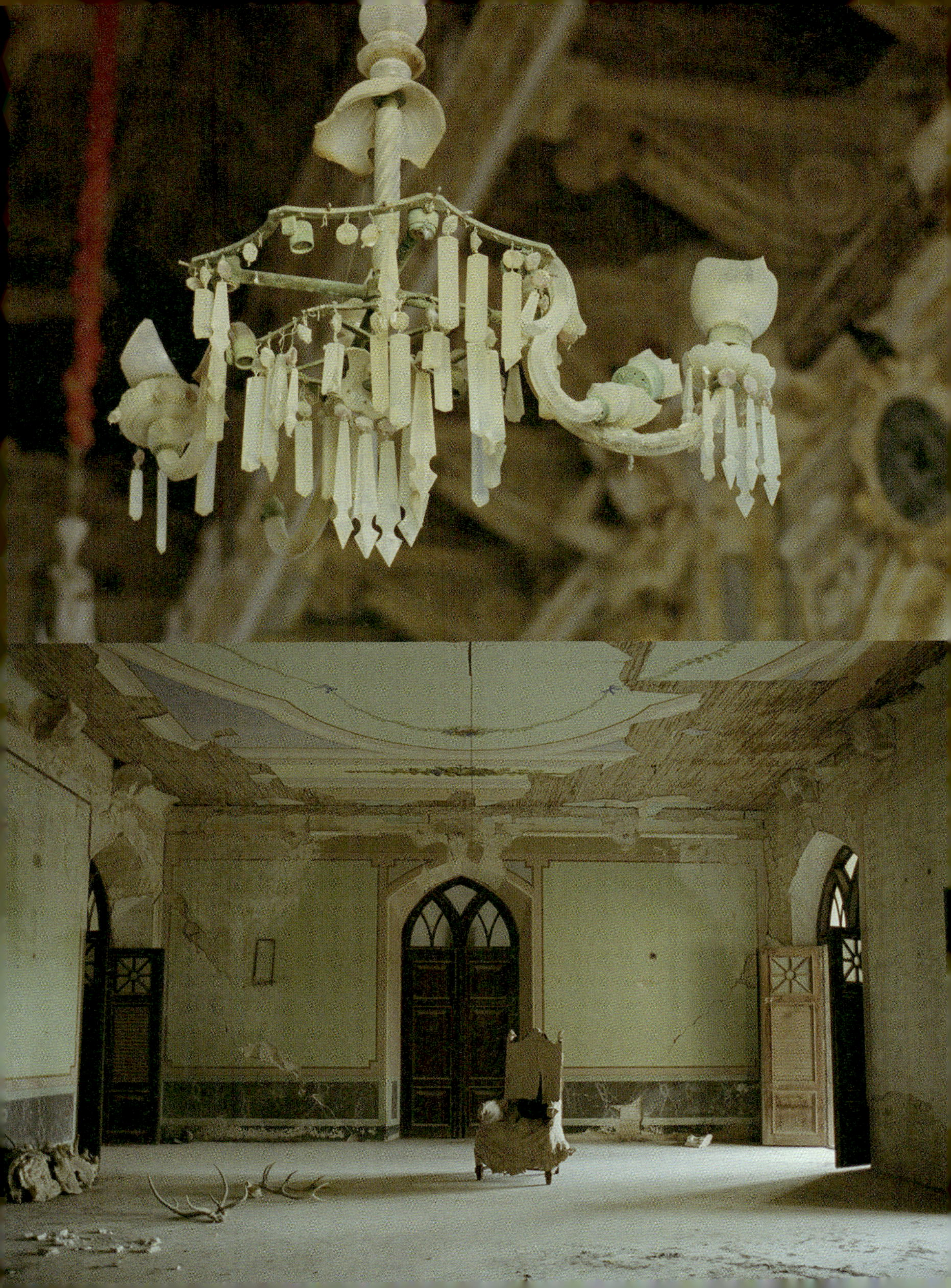

SAFEYA BINZAGR

Born 1940 in Jeddah, Saudi Arabia, where she lives and works

Turathuna (Our Tradition)
1997–99

Artist, teacher, and mentor, Safeya Binzagr has always cultivated a deep connection to her birthplace of Jeddah, although she moved away from the city as a child, attending school in Egypt and later receiving a degree in drawing and graphic arts from Central Saint Martins in London in the late 1960s. Returning to Saudi Arabia as an adult and witnessing the rapid modernization and urbanization transforming her birthplace, she began compiling and documenting local traditions and customs, capturing in her paintings and drawings aspects of Saudi Arabian culture that were quickly vanishing: tribal dress, marriage ceremonies, and everyday situations. In 1978 Binzagr, a pivotal figure in the emerging Saudi arts scene, was one of the few women to ever hold an art exhibition in the country, at a time when there were no commercial galleries. In 1995 she established Darat Safeya Binzagr, a museum, art school, and gathering place for artists in Jeddah, where she showcases her artworks and rare collection of traditional garments and costume jewelry from around the country. In 2017, she was awarded the First Class Order of King Abdulaziz for her contributions to Saudi culture.

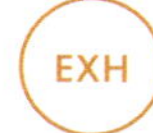

Turathuna (Our Tradition) (1997–99) is a series of detailed photogravure prints capturing the intricacies and richness of traditional dress from various tribes and regions of Saudi Arabia in thirty-nine images. The project was preceded by intensive research into the histories of the different garments as well as the styles, colors, embroidery, and textiles used in various parts of the country. Golden thread and silk adorn ceremonial garments from Hijaz, for example. Here a bride is shown crowned with an embroidered headpiece. In contrast, a woman from Aseer is portrayed in the linens and cotton fabrics typical of everyday attire and complemented by a straw hat as protection from the heat. Produced in a limited edition of thirty prints, such images are significant as detailed and extensive documents of Saudi Arabia's folkloric heritage. By comparison with the clothing of today, Binzagr's series inherently conveys the changes to traditional costumes that took place over the course of the twentieth century through the influences of mass production and globalization.

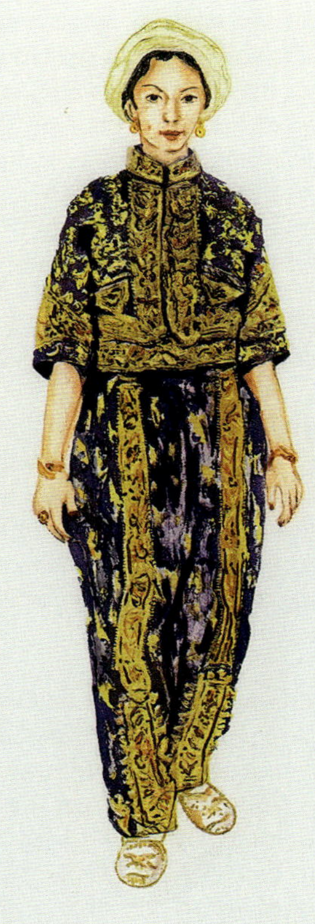

2/30

Safeya Binzagr

'98

IBRAHIM EL-SALAHI

Born 1930 in Omdurmán, Sudan, lives and works in Oxford,
United Kingdom

Fatima
1968

Dry Month of the Fast
1962

Untitled
1962

Ibrahim El-Salahi works with motifs from African, Arab, and Islamic art to create paintings and drawings that interrogate and invert common notions of Sudanese identity using a modernist vocabulary. Trained as a painter at Slade School of Fine Art in London during the mid-1950s, El-Salahi returned to teach at the College of Fine and Applied Arts in Khartoum in 1957. He was one of the initiators of the pioneering art movement known as the Khartoum School, which abstracted Indigenous, Islamic, and calligraphic forms to develop a visual language and identity reflecting postcolonial independence. In 1961, on a trip to Nigeria, he met the writers Chinua Achebe and Wole Soyinka, and forged ties with the pan-African modernist movement he too was a part of. El-Salahi served Sudan as a cultural diplomat in the early 1970s, first in London then in Khartoum, where he was imprisoned in 1975–76 on accusations of his involvement in plotting a coup. In prison he continued to secretly draw studies for paintings on miniscule pieces of paper, which he concealed in the sand. The experience informed his subsequent artistic practice in Qatar, where he lived after his release, and later in the UK, where he moved in 1998. He was honored with a retrospective at Tate Modern in London in 2013.

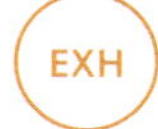

The paintings *Dry Month of the Fast* and *Untitled* (both 1962) demonstrate El-Salahi's inventiveness. The muted tones of his palette borrow from the dry desert hues of Sudan, accentuated with the suggestion of familiar shapes—figures, body parts, heads of birds—yet obscured again through their mutations into background, outline, and shadow. African motifs are evident in both works, with elongated figures reflecting traditional wood carvings and animal figurines. Despite their soft tones, the paintings evoke power, energy, and the supernatural, expressing both reflection and change. El-Salahi's formal commitment to the drawn line radiates in both works. *Fatima* (1968) builds on this visual language with organic and geometric shapes placed in formal composition and textural contrast, lending movement and dimensionality to the work. Grounded in Indigenous symbolism and motifs, the painting's abstract and masklike shapes morph into the surreal. This represents El-Salahi's transnational legacy as a pioneer of a visual language that repositioned African art in the global canon of modernism.

Untitled, 1962

DIRIYAH CONTEMPORARY ART BIENNALE 2024

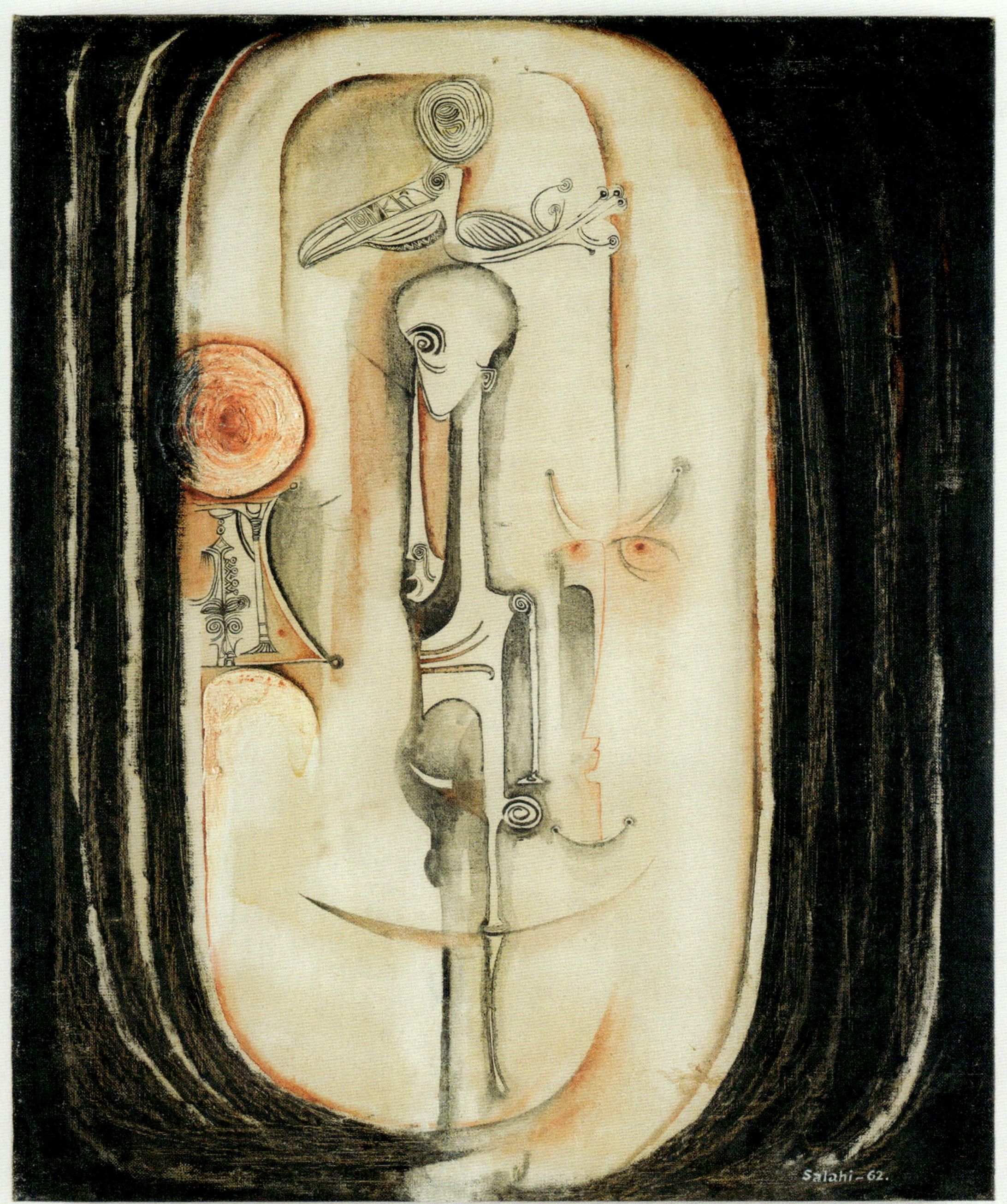
Salahi - 62.

HIND NASSER

Born 1940 in Amman, Jordan, where she lives and works

Selected works

1978–2021
(see p. 293 for details)

Hind Nasser is a Jordanian artist, a pioneering cultural activist, and a patron of the arts. She graduated from the Beirut College for Women (now the Lebanese American University, LAU) with a bachelor's degree in history and politics. Nasser led the establishment of several museum and cultural endeavors, including the Jordanian Association for Popular Arts and Crafts (1973 and 1996), the National Children's Society (1973), the National Music Conservatory (1983), and organization that would later become the Jordan Archaeological Museum. She began studying painting in 1976, when Fahrelnissa Zeid, the renowned Turkish artist active in the avant-garde scene of postwar Paris, settled in Amman and took her under her wing. Zeid launched Nasser's career in the art world. She went on to develop a body of work defined by a bold use of color and confident, gestural brushwork. Organic shapes and circling, spiraling lines give rise to canvases that can be read as both ominous and inviting.

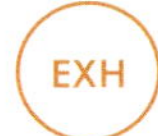

Whether figurative or abstract, her paintings are often an explosion of colors that compete with nature. She occasionally turns to whites and monochromes in her minimalist compositions. In her decades-long and evolving practice, Nasser's compositions of abstracted cultural motifs and impressionistic works on paper capture the natural terrains and varied cityscapes of Jordan. *Untitled* (1978) and the two works *Untitled* (2021), date from different points in the artist's career. *Untitled* (1978), an abstract landscape of rock formations, is one of her earliest paintings, from a period soon after she began her art training with Fahrelnissa Zeid at the age of twenty-five. The later works are abstract compositions that embody the artist's typical lively color palette. These are rendered in more self-assured and fluid lines, with occasional red streaks that create dramatic openings. *Petra I* and *Petra II* from 1987 exemplify the artist's sketches of rocky desert terrain. Nasser's works are a dialectic of interior and exterior landscapes, drawing inspiration from her surroundings: immense desert expanses, the mountains of Jordan, the wonders of Petra, seascapes, open skies, leafy trees, and flowers are rendered with a flow of abstracted lines and forms, which transform into the emotional landscapes of another realm beyond the visible world.

Untitled, 2021

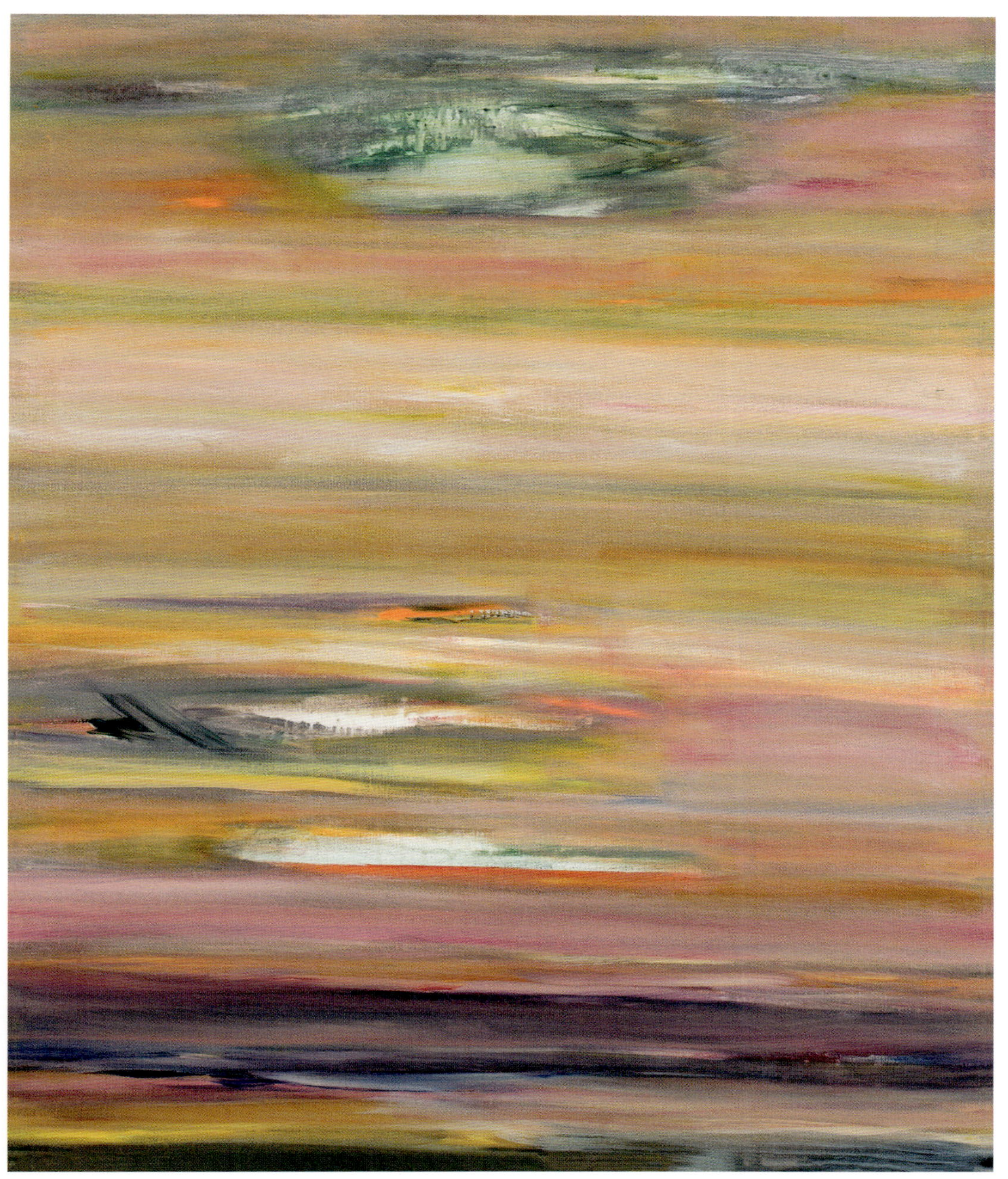

LALA RUKH

Born 1948 and died 2017 in Lahore, Pakistan

Selected works on paper

1983–2010
(see p. 294 for details)

Lala Rukh was one of the co-founders of the pioneering women's rights organization Women's Action Forum (WAF) as well as an abstractionist who worked with text-like symbols and graphite marks inspired by the notations of traditional Hindustani music and Islamic calligraphy. Trained in fine arts at the University of Punjab in Lahore and the University of Chicago, she often used her artistic practice to bring attention to social and human rights. During Pakistan's military dictatorship of the 1980s, when government-controlled printing offices in Lahore refused to print the WAF's protest materials, Rukh began designing and screen-printing the posters herself, calling for the equal rights and freedom of women. She later established printmaking workshops to aid women involved in similar movements across South Asia. A committed educator, Rukh taught for thirty years at the University of Punjab and the National College of Arts, where she also established an MA (Hons.) visual art program and helmed the school's art history department.

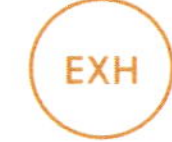

In contrast to her vivid, strident posters and activism, Rukh's artistic practice was grounded in Minimalist constraint. The five works on display, spanning the period between 1983 and 2010, are exemplary of the sparing precision that defined her language of mark-making. In *Untitled (2)* (1983–86) and *Untitled (6)* (1983–86), Conté crayon marks are reduced to fine, nominal curves of line on paper, studiously distilled yet gestural, dynamic, and bordering on the figurative, like a musical score. Her preoccupation with classical Hindustani music is evident throughout; the works presented collectively suggest both movement and the making of sound. In *Untitled* (2003) the repetitive lines reveal the evolution of her visual language. Far from popular ideas of Minimalism as stark, works such as *Untitled 1, 2* (2010), a diptych, and *Untitled* (2010) build on her early vocabulary of markings, while using a broader, more concentrated constellation of graphite lines and dots on carbon paper. The drawings suggest the specificities of the sky, sea, or horizon as well as a space of emergent possibility and interpretation. Rukh's work as a whole is framed by this commitment to the formal practice of drawing, ultimately forming an index of a lifetime spent looking, listening, and committing her own hieroglyphics to paper.

Untitled 1 (detail), 2011

DIRIYAH CONTEMPORARY ART BIENNALE 2024

HASSAN SHARIF

Born 1951 in Bandar-e Lengeh, Iran, died 2016 in Dubai,
United Arab Emirates

Selected works

1979–1984
(see p. 295 for details)

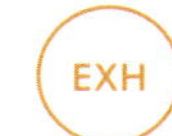

A central protagonist of Conceptual art in the United Arab Emirates, Hassan Sharif left a lasting impact in the Gulf and international art scenes with his explorations of performance that pushed the limits of artistic expression. In his work he explored repetition, landscape, and the body, reflecting on contemporary society through found objects and assemblage. After graduating from the Byam Shaw School of Art in London in 1984, Sharif returned to Dubai, where he worked as an educator, mentor, and facilitator, translating art books into Arabic and helping establish art spaces such as the Al Marijah Art Atelier (1984) in Sharjah and The Flying House (2007) in Dubai. A major retrospective of his work was curated by Catherine David in 2011 at Qasr Al Hosn, Abu Dhabi, and his work was presented in the United Arab Emirates pavilion at the Venice Biennale in 2009 and 2015.

While studying in London in the 1980s, Sharif became interested in the avant-garde Fluxus movement and developed his own methodologies: intervening in the public sphere and in nature as well as developing system-based approaches to making art. His works followed the Constructivist aesthetic, giving importance to order, geometry, and composition. In the 1980s Sharif produced a series of performances that centered around simple actions, which he documented with snapshot-like photographs mounted on paper and sometimes accompanied by instructions or notes.

Among the fourteen works on view is the documentation of *Throwing Stones* (1983), one of Sharif's most renowned works, in which he and a friend, fellow Emirati artist Mohammed Ahmed Ibrahim, tossed rocks into a desert landscape. Each time the rocks were thrown, a new configuration materialized and pointed to the ephemeral unpredictability of art-making. In *Performance is Good* (1984), Sharif sat on a bench in a hallway at his art school, and when a person walked past him, he recorded the activity within a system of rules he had outlined for himself. *Body and Squares* (1983) shows the artist laying on a grid drawn on the floor, calculating the multiple combinations of squares he can cover with his body. In these and other works, the artist uses his body as both subject and medium; the minimal, annotated records of the performances relay the artist's logic, calculations, and outcomes as an interplay of chance and order.

Body and Squares, 1983

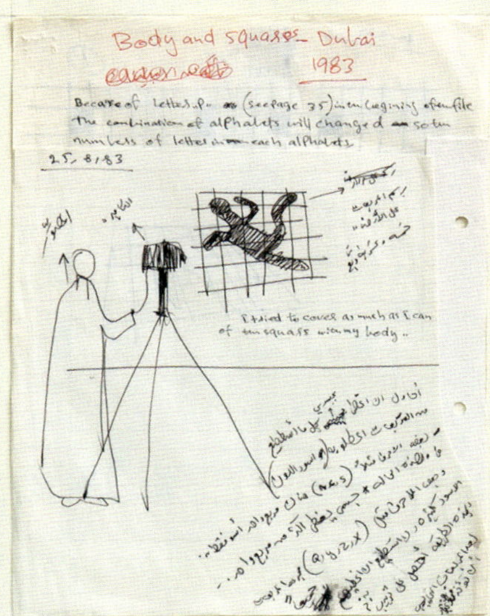

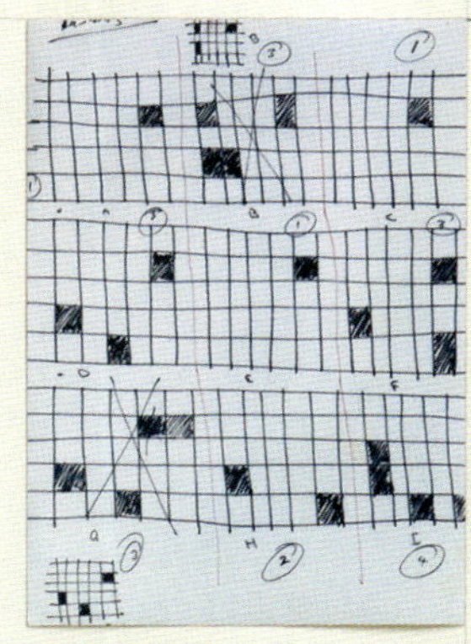

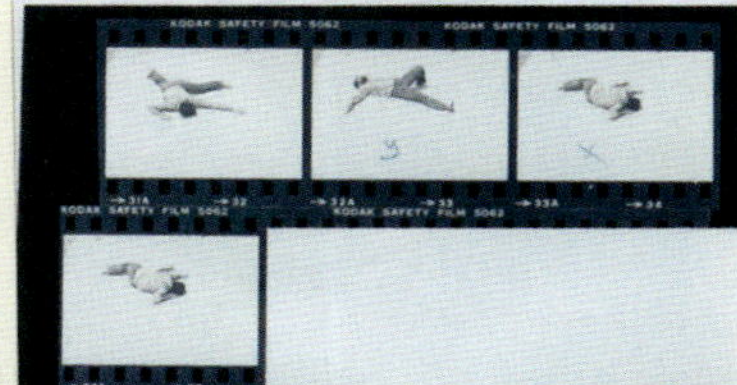

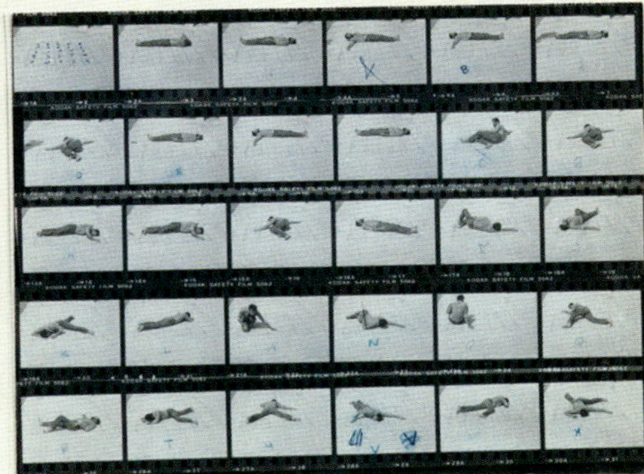

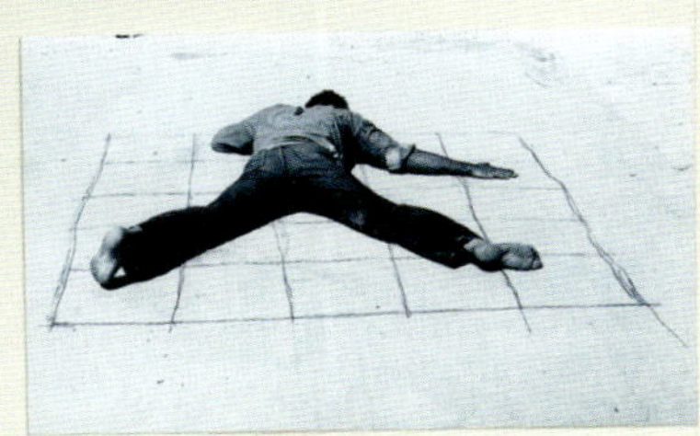

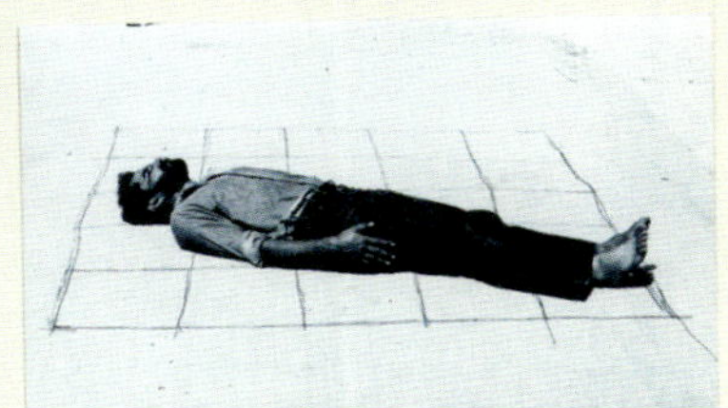

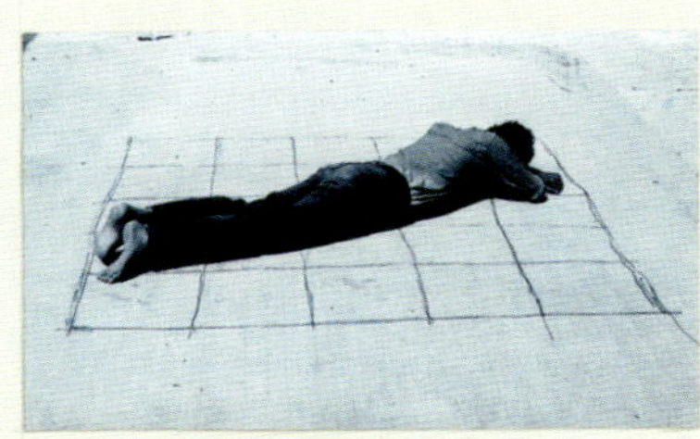

Body and Squares — 1983

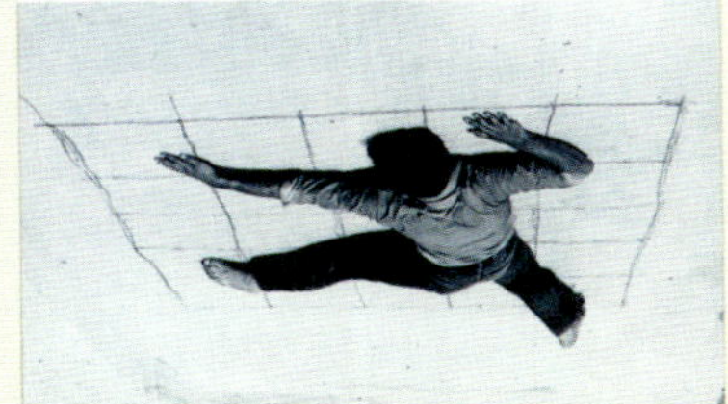

SAMIA ZARU

Born 1936 in Nablus, Palestine, lives and works in Amman, Jordan

Life Is a Woven Carpet
1995

Life Is a Woven Carpet
2001

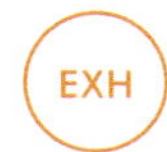

Samia Zaru's work encompasses a wide spectrum of media, from painting to sculpture, design, embroidery, and welding and casting. Her installations, public murals, and smaller-scale works probe questions of Arab identity, representation, and memory through abstract interpretations of traditional imagery and crafts. Across her much celebrated, decades-long practice, she has also employed materials such as wood, local dyes, ropes, and Palestinian embroidery work. Trained in fine arts at the American University in Beirut and then at the Corcoran School of Art and Design at the American University in Washington, DC, she was named Woman of the Year by the American Geographical Institute in 2000 and received the 2012 Takreem Award for Cultural Excellence. Zaru is also known for her role as an educator, having served as a UNESCO consultant on policies to enhance arts education and working tirelessly to revive traditional design in the Arab and Islamic world. Her educational activities have included lecturing and presenting television programs on the arts geared toward children, alongside her role as a professor of art at the University of Jordan.

Presented at the Biennale are two large-scale textile works with the same title: *Life Is a Woven Carpet* (1995) and *Life Is a Woven Carpet* (2001). Comprised of woven, netlike hangings of rope with various appended materials including fragments of textiles, pieces of clay used in the traditional buildings of Palestine, and glass fragments, the works reflect the artist's idea of life as a rich fabric of threads with knots, tangles, and empty spaces. The material accumulation of textures, atmospheres, colors, and lines becomes a metaphor for human experience and an expansion of knowledge. Reflective of Zaru's preoccupation with making works that break down social and religious boundaries, the openness of the woven netting and rope become a framework for free association—each viewer can choose an individual entry point for experiencing and surveying the work. In the words of the artist: "This, in my opinion, is the fourth dimension—interaction, and continuous wonder and engagement between one human production and another."

Life Is a Woven Carpet, 2001

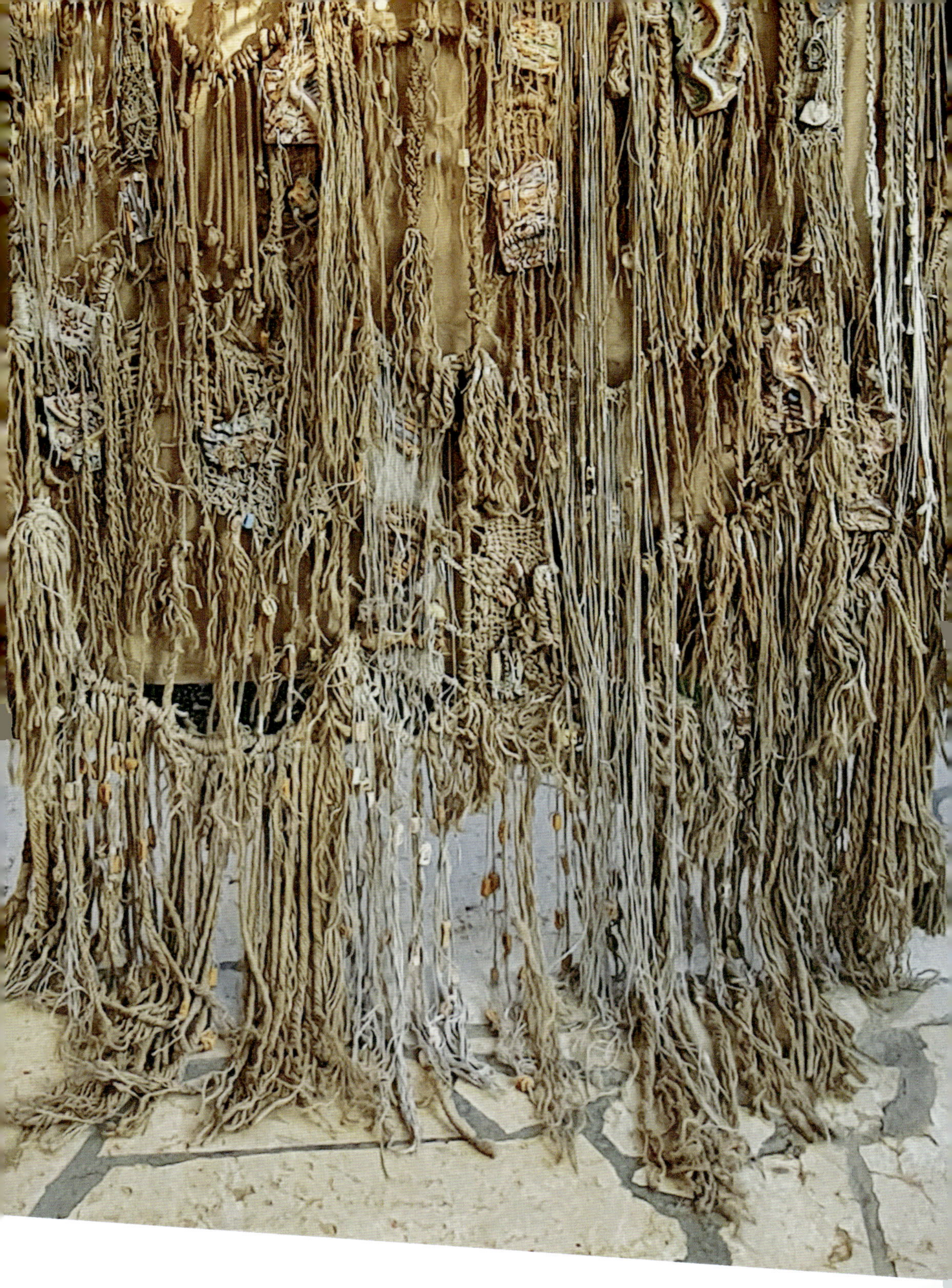

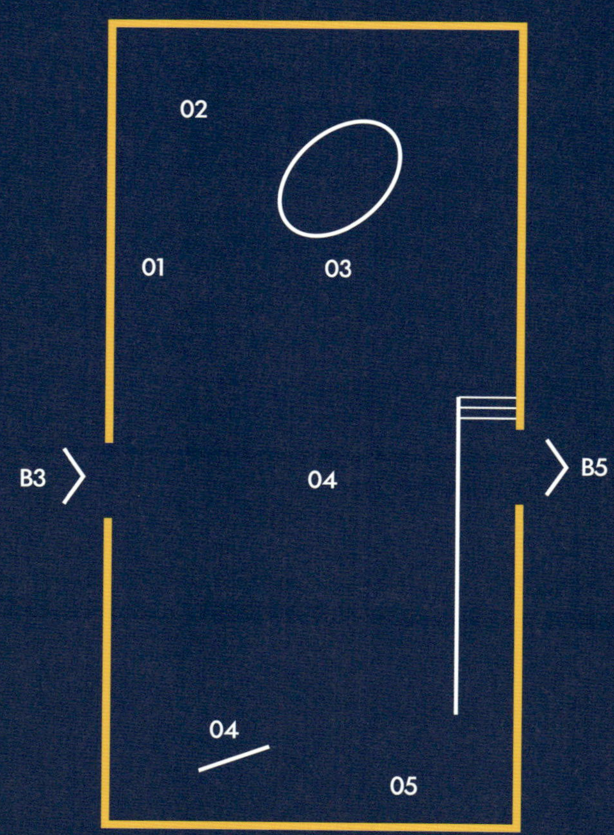

01   Hamra Abbas / p. 140
02   Dala Nasser / p. 144
03   Suzann Victor / p. 148
04   Alia Farid / p. 142
05   Anaïs Tondeur / p. 146

WATER AND HABITATS

This hall is dedicated to the existential necessity of water in its various forms as all life on this planet relies on this element to survive. Water is not only an irreplaceable resource; it also serves as a large storage of heat. This is very obvious in desert landscapes where water collects on the surface on a seasonal basis. After rain, the earthly scent of petrichor is generated when rain drops fall on dry soil. The selected works are a commemoration of water sources and springs, and are a call to protect our diverse ecosystems, whether marshlands, mountains, or other landscapes. These different art installations highlight the disparity in access to clean water, both in urban and rural contexts, while others point to its capacity to heal and revitalize.

HAMRA ABBAS

Born 1976 in Kuwait City, Kuwait, lives and works between Lahore, Pakistan, and Boston, MA, United States

Mountain 5

2023

Trained in the tradition of miniature painting at the National College of Arts in Lahore, Hamra Abbas explores historical techniques, while foregrounding questions of faith and devotion, and challenging Orientalist legacies. Having also lived in the United States and studied in Germany at the University of the Arts Berlin, she engages with a wide range of media, from the ancient Chinese painting style of *gongbi*, learned during a residency in Singapore in 2015, to paper cutting, video, sculptural installation, and, most recently, historical stone-inlay techniques. Abbas's work defies the perception of classical art forms as static in time and fixed to one culture. In her work different histories and worlds meet.

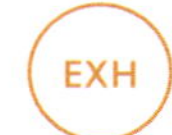

Mountain 5 (2023) is the largest work in a series of mosaic panels depicting the world's second highest peak, K2, which the artist started in 2022. Comprising ten panels that create the impression of a boundless, rocky landscape, this labor-intensive work combines two materials: the sturdiness of granite and the tonal variations of lapis lazuli. Based on Abbas's own drawing, *Mountain 5* was created by cutting and joining the lapis lazuli stone; this was followed by the inlay process, which required fixing the stone on a granite base and polishing it to reveal the final image.

This ancient Roman inlay technique of *pietra dura* (literally meaning "hard stone" in Italian) was revived during the sixteenth century in Florence. Some scholars have traced its way from there to South Asia, reaching a peak of development during the Mughal Empire. As art historian John Clark has argued, the dynamic of influences passing from Europe to Asia cannot be described as derivative. On the contrary, it has led to distinct art forms and modernisms. For example, *pietra dura*, called *parchin kari* in South Asia, evolved into a signature Mughal style defined by colorful, meticulous designs, idyllic landscapes, and garden motifs—exemplified in the seventeenth-century architecture of the Taj Mahal. Continuing the artist's investigation on representations of paradise and nature in Islam, *Mountain 5*, is a highly contemporary work, both in terms of its monumental scale and the expressive, almost painterly shadings of bright blues and grays used to create the mountain landscape—for the artist, a space of contemplation and harmony.

Hamra Abbas working on *Mountain 5*, Lahore, Pakistan, 2022

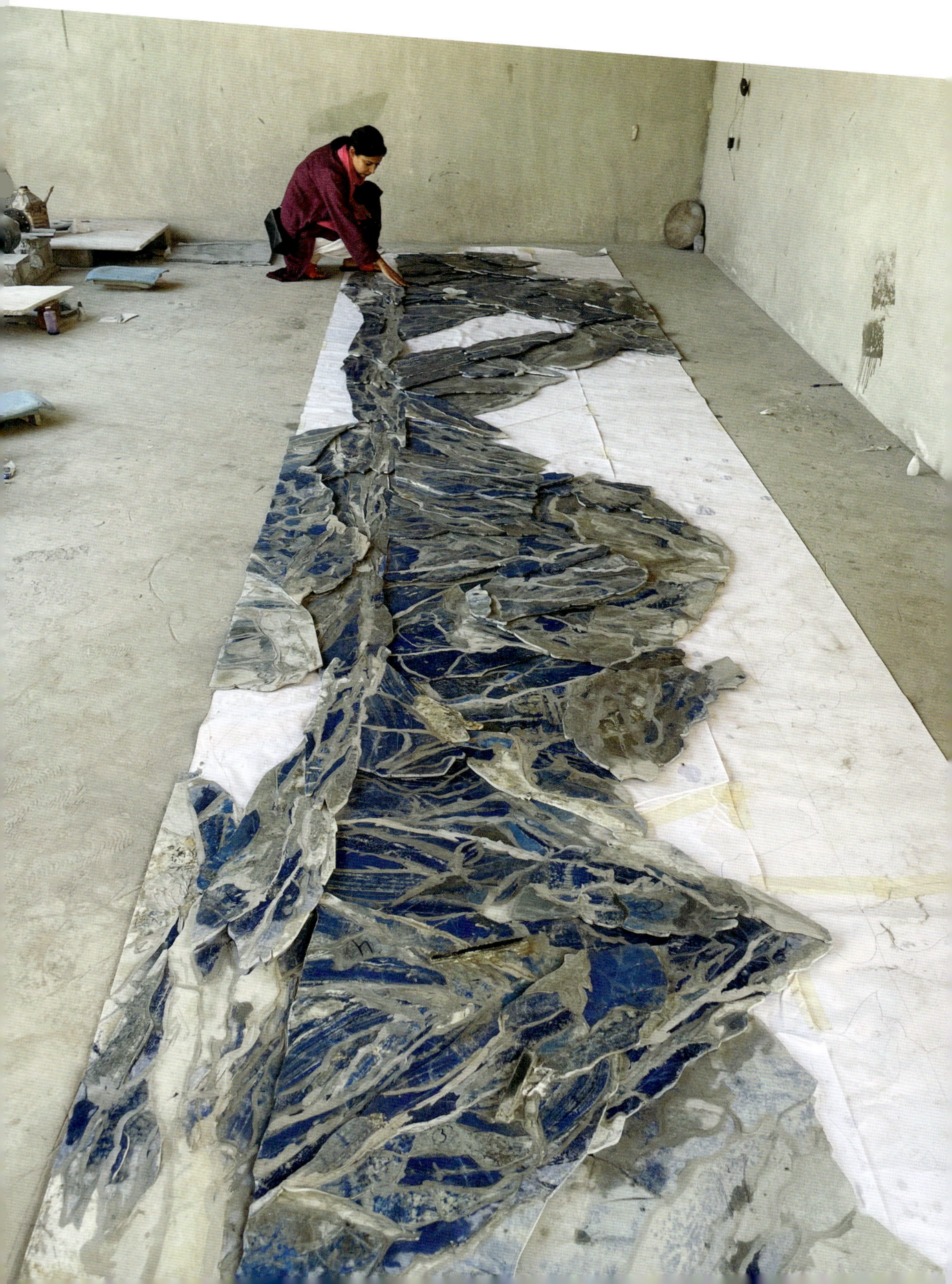

ALIA FARID

Born 1985 in Kuwait City, Kuwait, lives and works in Kuwait City
and San Juan, Puerto Rico

In Lieu of What Was
2019

Chibayish
2022

Chibayish
2023

Alia Farid works mostly in film and sculpture. Her work is an exploration of material entanglements and the information that can be gleaned from studying materials in relation to environmental and social histories of the Global South. She has a BFA in fine arts from the Escuela de Artes Plásticas de Puerto Rico, San Juan, a MS in visual studies from the Visual Arts Program in MIT, Cambridge, and a MA in museum studies and critical theory from the Programa d'Estudis Independents at MACBA, Barcelona. She received The Lise Wilhelmsen Art Award in 2023 and is currently the David and Roberta Logie Fellow at Harvard University's Radcliffe Institute.

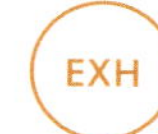

The presented works are part of a series that Farid has been developing on both sides of the Kuwait-Iraq border since 2019. *In Lieu of What Was* (2019) consists of five drinking fountain-sculptures in the shape of different vessel types used to store or carry water, including a traditional clay pot, a plastic water bottle, a vase-shaped *zamzamiya* (used for holy water from the Zamzam spring well in Makkah), an amphora-like *jarrah*, an emblematic Kuwaiti water tower, and a vernacular water-cooling system called a *heb*. Molded in lacquered fiberglass, the vessels mimic the shape and scale of public drinking fountains, called a *sabeel* in Arabic a distinctive feature of the urban landscape of Kuwait. Their reflective, glass-like surfaces radiate a fragility that invokes the complexities of freshwater resources in the country. Formerly transported on sailboats from the Shatt Al-Arab River in southern Iraq, fresh water today is largely a product of desalination plants.

Filmed at the confluence of the Tigris and Euphrates rivers in southern Iraq, *Chibayish* (2022) and *Chibayish* (2023) record the artist's interactions with three young marshland residents. The footage shows Riad Samir and the brothers Jassim and Qassim Mohammed caring for a water buffalo, describing their geography, naming members of their community, and traversing a marsh engulfed by oil infrastructure and industrial waste. Like much of Farid's work, the film echoes issues of cultural identity, history, colonialism, and the right to remain.

Above: Installation view of *In Lieu of What Is* at Portikus, Frankfurt am Main, Germany, 2022
Below: Video still from *Chibayish*, 2022

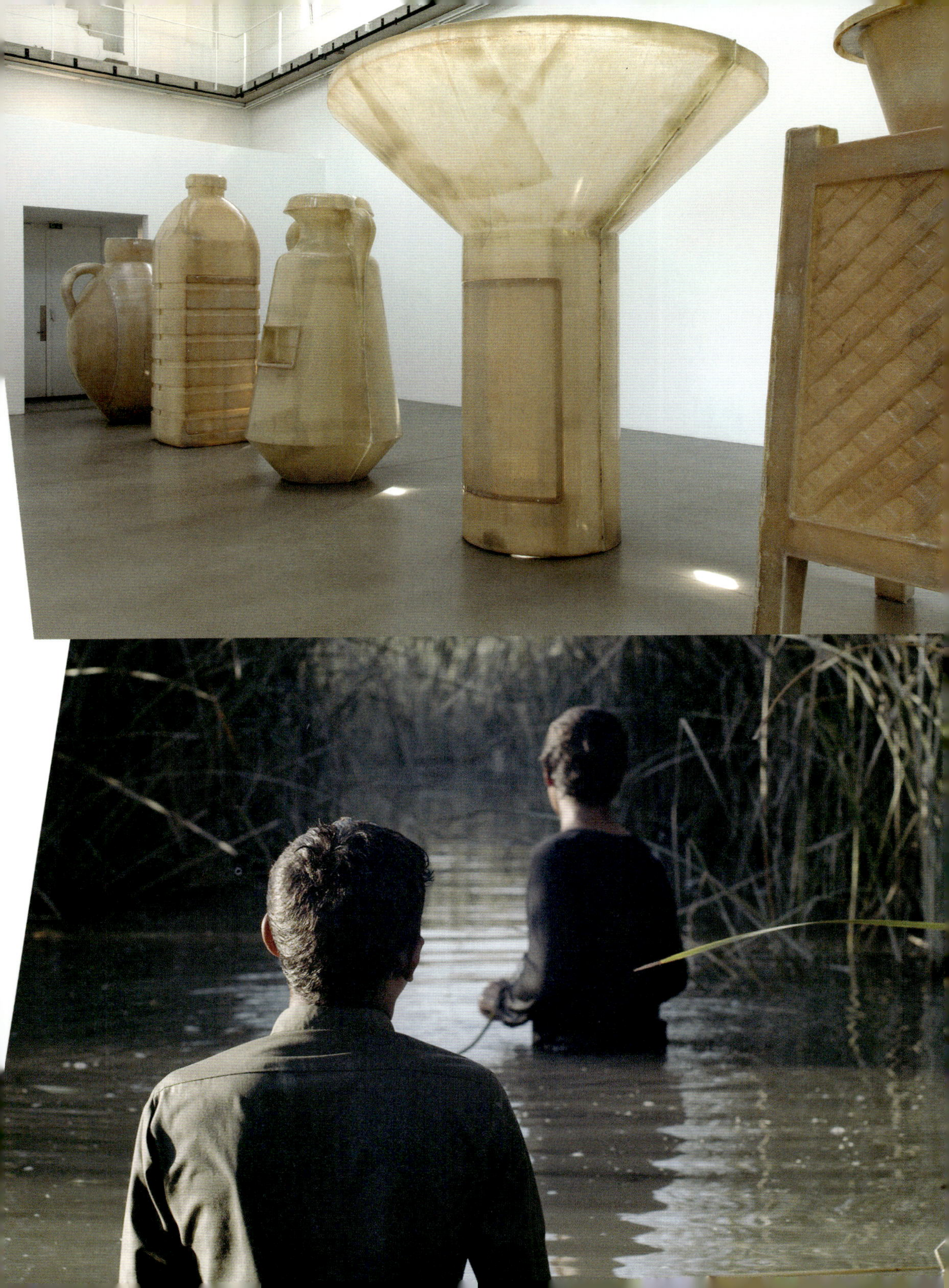

DALA NASSER

Born 1990 in Tyre, Lebanon, lives and works in Beirut, Lebanon

Mineral Lick

2019

Dala Nasser works with sound, performance, film, and painting to create immersive installations that emphasize material transformation over time and bear witness to places impacted by conflict and climate change. Trained as a painter at the Slade School of Fine Arts in London and the Yale School of Art in New Haven, she was awarded the 2017 Emerging Artist Prize at the Sursock Museum's 32nd Salon d'Automne in Beirut. While her work is multidisciplinary, Nasser draws on her practice as a painter and her family's heritage as farmland owners to respond to histories embedded in specific locations. Shown as fragments, as draped tarps, stretched on wood to form makeshift structures, or sometimes accompanied by sound, her canvases are the result of intensive processes of making and unmaking. Repeated actions of marking, soaking, burying, rubbing, and dyeing with plants from her own garden make her works indexes of place, alternate and abstracted views of the landscapes that themselves evolve with time. The weathering and deterioration of her working materials become the visual markers of systemic failure and environmental degeneration.

In *Mineral Lick* (2019) Nasser probes Lebanon's unique regional position as a water-rich nation to examine water distribution and toxicity in her hometown of Beirut. Using tap water from all sixty sectors of Beirut, which is known for its heavy rains that flow down the mountains and seep into an aging underground pipe infrastructure, Nasser creates her own abstracted hydromap of the city. The artist mixes equal parts dye and rock salt to each gallon of water before submerging fabric into each sample. The fabric autonomously grows its own salts in response to the varying acidity levels of each neighborhood's water supply. The installation suggests the poisonous impact of inaction and ineffectiveness in a shifting context where language and political legitimacy have lost value. During its first showing at an exhibition at Ashkal Alwan, The Lebanese Association for Plastic Arts in Beirut in 2019, *Mineral Lick* was displayed for a single evening before the street protests of the October 17 Revolution—in response to a series of cabinet-issued tax reforms—brought the country to a standstill.

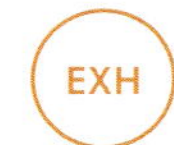

EXH

Installation view of *Mineral Lick*, from the exhibition *Homeworks 8* at Beirut Art Center, Lebanon, 2019

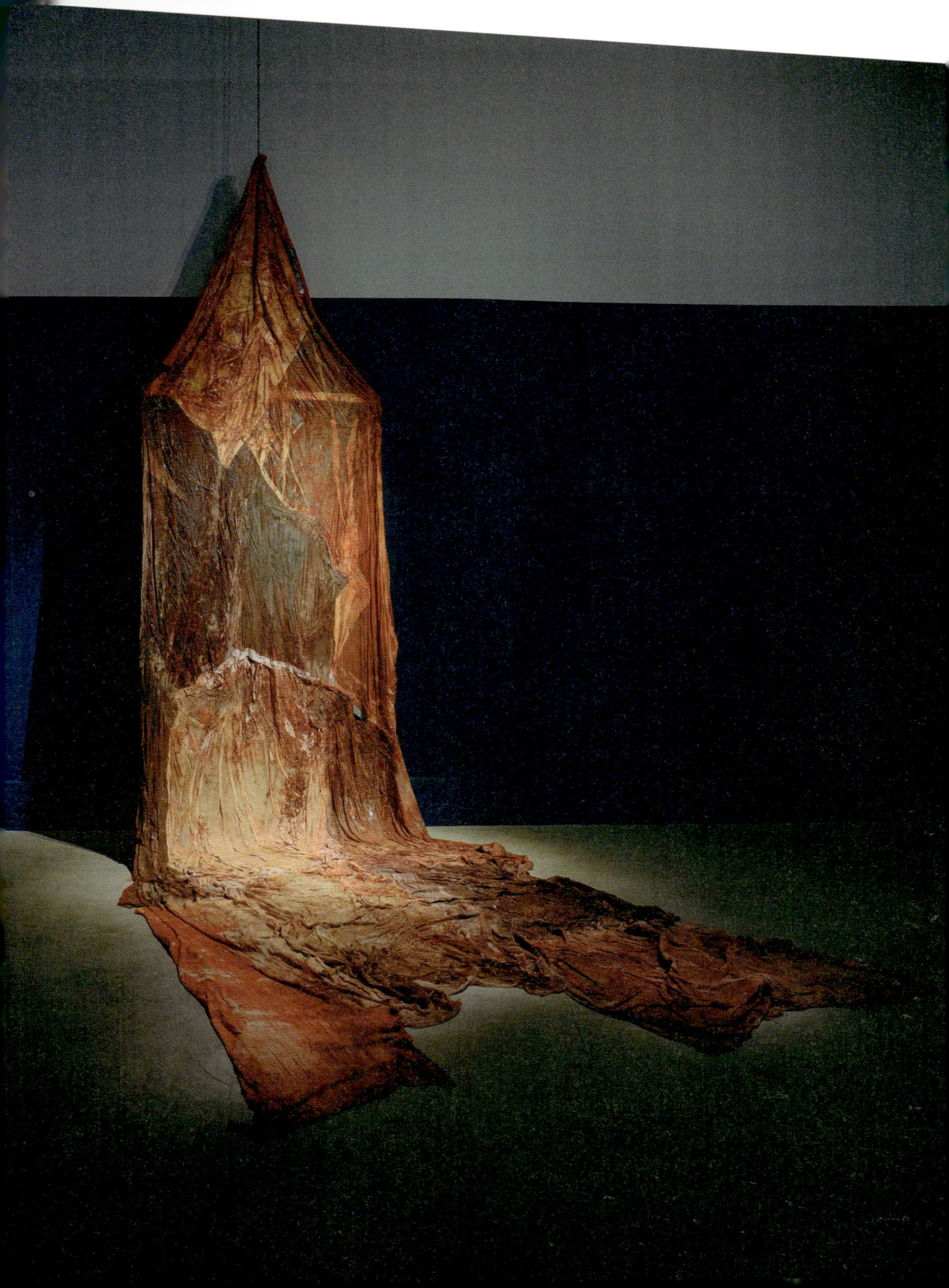

ANAÏS TONDEUR

Born 1985 in Paris, France, where she lives and works

Urban Petrichor
2015–ongoing

Fragments of Soil
2024
Re/Search

Anaïs Tondeur is an artist who uses image-based and olfactive investigations as anthropological tools. Her installations interweave fieldwork and fiction to consider the urban condition and its relationship to ecology. Having studied at Central Saint Martins and the Royal College of Art in London, she was awarded the Prix Photographie & Sciences (2023) and Prix Art of Change 21 (2021). She has also completed multiple residencies, including at the Musée des Arts et Métiers and the Muséum national d'Histoire naturelle in Paris. Exploring ways to reintegrate human life into the natural cycles of the earth, she creates protocols of attention focusing on soil, plants, and the atmosphere. Tondeur's research-based practice is driven by an interdisciplinarity approach, which have taken her on expeditions to places such as the boundaries of tectonic plates, the Chernobyl exclusion zone, and the infrastructure of tunnels beneath the city of Paris.

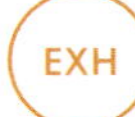

Urban Petrichor (2015–ongoing) stems from an investigation into the traces of petrichor, the smell of soil after rain. In her collaboration with anthropologist Germain Meulemans, the artist invited over one hundred inhabitants to turn their attention to the organic processes thriving in the cracks of city pavement. During collective walks through Paris and its immediate surroundings, they collected urban soils, which were then distilled using the traditional process of hydrodistillation. In the display, the soil distillates are shown in suspended Florence flasks. Their contents are continually transforming in a visible alchemy, while casting shifting shadows and reflecting light.

In this process they reenact a protocol of a nineteenth-century Parisian chemist who studied mud through scent, devoting years of research to the oxidized earth under and between the city's cobblestones. Creating the first olfactory palette of Paris soils, Tondeur and Meulemans are not searching to convey petrichor as a substance but as a process arising from a complex set of reactions between atmosphere, soil, and microorganisms in the earth. The metamorphic quality of the work urges reflection on how the ground and the sky, two entities that modern thinking about the city has tended to separate, may once again be brought into correspondence.

Above: View of working process, collecting soil, Montreuil, France, 2019
Below: Petrichor, soil distillates, 2017

DIRIYAH CONTEMPORARY ART BIENNALE 2024

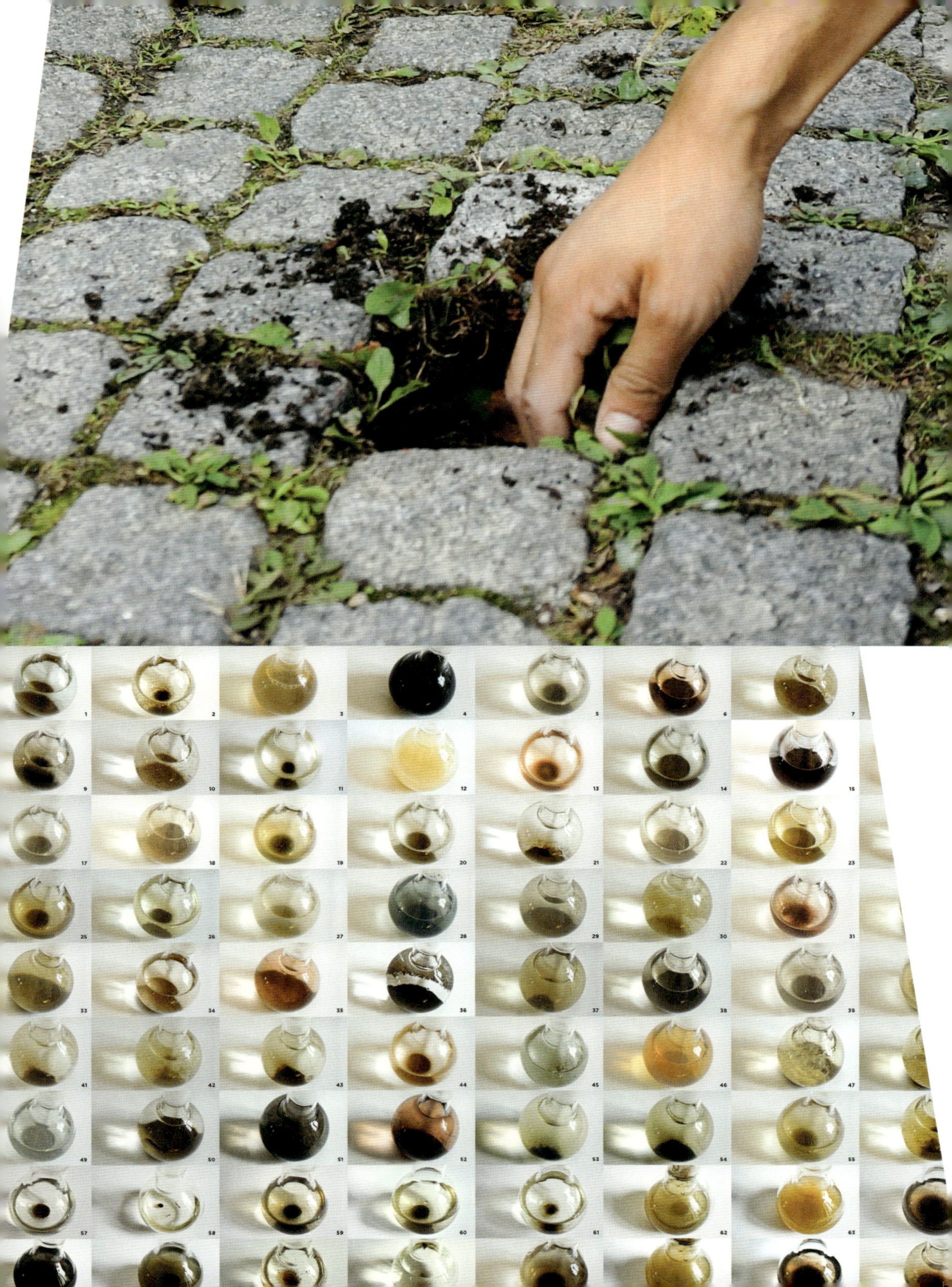

SUZANN VICTOR

Born 1959 in Singapore, lives and works in Blue Mountains, Australia

Strike
2021

For over three decades, artist Suzann Victor has probed the physical, sensorial, and political properties of space. Employing a diversity of materials, from the bodily and organic to metal and glass, Victor's artistic practice is defined by an ability to validate the fragility of being and reinforce the power of creativity. Trained at LASALLE College of the Arts in the late 1980s, Victor was the initiator of 5th Passage, an independent art space established in 1991 that played an integral role in artistic experimentation in Singapore in the 1990s, preceding major state-funded institutional developments. Victor received her PhD at the University of Western Sydney in 2009. She was the first woman to represent Singapore at the 49th Venice Biennale (2001).

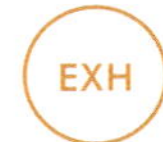

Strike (2021) is an interactive installation that stages a performance of sound and drawing in space through simple means. As with other kinetic installations by Victor inspired by physics, *Strike* operates as a lever device, trading force against movement. The work turns water-filled glass objects into musical instruments inviting the audience to participate in an ephemeral act of creation. With a simple tug, visitors can activate the sets of strikers—acrylic spheres situated at the end of long cables with counterweights. Swinging back and forth, the strikers hit against the glass releasing a sequence of sounds into the space, which have different tonalities and pitches conditioned by the water level in each vessel.

Throughout her artistic practice, Victor has stressed the potential of liminal spaces—a passageway, a drain, gaps between tiles—to accommodate the things for which society often leaves little space: creativity and difference. In *Strike*, the artist thoughtfully choreographs the gaps between each glass vessel so that the negative space carries sonic potential. Every activation creates a unique performance of sound that situates the act of creation at the intersection of many constraints and factors, including chance. In the 1990s, Victor advanced the notion of disembodied art in her installations that made use of kinetic elements to bypass what the state perceived as the "subversive" agency of the body and acts of performance art. For an artist who has persistently affirmed the virtues of creative expression, *Strike* not only reinstates agency but overtly transfers it to the audience.

Detail of the installation *Strike*, from the exhibition *Of Waters* at Galleries Curate: RHE, STPI Gallery, Singapore, 2021

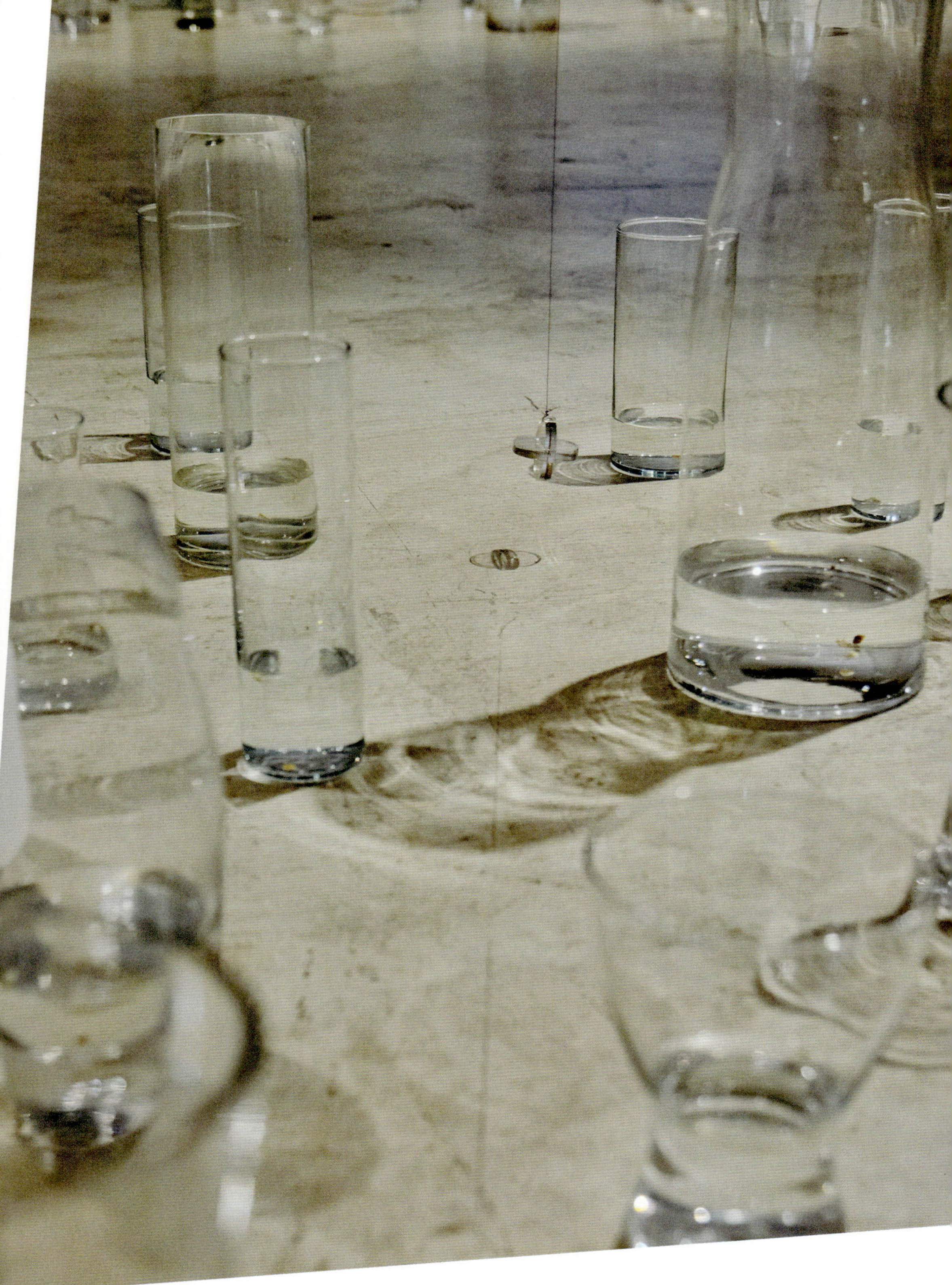

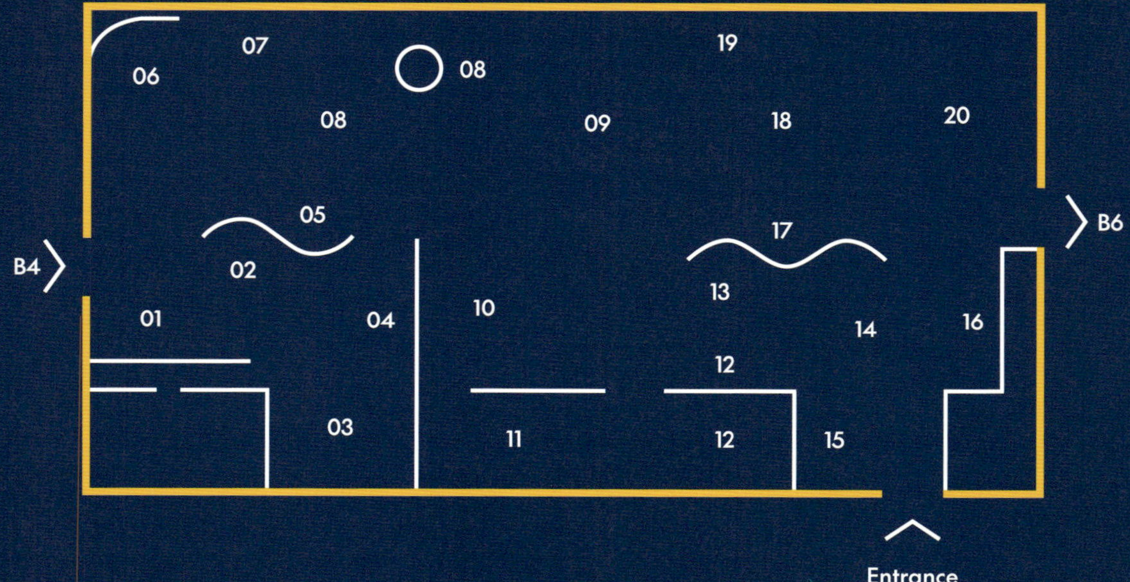
07
06
08
19
08
09
18
20
05
02
17
B4
B6
13
01
04
10
03
14
16
12
11
12
15
Entrance

KNOWLEDGE IN MATERIAL AND SPIRITUAL INTELLIGENCE

This hall is dedicated to the celebration of natural materials. Juniper, rattan, rubber, mulberry, camphor, lacquer, and organically dyed textiles are central to the creation of the works on view. Through a wide range of artistic expressions, artists bring the complex and often violent histories and circulation routes of natural resources to the fore. They trace the intelligence embedded in the natural world and the cultural significance of flora and fauna, underlining their ecological, economic, and spiritual relevance. As a whole, this hall serves as a reminder of the preciousness of traditional knowledge and craft, revealing the deep layers that make up cultural heritage and the way each layer serves as a witness of its time. Art has the capacity to make often painful circumstances tangible, it can touch upon our emotions and provide space to collectively develop empathy.

SARA ABDU

Born 1993 in Jeddah, Saudi Arabia, where she lives and works

Now That I've Lost You in My Dreams, Where Do We Meet?
2021/2024

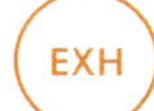

Sara Abdu's practice is grounded in an exploration of the subconscious, the self, memory, and mortality. Taking the form of installations, drawings, and videos, dreams have often inspired ideas that gave rise to work examining the experience of the infinite. Her practice has covered shifting topographies, probing the interplay between form and language, between our inner and outer worlds, the conscious and the unconscious, the material and the immaterial. She is known for creating meditative spaces of contemplation where language is translated into visual and sonic forms of her own. Born to Yemeni parents, she studied graphic design and digital art at the Future Institute of Higher Education Training in Jeddah, and English language and literature at the Arab Open University. In 2017 she was an artist in residence at Cité internationale des arts in Paris.

The installation *Now That I've Lost You in My Dreams, Where Do We Meet?* (2021/2024) is inspired by dreams of people from Abdu's life who are no longer present. An expression of her longing for moments of reunion, the installation became a place to examine these dreams as a space of reconciliation and acceptance; a space where new memories and encounters could be generated. Consisting of handmade soap bars stacked into a wall-like structure inspired by the traditional soap factories of the Levant, each brick-shaped bar is inscribed with one word from the work's title. Made from natural ingredients including sidr powder and camphor crystals, the materiality of the work is the artist's ode to the Islamic rituals of washing the body of the deceased before burial. Forming an architecture of the title's repeating phrase, the stacked blocks create a tower that visitors can walk around and absorb the permeating scent of the soap. By circulating the exhibition space, inhaling and re-inhaling, viewers absorb this scent associated with departure. For Abdu, memory, evoked by smell, is closely associated with healing. Open-ended and full of longing, the words of the title are repeated in an almost meditative pattern. Posing this unanswerable question—again and again—becomes a confrontation with finality and a simultaneous attempt to prolong the fleeting moment of farewell.

Now That I've Lost You In My Dreams, Where Do We Meet?, 2021
Above: Soap bars / Below: Installation view at Athr Gallery, Jeddah, Saudi Arabia, 2021

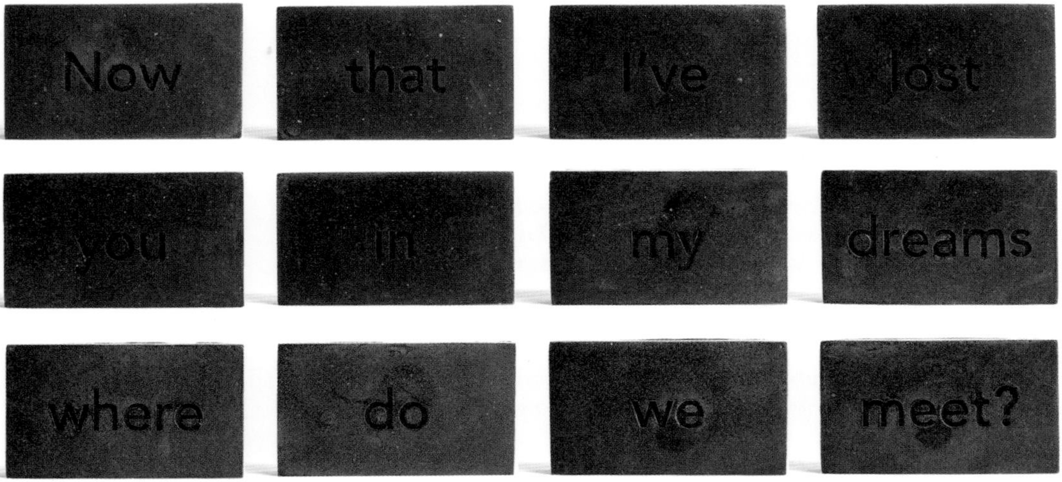

Now that I've lost
you in my dreams
where do we meet?

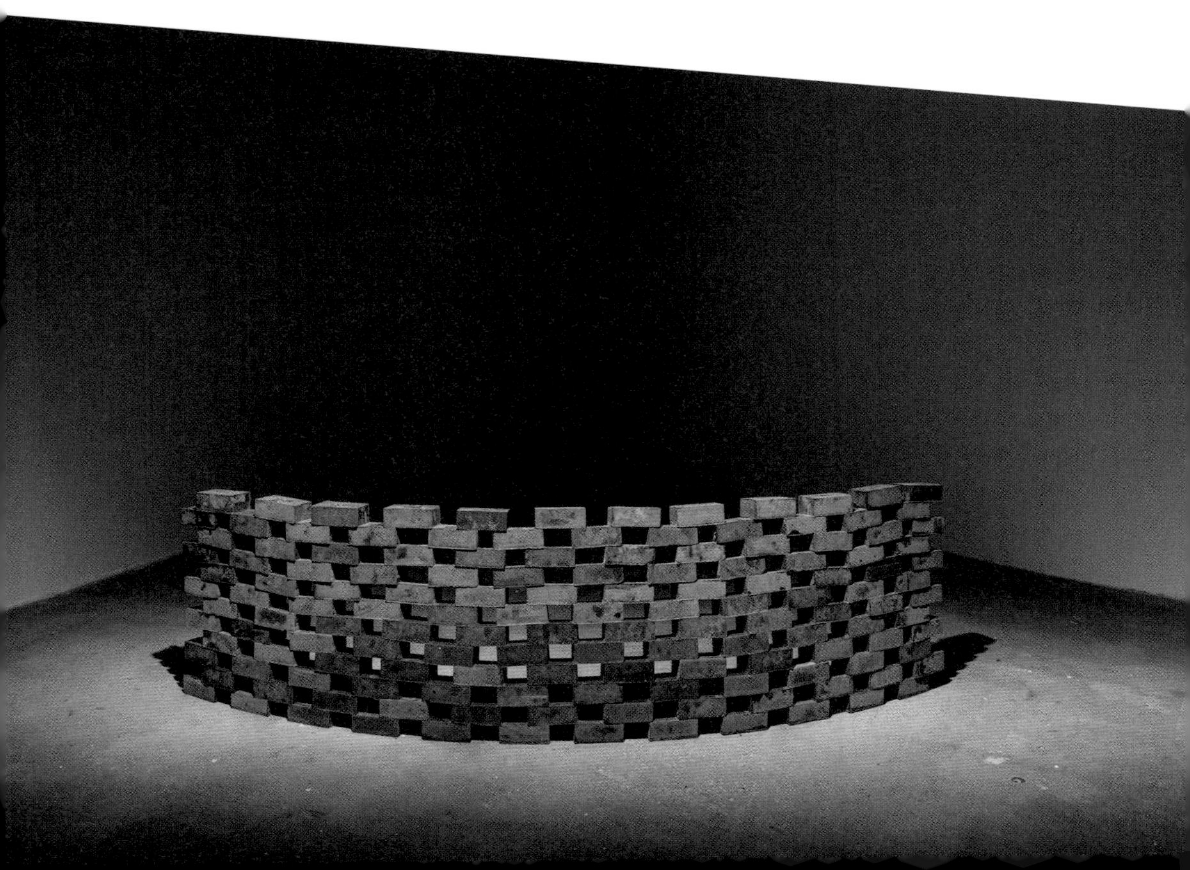

REEM AL NASSER

Born 1987 in Jizan, Saudi Arabia, where she lives and works

Blue Windows

2022

Reem Al Nasser's multimedia practice is steeped in the rituals and traditions of her native Jizan, a port city near Saudi Arabia's southern border to Yemen. Upon completing her degree in economics at Jazan University in 2011, she began exploring and documenting the long-standing customs of communities around her, gathering oral histories from elders. Al Nasser is not only interested in preserving the rich cultural history of her region, but also in unpacking and questioning social behaviors that define collective and individual identity.

Blue Windows (2022) is made up of charred and discarded branches of juniper—a tree known as *arar* in Arabic—from the woodlands of the mountainous Aseer Province. Stacked on shelves inside two large structures resembling metal grates, the wood bears witness to the fires that blazed through the region's Al Jarrah Park in 2021. Due to strong winds and steep slopes, the fires were hard to contain and ravaged large forests of mature juniper trees that were over one hundred years old. When the fires were finally put out, the artist traveled to Abha, the capital of Aseer, to witness the damage and pay her respects to the *arar* trees. She vividly remembers the sadness and emotional turmoil the forest fire wrought on the surrounding community.

The large installation pays tribute to one of Abha's most precious resources, used to produce juniper tar oil and furniture. As the title suggests, the flourishes and color of the metal containers recall the traditional windows of Abha, which are typically painted blue to denote the sky and heavens and to invite God's blessings into one's home. The multi-layered form of these containers mirrors the region's terraced mountains, a commemoration of ancient agricultural practices; they also recall the horizontal lines of stones typically found on building façades in Abha, which facilitate rainwater runoff. *Blue Windows* not only captures a dramatic moment of destruction but also tells a story of loss, mourning, and hope—within a changing ecology.

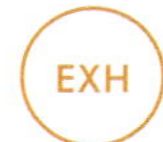

Above: Reem Al Nasser working on *Blue Windows*, Al Muftaha Village, Abha, Saudi Arabia, 2022
Below: Installation view of *Blue Windows* at JAX District, Riyadh, Saudi Arabia, 2022

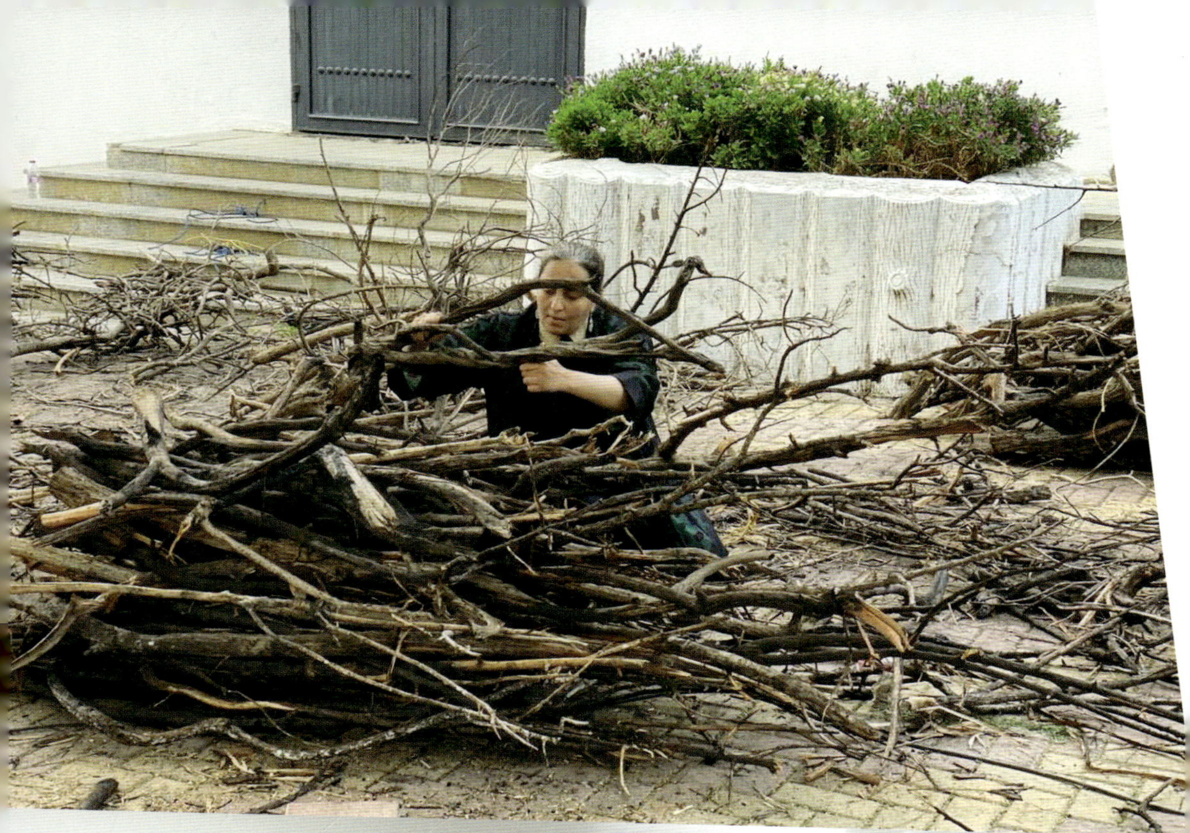

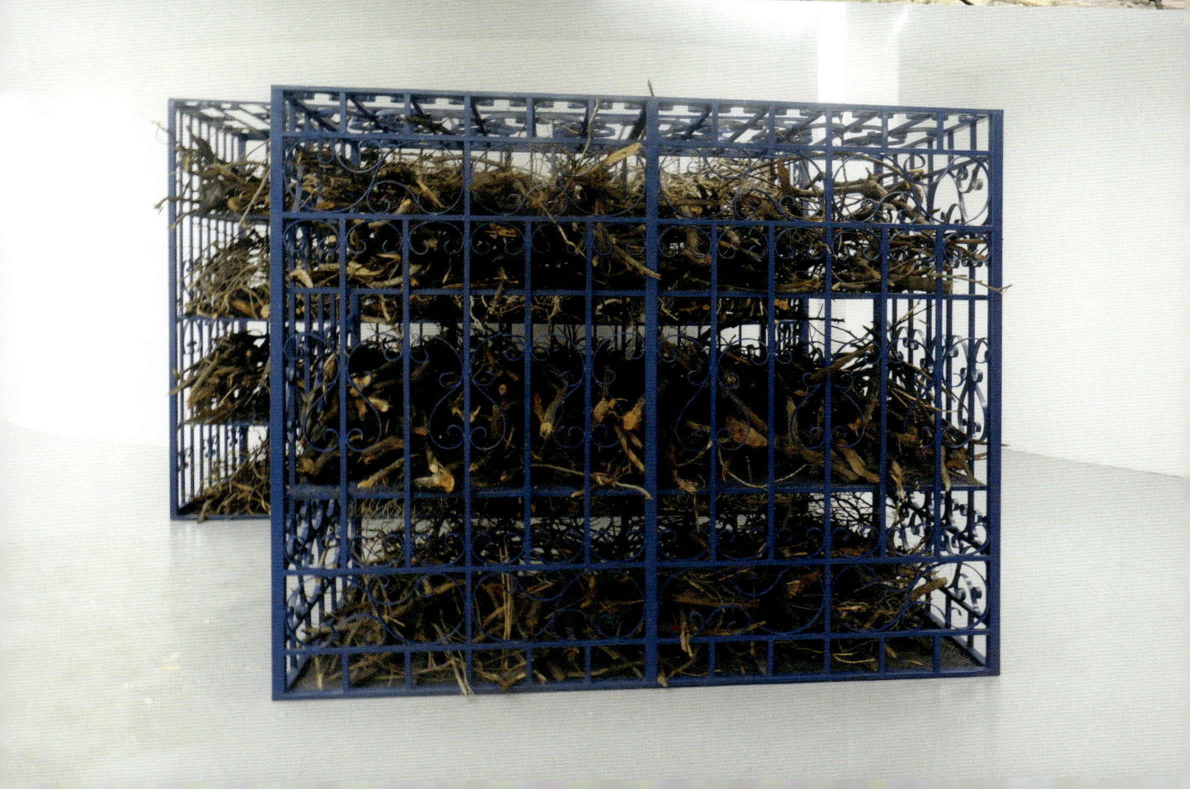

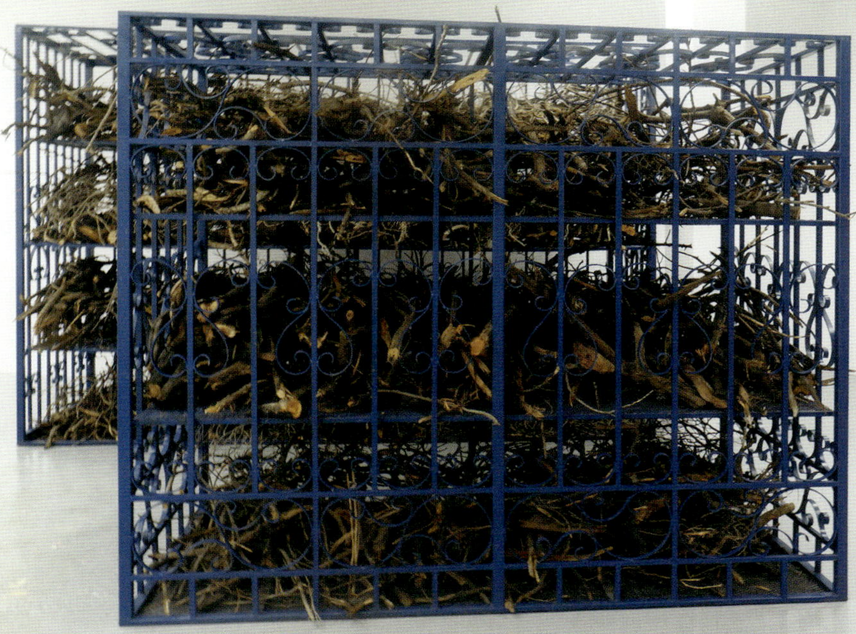

EL ANATSUI

Born 1944 in Anyako, Ghana, lives and works in Nsukka, Nigeria,
and Tema, Ghana

Logoligi Logarithm
2019

El Anatsui works with found objects and everyday materials to create imposing installations that interrogate colonial imports, consumption, and waste. Trained in art at the Kwame Nkrumah University of Science & Technology in Ghana, he rose to acclaim with his large-scale works made of bottle tops. He received the Golden Lion award for Lifetime Achievement at the 56th Venice Biennale (2015). While his work repurposes discarded resources such as bottle caps and cassava graters, it is his meticulous transformation of these scraps into precisely composed, tapestry-like sculptures that underscore the formal brilliance of his visual language. Anatsui spent four decades teaching sculpture at the Fine and Applied Art department at the University of Nigeria, Nsukka. He is a member of the Nsukka Group artist collective, which incorporates and adapts the traditional, abstracted designs of the Igbo people into contemporary practices.

The artist's installation *Logoligi Logarithm* (2019) borrows its title from a poem by the Ghanaian poet, and late friend of the artist, Atukwei Okai, who used the word *logoligi*—meaning "snakelike" or "indirect" in the Niger-Congo language of Ga—to suggest the bureaucratic obstacles that convolute a political system, making it an impenetrable mathematical equation. Anatsui's evocatively labyrinth-like structure comprises veils of intricately stitched patterns of bottle-cap seals draped on aluminum tubes to form pathways at once translucent and opaque. The "walls" do not define the space so much as serve as liminal demarcations of shifting spatial possibilities, pushing the boundaries of what Anatsui calls the "unfixed form."

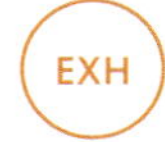

Installation view of *Logoligi Logarithm* at Haus der Kunst, Munich, Germany, 2019

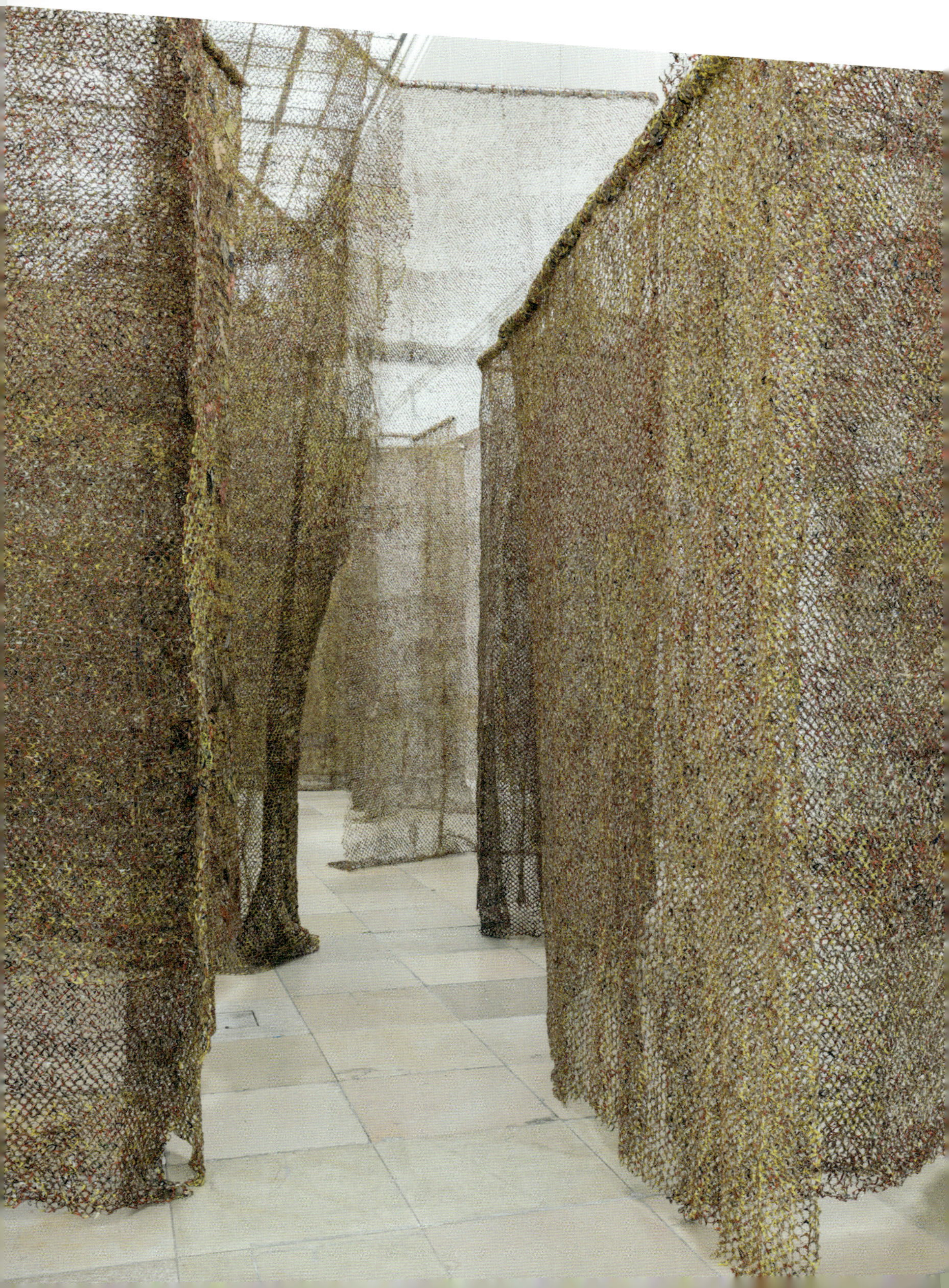

NAZGOL ANSARINIA

Born 1979 in Teheran, Iran, where she lives and works

Membrane (parts)

2014 / Selected works from the series
(see p. 283 for details)

Pillars

2014–18 / Selected works from the series
(see p. 283 for details)

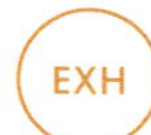

Born and raised in Tehran, Nazgol Ansarinia adopts a deconstructive approach, first developed during her graduate studies at the California College of the Arts in the early 2000s, to investigate the systems and networks that structure the urban everyday there, paying particular attention to architecture and language as expressions of power. Ansarinia's interest stems from the breakneck pace of expansion and gentrification in the city over the past few decades, a process that has left it in a disorienting state of eternal flux.

These cycles of demolition and construction often reveal, for a brief period, a fragment of an interior wall, providing access to a private sphere that is otherwise carefully guarded. Ansarinia's *Membrane (parts)* (2014) are sections of a one-to-one replica of one such wall molded using fragile white papier-mâché. On them we can make out traces of the architecture of everyday life: outlines of walls, floors and a stairway connecting two floors; the familiar staggered arrangement of cement blocks; neat, tiled grids; small depressions corresponding to electrical sockets and switches. Monumentalizing a momentary ruin, *Membrane* indexes and preserves the lives and memories of those who once inhabited these domestic spaces. These ghostly fragments evoke both skin and shroud, the surface of the city's ever-changing body, and an attempt to arrest that unrelenting process of transformation and to mourn what is lost as a result.

Ansarinia's *Pillars* (2014–18) is a series of cast resin sculptures that resemble capitals, sometimes attached to pillars. Each is based on an article from the Iranian Constitution, its mass the result of rotating the text around a central axis, its undulating exterior determined by the contours of Farsi script. Ansarinia intentionally leaves a gap in the resulting forms so that the text remains visible and legible. While her title acknowledges the foundational role that such statutes—which govern economic matters—play in society, Ansarinia transforms these texts into a type of Neoclassical architectural ornament that features prominently in the garish new construction that has overrun Tehran in recent years.

Above: Research photo for *Membrane*, Tehran, Iran, 2014
Below: *Article 49, Pillars*, 2014

DIRIYAH CONTEMPORARY ART BIENNALE 2024

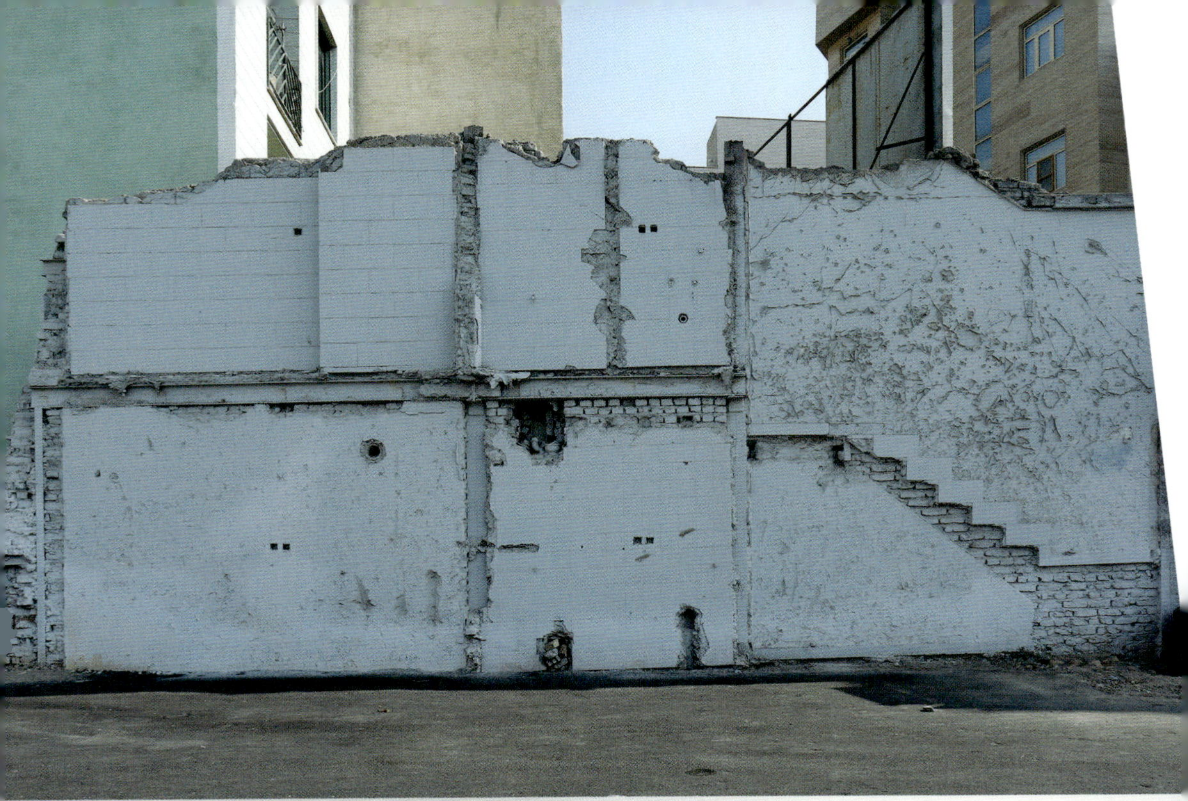

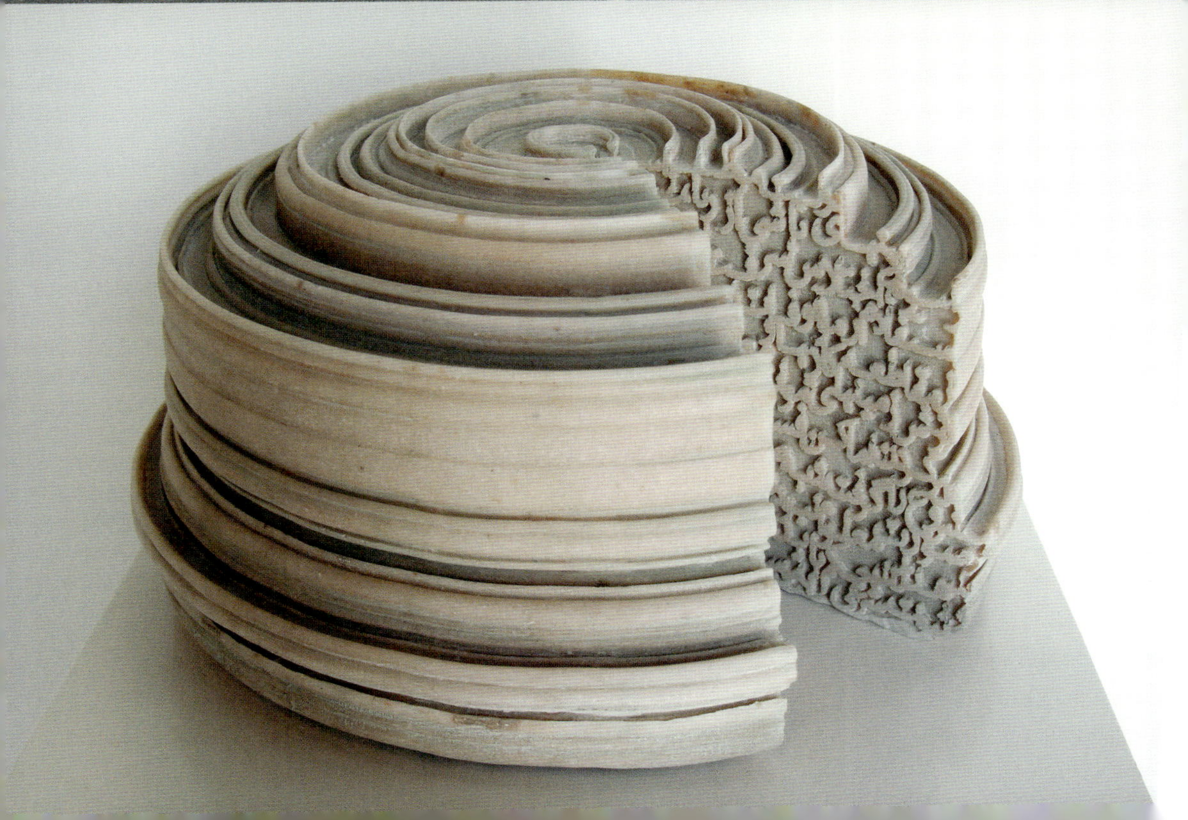

DANA AWARTANI

Born 1987 in Jeddah, Saudi Arabia, where she lives and works

Come, Let Me Heal Your Wounds
2020

Listen to my words
2020 / Video, 12 min 57 sec
Film Program

Dana Awartani is a Saudi-Palestinian artist who draws on the heritage of Islamic art and languages of abstraction to create works of philosophical depth. From drawings of sacred geometric patterns to textile works and multimedia installations, her works are expressions of reverence for the history of Arab culture, process, and craft. She often collaborates with artisans to carry forward traditional art forms, underscoring the importance of continuity with the past, while bringing these practices into contemporary discourse. Studying in London, she received a BFA (2009) from Central Saint Martins and an MA (2011) from The Prince's Foundation School of Traditional Arts. She is currently pursuing an *Ijazah* certificate in Islamic illumination.

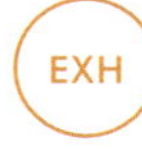

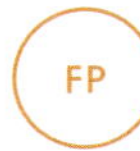

Come, Let Me Heal Your Wounds (2020) derives from research into Ayurvedic dyeing used to create clothing with healing properties. Awartani worked with dyeing workshops in Kerala to color pieces of silk in earthy hues—ochres, reds, and greens. The fabric was spanned on wooden frames and mounted on the wall as overlapping, semitransparent panels. The artist identified 355 sites of cultural loss caused by conflicts and acts of destruction since 2010, locating places where architectural heritage has been annihilated in Syria, Tunisia, Libya, Iraq, Egypt, and Yemen. Marking each location with a tear or hole, she created her own intuitive map on ten pieces of silk. Working together with local craftspeople, Awartani then repaired the pieces of fabric, darning each hole by hand. With its lightness and ephemeral quality, Awartani's work hints at the fragility of existing sites, while serving as a plea to safeguard ancient monuments and maintain our threads to the past.

In her animated film *Listen to my words* (2020), the gray screen gradually fills with a delicate geometric pattern. The artist draws from the ornamental motifs of *jali* and *mashrabiya*, latticed screens used in Islamic architecture to regulate light, airflow, and heat. *Jali* have also traditionally shielded women from the male gaze, confining them to the home. Awartani was inspired by Nur Jahan (1577–1645), the wife of a Mughal emperor and a woman who played a leading role in government from behind a *jali* screen. Accompanying the drawings, voices of modern-day Saudi women recite verses by Arab poetesses dating from the pre-Islamic era to the twelfth century, expressions of yearning and pride across time.

Installation views of *Come, Let Me Heal Your Wounds*. Above: Centro de Creación Contemporánea de Andalucía C3A, Córdoba, Spain, 2022 / Below: Museo Nacional Thyssen-Bornemisza, Madrid, Spain, 2020

DIRIYAH CONTEMPORARY ART BIENNALE 2024

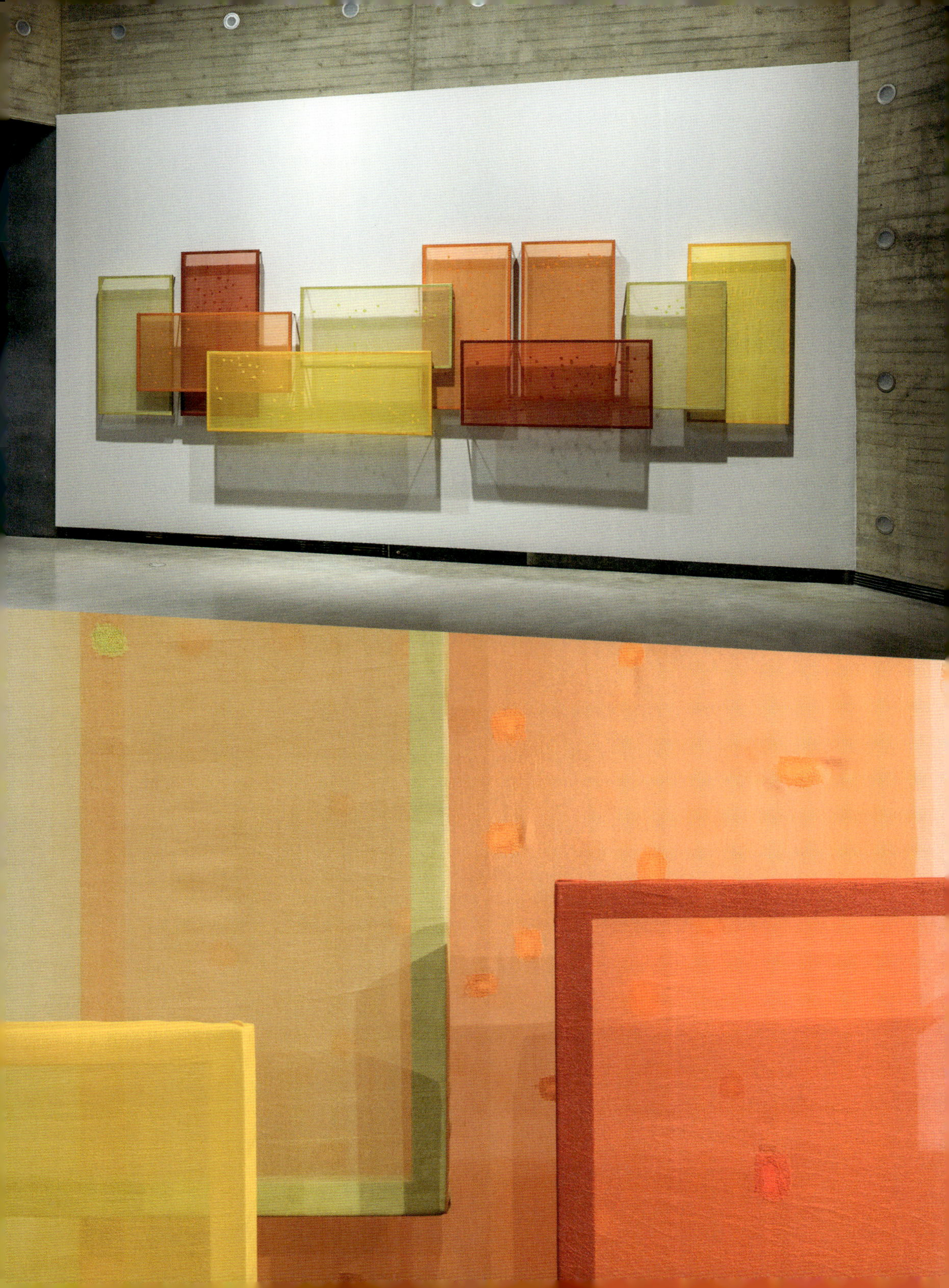

ASMA BAHMIM

Born 1979 in Jeddah, Saudi Arabia, where she lives and works

Fantasia

2022 / Selected works from the series
(see p. 285 for details)

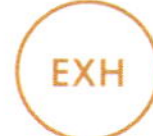

Asma Bahmim works with handmade paper, natural pigments, and organic materials to explore and revive the art of Islamic miniature painting. She studied at the King Abdulaziz University in Jeddah, first receiving a bachelor's in art education and then a master's in drawing and painting. Having obtained her PhD from the University of Jeddah, Bahmim views pedagogical methods as a foundation of her practice. Her deep grounding in historical research and use of references allows Bahmim to draw from contemporary situations to retell and compositionally reconfigure classical tales from old manuscripts by augmenting traditional miniature forms. A faculty member of the fine arts department at King Abdulaziz University, she is also a researcher in the philosophy of children's art and geospatial art.

The nine selected works on display, all from 2022, feature animals and borrow from ancient fables to address the current state of the world. From the golden-winged fox in *Neeran the Alopecia* and *Red the Fox* to the glimmering-feathered falcon and magpies in *Strong Wings* and *Magpie Tawaf* or the masked human-headed lioness in *By the Moon Pond*, these works combine gouache, gold leaf, gum arabic, banana leaves, and natural dyes to probe and invert well-known images from children's books, folktales, and the imagery of Islamic manuscripts into moral compasses for the present day. By combining fiction and nonfiction, the familiar and the unknown, Bahmim points toward stories that are recognizable and accessible while offering room for deeper interpretation, examination, and inquiry. The tiger protects the cornfields; the sharp-sighted, quick-witted peregrine falcon guards the horizon; and a chorus of beasts debate and reflect in the sparkling mirror of the pond. Sometimes figures from the world of pop culture merge with the animals, adding contemporary voices to the messages that they convey. American singer and songwriter Ariana Grande is recognizable in *By the Moon Pond*, wearing the rabbit mask from her *Dangerous Woman* (2016) album cover, while shown with a lionlike body. Twiggy, the British fashion icon of the 1960s, becomes a delicate bird in *Magpie Tawaf*. In this fantasy world, animals become the codes and models for a future through forms appropriated from an ancient heritage.

From the series *Fantasia*, 2022. Above: *Straightening* / Below: *Magpie Tawaf*

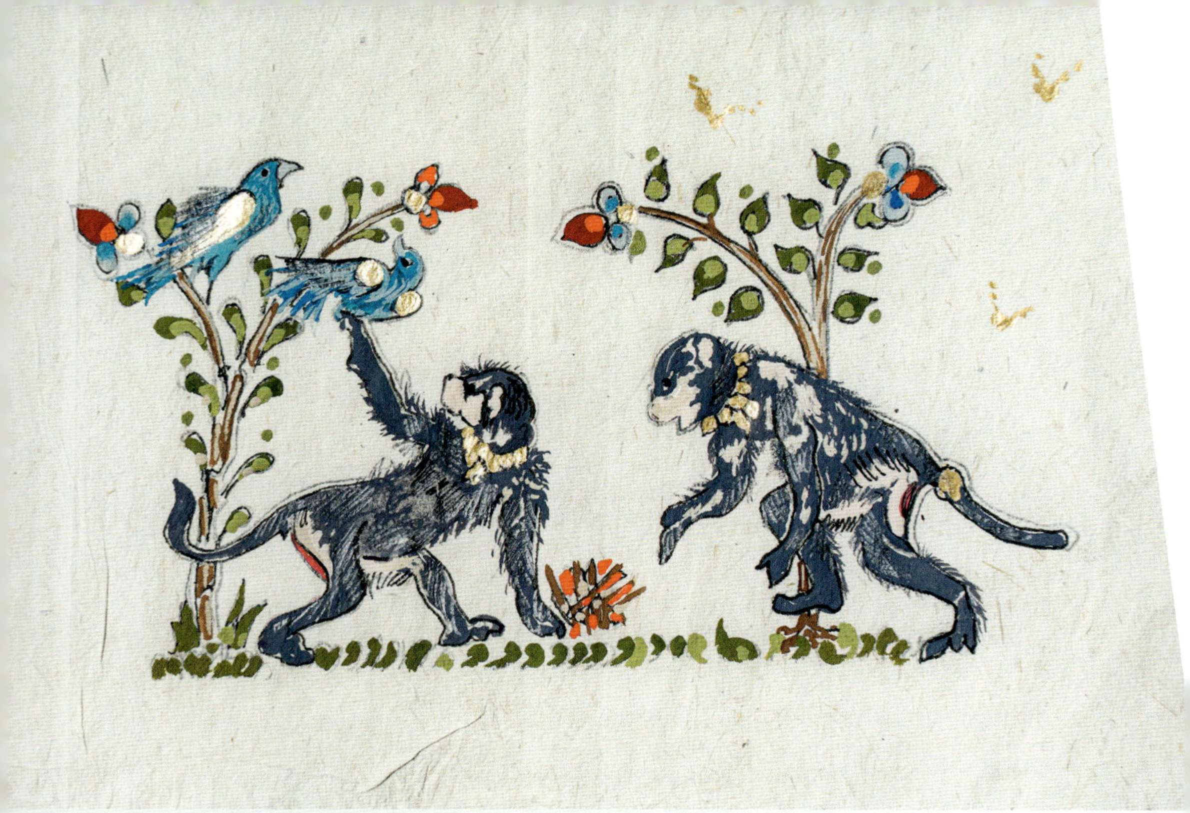

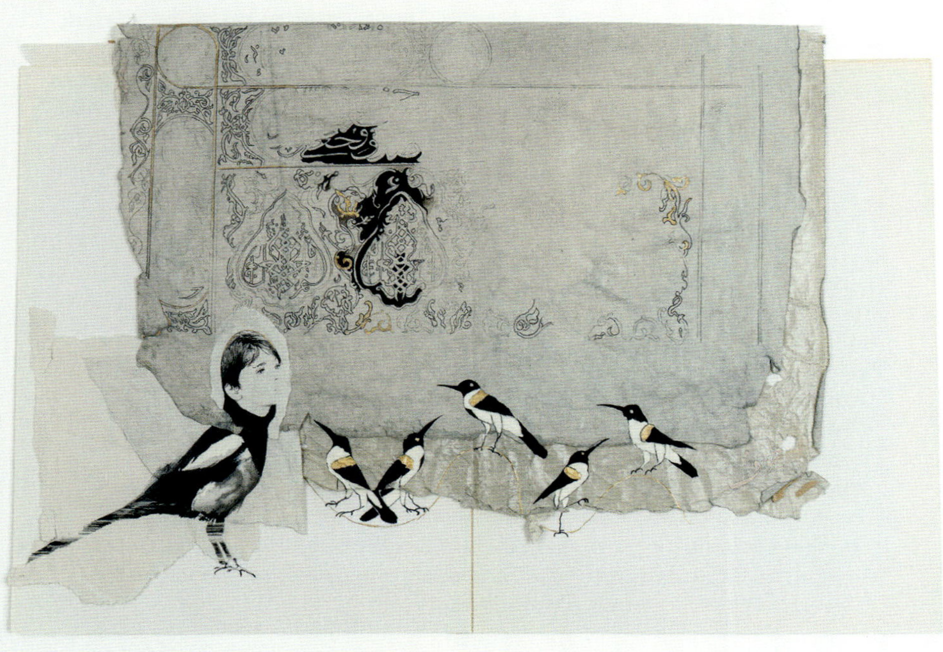

ROSSELLA BISCOTTI

Born 1978 in Molfetta, Italy, lives and works in Rotterdam,
the Netherlands

Annalies / Mei / Princess of Kasiruta / Sanikem—Nyai Ontosoroh—Madame Le Boucq / Surati / Maiko
2019–22

Rossella Biscotti excavates social and political systems of the modern era, laying bare the frameworks of power and uncovering alternate historical narratives. Her work has explored political movements of her native Italy, judiciary and penal institutions, the social structures of collaboration, and Dutch colonial archives. Underpinning her layered sculptures, performances, films, and installation are rigorous processes of fieldwork and research. Graduating from the Accademia di Belle Arti in Naples in 2002, she attended the Rijksakademie in Amsterdam in 2010–11. Her work was exhibited at dOCUMENTA 13 in Kassel (2021), and she has been an artist-in-residence with the DAAD in Berlin (2018) and the NTU Centre for Contemporary Art Singapore (2020).

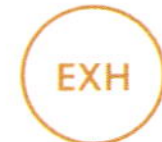

In her 2019 series of rubber works Biscotti draws from the patterns used in the wax-resist technique of hand-dyed batik. Laid across the floor or draped over wooden rods, the flat sheets have fleshy beige and reddish tints, which together with the pliable, tactile quality of the rubber implicate the human body. As intricate expressions of female labor and the domestic domain, the fabric motifs lend the work a strong feminine sensibility. This is underscored by the titles of the works, names borrowed from female characters in the writings of renowned Indonesian author Pramoedya Ananta Toer (1925–2006). Sanikem-Nyai Ontosoroh-Madame Le Boucq, Maiko, Annalies, Mei, Surati, and the Princess of Kasiruta all inhabit *The Buru Quartet* (1980–88), a series of four novels that Toer wrote while imprisoned in the Buru penal colony under Suharto's rule from 1969 to 1979 and published over a decade later.

Biscotti's longstanding fascination with *The Buru Quartet* revolves around its portrayals of colonial-era social and racial hierarchies, emerging anti-colonial movements, and the lives of different women, such as the insightful, concubine-turned-matriarch figure of Nyai Ontosoroh or the physically and mentally scarred character of Surati, who chooses to be infected with smallpox as a path out of servitude. Fabrics referenced in the novel are manifested as stand-ins for the transferable value of the female body in a narrative dominated by male protagonists. Biscotti casts the complexity and exploitation imprinted on these female biographies in the materiality of rubber—a product of historical forces such as forced migration, crop substitution, and inden-tured labor in Sumatran plantations.

Installation view of *Princess of Kasiruta*, from the exhibition *Indigo Waves and Other Stories* at Gropius Bau, Berlin, Germany, 2023

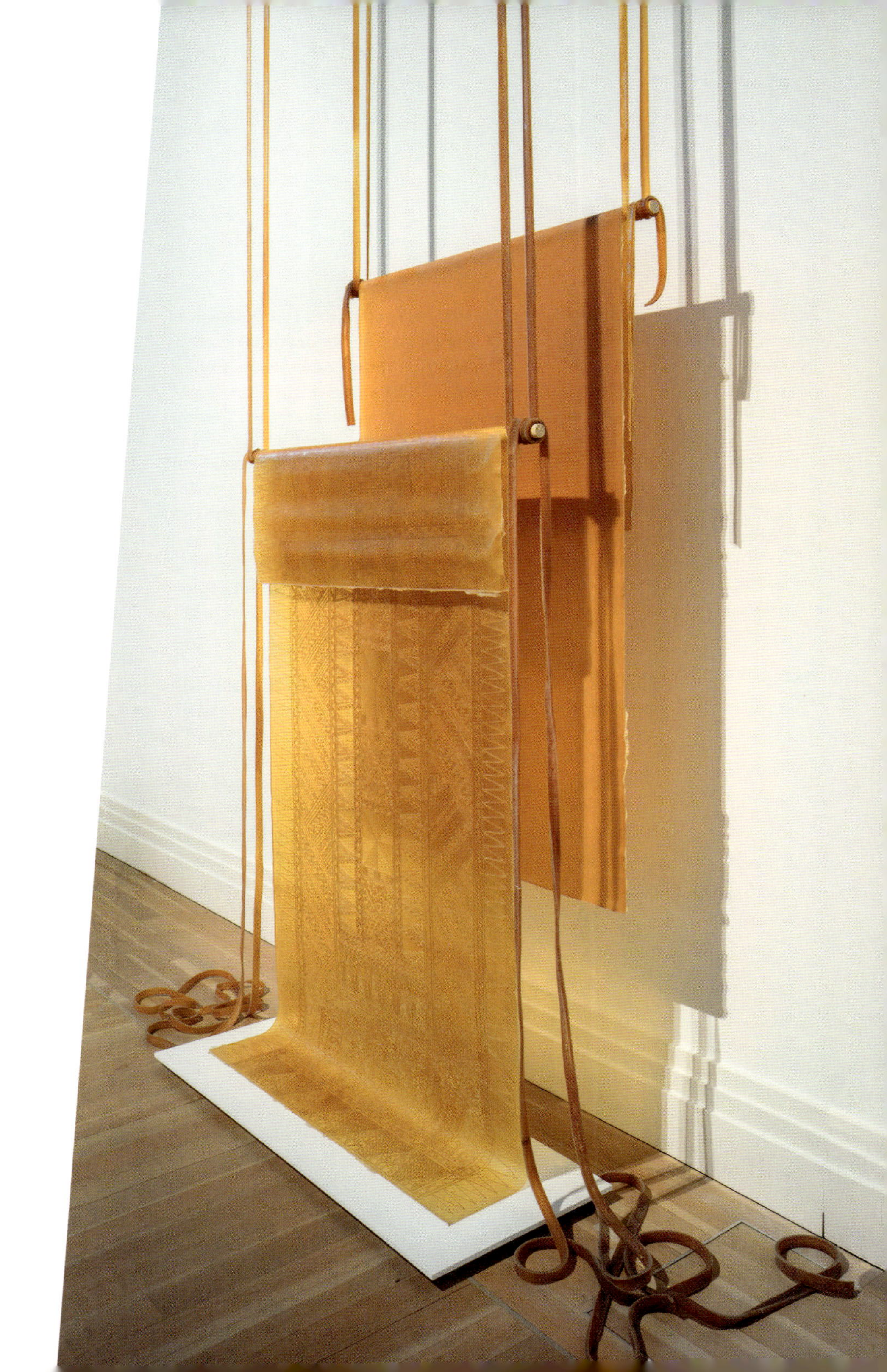

MUHANNED CADER

Born 1966 in Colombo, Sri Lanka, lives and works in Galle, Sri Lanka

Land and Water
2014

Muhanned Cader uses painting, drawing, and collage to make small-format works that are grounded in the personal observation and experience of natural landscapes. Cader studiously abstracts sites of nature—such as the inland forests of his homeland—transforming them into carefully rendered scenes or collages. He describes these works as "mapping all the ideas of a landscape," in which he often chooses to avoid the traditional rectangular framing of a canvas to create organically shaped views or peepholes into another world. Studying in the US, he received his bachelor's in fine arts from the Art Institute of Chicago in 1994. He was awarded Sri Lanka's Kala Suri in 2005—a national order of merit by the President for excellence in the arts—and has taken part in exhibitions such as the 1st Lahore Biennale (2018), the Kochi-Muziris Biennale (2014), and the Singapore Biennale (2006).

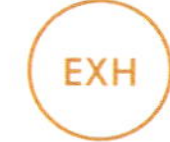

Land and Water (2014) comprises one of the accordion books that have become central to Cader's practice. Composed in a Moleskine notebook and extending almost two meters when fully unfolded, this work is an example of his signature visual language of collage, with its fluid, gestural arrangement of cut-outs and his ease with color. Sourced from personal snapshots and found materials, the composition of *Land and Water* suggests the transitions across transcontinental vistas. Forming an irregular but continuous path across not one but many landscapes, the work suggests points of juncture, where change has occurred. Starting at one end, the viewer wanders through different terrains, navigating along shapes and outlines. The shimmering sky blue that could point either to heaven or sea meets the earth tones of an evident desert followed by a sliver of green. This preoccupation with a view of land meeting water is found repeatedly in his work as a fundamental element of all natural scenes, occurring here at vertical interfaces instead of across the horizontal. While the stretched horizons of his landscapes and work titles sometimes have metaphorical undertones that suggest larger questions, in his open-ended practice, the artist is first and foremost preoccupied with finding formal language in color, shape, and form.

Installation and detail view of *Land and Water* at Grey Noise, Dubai, United Arab Emirates, 2014

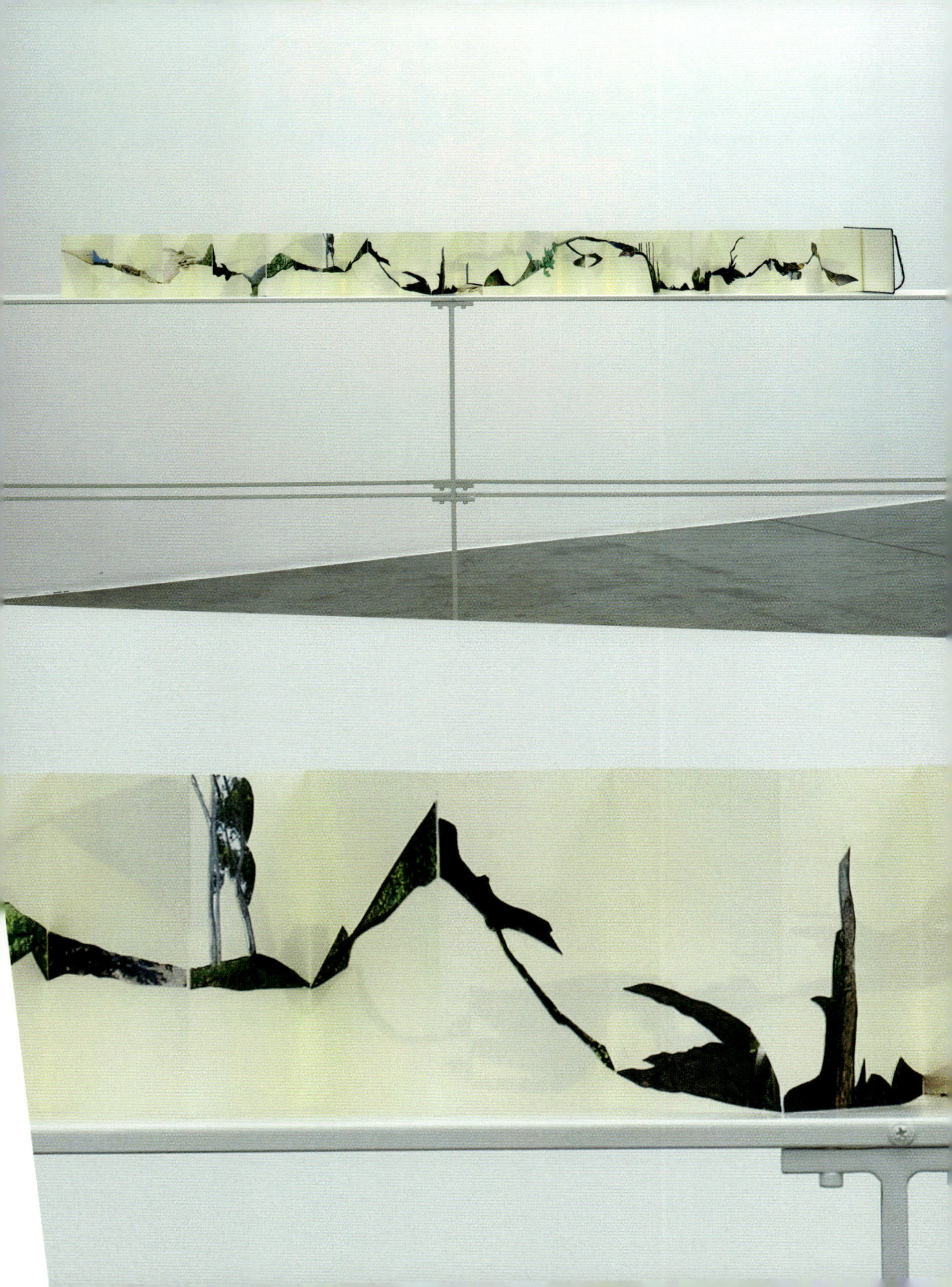

JOAN JONAS

Born 1936 in New York, NY, United States, lives and works in
New York and Nova Scotia, Canada

Reanimation
2010/2012/2013

Joan Jonas is a multimedia artist acclaimed for her dreamlike and
ever-evolving work emerging from her enduring fascination with myth
and ritual. Amid New York City's burgeoning art scene of the 1960s
and 1970s, Jonas came to be known for her radical experimentation
with video and performance using live-feed self-portraits to interrogate portrayals of female identity, at a time when women artists
were redefining their artistic paths by turning away from traditionally
male-dominated mediums such as painting and sculpture. Among
her many collaborators—dancers, musicians, storytellers—have been
the artist's canine companions, repeatedly appearing in her work as
drawings or impromptu performers. In 2015 Joan Jonas represented
the United States at the 56th Venice Biennale.

As with many of her works, *Reanimation* (2010/2012/2013) has taken
different forms over time, first as a performance in collaboration
with jazz musician Jason Moran in 2010, and then restaged as an
installation for dOCUMENTA 13 in 2012. The work is inspired by a
chapter of *Under the Glacier*, a 1968 novel by Icelandic author and
Nobel laureate Halldór Laxness, which tells the story of a young
church emissary sent to investigate strange occurrences in a remote
glacial village. Jonas's immersive installation comprises four videos
layering ghostly superimpositions of live projections from the original
performance, footage of the artist painting on snow or drawing with
ice, and an otherworldly Arctic landscape shot on the Lofoten Islands
in Norway. The videos are projected onto four large screens forming
a mystical and intimate viewing space. Here a delicate sculpture of
suspended crystal balls refracts light from the projections and scatters
luminous fragments around the darkened space to resemble the
celestial landscape of a starry night. The installation is enveloped
by a soundtrack that includes passages from Laxness's imaginative
prose, excerpts of Japanese Noh theater plays, traditional songs
of the Indigenous Sami people, and Moran's original compositions.
In an idiosyncratic language of performance, Jonas weaves these
images, props, sounds, and her own repeating, ritualized actions
into a complex tapestry. Through this flow of sensorial associations,
Reanimation invokes a nonlinear, expanded sense of time and the
miraculous nature of the world we inhabit—in the artist's words, "the
fragility of life in a rapidly changing situation."

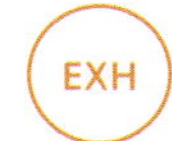

Above: Installation view of *Reanimation* 2010/2012/2013, Gavin Brown's Enterprise, New York
Below: Video still from *Reanimation* 2010/2012/2013

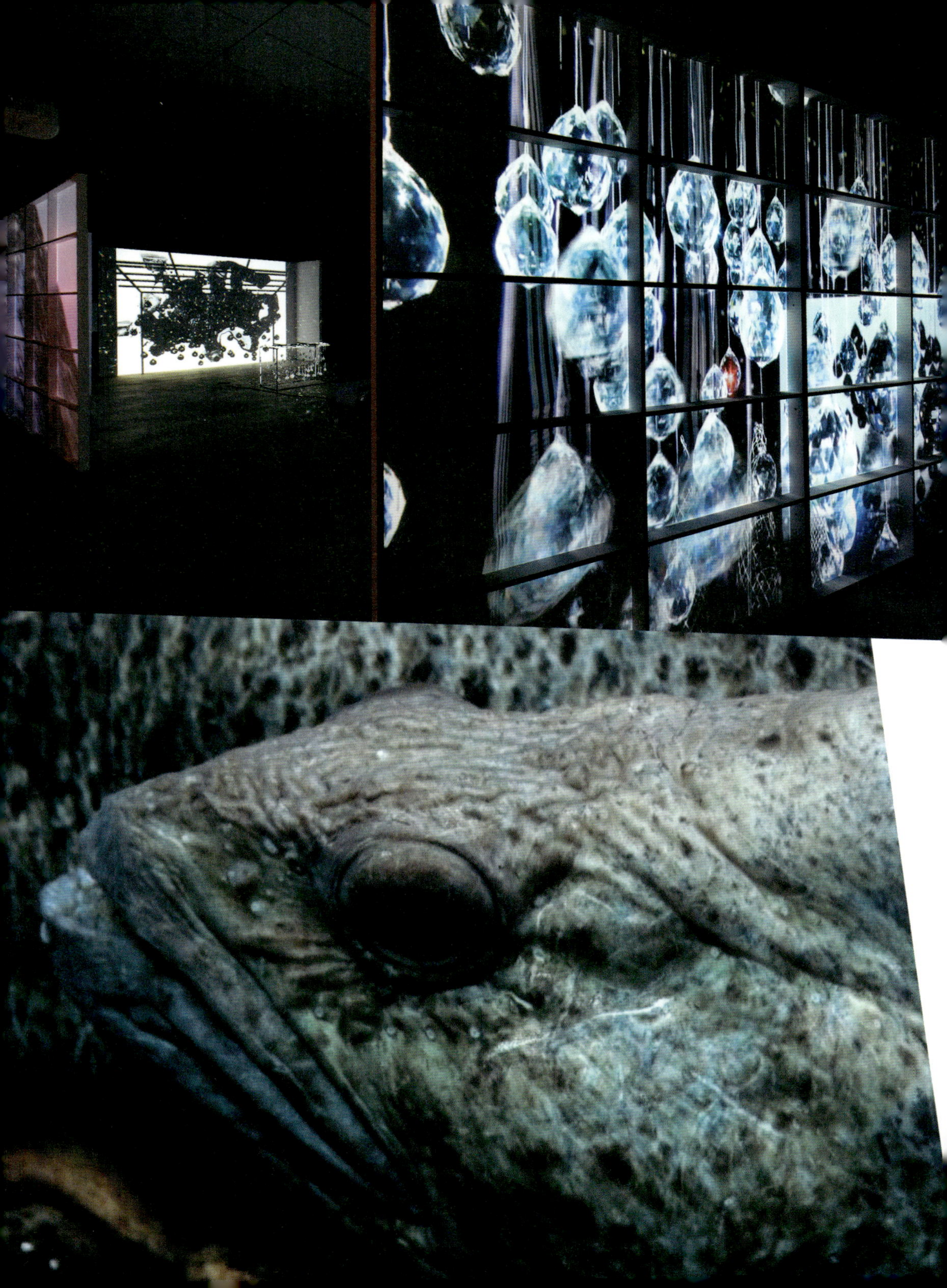

LIANG SHAOJI

Born 1945 in Shanghai, China, lives and works in Tiantai, China

Lonely Cloud
2016

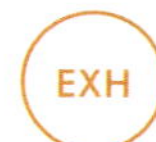

For over three decades, Liang Shaoji has been breeding silkworms and integrating their silk and life cycles into his practice. His deep affinity for these insects and their work is expressed in the poetic and meditative quality of his sculptures, installations, paintings, photography, videos, and performances. Liang graduated in 1989 from the Zhejiang Academy of Fine Arts, where he studied soft sculpture with renowned Bulgarian fiber artist Maryn Varbanov. Soon after, he became fascinated by the possibility of working with live silkworms and gradually developed his unique form of silk farming into a generative and collaborative artistic process.

Liang closely observes the ways silkworms live, breed, and transform, investigating their responses to a myriad of different materials. Silkworms—commonly associated with renewal and rebirth—naturally cover everything with the silk they spin. For Liang, their soft but strong fiber represents a celebration of life's vigor. At the same time, the artist incorporates rusted iron and other industrial waste in his sculptural work, often using metal as a symbol of industrialization and machines, which are coated and "healed" by the natural silk. His choice of subjects is inspired by the socioeconomic context of today's China and its people's collective, psychological experience of rapid modernization. He also draws ideas from traditional Chinese architecture, especially temples and similar spaces conducive to introspection and quietness.

Meditation, the practice of emptying one's mind to experience peace, is an important element of Liang's life and art, and the foundation of his connection to Zen and Buddhist philosophies. The mountain where he lives and practices his sericulture art is the home of Tiantai Buddhism. For *Lonely Cloud* (2016), Liang used camphor wood, usually carved into Buddha statues, as a ground for his silkworms. The large, heavy piece of wood is held up by a structure of rusted steel pipes, which the artist found at a construction site. In its raised position, the trunk's form, wrapped in translucent, white silk threads, is reminiscent of a cloud. Liang has likened the way silkworms secrete strands of silk from their salivary glands to breathing or "cloud-forming." Reoccurring throughout his work, clouds—regarded as sacred in Tiantai for their nobility and strength—embody the spiritual in nature.

Above: Artist sketch of *Lonely Cloud* / Below: Installation view of *Lonely Cloud* from the exhibition *Holzwege* at ShanghART Shanghai, China, 2016

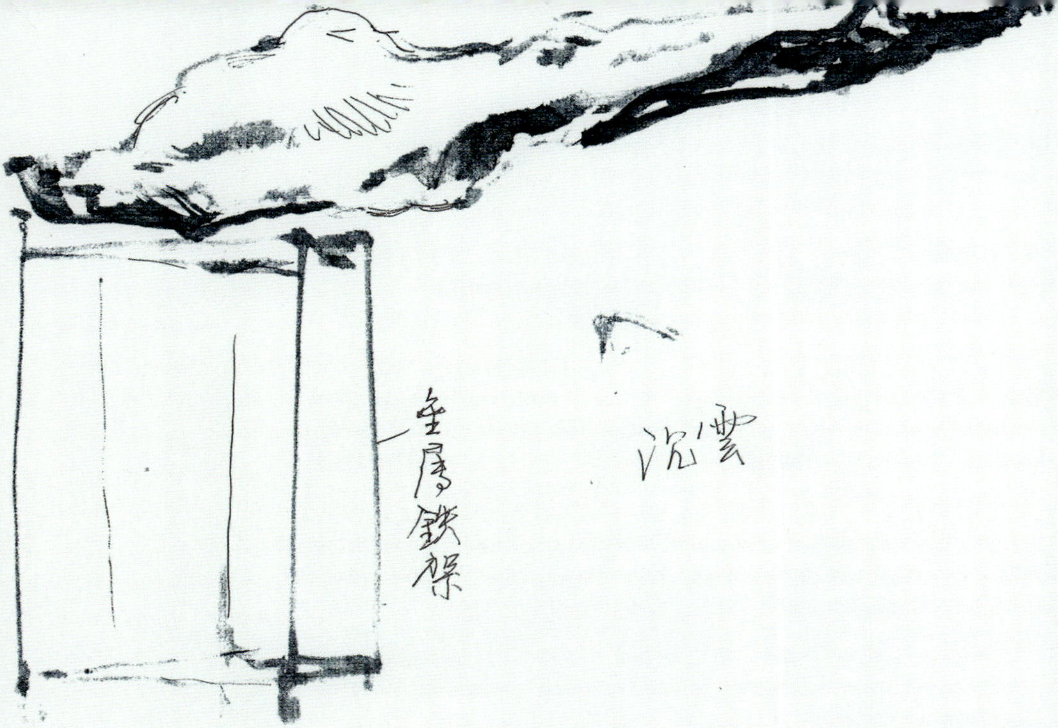

金屬鐵架
沈雲

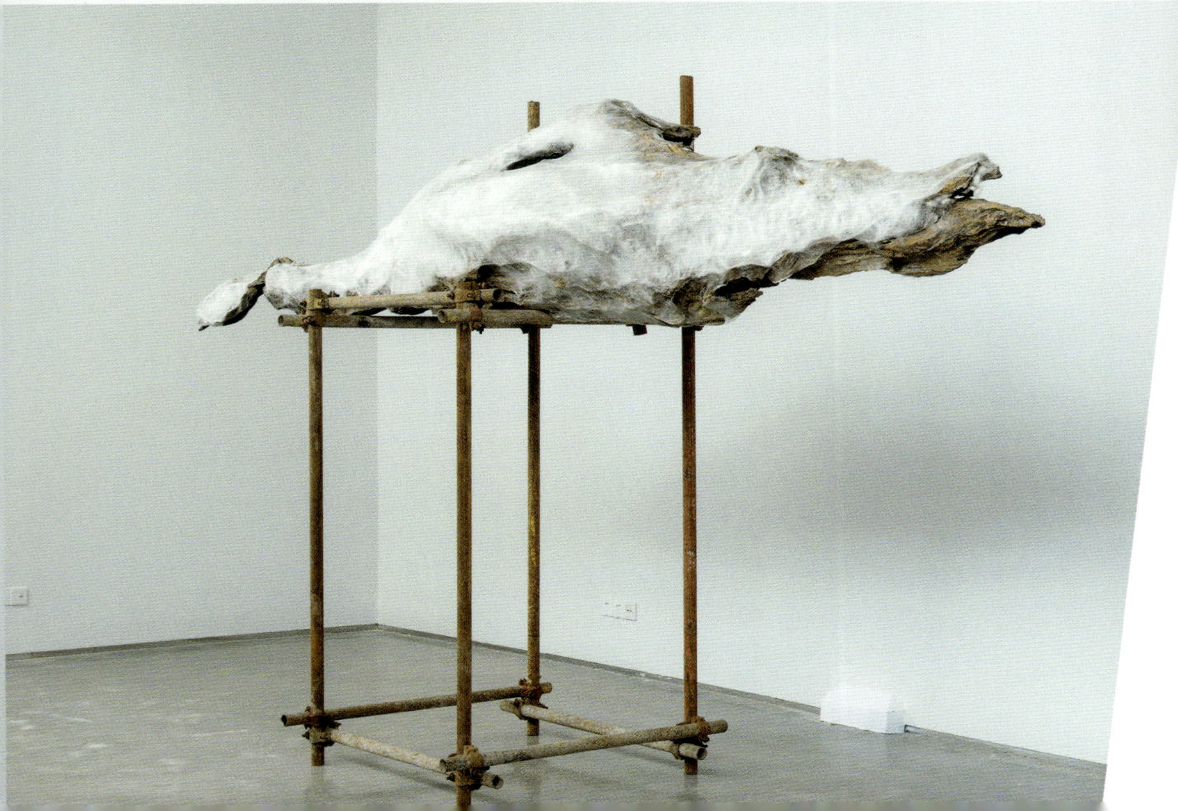

REGINA MARIA MÖLLER

Born Munich, Germany, lives and works in Berlin, Germany

DIE MOTTE (The Moth)

2018/2024

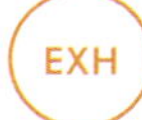

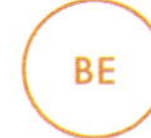

Regina Maria Möller is an artist, writer, and educator. In 1994 she founded the magazine *regina*—an artwork utilizing the format of popular women's magazines to question the construction and representation of female identities. In the same year she started her label *embodiment*, under which she produces prototypes of clothes and interior objects as limited-edition wearable sculptures and works of art in use. *embodiment* operates within the undefined space between the body and environment, probing the social and cultural codes embedded in these interfaces. Möller also develops multilayered installations and research projects; most recently she collaborated with scientists on *The Mask—Arrayed* (2020–22), an investigation of the face mask hosted by the Max Planck Institute for the History of Science in Berlin.

In the installation *DIE MOTTE* (The Moth, 2018/2024), Möller creates a stagelike space defined by a set of moveable curtains that reference different historical theater curtains. The central protagonist in this setting is the elusive and enigmatic character of the common clothes moth. Generally disliked for its destructive habits—its larvae feed on the keratin present in high-quality fibers such as wool and silk—the insect is also a guarantor of quality. For the artist, it is a sign of the natural and the physical in our obsessively synthetic and digital times. The insect is announced with top billing in large lettering on a nettle curtain. It appears again, highlighted as embroidery on a two-sided portal curtain; on the one side, it is shown flying into the light, and on the other, vanishing into the golden ochre of the velvet fabric. The moth can also be discovered as a painted motif, mysteriously crawling on a porcelain vase that is displayed in a glass cube and superimposed with a QR-code. This code and others placed nearby permit the viewer to seek out additional porcelain vases with moth motifs, but only in the disembodied realm of the digital.

A play between presence and absence, *DIE MOTTE* is a reminder of our physical impermanence. Viewers are invited to walk through the spot-lit space and move the theater curtains while watching others and being watched—as shadows projected onto the fabric. This animated show of bodies, lively but immaterial, visualizes the dissolution of the physical in the increasing digitization of our everyday experiences.

DIE MOTTE (The Moth) at Gallery Michael Janssen, Berlin, Germany, 2018
Above: Installation view / Below: Detail view of *Hauptvorhang* (Portal Curtain)

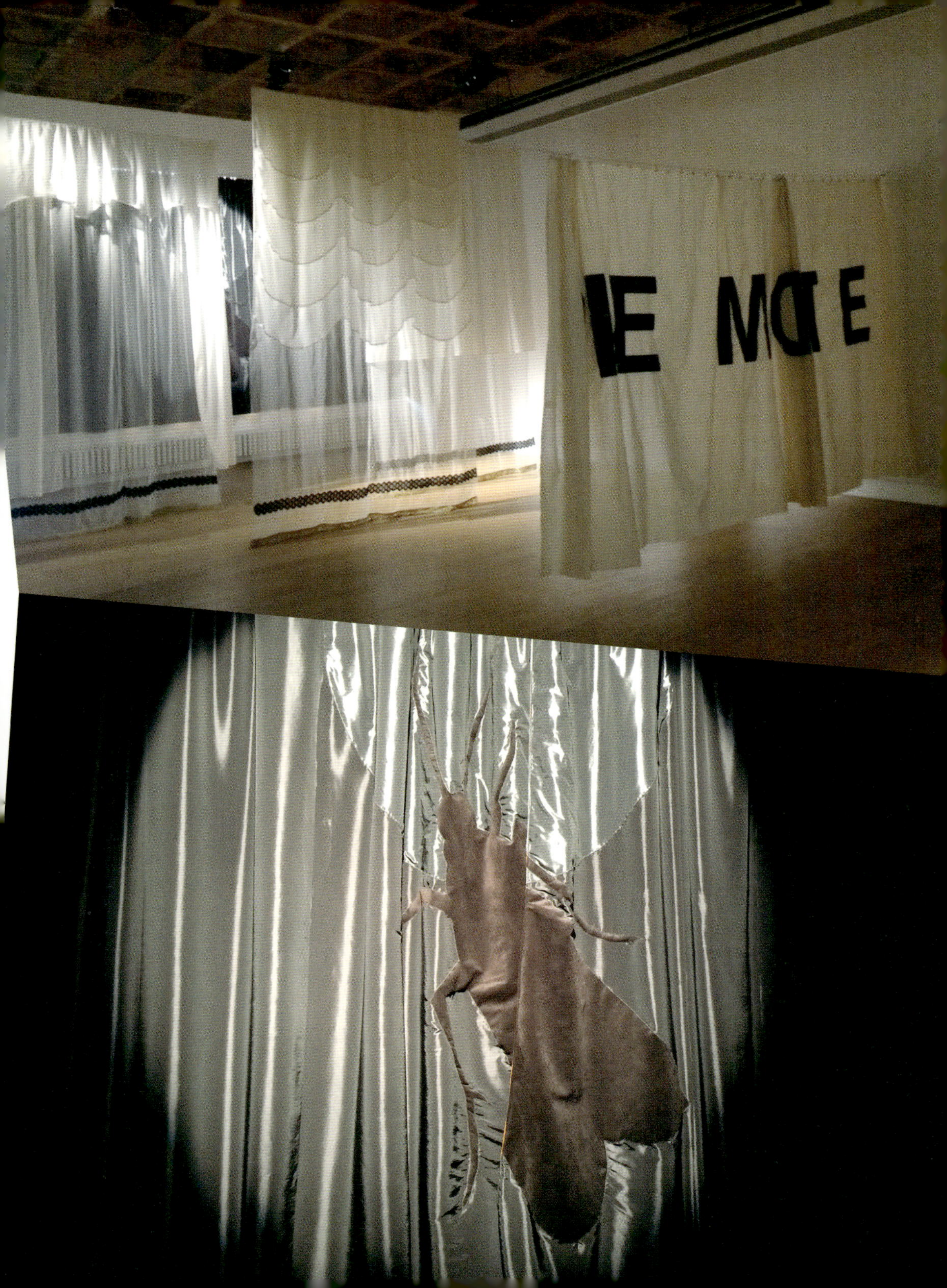
E MOE

PHI PHI OANH

Born 1979 in Houston, TX, United States, lives and works in Da Nang,
Vietnam

A Light Exits in the Spring
2023

Phi Phi Oanh has been working with Vietnamese lacquer painting (*tranh sơn mài*) for two decades. With a background in painting, she explores this historical technique, engaging its materiality and expanding its form. In 2004 Oanh was awarded a Fulbright scholarship to study traditional *tranh sơn mài* in Hanoi, now a key medium in her practice and research. Drawing from the hybrid nature of her Vietnamese-American history, she reconfigures the culturally specific lacquer medium to create familiar yet distinctive, immersive yet intimate installations.

Formed from the sap of the versatile *Rhus succedanea* tree native to northern Vietnam, lacquer has an ancient history, used to cover utilitarian wooden objects and temple interiors for protection from termites and humidity. In the 1930s, Vietnamese lacquer was introduced as a painting medium at the École Supérieure des Beaux-Arts de l'Indochine, established in Hanoi by the French colonial government, resulting in a hybrid between age-old craft techniques and Western art: the modern *tranh sơn mài*. Oanh is interested in expanding this process of acculturation by combining *sơn mài* (lacquer) with new materials and display methods to reflect on not only the medium itself but also cross-cultural histories.

Oanh sees certain metaphors as inherent to the medium. In the same way that lacquering requires multiple applications of varnish on wood, as well as repeated sanding and polishing, memory is formed through an accumulative process, or as the artist puts it, a "sanding away of time and perception." This focus on memory positions *sơn ta* (natural lacquer) as a cultural medium, witness, and marker of the changes in Vietnamese society.

A Light Exists in the Spring (2023) from the series *Palimpsest* (2013–ongoing) is an attempt at the total dematerialization of the medium, while highlighting the details of its "material qualities ... the deep colors and ever-changing light." The artist's Lacquerscope machines, adapted from old slide projectors, render small, multicolored images on a large screen in a manner suggesting telescopic views. In display cases, miniature paintings and lacquer "skins" (*tranh sơn mài* on clear film) are rescaled through magnifying lenses, recalling microscopic images of infinitesimal worlds. This play between light, surface, scale, and perspective situates *sơn ta* between painting and photography, all within an innovative sculptural arrangement.

Installation view of *Palimpsest*, from the exhibition *Trees of Life – Knowledge in Material* at NTU Centre for Contemporary Art Singapore, 2018

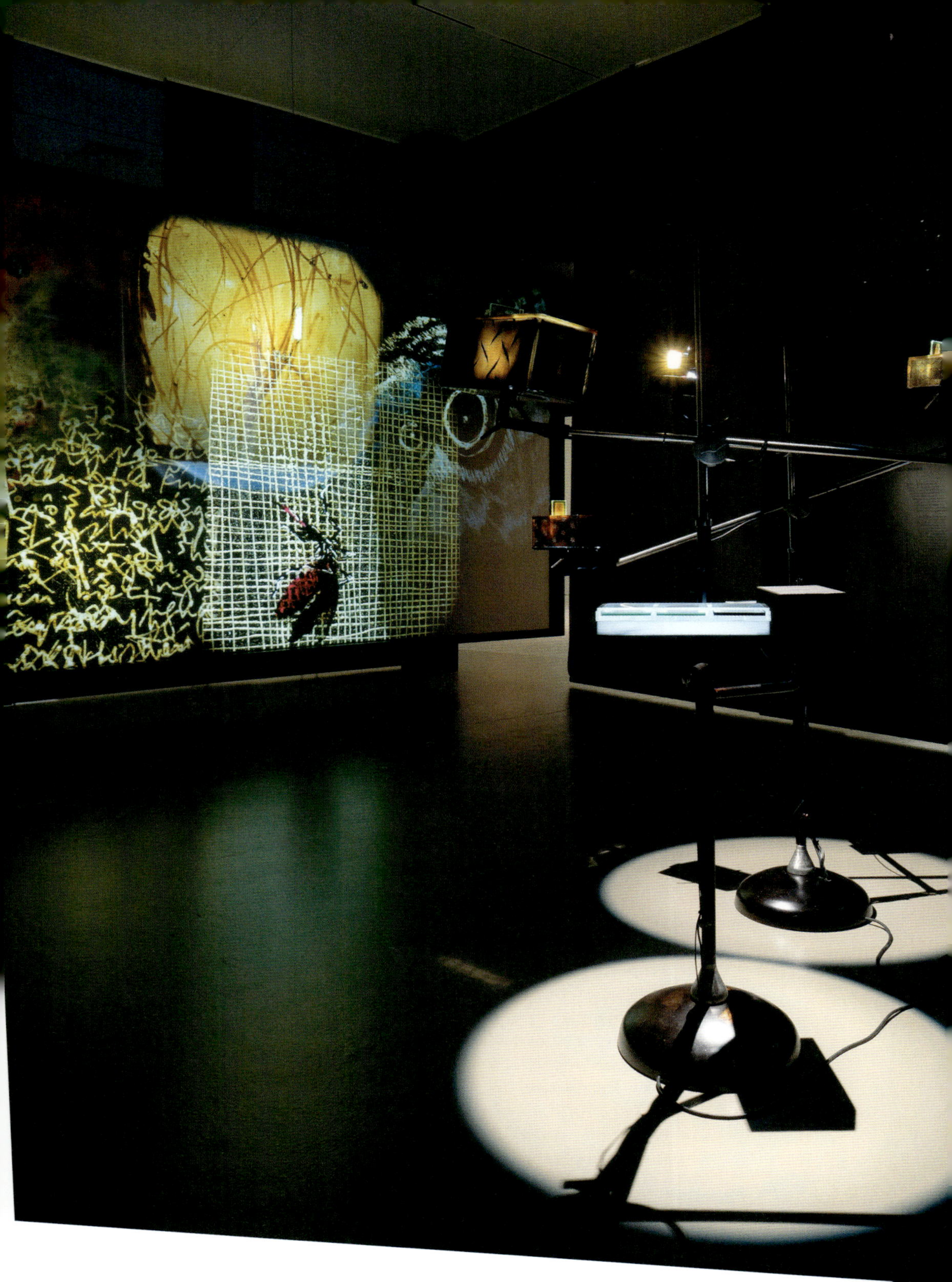

JORGE OTERO-PAILOS

Born 1971 in Madrid, Spain, lives and works in New York, NY,
United States

A Library of Earthen Architectures

2024 / With contributions by: Daniah Alsaleh, HRH Nawaf Bin Ayyaf, Bricklab,
Ahmed Mater, Filwa Nazer, syn architects, Alaa Tarabzouni & Fahad Al Saud

Jorge Otero-Pailos is an American-Spanish artist, preservation architect, scholar, and educator renowned for pioneering experimental preservation practices. Alongside his artistic practice, he is Director and Professor of Historic Preservation at Columbia University's Graduate School of Architecture, Planning, and Preservation (GSAPP), where he also directs the Columbia Preservation Technology Lab, and where he founded the first PhD program in Historic Preservation in the US. His works have been commissioned by and exhibited at major heritage sites, museums, foundations, and biennials, including the Chicago Architecture Biennale (2017), Artangel's public art commission at the UK Parliament (2016), the V&A Museum (2015), and the 53rd Venice Biennale (2009). He is the recipient of a 2021–22 American Academy in Rome Residency in the visual arts.

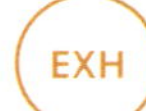

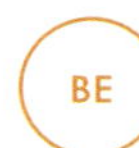

Otero-Pailos employs artistic methods—informed by advanced technologies, materials research, and interdisciplinary collaborations—to expand the range of objects that are valued as cultural heritage and to develop new ways of caring for those objects. His wide-ranging artistic practice finds expression through materials such as airborne atmospheric dusts, smells, sounds, and architectural fragments. His series *The Ethics of Dust* (2008–ongoing) consists of large-scale latex casts and utilizing the dust and pollution residues found on landmarked monuments to highlight how the different kinds of dusts sedimented on buildings function as repositories of previously unexamined environmental histories and collective memories.

For the Biennale, Otero-Pailos collaborated with Saudi artists and heritage experts in charge of Saudi World Heritage sites to create *A Library of Earthen Architectures*, which includes artifacts representative of Saudi cultural memory. Accompanying each artifact is an audio recording of a conversation between the artists discussing its importance, what makes it worthy of care, and how it expands the range of materials and meanings associated with earthen World Heritage sites such as At-Turaif. The library is a collective open-ended work that centers the role of artists in the physical documentation, interpretation, and presentation of World Heritage sites in Saudi Arabia. It documents the emergence of a multigenerational conversation between Saudi artists exploring experimental preservation methods. The interviews can be accessed through The Learning Garden, the digital extension of the Biennale.

Dust Cloud, 2024. Produced in the context of the Diriyah Contemporary Art Biennale 2024 as part of research on dust manufacturing technologies for the production of artificial rain in Saudi Arabia.

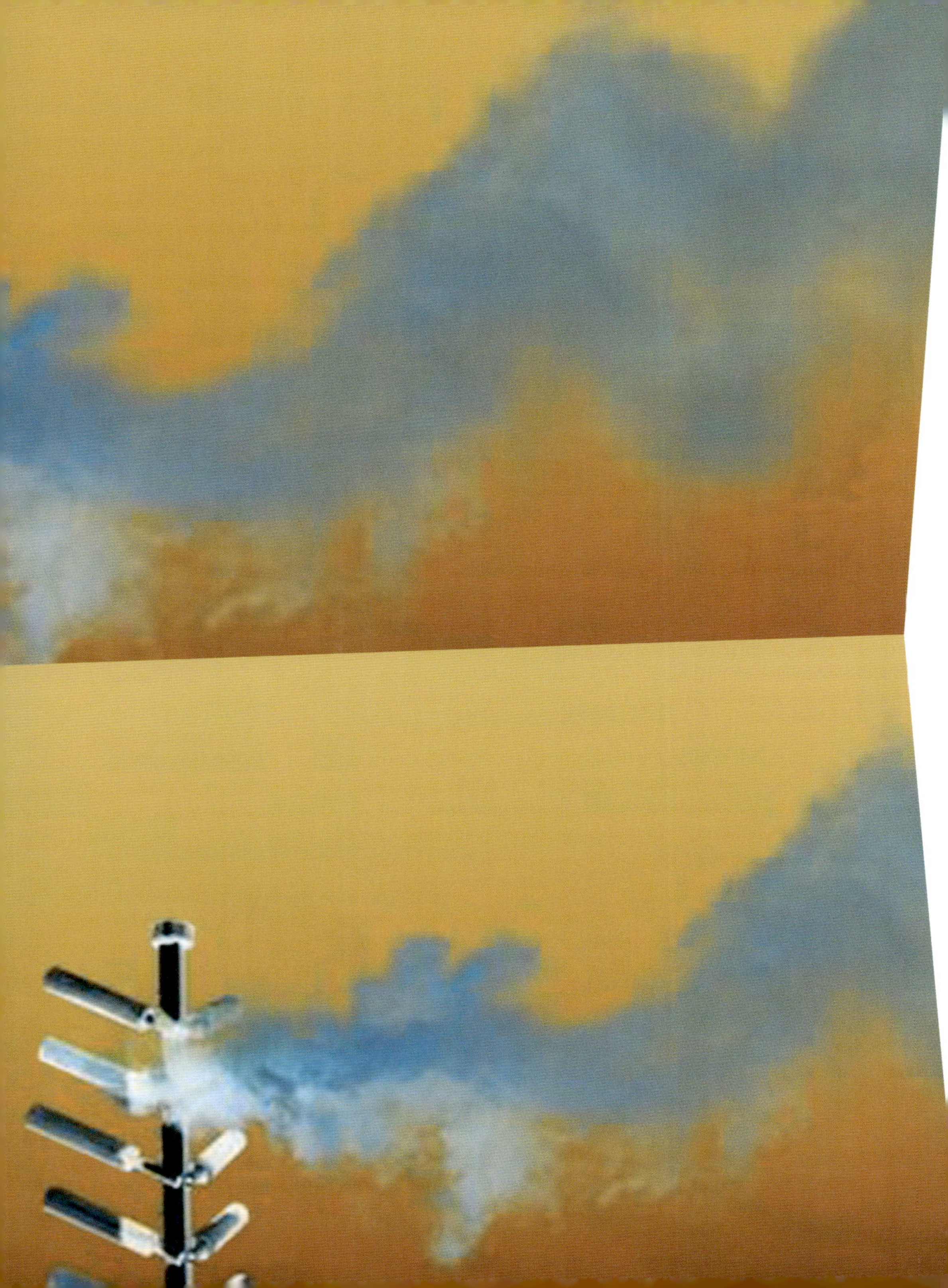

SOPHEAP PICH

Born 1971 in Battambang, Cambodia, lives and works in Phnom Penh, Cambodia

Amulet (Hevea Afzelia)
2023

Rang Phnom Flower
2015

Sopheap Pich is known for large-scale, organically inspired works made from natural and traditional materials, such as rattan, bamboo, and burlap. Having left Cambodia with his family as a refugee in the late 1970s, he eventually settled in the United States. There, he received an MFA in painting from the School of the Art Institute of Chicago, subsequently deciding to return to his homeland in 2002. Today, he produces his works together with a team of assistants in his studio outside of Phnom Penh.

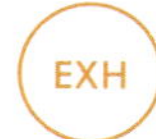

Rang Phnom Flower (2015) developed from the idea of creating an oversized, flowering cannonball tree (*Couroupita guianensis; rang phnom* in Khmer) and was inspired by the artist's trip to Ratanakiri in northeastern Cambodia, where the landscape is full of these big trees with magnificent bright flowers. Because of their resemblance to the sal tree, under which the Buddha is believed to have been born, they are often planted near Buddhist temples, and so the trees—native to the Americas—spread across Southeast Asia. These rang phnom are seldom cut down, since the wood is not desirable, and they are believed to have spirits living in them. The sculpture is made of hundreds of strands of woven rattan. Through its delicate crafting and amplification of the plant's budding forms, the work conveys the power of nature and its fragility—a balance rendered in monumentality.

Amulet (Hevea Afzelia) (2023) displays the greatly enlarged seeds of the Cambodian Beng and rubber trees, which are strung along a thick rope, like beads, recalling the bracelets worn by Buddhists as a sign of faith and devotion. The work incorporates a new material for the artist; common seeds are recreated in handblown glass. The Cambodian Beng tree (*Afzelia xylocarpa*) is an endangered species native to Southeast Asia. Its edible seeds are used for medicinal purposes; its wood is highly valued. The rubber tree (*Hevea brasiliensis*) is linked to the history of colonialism and monoculture. Although native to South America, it has been cultivated for over a century in Southeast Asia, where most of the world's rubber plantations are now located. Pich magnifies the seeds, and their complex histories, while hinting at the magnificent life-power within such small capsules, which can transform into giants.

Above: Amulet (Hevea Afzelia), 2023 / Below: Installation view of Rang Phnom Flower at Sopheap Pich studio, Phnom Penh, Cambodia, 2015

DIRIYAH CONTEMPORARY ART BIENNALE 2024

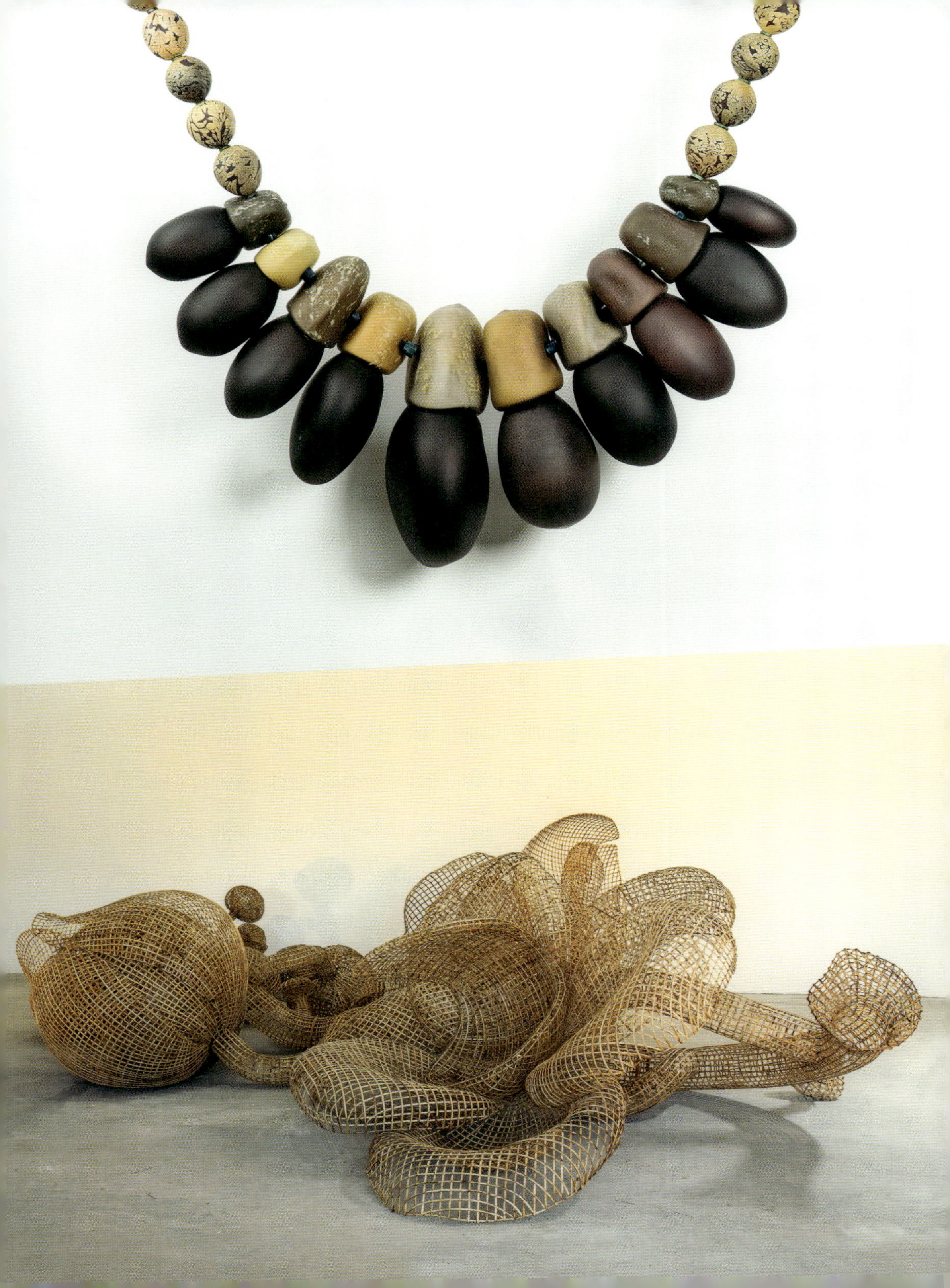

ARIN RUNGJANG

Born 1975 in Bangkok, Thailand, where he lives and works

Golden Teardrop

2013

Arin Rungjang is known for video and installation-based works that revisit minor and major histories. His works read history not as a linear trajectory or grand narrative but a complex network of stories traversing the past, present, personal, and political. After graduating with a BFA in graphic arts from Silpakorn University in 2002, Runjang went on to participate in landmark regional and international exhibitions, notably representing Thailand at the 55th Venice Biennale in 2013. Rungjang received the Silpathorn Award in visual art from Thailand's Ministry of Culture in 2020.

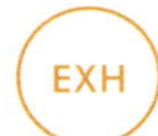

"History is like the yolk that was thrown away, like the birth of *ovos moles*," Rungjang muses aloud in a letter to a friend, one of two voiceover tracks narrating the single-channel film and installation *Golden Teardrop* (2013). Telling the story of the link between this Portuguese egg-yolk sweet and the popular Thai dessert *thong yod*, food becomes a thematic apparatus through which the artist interweaves disparate biographies and geographies across time. The film begins with the personal story of a Japanese woman living in Thailand, recounting her life as marked by a matrilineally inherited love of culinary exploration and a family history haunted by the experiences of the Hiroshima and Nagasaki bombings. Incongruently but profoundly, her story intersects with that of Maria Guyomar de Pina, a Catholic woman of Japanese, Portuguese, and Bengali ancestry who was born in Ayutthaya during the reign of King Narai in the seventeenth century. She was married to the infamous Greek adventurer Constantine Phaulkon, who was brutally executed during the 1688 Siamese Revolution for his role in seeding French influence in the Ayutthaya Kingdom. After unsuccessfully fleeing Ayutthaya, the widowed Guyomar de Pina became a cook for the Siamese court. It is believed that the popular Thai dessert *thong yod* originates from her incorporation of traditional Portuguese dessert recipes combining egg yolk and sugar, such as the fifteenth-century *ovos moles*, into the royal menus.

Cutting across five centuries of trade, war, and revolution, the story of *thong yod* unravels little-known fragments of Siamese history and its early forays in world politics and international trade. The desert, literally meaning "golden teardrop," is given another form by Rungjang in his spherical installation of six thousand suspended drop-like brass shapes, a sculptural articulation of silent tears, evoking Thailand's fraught past.

Installation view of *Golden Teardrop* at Singapore Art Museum, 2013

 DIRIYAH CONTEMPORARY ART BIENNALE 2024

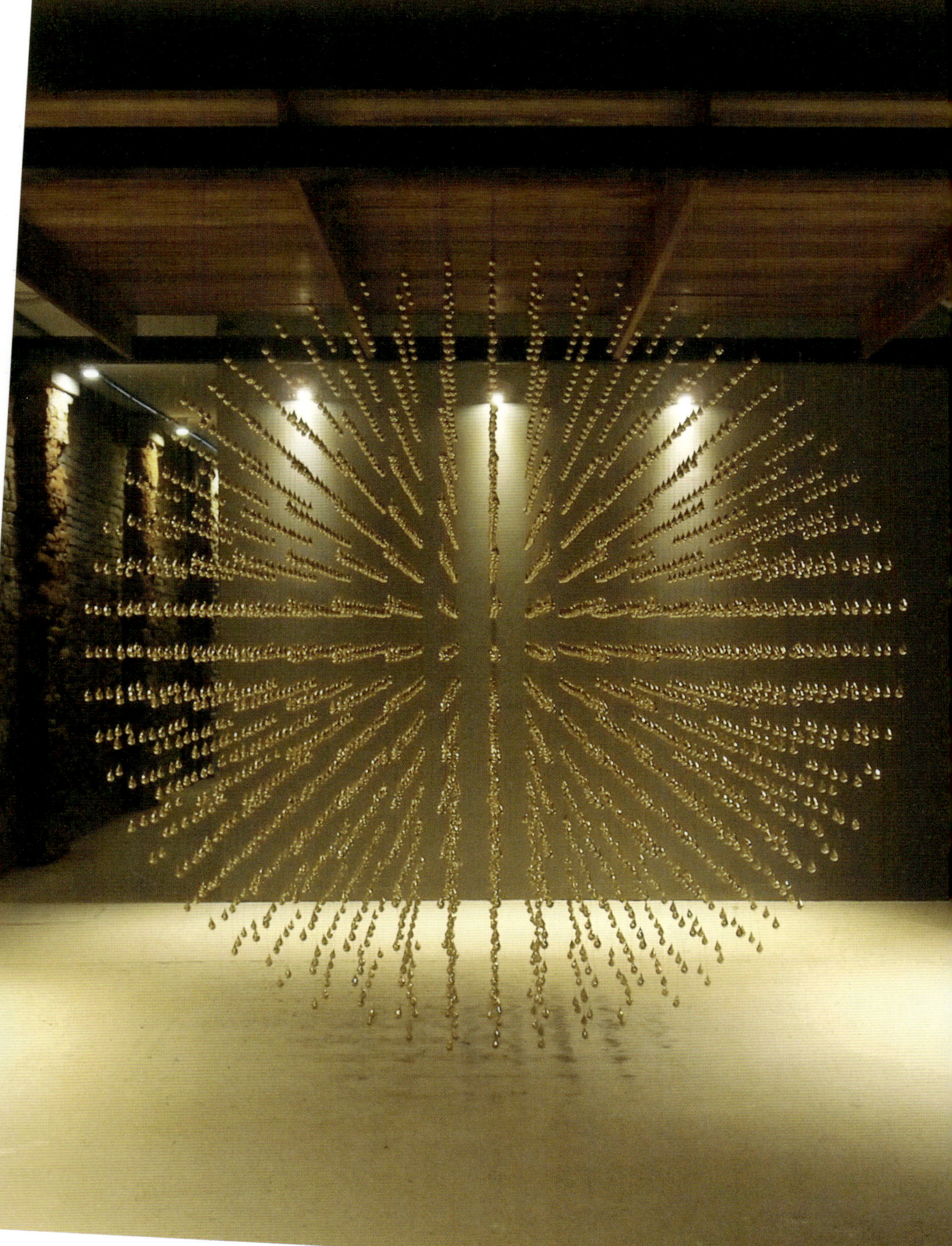

TOMÁS SARACENO

Born 1973 in San Miguel de Tucumán, Argentina, lives and works
in Berlin, Germany

Hybrid dark semi-social Cluster GC 12406 built by: a duet of Cyrtophora citricola—eight weeks, rotated 180°
2019

An Open Letter for Invertebrate Rights
2020

Fly with Pacha, Into the Aerocene
2023 / Video, 67 min 15 sec
Film Program

Tomás Saraceno's pioneering and visionary artistic practice spans various fields of knowledge from astronomy to ecology and music. Informed by his background in architecture, Saraceno's visually impactful and interactive structures are inspired by natural forms that can represent complex macro-cosmic structures. His *Spider/Web Pavilion 7* (2019), at the 58th Venice Biennale in 2019, exemplifies his long-term fascination with the spiderweb, often employed as a visual analogy to represent the origins of the universe. In collaboration with leading arachnologists and researchers, Saraceno was the first to scan, analyze, and reconstruct a three-dimensional spider-web, highlighting how these webs have yet to be properly explored and measured in terms of their exceptional architectural and physical properties.

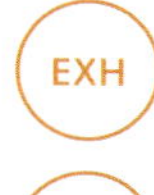
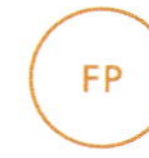

Hybrid dark semi-social Cluster GC 12406 built by: a duet of Cyrtophora citricola—eight weeks, rotated 180° (2019) is part of Saraceno's ongoing *Hybrid Webs* series that further investigates the world of spiders through direct "collabo-ration" with arachnids. Spiders from different species are allowed to interactively weave webs in a shared space, creating hybrid environments of coexistence. The title is a detailed description of the components involved in the web sculpture, including the type of collaborating spiders and the time needed to create the web. As in many of Saraceno's interventions, community, sharing, and appropriation for the good of all are central concepts. He emphasizes "DIT" (doing it together) as key to improving the ecosystem: "We come from different worlds, but work together to make a better future." Saraceno is also intent on raising awareness of the rights of invertebrates, who have inhabited the earth for over 380 million years in comparison to the mere 200 thousand years of human presence. In an open letter to the world, he encourages a shift from arachnophobia, a fear of spiders, to arachnophilia, an appreciation of these arachnids, as part of a growing interdisciplinary, research-driven initiative to support our common struggle against extinction.

Also screening during the opening week of the Biennale is Saraceno's film *Fly with Pacha, Into the Aerocene* (2023), which chronicles the record-breaking, fuel-free flight of the Aerocene Pacha hot-air balloon, lifting off from the salt flats of the Salinas Grandes, Argentina, as well as the struggle of local and Indigenous communities against prospective Lithium mining in the region.

Detail of the installation *An Open Letter for Invertebrate Rights* at Down to Earth Festival, part of Berliner Festspiele's *Immersion* series at Gropius Bau, Berlin, Germany, 2020

Martin-Gropius-Bau
Niederkirchnerstraße 7
10963 Berlin

13.82020 billion.
ABB (After Big Bang)

AN OPEN LETTER
FOR INVERTEBRATE RIGHTS

Dear Martin Gropius Bau,

We would like to start by thanking your entire team and the team of *Down to Earth* for recognizing our rights to inhabit and exhibit in this museum and for not labelling us "urban pests"* as many others do. We hope that after this exhibition ends, Gropius Bau would consider allowing our continuing but threatened, unlimited existence.

Your scientific name for us is *Holocnemus Pluchei*, though we call ourselves differently in our vibrational language. On the 17th of January 2020, you spotted our presence in the upper-left corner of a window in Room 1.9. Now, for over a period of eight months, and with a pandemic in between, you have shown good will of co-existence by not sweeping us away. We are happy that you continue to recognize us and our contributions, even after so many anonymous exhibitions.

We could grant you a certificate of co-existence for a perpetual loan of our collection to be exhibited permanently, under the terms agreed to respect our rights! We have lived on earth for more than 380 million years, while some of you humans, only 200 thousand years. Can the minority learn to live with the majority of us? We are the 95% of all animals on planet earth asking for the right to weave synanthropically, yet we are threatened into extinction by such a small number of individuals.

Do not be afraid. Let us move from arachnophobia to arachnophilia by sensing new threads of connectivity, or else face the eternal silence of extinction.

At-ten(t)sion to invertebrate rights!
Signed,
Spider/Webs**

Title: Invertebrate Rights for "Down to Earth"
Year: 13.82020 billion, ABB (After Big Bang)
Co-Author: Spider/webs, Holocnemus Pluchei & Tomás Saraceno,
founding member of Arachnophilia
Edition: Still ongoing but threatened
Material: Dome Spider/Web endemic to Gropius Bau sensed and
felt at 1-300 Hz, sunlight, air, mirror, open letter.
Dimensions: Variable.
Diet: Please do not feed us, we eat just about anything
caught in our webs, including wasps, mosquitos, large jumping
spiders. We survive pandemics.

* Urban Pest acc. http://idtools.org/holocnemus-pluchei
** This letter was translated into English from the original vibrational language of 1-300 Hz thanks to the Arachnophilia.net community and their archives of non-human languages. Tomás Saraceno would like to give special thanks to those working together to give voice to the spiders in their fight against arachnophobia, including the members of Studio Tomás Saraceno, the Arachnophilia, Arachnomancy and Aerocene communities, and the teams of Berliner Festspiele, Martin Gropius Bau, and *Down to Earth*. Join the Arachnophilia Community and sign the petition in support of this open letter at Arachnophilia.net. Let your future be read by a spider/web with the Arachnomancy App.

CITRA SASMITA

Born 1990 in Bali, Indonesia, where she lives and works

Timur Merah Project XII: Rivers With No End

2023

Citra Sasmita is a Balinese multidisciplinary artist, whose work unravels myths and misconceptions about Balinese art and culture with a particular focus on building female-centered narratives that counter colonial legacies. Sasmita's paintings, sculptures, and installations draw from the style of traditional Kamasan painting and its figurative and narrative compositions. Populating masculine mythologies with female protagonists, she reimagines this cultural heritage. Her work was included in Biennale Yogyakarta (2019) and is being presented at the Thailand Biennale in Chiang Rai (2023–24). Sasmita was a Gold Award Winner UOB Painting of the Year in 2017.

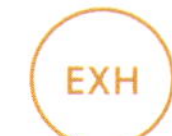

The installation *Timur Merah Project XII: Rivers with No End* (2024) is the most recent iteration of Sasmita's long-running *Timur Merah Project*, which she began in 2019. Meaning "the east is red," the work follows the propagation of maritime Islamic culture across the agrarian Indonesian archipelago and is described by the artist as "a historical pilgrimage and ancestral narrative." Sasmita explores Islam's arrival through sea routes, beginning in the eigth century CE, and specifically the relevance of the port of Nusantara, tracing its influence on both the spiritual and material culture of the region. The work utilizes architectural elements typical of Nusantara, where the historical traces of Islam remain imprinted upon the architecture of the city. In the work, wooden pillars carved in a traditional style with minimalist floral carvings are shown at a horizontal, symbolizing rivers, the flow of knowledge, and the fluid Islamic and Hindi civilization of Bali. Attached to these pillars are embroidered tapestries and flags. The floral tapestries that comprise the work are taken from decorations traditionally found on the sails of ships belonging to the Bugis people.

To produce this work, Sasmita collaborated with a women's community in Jembrana, Negara, West Bali to create the floral embroidery featured hanging from the antique-style pillars of the piece. The first Islamic society developed in Bali was located in Jembrana, Negara, West Bali, and still holds religious and spiritual significance due to this history. The inclusion of this craftwork reflects Sasmita's ongoing commitment to reinserting Balinese women into historical narratives.

Decoration of fishing boats, Perancak, Jembrana, West Bali, 2020

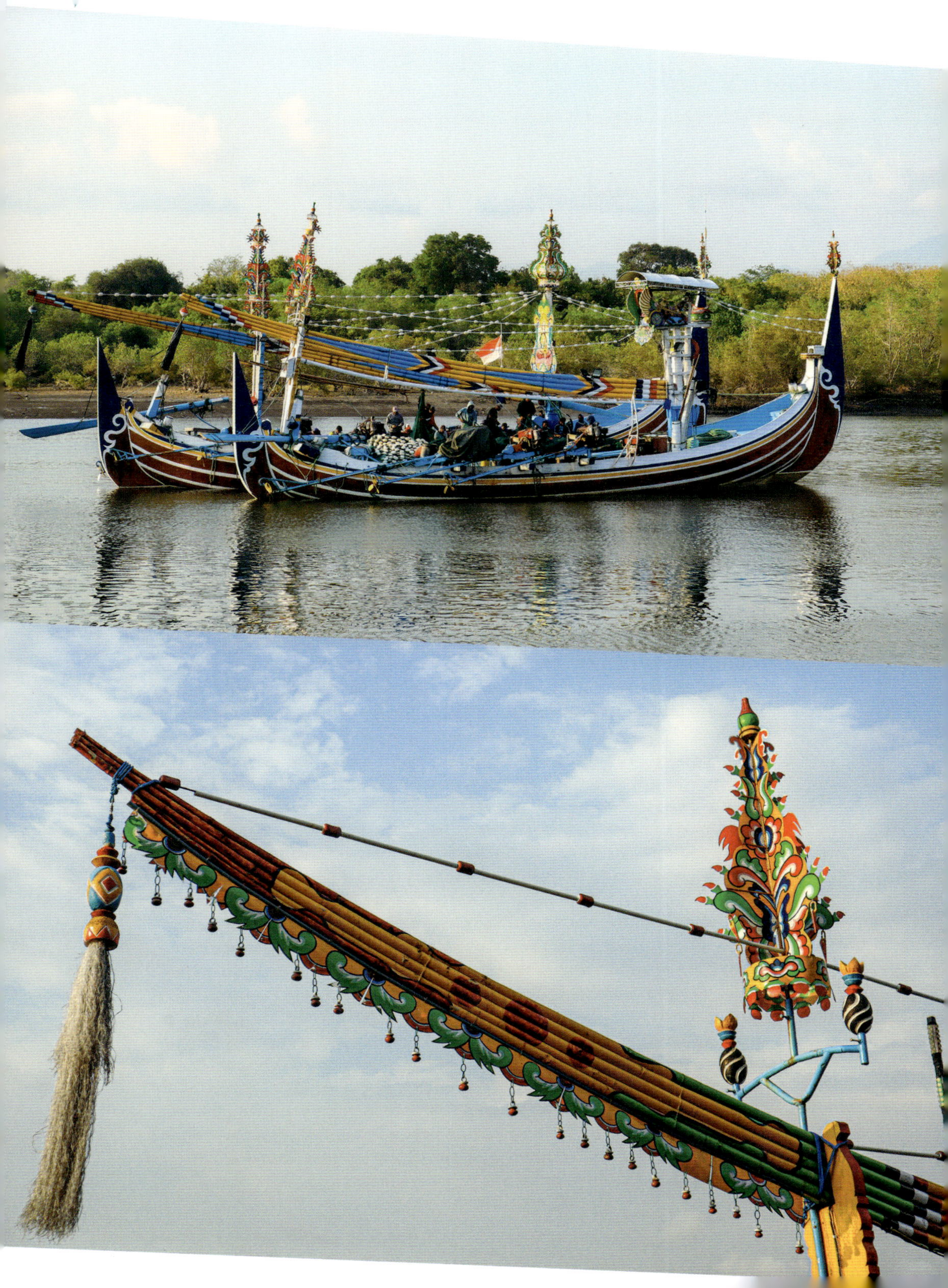

YANG FUDONG

Born 1971 in Beijing, China, lives and works in Shanghai, China

Blue Kylin
2008

On the Double Dragon Hills
2012

Working across film, photography, and installation, Yang Fudong is part of China's pioneering generation of avant-garde contemporary artists who emerged in the 1990s. He first started experimenting with 35 mm film while studying painting at the China Academy of Art in Hangzhou, from which he graduated in 1995. Yang's practice spans a wide spectrum of aesthetic and critical influences, from traditional scroll painting and the golden age of leftist Chinese cinema in 1930s Shanghai to the expressionism of global New Wave cinematic movements. Known for his highly stylized and formally abstract commentaries on historical, social, and political developments, Yang has since shown in prestigious international group shows such as the Sharjah Biennial (2013), the Venice Biennale (2003, 2007), and documenta11 (2002), and has had numerous solo institutional surveys.

A pivotal period of Yang's genre-defying photographic and filmic practice was the making of his first feature film, *An Estranged Paradise*, which he first shot in 1997 but only completed in 2002, when it was shown as part of documenta11. It followed the life of a disillusioned young Chinese intellectual in Hangzhou, plagued by an unnamed malaise of profound discontentment shared by many youths of his post–Cold War generation. With the same documentarian eye to the quotidian while reflecting the unsettling atmosphere of China's rapid modernization, Yang's *On the Double Dragon Hills* (2012), which is presented here, records the livelihoods of stone craftsmen in Shandong Province, an area known for its rich natural abundance of bluestone, which is seen as a signifier and bringer of prosperity in China.

The film portrays the routine labor of workmen in one of the region's stone quarries. Their unscripted movements, from handling machinery to standing or sitting and resting, take on the quality of theater, a choreography that unfolds before the backdrop of the quarry's dramatic natural landscape. Yang's edited sequences flit across two screens in silent, black-and-white frames. The unheard loudness of the shown activity starkly contrasts the silence of the artist's double-channel composition—underscoring the film as both a documentary and carefully crafted, artistic work. Together with two photographs from Yang's earlier series *Blue Kylin* (2008), also documenting the quarry, the film offers a window into the livelihoods and performances of labor that have defined China's participation in the globalized economy.

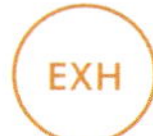

Above and below: Blue Kylin, 2008

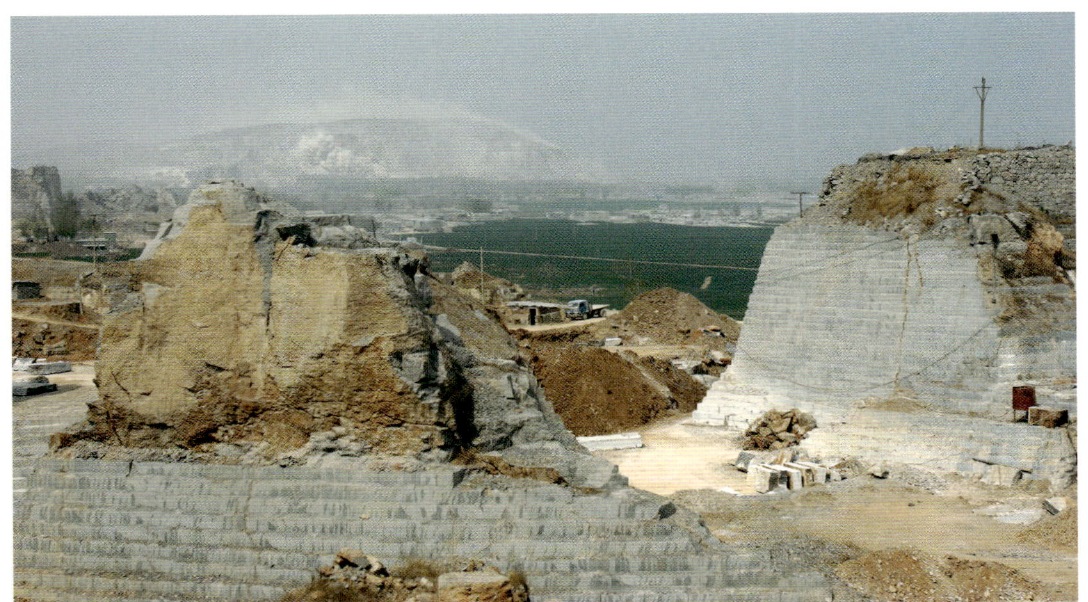

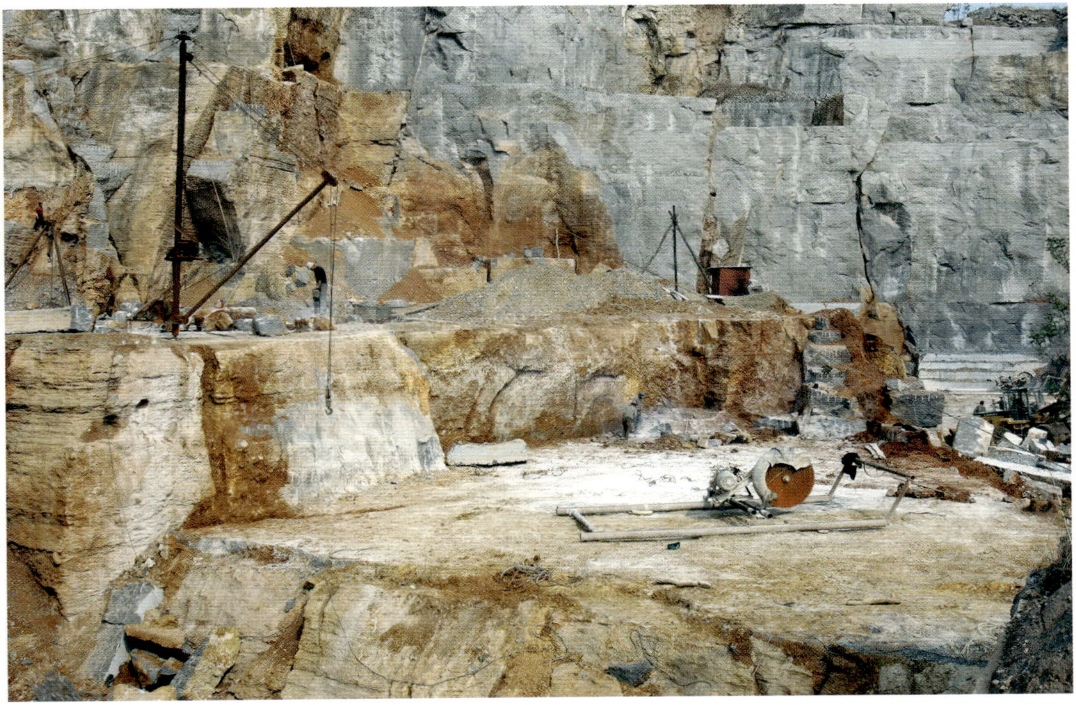

EXHIBITION HALL B6

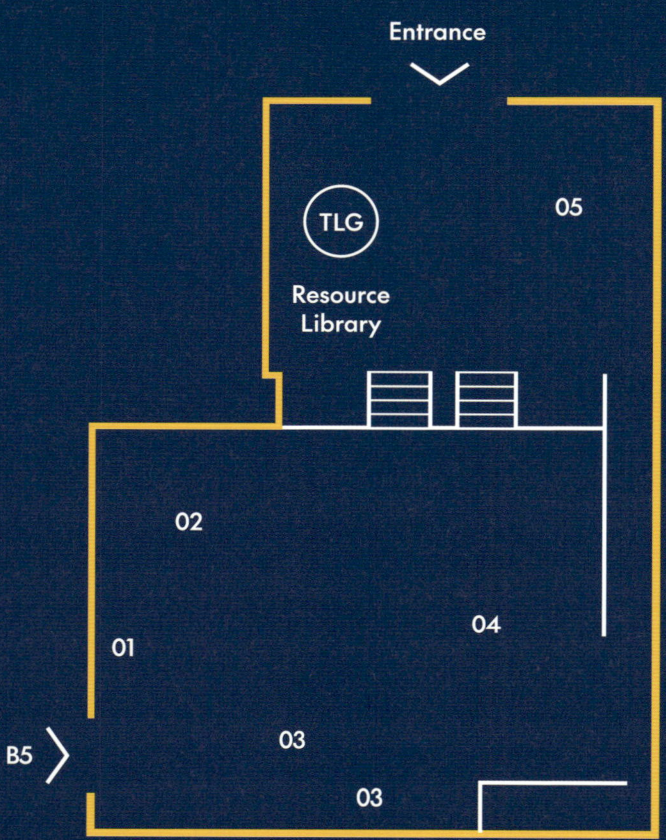

01   Priyageetha Dia / p. 190
02   Tania Mouraud / p. 192
03   Seher Shah / p. 194
04   Tang Da Wu / p. 196
05   Mona Vătămanu & Florin Tudor / p. 198

TIME AND SPACE

The featured works provide a critical perspective on our built and urbanized environment. Large-scale installations reflect on the absurdity of technocracy, while another encompasses a meditative space and soundscape providing room for retreat. Graphite-dust drawings deconstruct the aesthetics of brutalist architecture, and relics from the past question what heritage and conservation means for the writing of history.

On an elevated floor, mirroring the stories and histories unfolded in the beginning of the exhibition parcour, a platform covered with historical kilims serves as a space for social gatherings and conversations. This space marks both an ending point and an embarkation as underscored through the tree of life motif in which every ending is also a beginning.

The hall's open library is an invitation to engage more deeply with the featured works of art and the topics suggested in *After Rain*. It invites the visitors to allow deeper reflection of what they experienced through the journey created by this Biennale.

PRIYAGEETHA DIA

Born 1992 in Singapore, where she lives and works

Spectre System
2024

Mesh: Prelude to Spectre System
2024

Through site-specific interventions, speculative narratives, and acts of appropriation, Priyageetha Dia addresses the plantation histories of Southeast Asia and their contemporary legacies. Dia studied fine art at LASALLE College of the Arts in Singapore. Working with computer-generated imagery (CGI), Dia has developed a digital vocabulary that traces the links between technology, labor, and environmental destruction. Her sensorial environments translate colonial histories into a space of visceral experience.

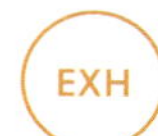

Employing 3D animation and game-engine software, *Spectre System* (2024) marks a new chapter in the artist's research on plantation corporatism and labor migration on the Malay Peninsula. One of the British Empire's most profitable colonies and the world's largest exporter of rubber in the mid-nineteenth century and early twentieth century Malaya relied on the indentured labor of hundreds of thousands of workers from South India. Such socioeconomic structures have persisted in the region's longstanding sugarcane and rubber production and endure in other cash crops, such as palm oil. Building on previous animations by the artist, the work creates a space where the real and imaginary merge; the psyche of labor, environment, and capital intersect. A computer-generated, elusive protagonist conjures memories of the land, people, and other entities. Morphing into the space, the figure reveals the terrain as a repository of memory and site of racialized dispossession—a geology of histories and stories. These memories and artifacts gradually break down into data and information, and an arc is spanned from the colonial labor of the past to the digital economies of the present.

The animation extends into the physical space through a large vinyl print on the wall, *Mesh: Prelude to Spectre System* (2024). Images of elongated hands with gleaming skin seem to guide, embrace, or entrap viewers. Through this immersive vinyl, the artist strives to dissolve the boundaries between the body and space. The gesture underscores to what extent the environment we inhabit is a container of countless histories and handprints.

Video still from *Spectre System*, 2024

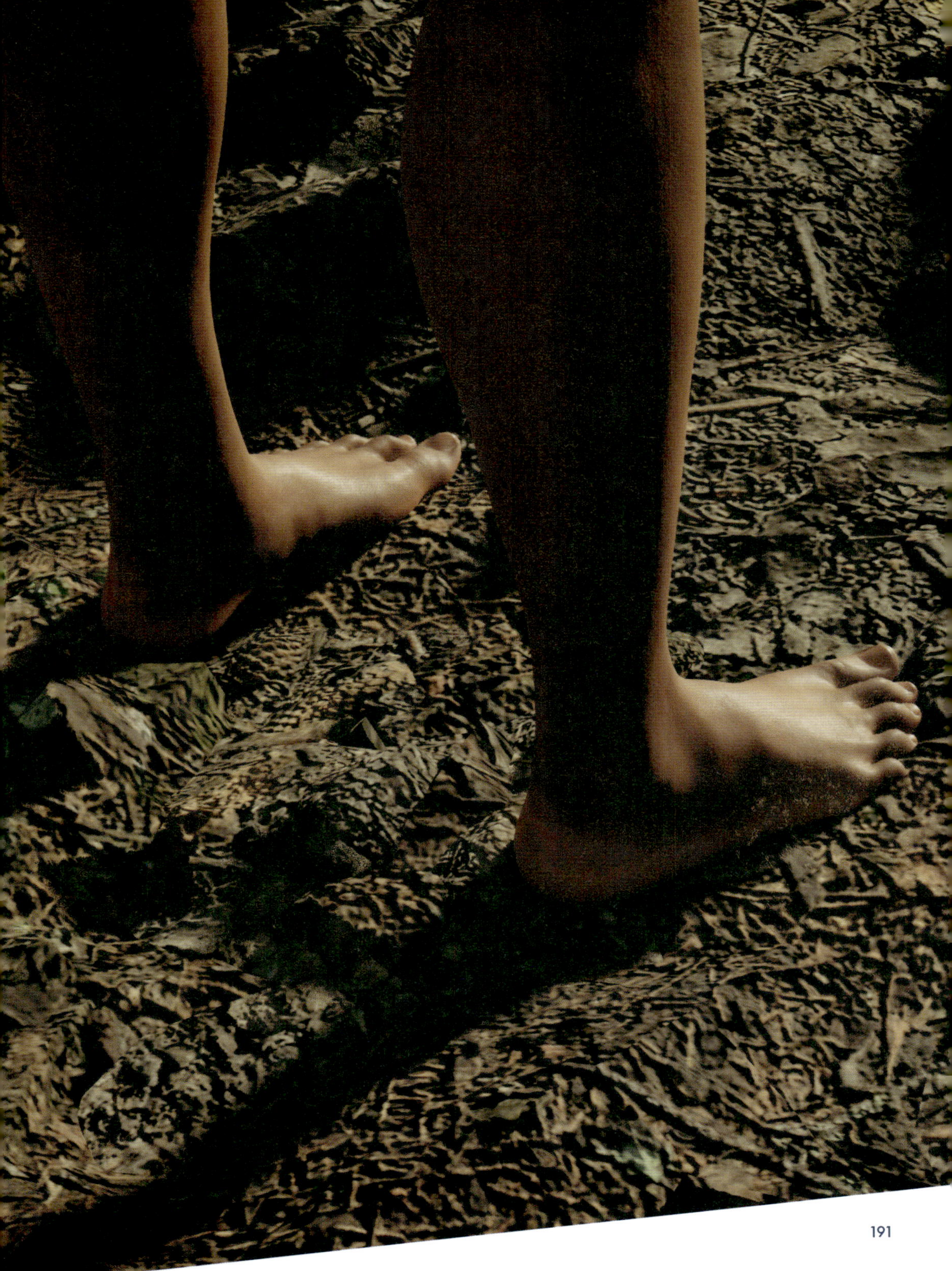

TANIA MOURAUD

Born 1942 in Paris, France, where she lives and works

Initiation Room N°2
1971/2022/2024

Tania Mouraud's extensive body of work—ranging from painting to
public art, conceptual writing, installation, videos, sonic works, and
performances—has addressed artistic and humanistic themes, such
as the plasticity of language and the individual's own perception and
self-awareness, as well as a broader set of ethical and sociopolitical
issues, confronting persistent inequalities and our treatment of the
environment. A key figure of contemporary French art, Mouraud has
engaged with diverse art scenes, vocabularies, and movements, thus
evading any facile classification of her practice. She has exhibited in
countless individual and collective exhibitions across the globe and
has permanent installations at prestigious institutions such as the
Centre Pompidou in Paris and the Collection FRAC Lorraine in Metz.

In 1969 the artist began creating so-called initiation rooms: psychosensorial
environments that could be built within homes or public buildings as places
of refuge to escape the hectic rhythm of the outside world. An early iteration
of this series in 1970 featured a cavity in the floor that corresponded to the
dimensions of Mouraud's own body: "I am building a world where I could die in
peace," she stoically declared. Inspired by a Tang Dynasty statue of the Buddha,
Initiation Room N° 2 (1971/2022/2024) is a low-ceilinged, luminous white space
that beckons visitors to sit inside in quiet contemplation. The effect of the diffused
lighting along with the reflective quality of the glossy white paint applied to the
walls, floor, and ceiling creates the illusion of an infinite space—a metaphor for
the expanded human consciousness said to result from the practice of meditation.
To help facilitate this state of quiet wakefulness, the peaceful, hypnotic sound
of a 200-hertz sine wave is continuously emitted throughout the room, its tone
varying slightly according to the movement of bodies as they enter and exit.
Mouraud's installation is a generous, participatory work of art, meant not to be
looked at (and admired), but rather to provide an immersive experience that
allows us, the viewers, to look within ourselves.

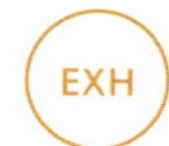

Interior of the installation *Initiation Room N°2*, 2022

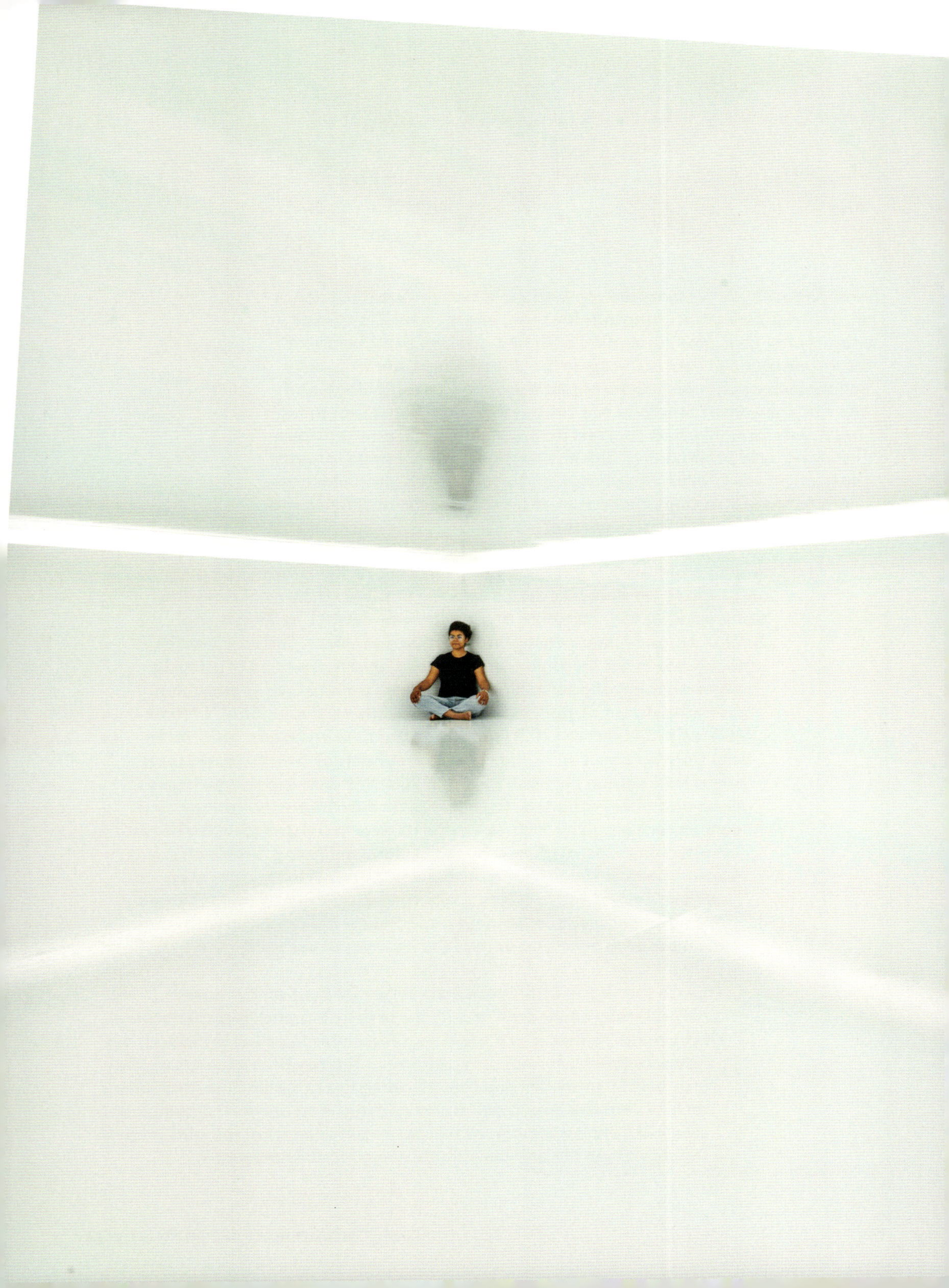

SEHER SHAH

Born 1975 in Karachi, Pakistan, lives and works in Barcelona, Spain

Notes from a City Unknown
2021

Of Dust and Measure (5–9)
2019–21

Seher Shah adapts the tools and conventions of architecture (graphite, ink, paper, perspective, plan, and elevation) into an artistic language uniquely her own. Having studied both fine arts and architecture at the Rhode Island School of Design in the United States, her long-term collaborations with architectural photographer Randhir Singh and the Glasgow Print Studio in the United Kingdom represent meeting points for her varied interests across architecture, photography, drawing, and printmaking. She has engaged monumental formats in her past work, which have ranged from large-scale graphite drawings to series in various media that deconstructed the aesthetics and ideologies of Brutalist architecture.

Shah's recent work is more intimate, focusing on the overlooked gaps and ruptures in domestic space and the familiar rhythms of daily life, while working with literature and poetry—by Jorge Luis Borges, Agha Shahid Ali, and others—for both inspiration and solace. This turn inwards coincided with her time living in New Delhi, during a period of growing authoritarianism and surveillance. It was both an act of self-preservation and of resistance. A portfolio of screen prints on paper, Shah's *Notes from a City Unknown* (2021) reflects on her time in the city. Inspired by Italo Calvino's *Invisible Cities* (1972), it consists of twenty-seven short poetic texts written between 2014 and 2021 that weave personal impressions and observations with reflections on architecture, history, and contemporary politics. Each spare but allusive text is paired with a heavy architectonic abstraction, a juxtaposition continuing Shah's ongoing explorations of weight—of a mark, of a shape, of language, of history. In this prismatic portrait, New Delhi remains unnamed and, ultimately, incomprehensible, a contentious and complex palimpsest in wich current injustices both echo and exceed the traumas of the past.

Though the line in Shah's drawing series *Of Dust and Measure (5–9)* (2019–21) references both architectural drawing and musical notation, it structures neither space nor time. Often interrupted or deflected, it is instead a tool for formal play, serving as figure within grounds of misty gray built up gradually and carefully using fine graphite dust. Meditations on how we mark time, these drawings are poised between accumulation and inscription, memory, and history—between what remains unquantifiable about life and our stubborn need to still measure it.

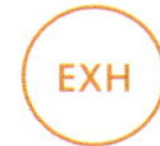

Of Dust and Measure (8), from the series Of Dust and Measure (5–9), 2019–21

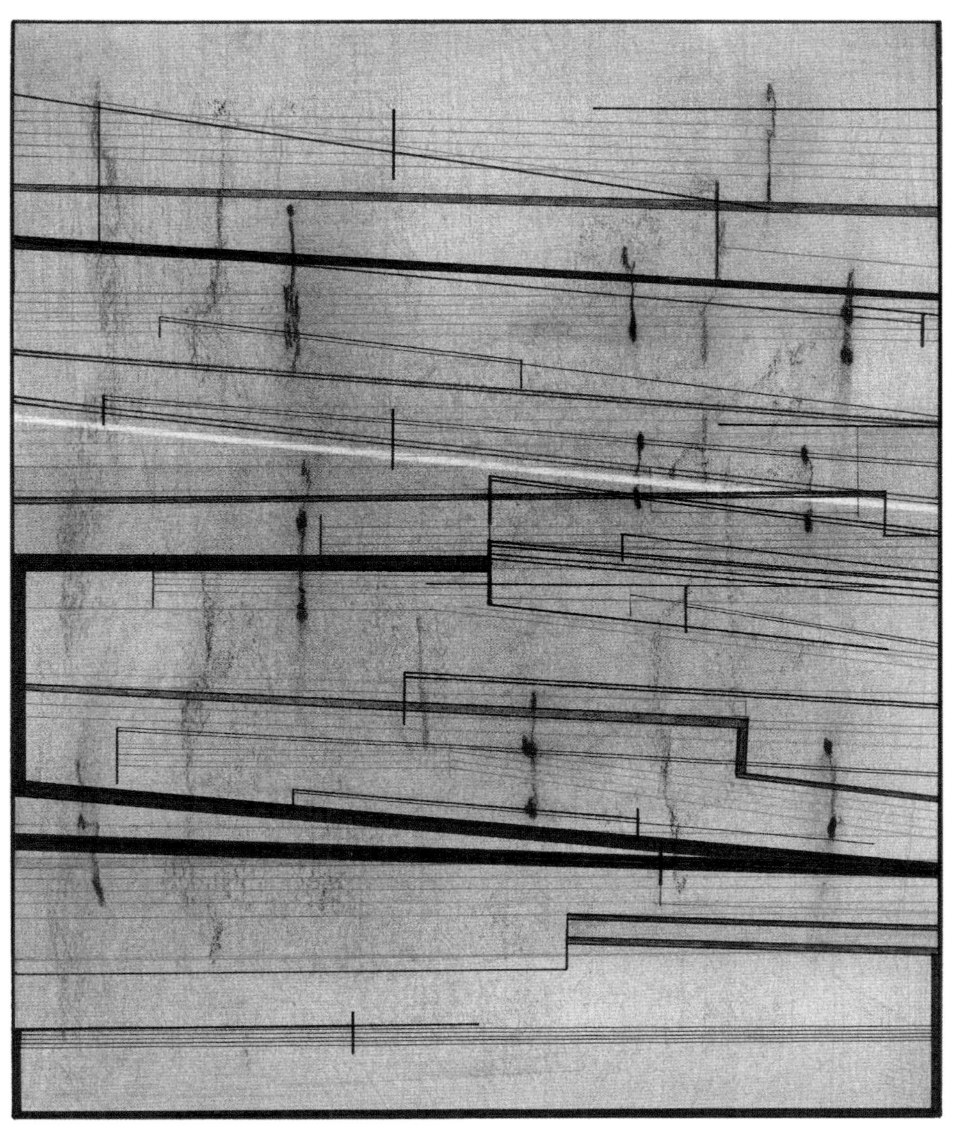

TANG DA WU

Born 1943 in Singapore, where he lives and works

On Tuesday the Delivery Vehicle Number is ER II, and on Monday is BG I
2022

Tang Da Wu has been a prominent and tireless presence in the development of Singapore's contemporary art scene since the 1970s. Over his five-decade-long career, he has moved between painting, drawing, installation, and performance. He studied sculpture at Birmingham Polytechnic and Central Saint Martins, eventually receiving an MFA from Goldsmiths, University of London, in 1985. In 1988 he founded The Artists Village, a collective promoting experimental art, originally at an artists' colony on a farm—the first organization of its kind in Singapore. In his work he explores social and environmental concerns, including deforestation, extinction, and urban transformation. Tang has taught at Singapore's National Institute of Education for the past twenty-plus years.

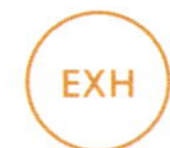

In his work Tang draws upon local mythologies and art history to explore societal issues. His featured large-scale installation alludes to the idea of the wagon as a messenger and vehicle of progress. Six large scrolls of paper hang loosely from the ceiling; their eerie blankness hints at a warning from the sky. The metal cart is deconstructed in space and time, consisting of three parts: one pair of large wheels and two pairs of smaller ones, each set seeming to be moving at different speeds. The bureaucratically intoned title *On Tuesday the Delivery Vehicle Number is ER II, and on Monday is BG I* (2022) suggests a certain absurdity to governing processes and administrative minutiae, even as it poetically inverts the order of the days. Scattered around, glass structures reflect the audience into the sculpture, implicating them as part of the collective body.

The artist's play on usual arrangements and objects highlights a sense of confusion in a society undergoing rapid change. Since its independence in 1965, Singapore has been expanding continuously. Rehousing programs have dismantled entire communities. Here, the transformations of globalization have been exceptionally rapid and, for many, devastating. As Tang warns in many of his works, human activity is destroying the planet we inhabit; the wheels of cause and effect have been set in motion, moving us not toward a brighter future but, in fact, death.

Installation view of *On Tuesday the Delivery Vehicle Number is ER II, and on Monday is BG I*, from the exhibition *Art School SG: This One is Dangerous* at Nanyang Academy of Fine Arts, Singapore, 2022

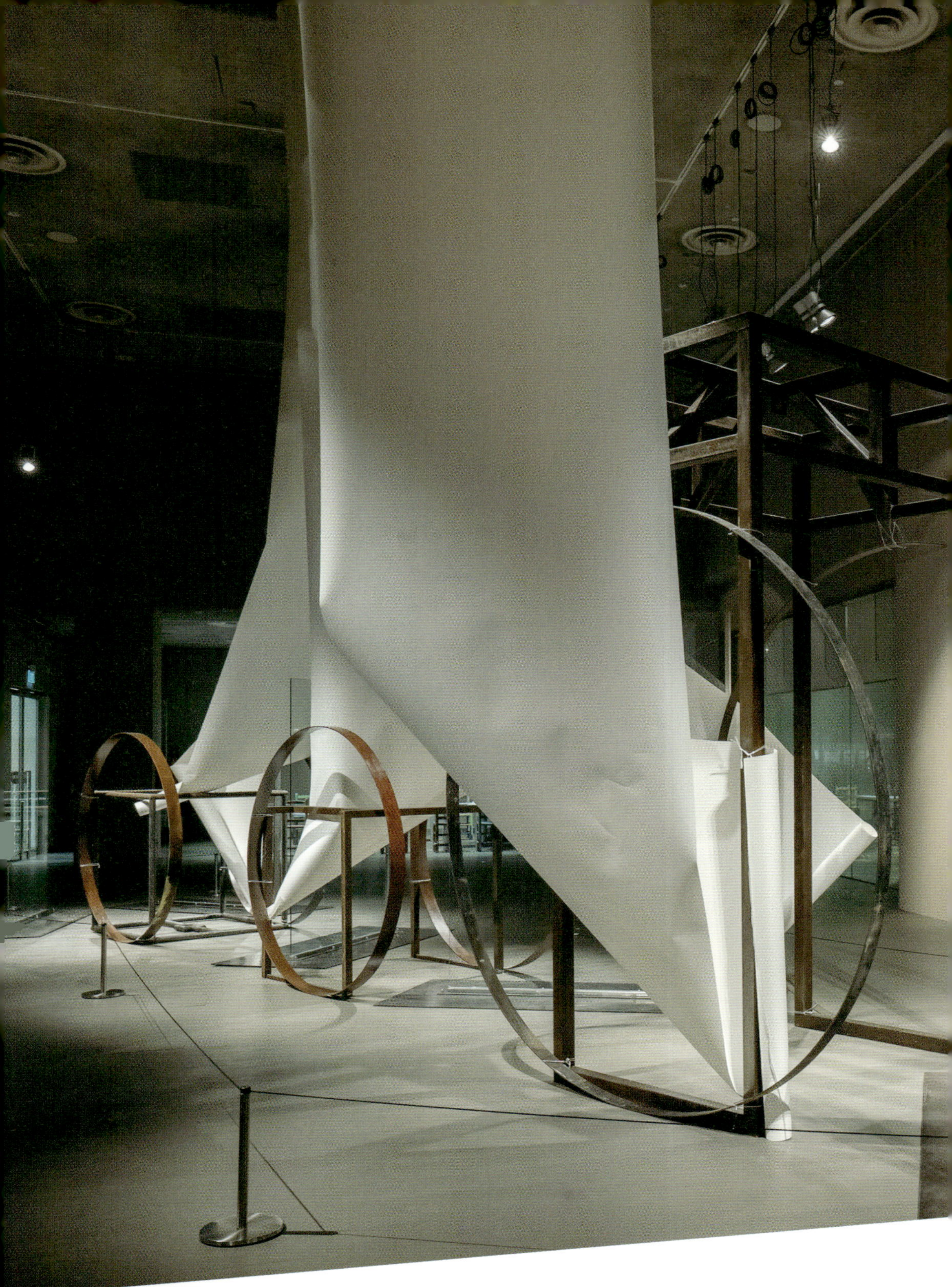

MONA VĂTĂMANU & FLORIN TUDOR

Mona Vătămanu, born 1968 in Constanta, Romania, lives and works in Bucharest, Romania
Florin Tudor, born 1974 in Geneva, Switzerland, lives and works in Bucharest, Romania

The Tree of Life / How Do We Read Signs We Cannot Understand?

2023 / Activations on February 20 and May 24, 2024

Working together for over two decades, Mona Vătămanu and Florin Tudor address the theme of history in films, installations, and performative actions that revisit ideologies, utopias, and grand modernist projects. Their collaborative work traces the impressions that past ideologies have left on architecture and living environments, which underlie the shifting conditions and injustices of the present. Defining their artistic process is an intellectual affinity with various critical thinkers, historians, and philosophers that connects their inquiries to broader cultural discourses and global concerns. Their work has recently been shown in the 5th Kyiv Biennial, Vienna (2023), the Kathmandu Triennale 2077 (2022), and the Baltic Triennial 14, Vilnius (2021).

The Tree of Life / How Do We Read Signs We Cannot Understand? (2023) is an installation embodying what art can do at its best: create a space for reflection at the meeting point of different cultures and historical experiences. The artists refer to the installation as "the idea of a school under a tree." Various kilims and woven rugs spread across the floor welcome visitors to sit and rest. Collected from different regions of the Balkans and Central and Western Asia, the rugs share a distinct iconography present in many cultures and geographies throughout time, the archaic motif of the "tree of life," in which a central, majestic tree is portrayed as the source of vitality and nourishment. For example, a kilim, most likely from Dobruja, a region bordering the Black Sea, features an emblematic composition: depicted upright, the tree trunk occupies the central part of the rug, with its emanating branches laden with birds and fruits, while a multitude of eyes or stylized scorpions at the edges of the kilim ward off evil spirits.

Resonating with the function of a traditional *majlis*, the cultural and social space of community gatherings across the Arab peninsula, the installation is activated throughout the Biennale as a meeting point for conversations around ways of living together in a dire time of climate change and war. This series of events derives from a workshop conducted by the artists within the Biennale Encounters program, which explored the symbolism of the tree from an ecological perspective as well as the making of kilims, a textile tradition deeply connected to the livelihoods of nomadic communities.

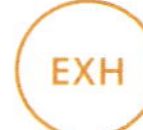
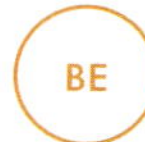

Installation view of *The Tree of Life / How Do We Read Signs We Cannot Understand?*, from the exhibition *Chronic Desire – Sete Cronica* at Corneliu Miklosi Museum, Timișoara, Romania, 2023

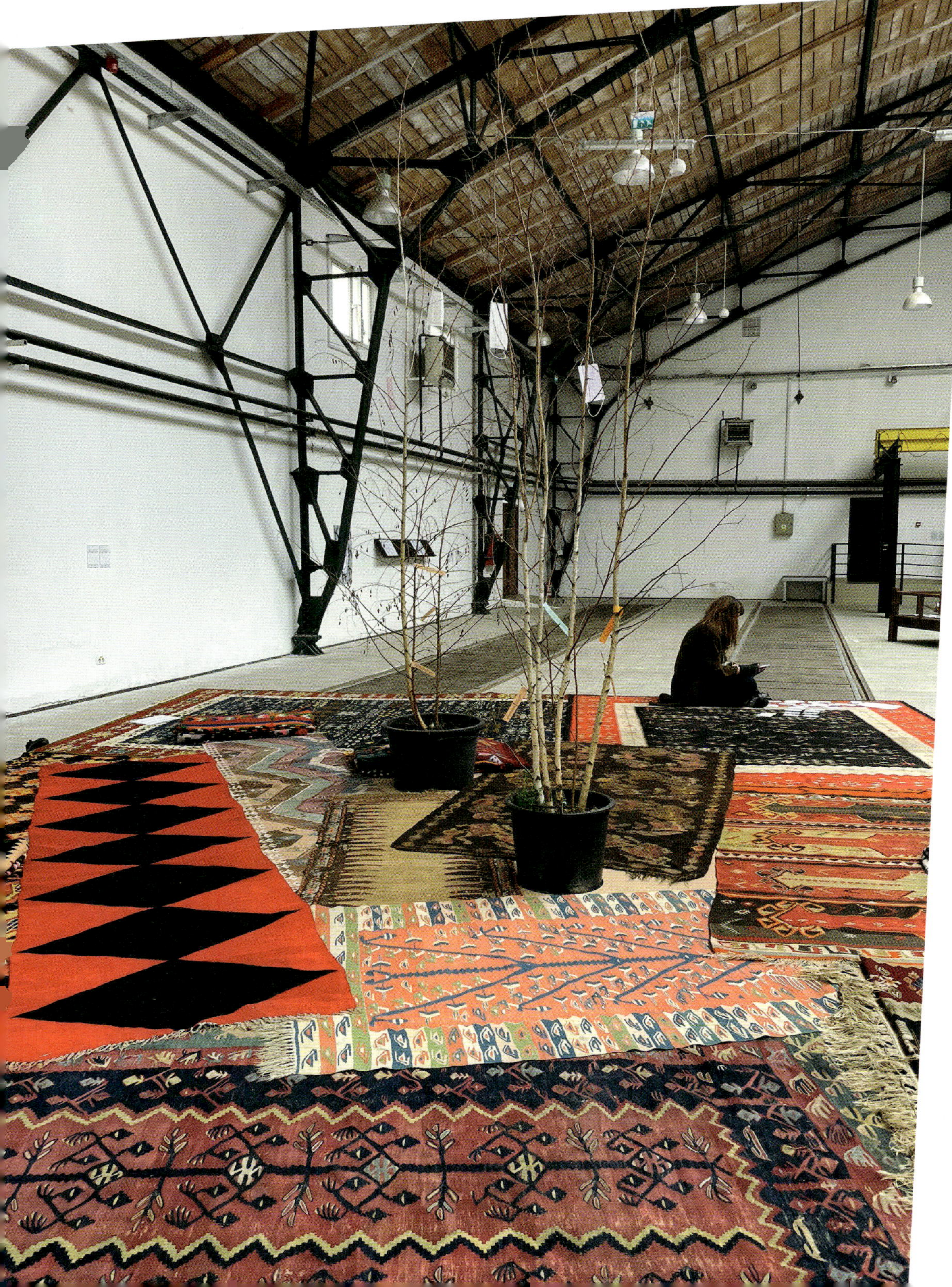

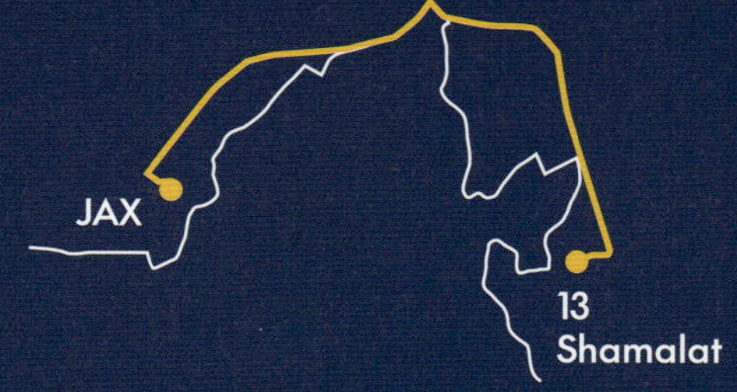

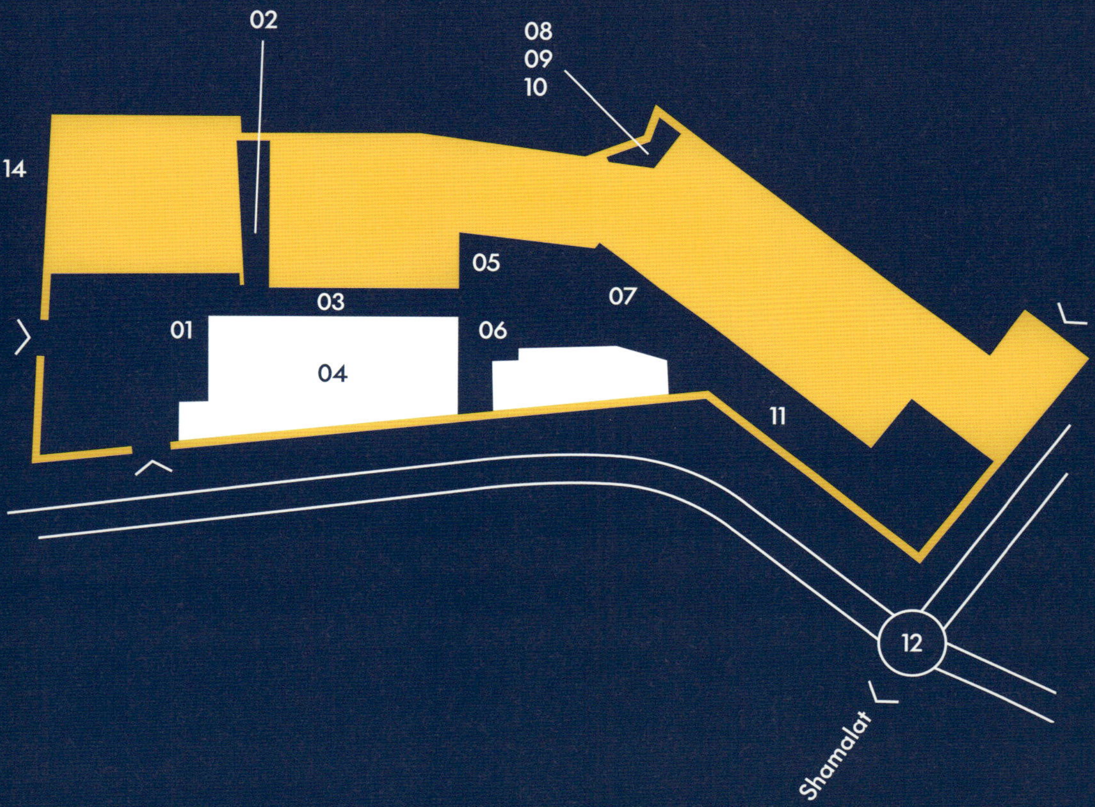

Courtyards and Terraces

Off-site

ELEMENTAL AND COMMUNAL

Multiple commissioned projects presented on the terraces and outdoor spaces of the JAX District are both works of art and social spaces. Ranging from a communal kitchen to a juice bar, various ways to provide shaded sites to gather are introduced. Reflected in these projects are the basic human need for shelter and food. These also serve as sites that embody our wishes and aspirations, constituting spaces of enjoyment and play. Engaging a multitude of senses, including the experience of texture, taste, and smell, the visitor once again becomes an integral part of the work of art. This approach extends to works presented elsewhere in Diriyah. At Shamalat, an artist-initiated cultural center in Old Diriyah, visitors are invited to take a walk that talks in a poetic way about the potential of the traditional use of local medicinal plants. Native flora to the Najd region is also highlighted in a communal dinner that takes place one night.

AZRA AKŠAMIJA

Born 1976 in Sarajevo, Bosnia and Herzegovina, lives and works in
Boston, MA, United States

Abundance & Scarcity

2024

Azra Akšamija is an artist and architectural historian whose artistic
practice and academic research leverages critical methods to restore the
social value of cultural heritage. In her multidisciplinary work, Akšamija
embodies the politics of identity and memory into objects such as clothing and wearable technologies. Her recent research work focuses on
the representation of Islam in the West. She is the director of the Future
Heritage Lab and the Art, Culture and Technology program, both at
MIT. She has not only published widely but has also recently shown
her work in major international exhibitions, including the 17th Venice
Architecture Biennale (2021), The Aga Khan Museum, Toronto (2020),
and Kunsthaus Graz (2019).

Situated on an outdoor terrace, the commissioned work *Abundance
& Scarcity* (2024) consists of a shading canopy made of refugee blan-
kets and felt recycled from the 2023 Islamic Arts Biennale in Jeddah.
Particularly suited for extreme environmental conditions of the desert,
its construction is based on a modular textile system borrowed from
the Saudi Arabian fabric known as *bisht*, traditionally made from goat
wool and camel hair. These textile components are arranged in strips
and sewn into larger coverings, which are spanned over a simple metal
frame. The effect is a vibrantly colored pavilion. As a shelter made of
cloth, it is also inspired by the traditions of nomadic cultures, including
Saudi Arabian nomadic tribes. Sculptural and decorative elements
are created by a technique of slashing, folding, and reverse appliqué.
In collaboration with local plant experts, native desert plants such as
medicinal plants, spices, and fragrant flora are integrated into the installation in sewn-in sachets of potpourri, which generate a refreshing scent.

Abundance & Scarcity is rooted in Akšamija's notion of performative
preservation, which prioritizes the revitalization of living social practices
that underpin the creation of material artifacts and monuments. Beyond
the exhibition, the surplus felt fabric will be donated to refugee camps,
allowing the artwork to continue its environmental and social mission
post-exhibition. This initiative underscores the transformative role of
art in advocating positive practices and interventions to address both
societal challenges and environmental issues. Akšamija's approach as
a whole is committed to addressing the complex challenges faced by
communities affected by conflict, displacement, and ecological crises.

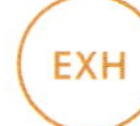
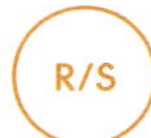

Above: Rendering for the project *Abundance & Scarcity*, 2023
Below: Photomontage of cloth for the project *Abundance & Scarcity*, 2023

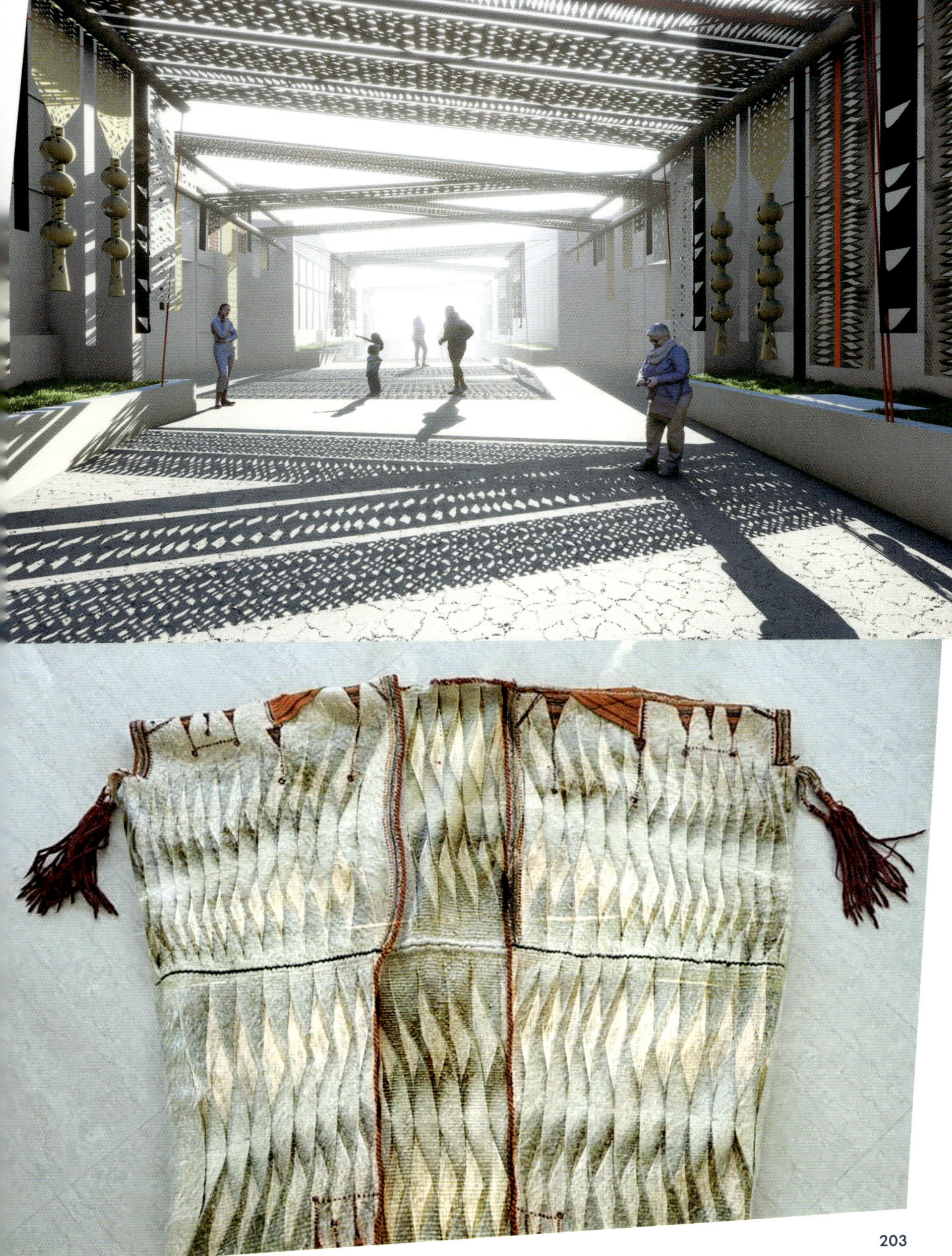

MOHAMMAD ALFARAJ

Born 1993 in Al Ahsa, Saudi Arabia, where he lives and works

The Whispers of Today Are Heard in the Garden of Tomorrow

2024

Mohammad AlFaraj is an artist, film director, storyteller, and writer, who graduated with a BA in mechanical engineering from King Fahd University of Petroleum and Minerals (KFUPM) in Dhahran in 2017. After his studies, he began turning his attention to the natural world and making art steeped in metaphor, drawing on agricultural practices, oral histories, and legends recorded from the elders of his community. Fantastical creatures as well as the fauna and flora of his environment appear in his work. By using local and natural materials, such as soil, palm fronds, and date extracts, AlFaraj conveys a deep-rooted connection to the oasis of Al Ahsa, where he was born and raised and where much of his exploration began.

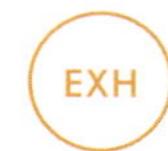

The Whispers of Today Are Heard in the Garden of Tomorrow (2024) is a newly commissioned work installed outdoors, which comprises sculptures, drawings made with natural materials, and photographs installed in a wooden pavilion enclosed on all sides with the heavy tarps typically used in agriculture. The floor is covered with soil. Recreating the environment of an open field, the setting reflects AlFaraj's conception of life and human history as a garden filled with memories and experiences. Like the plants, trees, and creatures that populate it, this metaphorical garden needs nurturing and care to enable beauty and goodness to flourish. Elements from a previous work, *Fossils of Knowledge* (2020), have been placed on the floor. Made from palm branches, they recall the backbones or fossils of large animals, and for the artist they are a eulogy to a past that needs to be overcome. New sculptures—made of sprouting baby palms covered in a mix of date syrup and gum arabic and then sealed with resin—sit on metal plinths, rising to the sky to suggest rejuvenation and growth. The walls are covered with drawings and ghostly imprints of words. For AlFaraj, the essence of the work is a deconstruction of the past to build the future. Past, present, and future form a dynamic continuum of shared responsibility and hope.

Research photo for the sculpture *The dancer who never stops,* from the series *New Palm,* Al Ahsa, Saudi Arabia, 2022

DIRIYAH CONTEMPORARY ART BIENNALE 2024

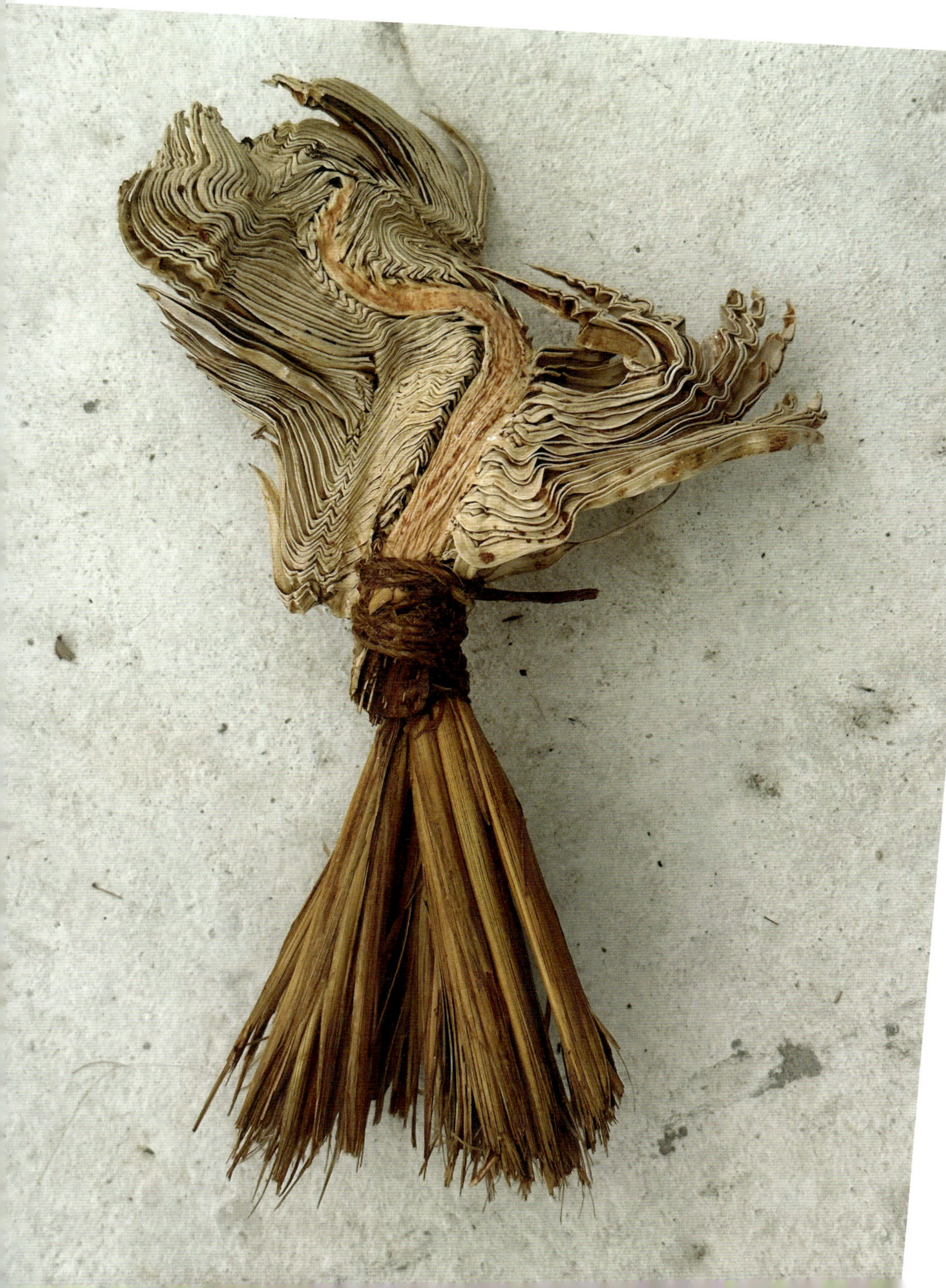

BRITTO ARTS TRUST

Established 2002 in Dhaka, Bangladesh

Palan & Pakghor
(The Kitchen Garden & The Social Kitchen)
2024

What started in the living room of artists Tayeba Begum Lipi and Mahbubur Rahman in 2002 as a place for gathering has become a stable organization, which, with the support of the Triangle Network, has filled gaps in the Bangladeshi art scene for over two decades. Britto Arts Trust is now a longstanding artists' collective that operates a permanent space in Dhaka but is active in many places throughout Bangladesh. Fostering artistic practice and community engagement, it offers alternative education programs, where formal structures are absent, and hosts artists' residencies in Dhaka that have facilitated connections between local and international practitioners. During the COVID pandemic, Britto Arts Trust initiated the project *ZERO WASTE—FoodArt* (2020), which involved national and international participants in growing and distributing locally grown foods.

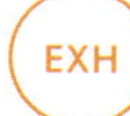

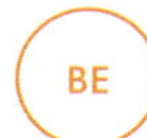

In Diriyah, Britto Arts Trust welcomes visitors into an ecological, social, and diasporic space defined by the structures of the Bengali *palan* and *pakghor*. The *palan* is a traditional kitchen garden usually looked after by women and children, which supplies the *pakghor*, a living-room-like family kitchen. The *palan* grows vegetables and culinary herbs supplied by Alzahrani Farm in Diriyah, while the pakghor is activated by volunteers from different parts of Riyadh, who sign up to cook for Biennale visitors. A further iteration of the project developed for documenta fifteen in 2022, this social space for cooking and gathering has been built in collaboration with Bengali bamboo craftsmen. This renewable material with the strength of steel is integral to the livelihoods of Indigenous communities in the Indian subcontinent. Bamboo stilts, woven panels, dome-shaped rooftops, and other substructures were produced with artisans from the Manikganj district in central Bangladesh, shipped to Saudi Arabia, and assembled on site in Diriyah. The displacement of material evokes other forms of migration and cross-cultural encounters that are integral to this work. Situated outside on one of the terraces of the JAX District, the garden and kitchen of Britto Art Trust provide a space for communal activities and conversation centered around cooking traditions. Welcoming visitors and participants, the project offers food and hospitality to create shared, participatory experiences and informal opportunities for reflecting on cultural identity and difference in a rapidly changing urban environment.

Above: Sketch of Palan & Pakghor, 2023
Below: Working time at Studio Mahbub & Lipi, Hasnabad, Dhaka, Bangladesh, 2023

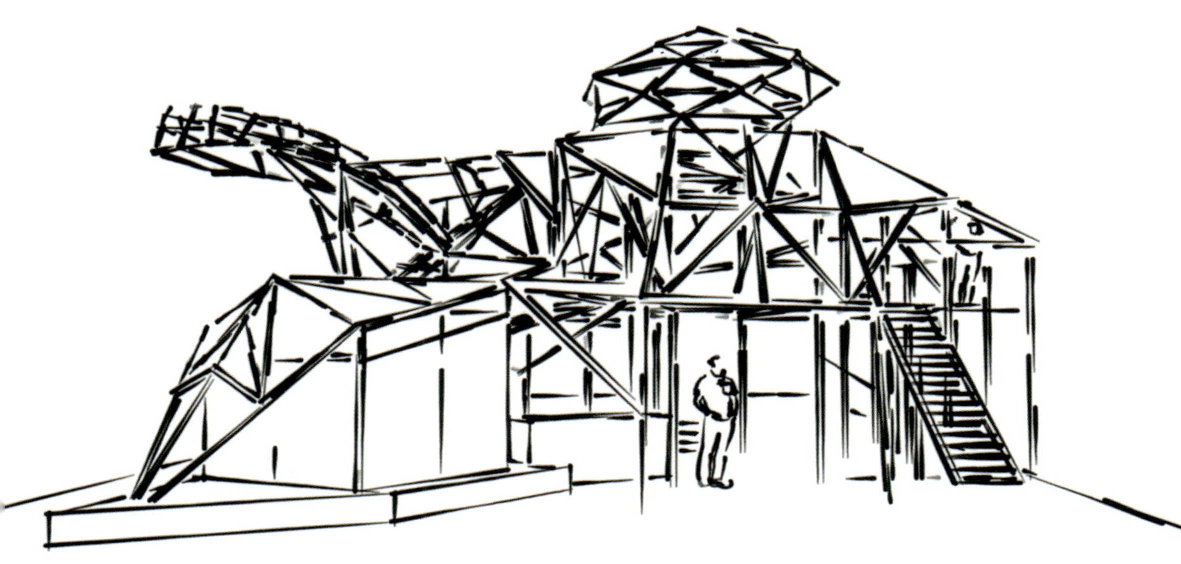

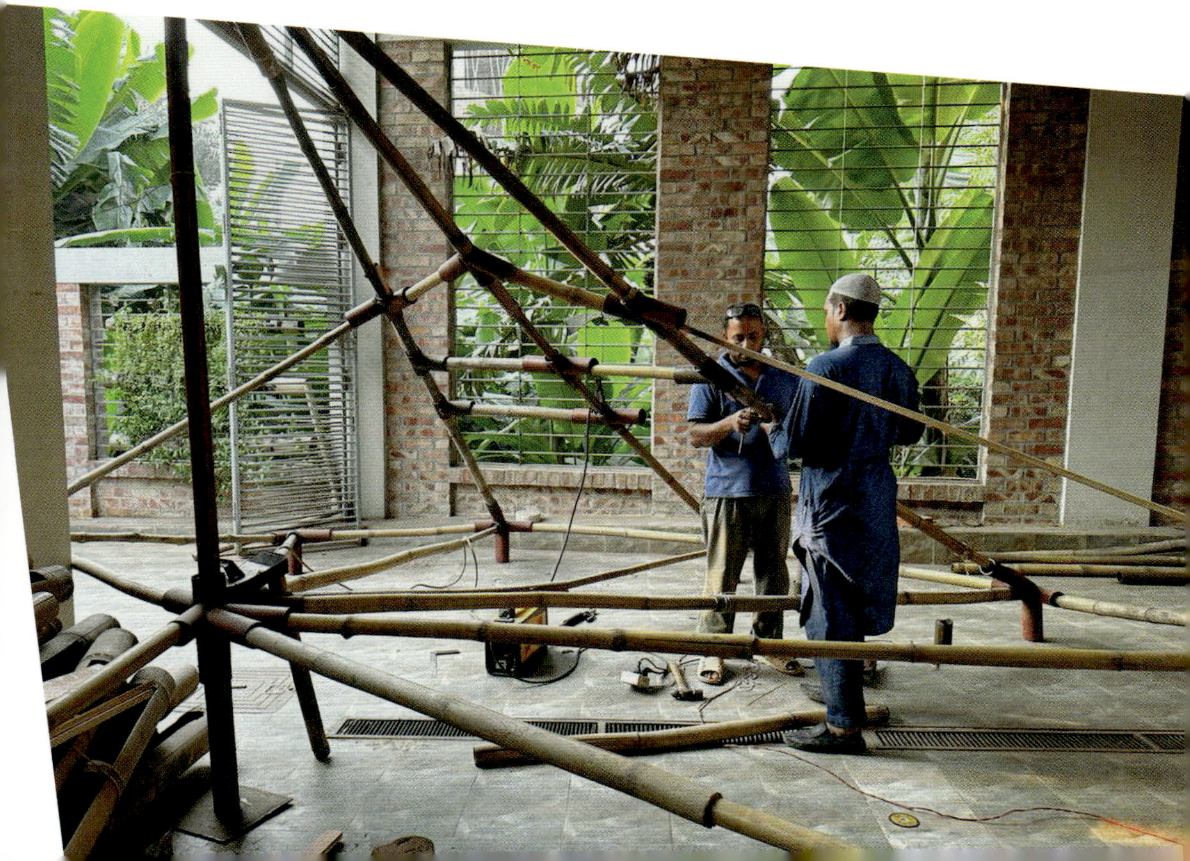

RACHAPORN CHOOCHUEY

Born 1970 in Bangkok, Thailand, where she lives and works

Set the Control for the Heart of the Sun 2.0
2024

Rachaporn Choochuey is the design director of all(zone), which she co-founded in 2009 as a group of Bangkok-based design professionals who are inspired by ever-expanding mega-metropolises and wish to create vernacular environments that can be places of solace and comfort. Choochuey received a BArch from Chulalongkorn University, Bangkok (1993); an MS in Advanced Architectural Design from Columbia University, New York (1998); and a PhD in Architectural History from the University of Tokyo (2002). She was a faculty member at Chulalongkorn University (2002–22), Louis I. Kahn Assistant Visiting Professor at Yale School of Architecture (2022), and she will be an adjunct professor at the Graduate School of Architecture, Planning and Preservation, Columbia University, in 2024. In 2016 all(zone) inaugurated the MAIIAM Contemporary Art Museum in Chiang Mai, which won the Best New Museum of Asia Pacific Award in 2017.

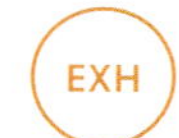

The new commission for the Biennale is a continuation of a series of canopies all(zone) has presented as temporary, mobile architecture since 2017, when they designed *Marmalade Sky* at Wonderfruit festival in Thailand, using translucent fabric to provide shade while effectively coloring the sky. This research was further developed for the 2019 Sharjah Architecture Triennial, where all(zone) created a transitional climatic space to bridge the variation in temperature between the air-conditioned indoor space and the hot exterior by using a passive cooling technique. In 2022 all(zone) was commissioned by the MPavilion in Melbourne, where their goal was to create a meeting place that conveyed a feeling of being under a large tree, with the light coming through its leaves. Three integrated layers of fabric, interwoven into a striking bright-colored waffle pattern, move with the breeze.

In Diriyah, simple steel tent poles hold up a lively canopy. During the day, the shade reduces the air temperature, while during the night, the fabric helps contain the heat that comes from the ground, in both cases optimizing thermal conditions. The porous pattern of the fabric roof creates a light environment, and its temporariness raises questions about the expected life span of architecture in relation to material choices and building methods. For all(zone), the priorities are sustainability and the engagement of the public, who use the created spaces to convene, converse, and celebrate.

Tectonic studies for Set the Control for the Heart of the Sun 2.0, 2024

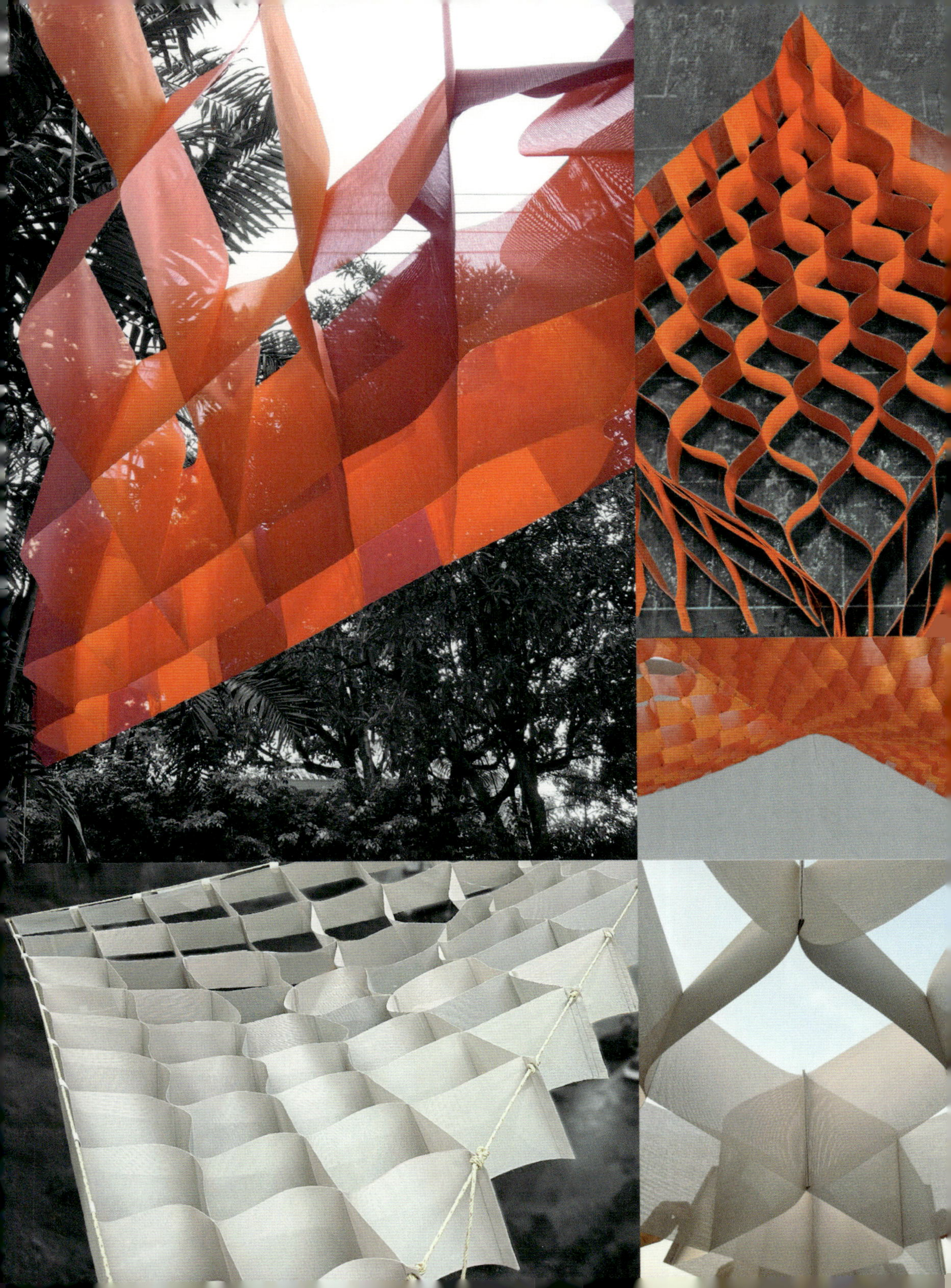

ÂNGELA FERREIRA

Born 1958 in Maputo, Mozambique, lives and works in Lisbon, Portugal

Zip Zap Circus School

2000–ongoing / Activation on February 20, 2024

Born in Mozambique when it was still a Portuguese colony, Ferreira grew up and studied in South Africa, receiving her MFA from the Michaelis School of Fine Art, University of Cape Town. She now teaches fine art at Lisbon University in Portugal. Her background constitutes the root of her work, which probes the relationship between Africa and the West through the lens of European modernism and the twentieth-century technologies of film and radio. Much of her practice centers on modernist architecture within the African continent, which Ferreira uses as a springboard for exploring both the utopian ethos of this global aesthetic movement and its deep entanglement with the European colonialist project.

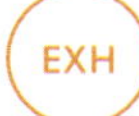
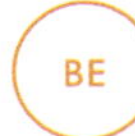

Zip Zap Circus School (2000–ongoing) began life as a material manifestation of an unrealized architectural design from 1994 by Portuguese-Mozambican architect Pancho Guedes (1925–2015): a plan for a possible school to shelter and provide alternative education for children in Cape Town, South Africa, developed at the invitation of a local nongovernmental organization, still operational today, from which Ferreira's work takes its name. Her model of Guedes's unbuilt school references another unfulfilled architectural plan: Mies van der Rohe's (1886–1969) unsuccessful design proposal for the Kröller-Müller Museum in the Netherlands in 1912. Although the German-American architect's design never became a larger-than-life museum, the shadow of its idea existed briefly as a life-size, wood-and-cloth model on wheels—a ghost of a building that never was—parked on the Kröller-Müller country estate and documented by van der Rohe in photographs.

Always rendering a portion of Guedes's original design while retaining the mobile and perishable nature of van der Rohe's model, Ferreira's *Zip Zap Circus School* is remade anew in each location, and then destroyed—"a ruin," in the words of the artist, and a projected utopia that rematerializes each time the work is shown. At times, the tent-like structures are activated by live circus skills workshops, offering a temporary glimpse of the building's original purpose. Revisiting two vastly different and unrealized modernist utopias, Ferreira's work acts as a go-between, while highlighting the tension still spanning contemporary reckonings with histories of settler colonialism, occupation, and democratic emancipation.

Zip Zap Circus School, Foreshore, Cape Town, South Africa, 2002

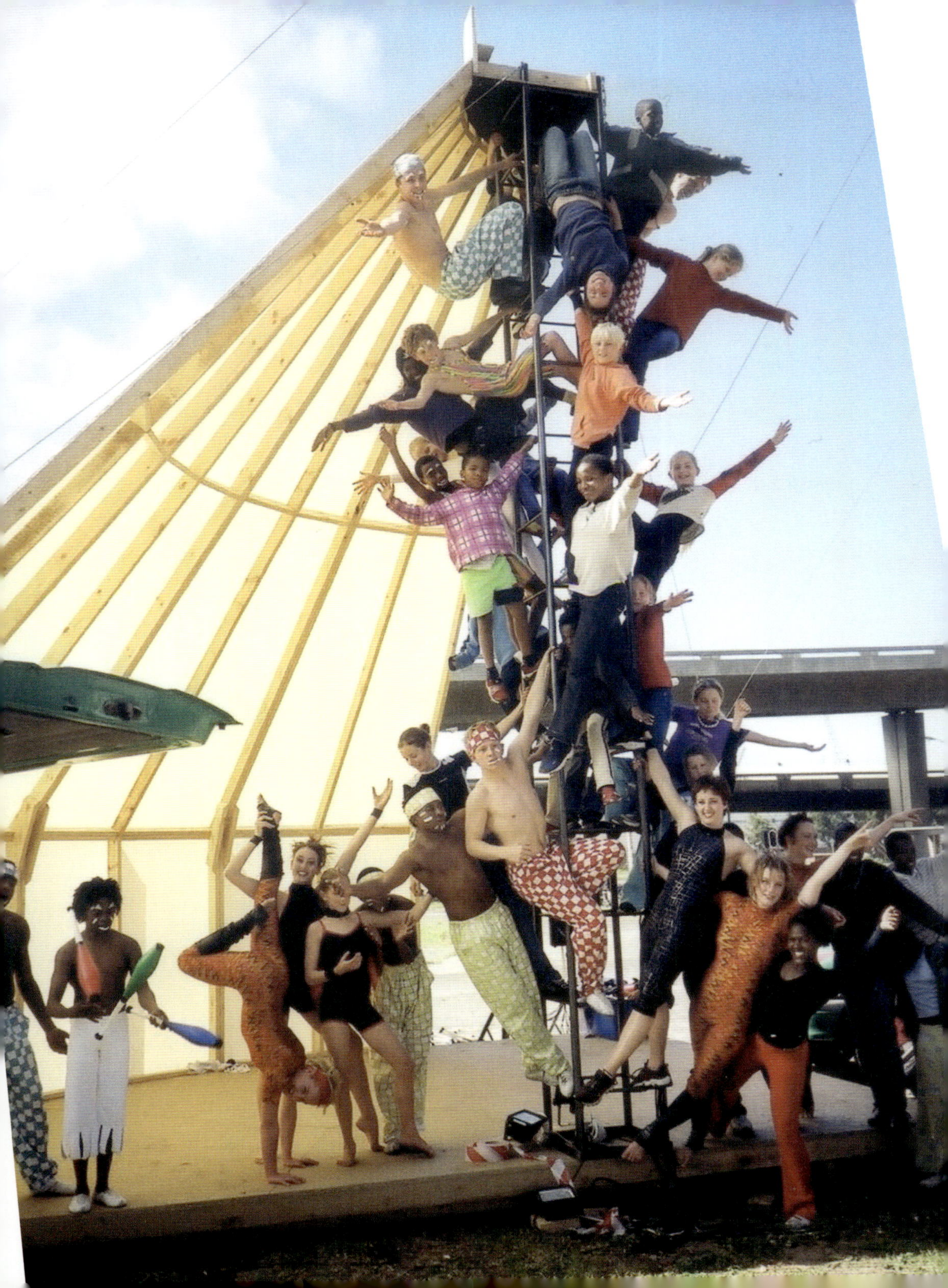

ANNE HOLTROP

Born 1977 in Tiel, the Netherlands, lives and works in Muharraq,
Bahrain and Amsterdam, the Netherlands

Glass to Stone
2024

Anne Holtrop studied architecture at the Academy of Architecture,
Amsterdam University of the Arts, and founded his own studio in
2009, developing a reputation early on with explorations of form
and material in projects like *Trail House* (2009) and *Batara* (2013).
After winning the competition to design the Bahrain Pavilion at the
Milan Expo 2015, Holtrop set up an office in Muharraq, Bahrain. He
has subsequently been involved in numerous cultural projects in the
Arabian Gulf, most notably the UNESCO-listed Bahrain Pearling Path
projects and the Misk Art Institute in Riyadh—exploring novel means
to use standard construction materials. Holtrop is also a professor of
architecture at ETH Zurich.

Glass to Stone (2024) is a work commissioned for the Diriyah
Contemporary Art Biennale 2024. The three-meter-high and five-
meter-wide wall-like structure has a steel tubing framework, which
supports fifteen overlapping panels of fused glass on one side.
Both a sculptural installation and material study, the work is a continuation of Holtrop's exploration of glass, which began with prototypes for his design of the curtain wall façade for Misk Art Institute.
Holtrop is interested in exploring the reuse of waste glass products
as a means of enhancing sustainability through advances in glass
technology, a particularly relevant building material for Saudi Arabia
due to the availability of fine sand.

For his installation at the Biennale, he collaborated with regional glass
manufacturers to create panels made of fused, recycled glass. In this
process, shards of waste container glass, originating both from production and waste facilities, were layered in reusable metal molds and
then fired in a kiln. Holtrop experimented with different sized shards and
temperatures of the kiln to achieve a range in visual effects. Holtrop's
recent work with glass is characteristic of his experiments with materials
and aesthetics and his implementation of building materials to convey
the feel and texture of natural surfaces. The opaqueness of the panels
creates a soft, filtered light. Over the course of the day the wall creates
shifting impressions due to the way the glass diffuses the sunlight: in
early morning it mimics salt crystals on coastal flats; at noon, ice crystals
in frozen water; and at sunset it has a warm reddish glow.

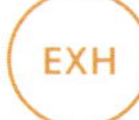

Above: Float glass, fused and resin laminated, Riyadh, Saudi Arabia, 2023
Below: ASAMCO Almarbaie, silica mining site, Tayma, near Madinah, Saudi Arabia, 2010

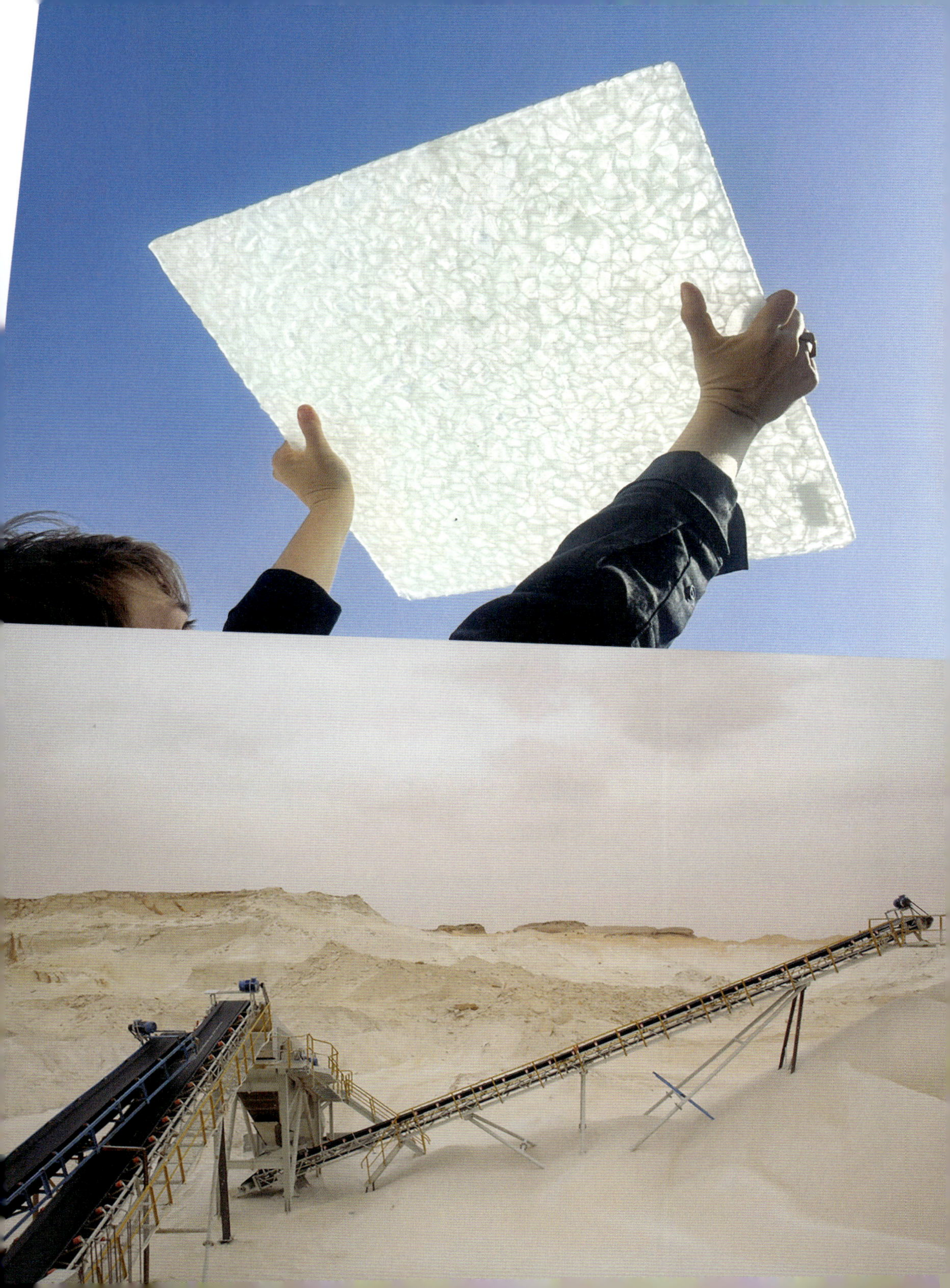

MARIAH LOOKMAN

Born 1973 in Karachi, Pakistan, lives and works in Karachi and Galle,
Sri Lanka

a Mirage: rivers meet the sea; fresh and salt waters may intermingle; an ocean remains distinct, and Poets have forgotten words for love

2024 / Offsite, Shamalat, 4102, 6089 King Faisal Rd., Al Diriyah, Riyadh 13713

Mariah Lookman is an artist and educator with a research-based practice. Her work is grounded in recuperating knowledge systems and technologies devalued by colonialism. As an educator, she is engaged in institution building, curricula innovation, and areas of post-conflict reconciliation through the arts. She is also the founder of Wellness Fund Galle Trust, a platform for philanthropy and activism that bridges art production and health. Mariah Lookman holds a D.Phil. from the Ruskin School of Art, University of Oxford.

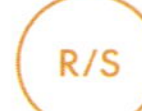

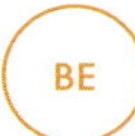

Mariah Lookman's commission is a multilayered work that draws from the historical spice trade and the enduring traditional healing practices produced through its routes across South and Southeast Asia and the Arabian Peninsula. Situated at Shamalat, an artist center initiated by Saudi artist Maha Malluh, the work consists of a water channel running along the sidewalk in front of Shamalat in the shape of a meandering river that cuts through the typical yellow stone of Riyadh and winds into a garden bed. This channel is a visual metaphor for the wadis that formed the paths traveled by pilgrims, sailors, and trading caravans. The garden bed holds a variety of medicinal plants that include species native and endemic to the Arabian Peninsula. Maps with recipes and remedies by the artist trace old spice routes, maritime histories, and navigation by the stars—all linked to the discovery of medicinal plants.

The sound walk gathers stories along the spice routes. These accounts were collected during the artist's research in Saudi Arabia, for which she traveled to regions from Riyadh to Jazan and the Hasher mountains. Visitors are invited to listen while strolling in the vicinity of Shamalat, which is located along the old caravan route of Wadi Hanifah. The artist's poetic narration is inspired by the stories of healers and merchants at the souks, and those of mothers and grandmothers. Storytelling becomes a method of recuperating a knowledge of plants that is passed on orally from one generation to the next. The work is an embodied and holistic experience of cross-cultural encounters and vernacular knowledge that has endured over distance and time. As a permanent installation at Shamalat, the water channel and garden will remain and outlive this edition of the Biennale.

Sketch for the sound walk *a Mirage: rivers meet the sea; fresh and salt waters may intermingle; an ocean remains distinct, and Poets have forgotten words for love*, 2024

DIRIYAH CONTEMPORARY ART BIENNALE 2024

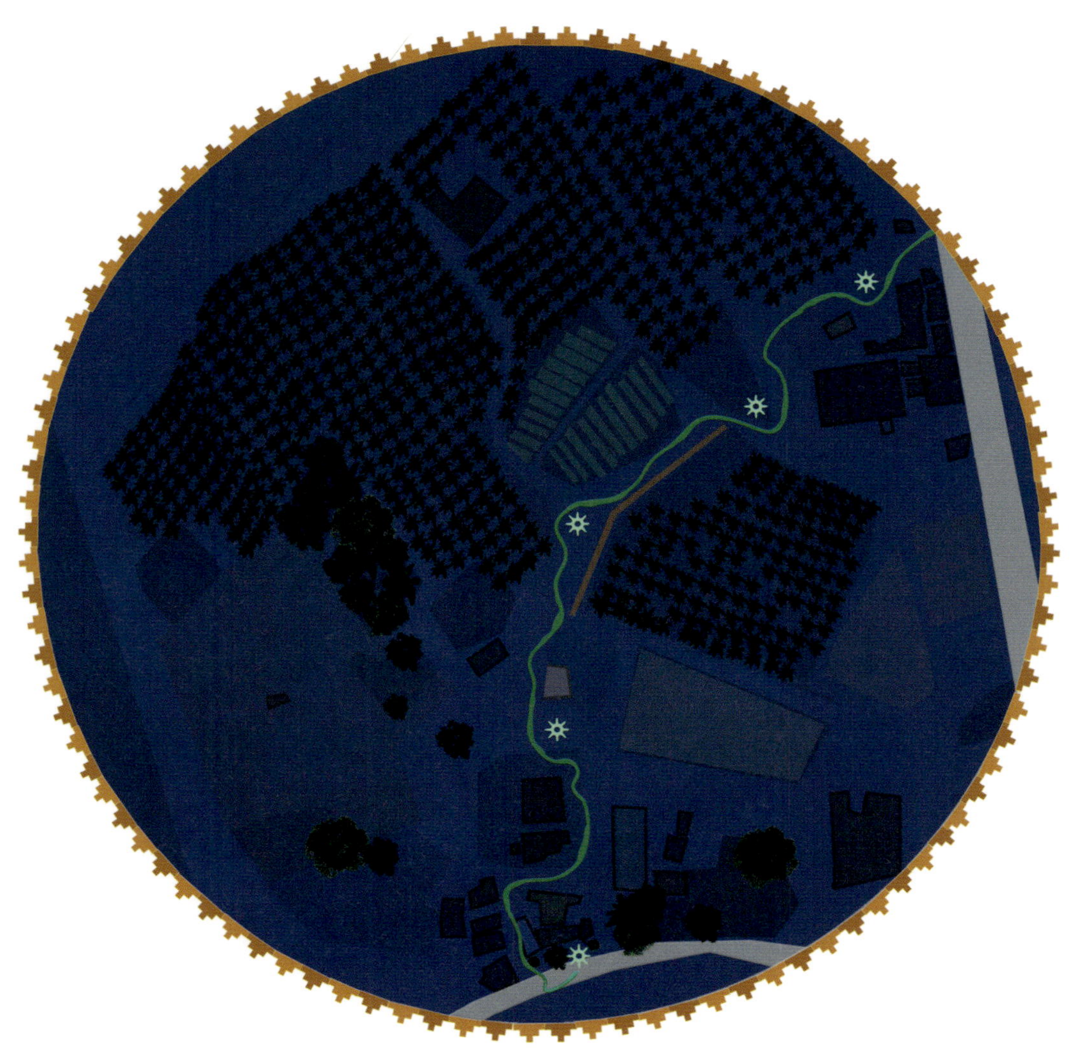

TANIA MOURAUD

Born 1942 in Paris, France, where she lives and works

Dream
2004–ongoing

Tania Mouraud's extensive body of work—ranging from painting to public art, conceptual writing, installation, videos, and sonic works and performances—has addressed artistic and humanistic themes, such as the plasticity of language and the individual's own perception and self-awareness, as well as a broader set of ethical and sociopolitical issues, confronting persistent inequalities and our treatment of the environment. A key figure of contemporary French art, Mouraud has engaged with diverse art scenes, vocabularies, and movements, thus evading any facile classification of her practice. She has exhibited in countless individual and collective exhibitions across the globe and has permanent installations at prestigious institutions such as the Centre Pompidou in Paris and the Collection FRAC Lorraine in Metz.

Borrowing from Martin Luther King Jr.'s famous 1963 speech on civil rights, Mouraud's vinyl print mural *Dream* (2004–ongoing) adapts the refrain of his passionate vision using bold, nonstandard Arabic script, transforming the words into a powerful visual statement. The work is part of a series of wall paintings exploring architecture and language that the artist began creating in the late 1980s. While the giant lettering has the scale of a billboard, the typography verges on the illegible. It is up to the viewer to decipher this world-famous phrase. This play between decoding the text and rethinking its meaning encourages readers to engage in a moment of reflection—and consider the message from a fresh perspective.

Realized as a wall work and billboards in Arabic, English, and Urdu versions, *Dream* is presented on a wall outside the exhibition halls and in the roundabout at the entry to the JAX District.

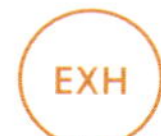

Installation views of *Dream* (2004–ongoing) from the exhibition *Art Grandeur Nature* at La Courneuve, France, 2004. Above: In Arabic / Below: In English

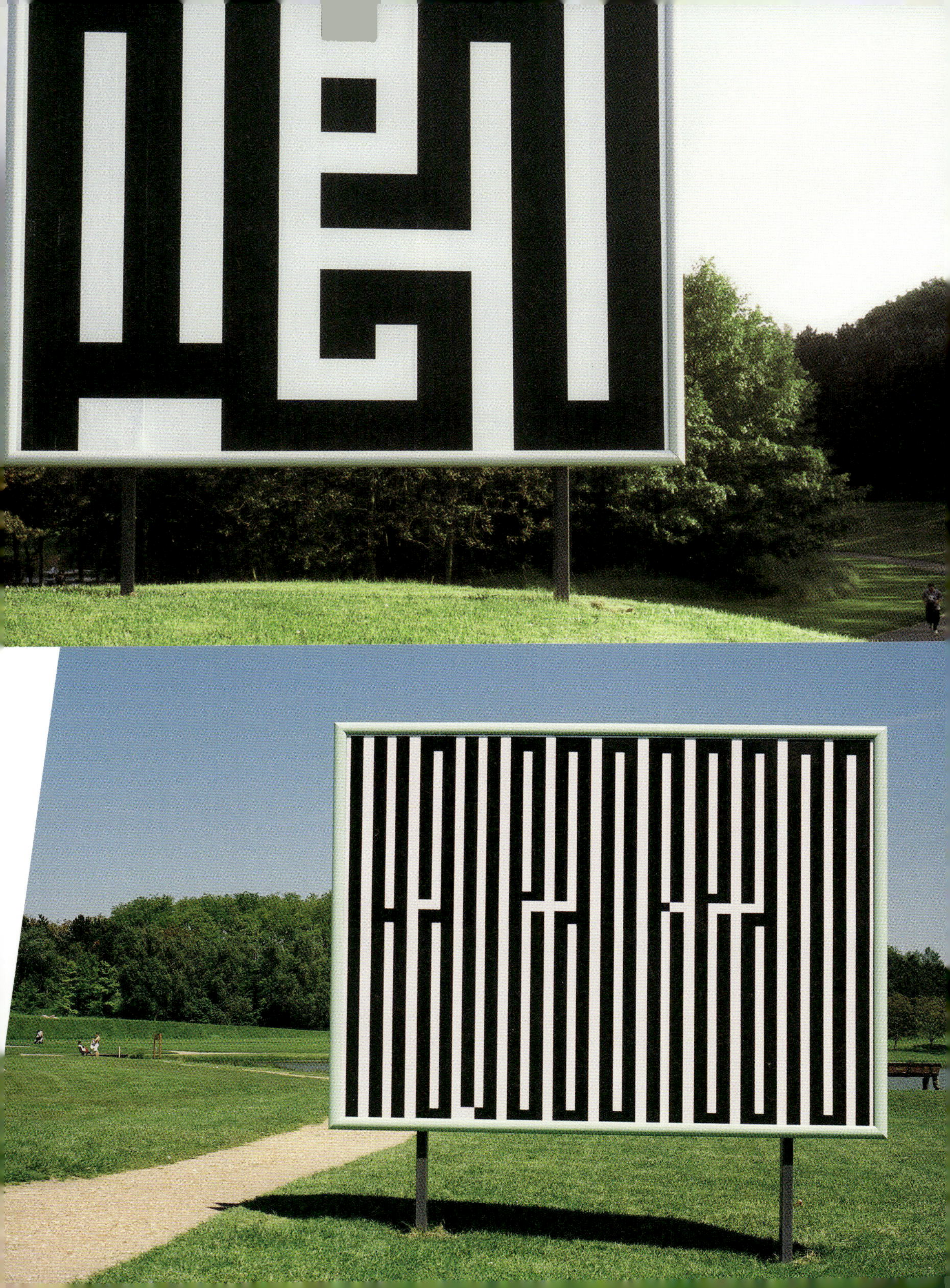

NJOKOBOK

Apolonija Šušteršič, born 1965 in Ljubljana, Slovenia, lives and works in Oslo, Norway
Youssou Diop, born 1970 in Kaolack, Senegal, lives and works in Oslo, Norway

NJOKOBOK BAR
2024

Storytelling Sessions
February–May 2024

EXH

BE

For over three decades, artist, architect, and educator Apolonija Šušteršič has shown a longstanding commitment to social and spatial practice in contemporary art. Šušteršič's projects are embedded within communities and take shape through a constant flow of exchange between different constituencies. The title of Šušteršič's recurrent projects *Suggestion for the (Next) Day* (2000–ongoing) is reflective of her dedication to explorations of present-day living environments as a means of producing alternative possibilities for the future. Education is integral to the artist's practice, and she is the founder of the MFA program Art and Public Space at the Oslo National Academy of Arts. In 2016 Šušteršič and chef and community activist Youssou Diop started the long-term project NJOKOBOK, initially in Slovenia and Senegal and then in Norway. Meaning "You are welcome/We share it" in the Wolof language, NJOKOBOK is a restaurant and a community space in one of Oslo's rapidly changing neighborhoods.

NJOKOBOK BAR is a social platform for gatherings and community storytelling sessions over juice, Senegalese tea, and *qahwa* (Arabic coffee) throughout the duration of the Biennale. The bar serves four types of cold-pressed juices free of charge to Biennale visitors: ginger, hibiscus, baobab, and turmeric, all having medicinal properties. The menu is complemented by Senegalese tea and *qahwa*, which are particularly refreshing on the cool evenings of February and during the nighttime gatherings of the month of Ramadan. Several key ingredients for the juices and tea—such as mint—are sourced from the Alzahrani farm in Diriyah, which played a key role in developing this project and fostering engagement with local producers and the community. The approximately eight-meter-long bar, chairs, and color of the interior were designed by Šušteršič. The colors correspond to the four juices on offer. Elements of the design reference one of the artist's earlier projects, the *Bonnevoie? Juice Bar* that she created in 1992 for Manifesta 2 in Luxembourg. During the Biennale, the bar will be activated with a series of storytelling sessions inspired by Arabic traditions of vernacular literature and the role of the *hakawati*. *Hakawati* means "storyteller" in Arabic and describes people who go around coffee shops and souks to tell stories and engage audiences in their tales. A continuation of the sharing session that took place as part of the Biennale Encounters, NJOKOBOK Bar invites *hakawati* from different communities—Palestinian, Senegalese, Indonesian and others—to share stories of belonging and migration that reflect the layered social fabric of Diriyah and Riyadh.

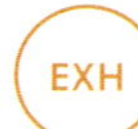
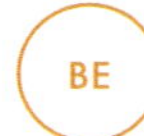

Above: Production of furniture for *NJOKOBOK BAR* at Fellesverstedet, Oslo, Norway, 2023 / Below: NJOKOBOK Restaurant, Oslo, Norway, 2022

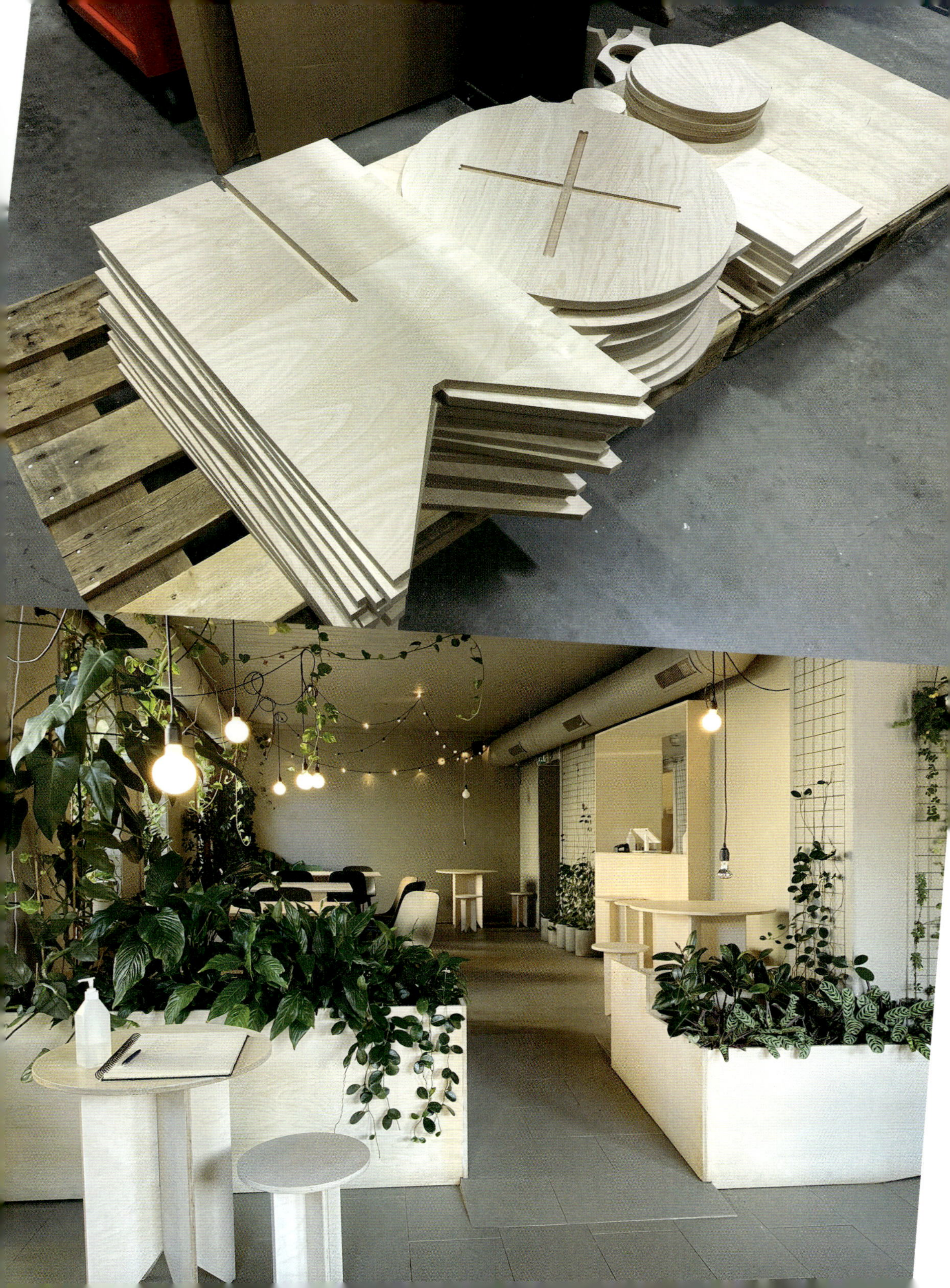

LUCY + JORGE ORTA

Lucy Orta, born 1966 in Sutton Coldfield, United Kingdom
Jorge Orta, born 1953 in Rosario, Argentina
Live and work between Paris, Seine-et-Marne, France, and London, United Kingdom

70 × 7 The Meal, Act XLVI

2024 / Meal on March 16, 2024

Lucy and Jorge Orta work as a collaborative multimedia visual arts practice to address critical social and ecological challenges such as water scarcity, corporate control of resources, and the impacts of climate change on migration. Taking form in works that include drawing, sculpture, and performance, their installations have investigated the possibilities of portable eco-minimal habitats and alternative models of community building. In recognition of their commitment to sustainability, they received the 2007 Green Leaf Award for Artistic Excellence, presented by the United Nations Environment Program in partnership with the Nobel Peace Center in Oslo and the Natural World Museum. Their collaborative process involves working with artists, architects, designers, craftsmen, and technicians to realize their installations. As an extension of this practice, the duo founded the community-based artistic research and production complex Les Moulins in the French countryside in 2000.

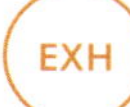
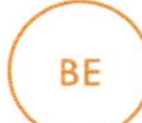
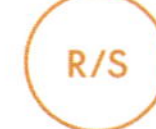

The artists' community conscious, context-specific practice is exemplified by their Biennale commission *70 × 7 The Meal, Act XLVI* (2024). For the last two decades the meal series has drawn attention to locally rooted topics. This 46th iteration explores native plants in relation to regional cuisine and the cultural traditions of sharing food. The meal will be staged as a Ramadan Suhoor prepared by local chefs. The food served is based on traditional recipes passed down by oral transmission and included dishes using plants native to Saudi Arabia. Over fifty native species from Wadi Hanifah were studied and identified by the Ortas on field trips within the Najd region through the help of botanists from Saudi National Center for Vegetation Cover Development and Combating Desertification. A table set for three hundred invited guests celebrates the rituals of feasting together in an eco-conscious setting. The meal is served on a set of special edition Royal Limoges porcelain plates and features table centerpieces designed by the artists and representing an idealized and rewilded native landscape.

70 × 7 The Meal, Act XXXIV, Thomas Paine Plaza, Philadelphia, PA, United States, 2013

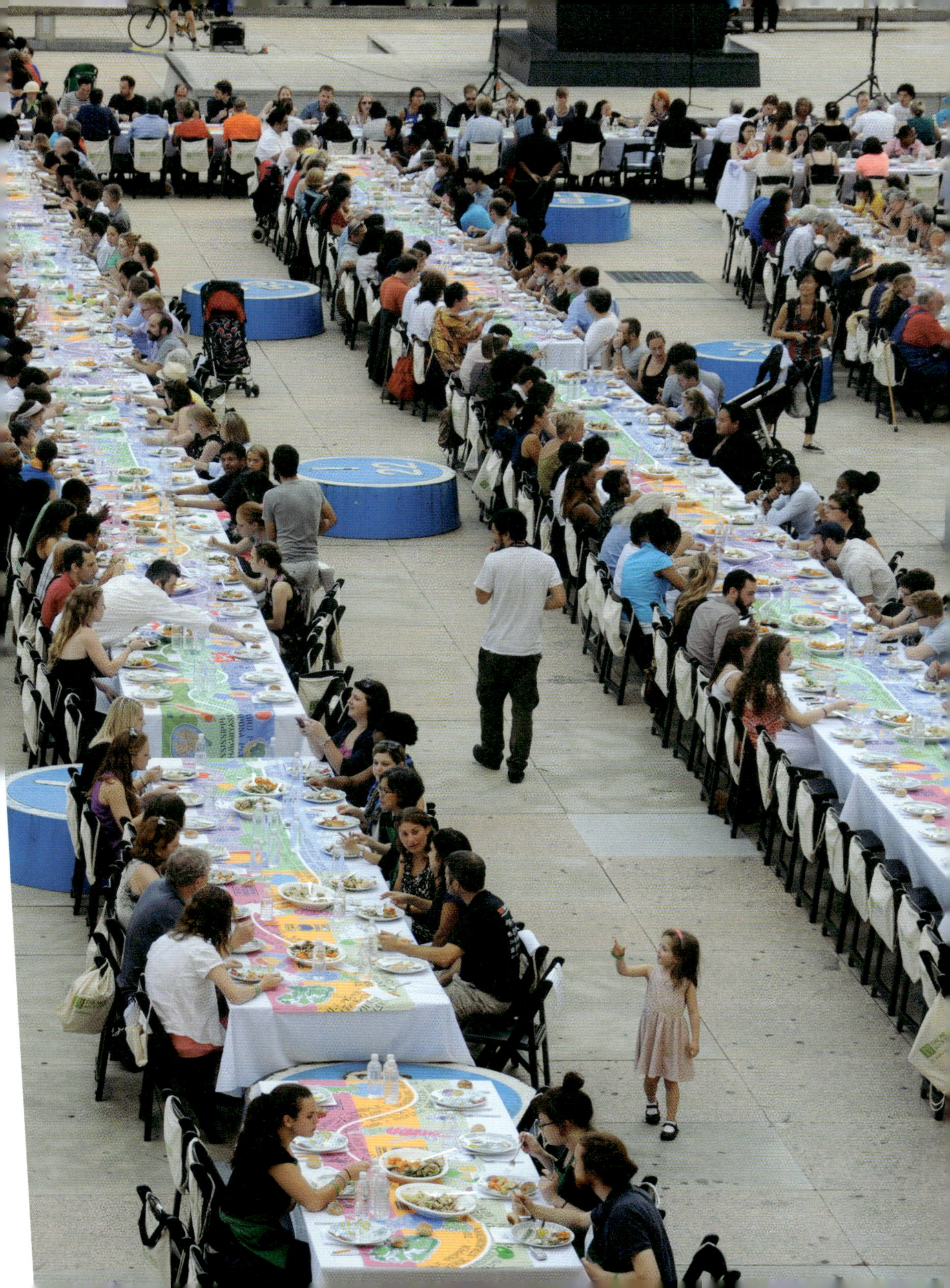

TAYYŪN

Founded 2018, based in Amman, Jordan
Deema Assaf, born 1984 in Amman, Jordan, where she lives and works
Yaman Amr, born 1989 in Amman, Jordan, where he lives and works

Insect Hotel
2024

TAYYŪN is a research studio founded and directed by architect, researcher, and urban forester Deema Assaf, whose practice focuses on the regeneration of urban ecosystems through native forest creation and cross-species architecture. Trained as an architect at the University of Jordan, she is a qualified practitioner of the Japanese Miyawaki Method, which can restore lost native forests ten times faster than natural ecological succession through the creation of locally sensitive microenvironments dense in biodiversity. Yaman Amr is the studio's managing partner, and an artist, architect, regenerative design expert, and permaculture teacher. Inspired by permaculturist Geoff Lawson's revitalization of a two-thousand-year-old forest in Morocco, TAYYŪN started its reforestation program with an initial private plantation site of 107 square meters in 2018. It has since planted four native forests in Jordan, which together comprise 2,700 native plant seedlings. Alongside forestation projects and the reintegration of wildlife into the city, the studio's practice involves the creation of a native forest database, as well as in-depth research and testing about how to adapt planting techniques and soil engineering interventions in specific localities.

The work *Insect Hotel* (2024) presented at this Biennale is part of a larger inquiry and series of interventions that explore possible structures for cultivating urban wildlife. Comprised of a three-meter-high wooden tower perforated with hundreds of insect nest tubes and carved with a bird nest cavity at its top, the installation is "urban acupuncture," which aims to draw wildlife back into the considerations of city planning. Installed outdoors, *Insect Hotel* will become a permanent installation and the nucleus of the studio's urban rewilding intervention in Saudi Arabia. As part of a larger project of such possible structures, including a previous work called *Urban Pigeon Tower* (2019), the installation serves as a call to expand what the studio describes as "the urban compassion footprint" and to rewild cities as rich, multi-species, biodiverse ecosystems. TAYYŪN also presented a rewilding workshop, which looked at the diversity of indigenous plants in Saudi Arabia to highlight and address possible reforesting and rewilding interventions impacting vegetation, soil, and water.

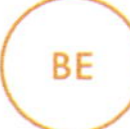

Installation view of *The Insect Hotel*, from the exhibition *Re-rooting* at Darat Al-Funun, Amman, Jordan, 2022

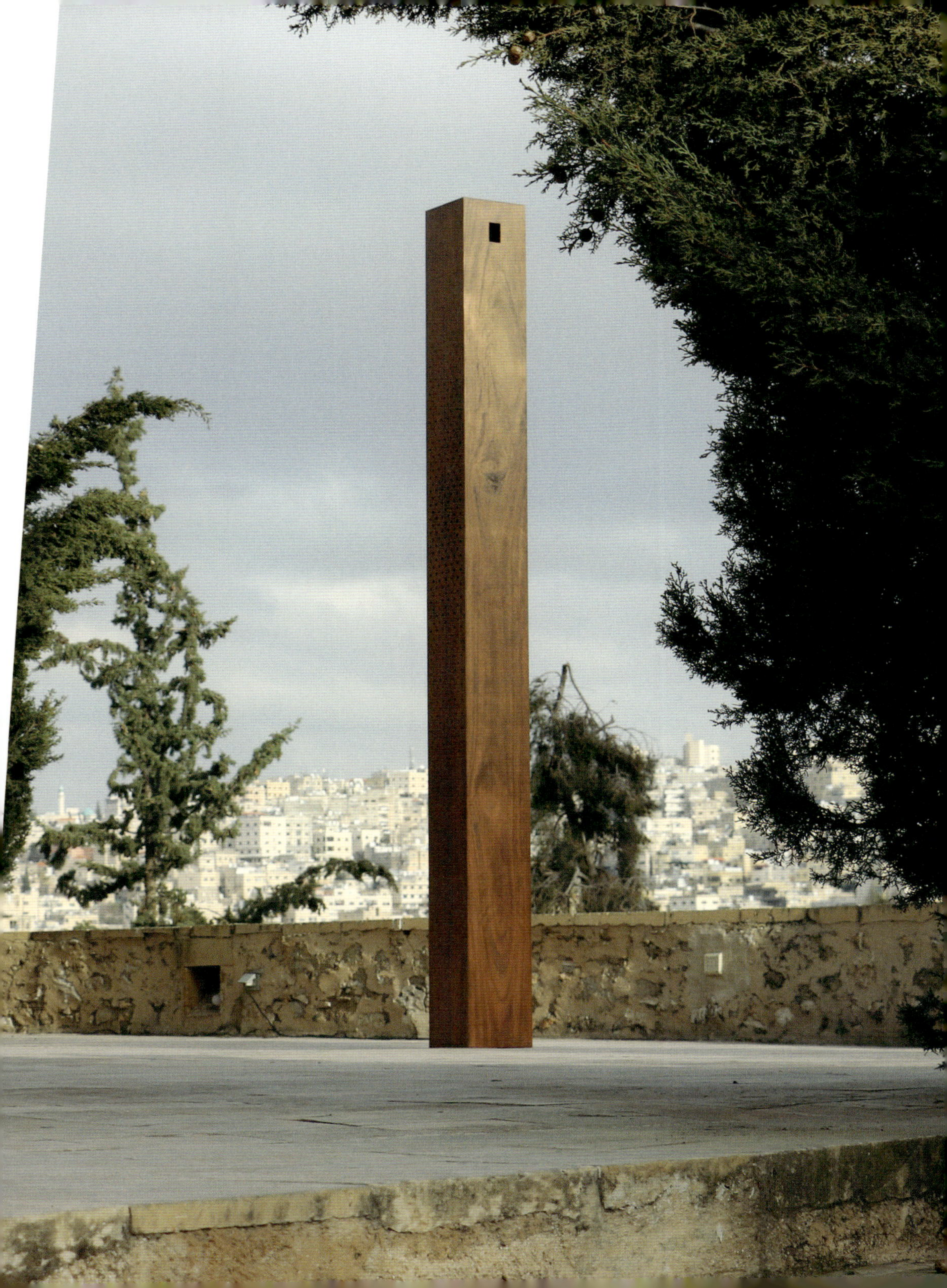

SISSEL TOLAAS

Born 1965 in Stavanger, Norway, lives and works in Berlin, Germany

IN_side_OUT_edis_NI تربة
2024

Sissel Tolaas is a smell researcher and artist who has been collecting and researching smells from around the world since 1990. With a background in mathematics, forensic chemistry, linguistics, and art from universities such as Moscow State University, the University of Oxford, and Princeton University, she has become a sought-after researcher and creator of smells. In 2004 she founded the SMELL RE_searchLab Berlin, one of the world's largest sources for artificial smells, equipped with an arsenal of ongoing smell-related archives.

Chemical communication, the planet's first and fundamental form of inter-action, fuels Sissel Tolaas's cross-disciplinary inquiries and extended pro-jects. She probes the smells that underpin human-to-human connections and plant-animal communication, unraveling the complexities of olfactory interactions. For Tolaas, smell is about opening up the complex world, of which we all are a part, and to which we all contribute: air is a shared endeavor. Where there is air, there are smell molecules—and there is life. Every day, we breathe in millions of molecules that provide a wealth of information to our subconscious minds. Smell is an omnipresent form of communication deeply linked to emotions and memory. Smelling the world is different than looking at the world. Every action is the source of an emotional reaction.

Tolaas records smell molecules from their original contexts, replicates them pre-cisely, and introduces them into specific situations or objects depending on the given content and context. Tolaas calls this the "decontextualization of smell." This provocative approach challenges culturally ingrained notions of "good" or "bad" smells, aiming to revive the richness of sensory information and its unique potential for information, communication, education, and even healing.

For the Biennale, Tolaas has been commissioned to create a smell derived from petrichor, the distinctive, earthy smell produced when rain falls on dry soil. The smell molecule has been shown to boost levels of serotonin and norepinephrine in humans, acting in a manner similar to antidepressants. Visitors can experience Tolaas's smell as a thread—as an invisible AIR wayfinder throughout the exhibition—introduced by mobile dispenser units. An outdoor area is dedicated to this unique molecule, inviting visitors to contemplate, rest, and share stories evoked by the smell molecule. In the Re/Search area, Tolaas presents her work on the study of the petrichor smell molecule and its scientific foundation.

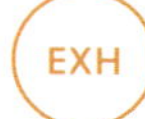
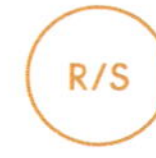

Above: Fieldwork: sampling of elements / plants emitting from or found in soil, South Alps Wetland, Nantesbuch, Germany, 2020 / Below: Smell molecule recording from soil sample, Bordeaux, France, 2022

DIRIYAH CONTEMPORARY ART BIENNALE 2024

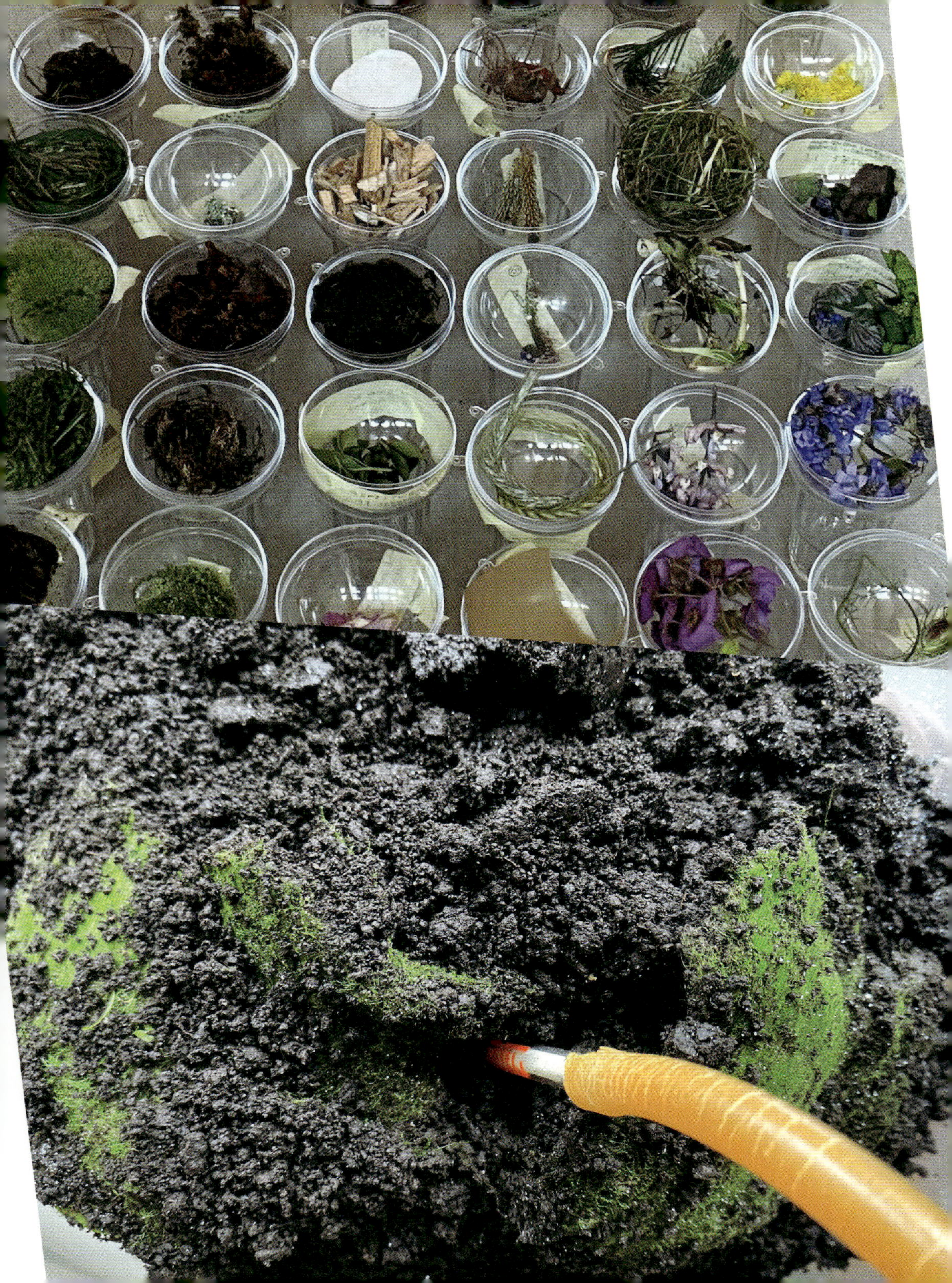

BIENNALE ENCOUNTERS
April 2023 – May 2024

Biennale Encounters is a yearlong series of events—talks, workshops, performances, collective walks, storytelling sessions, and musical intervals. It is a meeting point for the artists and audiences of *After Rain*. The program highlights different ways of creating and experiencing contemporary art. Biennale Encounters is guided by the notion that art-making and discourse production do not happen in isolation but rely on an active interweaving of ideas, cultures, and experiences.

Starting in April 2023, Biennale Encounters has made the development of the Biennale transparent and participatory. Before the Biennale exhibition opened its doors, twenty-six talks, workshops, and sharing sessions gradually introduced Biennale artists to the local community. Maximizing the possibilities of direct exchange between visiting artists and local audiences, Biennale Encounters embedded the development of commissions and existing works within the social context and natural environment of Diriyah and the wider Riyadh region. Planting the seeds of this 2024 edition, Biennale Encounters has prompted consistent discussions and activities around key themes, from the politics of water and food to interdependencies of all life forms and sonic fieldwork.

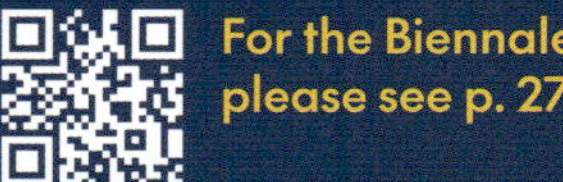

For the Biennale Encounters Schedule,
please see p. 270 or scan the QR code

A defining aspect of Biennale Encounters is the workshop format as a means for introducing artistic processes and methodologies within a collective learning experience. Artists committed to education were offered a platform to share their specific ways of working and perceiving the world. These include interdisciplinary investigations, archival research, photographic typologies, hacktivism, patchwork, urban rewilding, field recording, deep observation and listening, drawing, publishing, and storytelling. With participants attending from different regions across Saudi Arabia, the program has been shaped by principles of learning together, trial-and-error, and the pursuit of active, collective engagement in artistic production.

Moving into the period of the exhibition, Biennale Encounters has continued to unfold and evolve. During this period, the series has been expanded to include a program of live activations and performances, storytelling sessions, and musical events. Artists create sonic, theatrical, and social interventions that complement the exhibition with time-based formats. Taking place across the exhibition site and in different locations in the city, the program is an exploration of live interaction, ephemeral physical and durational experiences; poetry readings that conjure sculpture; activations of an installation-turned-theater set; audience-accompanied processes of drawing and filmmaking; and live sonic performances. The program is defined by an expansiveness of media and materials. Many of these contemporary performances have storytelling at their heart and take inspiration from diverse narrative-based traditions, whose roots extend back in time and across broad geographical cultural horizons. The program explores this diverse set of historical and contemporary ways of gathering and engaging with the world as a means of creating shared memories and maintaining communities and collective experience.

JUMANA EMIL ABBOUD

Born 1971, Palestinian, lives and works between Jerusalem and
London, United Kingdom

Gazelle in a Mother's Eye

2024 / Performance

Jumana Emil Abboud works with drawing, video, installation, and performance to explore intangible heritage interwoven through narratives surrounding nature and landscapes—specifically water sources. Having studied fine arts in Toronto and Jerusalem, she is currently a practice-led PhD candidate at London's Slade School of Fine Art. Drawing on her Palestinian origins and the entanglement of folklore, community, and storytelling, Abboud revisits the prism of resources, people, and places that emerge out of history's depths to imagine reciprocal futures. She focuses on waterscapes as integral sites of story, as the bearers and guardians of collective memory and future cultural legacy. Working across different media, Abboud uses materials as varied as beeswax, turmeric, lace, embroidery, found papers, natural pigments, oral histories, journal entries, drawings, performance, and video. Her practice reflects the urgency for continuity of culture amid measures of disruption and erasure. At the same time, it suggests a process of ongoing metamorphosis and the possibility for poetic repurposing to tap undercurrents of rooted narratives and redefine our survival.

In the performance work *Gazelle in a Mother's Eye* (2024), Abboud turns her focus to the landscapes of Saudi Arabia to examine how historic relationships with natural sources, primarily water, have informed present-day legacies. Using the research methods central to her practice, she navigates bodies of water in and around Riyadh, excavating tradition, myth, and oral customs in creating a new work that recognizes the intricate plurality of alignment with the manifest world we call home. Through an immersive study of local folktales and the experience of embedding herself in community contexts and intergenerational collaborations, Abboud invites us to reconsider water entanglement and its co-authored ways of being. What emerges is a site-specific work articulated into spoken word, video, movement, and live drawing, accompanied by metaphor and unfolding truths. The multimedia, multi-iteration artwork involves local participants sharing an extended story of variable parts that hold water close, probing connectivity, remembrance, and the enchantment of belonging.

BE

Above: Video still from *I Feel Everything*, 2021
Below: *A study in carrying water*, rehearsal for a performance, 2021

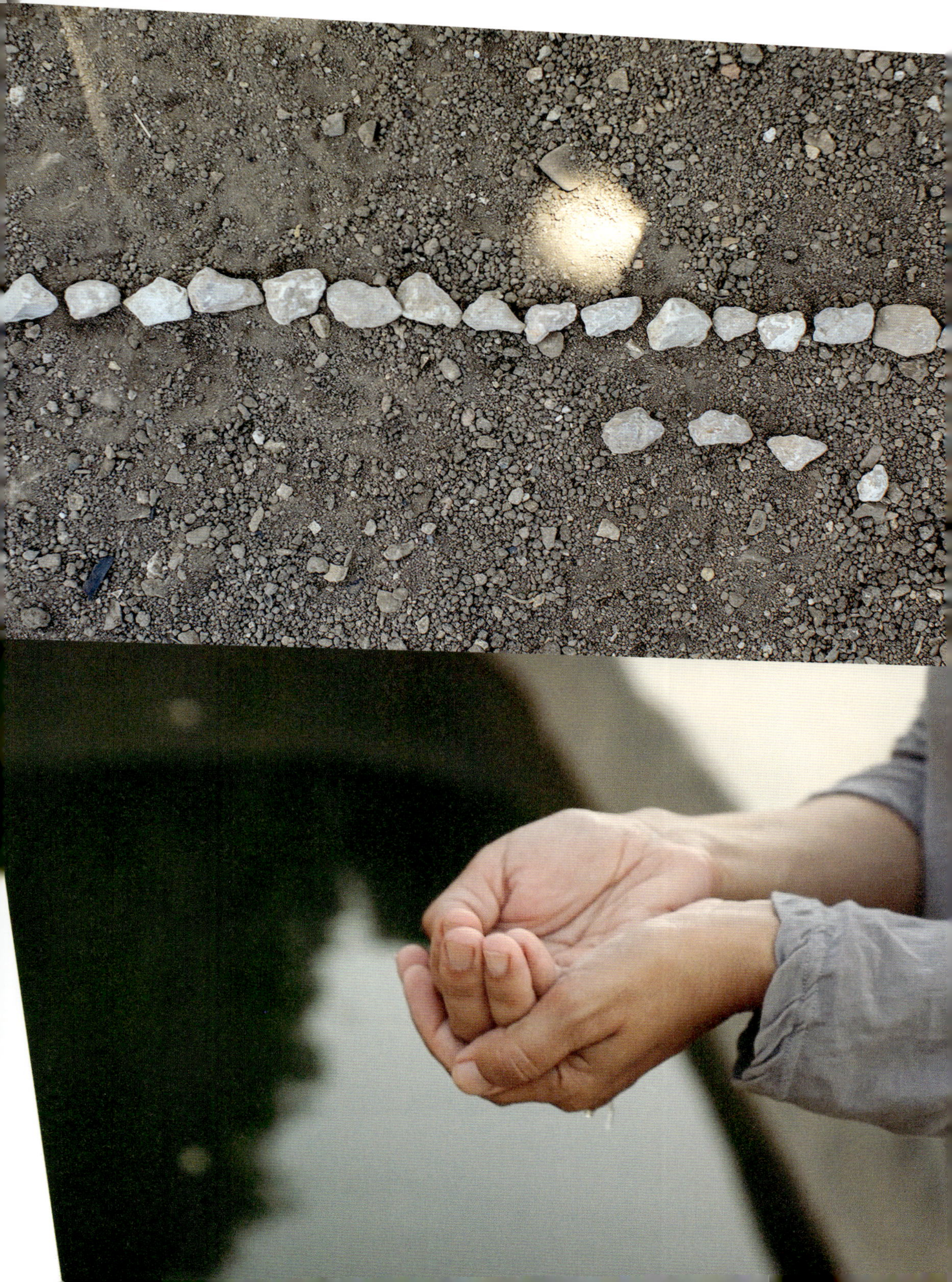

IRENE AGRIVINA

Born 1976 in Yogyakarta, Indonesia, where she lives and works

Open Material / Open Hardware

Two workshops on November 3 and 4, 2023

Domestic Hacking / Collective Making

Artist Talk on November 4, 2023

Irene Agrivina is an open-source advocate, artist, and educator committed to democratizing access to technology and empowering women in science. After studying graphic design at the Indonesia Institute of the Arts Yogyakarta, she co-founded the House of Natural Fiber (HONF) in 1999, during the post-Suharto era of reform, a time of political and social opening. At HONF, Agrivina took a leading role in the education program, facilitating interdisciplinary workshops based on the principles of DIY and DIWO (Do It Yourself and Do It With Others). In 2013 Agrivina co-founded XXLab (named after the female chromosome), a collective of women from different disciplines working at the intersection of art, science, and technology. In 2015 XXLab was awarded the Prix Ars Electronica for its project *Soya C(o)u(l)ture*.

Agrivina's workshops for Biennale Encounters are grounded in the spirit of "critical making" within art and design, and the needs of a community rather than the market. The first is dedicated to designers and practitioners from the field of fashion. Embedded in the context of Diriyah, it explores the use of date-palm leaves as a possible alternative material for clothing. This biochemical experiment is an extension of the ongoing project *Soya C(o)u(l)ture*, initiated in 2014, in which the artist and her XXLab peers generated a biomaterial from soya waste by using bacteria and tissue culture. The project not only responds to the need for sustainability in fashion, one of the world's most polluting industries, but also addresses environmental concerns in the artist's local context. Fermented into tofu and tempeh, soybeans are a staple across Indonesia, yet their large-scale production involves a liquid waste that poisons rivers.

In keeping with Agrivina's commitments to minimizing the gender gap in technology and mediating playful encounters with science, the second workshop introduces female participants to electronics, an open-source software (Arduino), and hardware devices. Using electronic circuits, participants create replicable DIY audio devices and a participatory installation that generates sound from leaves. "Hacking for us is a way of living," says Agrivina, whose credos are that art, science, and technology should benefit society, and women and girls can be at the forefront of generating alternatives for a more sustainable future.

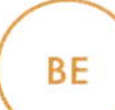

Documentation of the Open Hardware workshop at Diriyah Biennale Foundation, Riyadh, Saudi Arabia, 2023

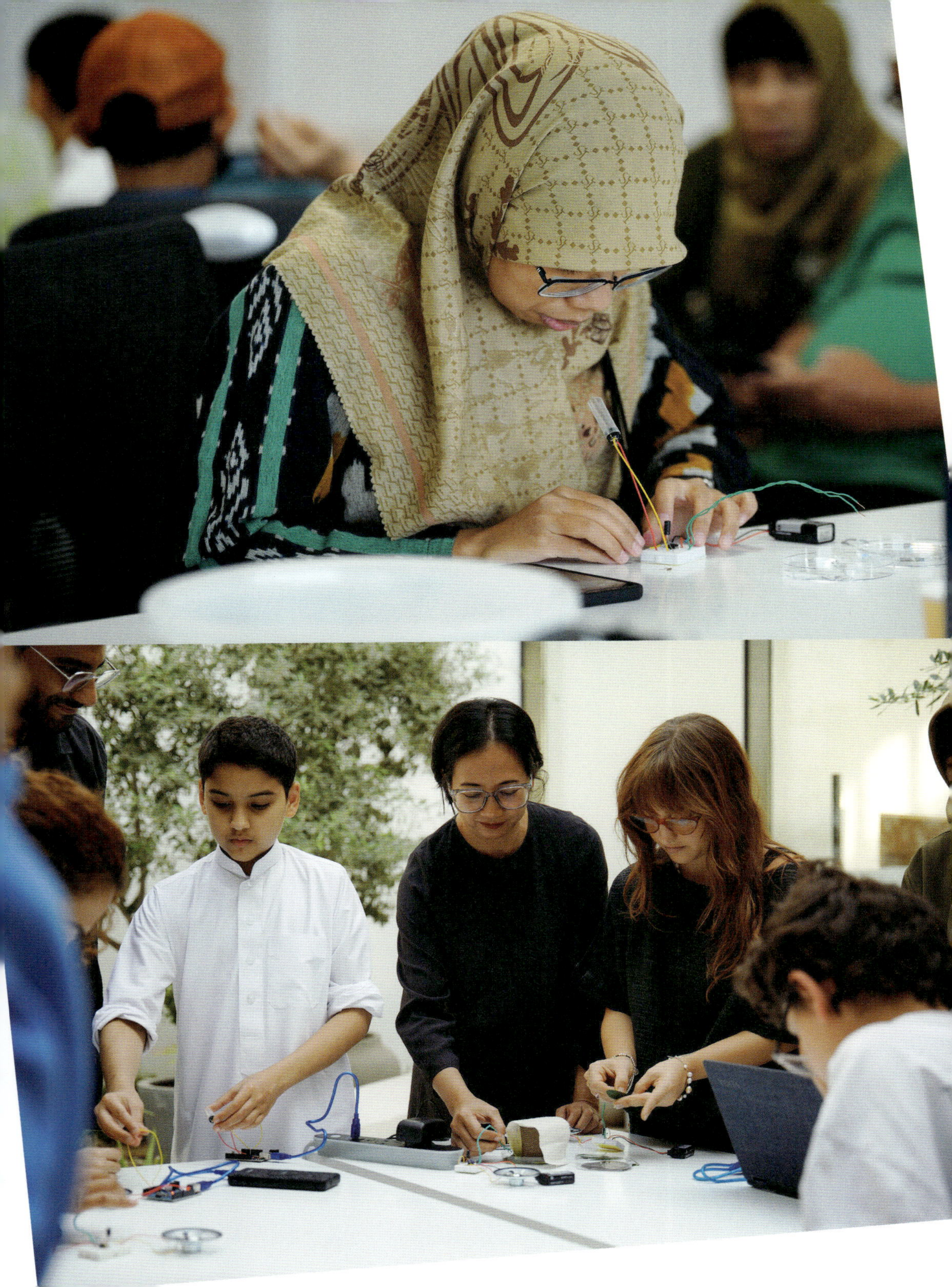

RASHA AL-DUWAISAN

Born 1983 in Washington, DC, United States, lives and works in
Dubai, United Arab Emirates

Buckets and Waterskins

2024 / Poetic interactions on March 22 and 23, 2024

Rasha Al-Duwaisan is a writer, poet, and historian who works with sound and oral history to examine and represent overlooked histories of the Arabian Peninsula, in particular in relation to her native Kuwait. Trained in public policy at Princeton University, she spent a year living with a family in Udaipur, India, working on local community issues with the Foundation for Sustainable Development, and then later at a shelter for donkeys, before returning to the United States to pursue graduate research. At Harvard University's Center for Middle Eastern Studies, she conducted an extensive oral history of the Kuwaiti community in India from the 1940s to the 1960s. The child of a diplomatic, nomadic upbringing, Al-Duwaisan's practice as both oral historian and poet is preoccupied with multiculturalism and absences or lapses in representation. Her choice of oral history as both method and form is rooted in a regional experience of histories where documentation and the archive are undervalued or absent. As a poet, she has published in journals including *The Cincinnati Review*, *Willow Springs Magazine*, *The Adroit Journal*, and *Michigan Quarterly Review*, which nominated her poetry for Best New Poets, 2023. Selections of her poetry were included by Jenny Holzer in her 2022 light installation at the Louvre Abu Dhabi on the occasion of the museum's fifth anniversary.

In a performance commissioned for the Biennale, *Buckets and Waterskins* (2024), Al-Duwaisan will juxtapose historic and contemporary responses to rain in the Arabian Peninsula, combining spoken word, poetry, and sound. The role of rain in our everyday lives has evolved dramatically over the last century. What was once desperately longed for as a source of life is now often considered a refreshing turn of weather or even a nuisance. Through the lens of historic adaptations to rainfall, Al-Duwaisan will narrate vignettes of modern domestic and social life. Using layered imagery centered on material objects, the landscape, and architecture, she will question how our interactions with nature have changed and how that has affected our sense of self and the world around us. She will share her words in an intimate, atmospheric space, where listeners are encouraged to think about their place in history.

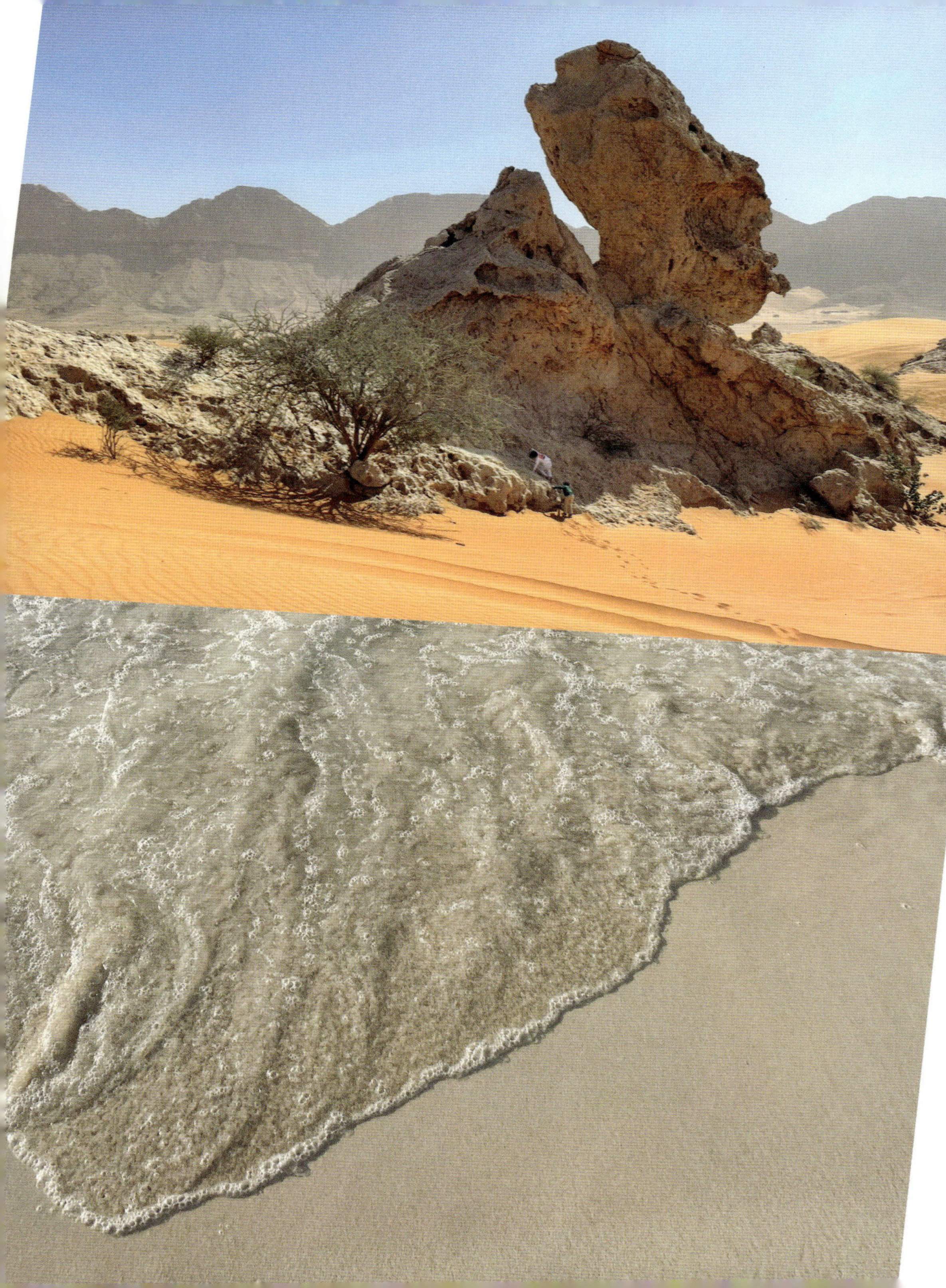

ANDRIUS ARUTIUNIAN

Born 1991 in Vilnius, Lithuania, lives and works in
The Hague, the Netherlands

Kayīb

2023 / Performance on March 9, 2024

Andrius Arutiunian works with hybrid forms of music and media to probe the politics of sound and how it shapes our experience of the world. Trained in composition and sonology at the Royal Conservatoire in The Hague, he represented Armenia at the 59th Venice Biennale in 2022 and is currently a DAAD fellow in Berlin. His practice is grounded in the principle of sound as a system of order, which he inverts, reorders, and disrupts. These interventions, as acts of sonic dissent and reattunement, take the form of sound installations, film, ritualistic gatherings, performance, and vinyl records. By combining sounds that range from hypnotic structures and vernaculars to modified historic incantations, non-Western tunings, and synthetic sources, his work has examined the politics of algorithms and AI, while offering meditations on strangeness, resonance, and the dynamics of political engagement. His reordering of political histories and musical forms encourage a new way of listening and offer entry to other worlds.

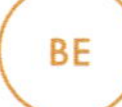

The performance *Kayīb* (2023) is a multilayered exploration of the hidden connections and forgotten stories that shape our world. Built on songs that have been banned and the sounds of secret societies, Arutiunian merges the sonic entanglements of oil extraction with histories of charlatanism to explore musical and political peripheries. Running a series of hypnotic and repetitive sonic movements through the bodies of self-made brass instruments, the performance unfolds as a complex interplay of multiple illicit voices and fictitious encounters between a cast of speculatively interrelated characters and musical figures. The work integrates protagonists such as George Ivanovich Gurdjieff (1867–1949), the Armenian-Greek mystic active in Paris in the early twentieth century and renowned practitioner-teacher of techniques aimed to produce higher states of consciousness, and Haile Selassie (1892–1975), the emperor of Ethiopia fascinated by Armenian musicians. Arutiunian creates a hypnotic, immersive experience that challenges listeners to think critically about history, power, and the nature of reality. The piece exemplifies his novel approach in combining musical harmony and rhythm with the study of underground communities and esoteric movements in a search for political and musical attunement.

Documentation of the performance *Kayīb* at Lithuanian National Drama Theatre, as a part of the exhibition *Counterfates* at Meduza gallery, Vilnius, Lithuania, 2023

DIRIYAH CONTEMPORARY ART BIENNALE 2024

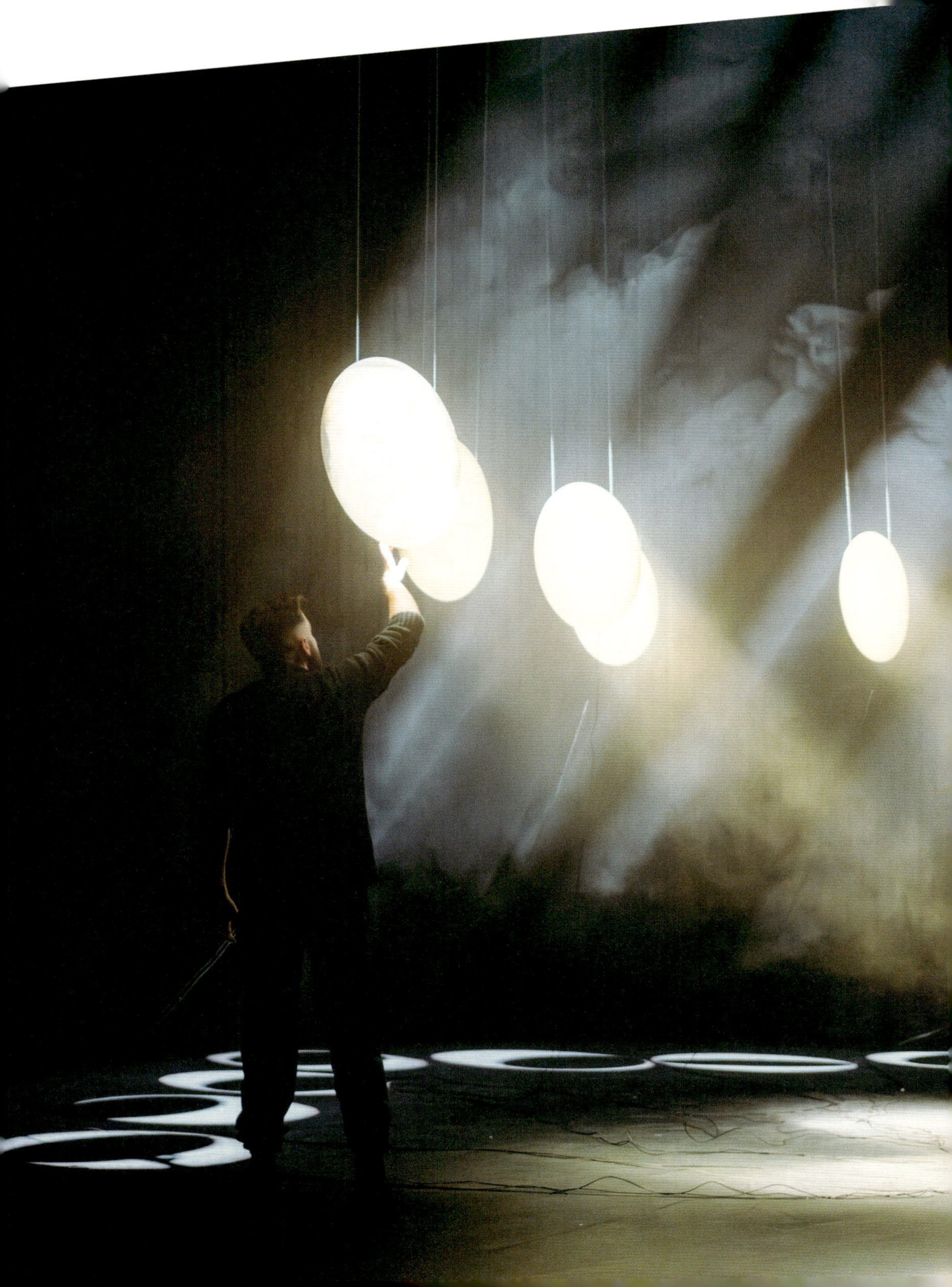

TAREK ATOUI

Born 1980 in Beirut, Lebanon, lives and works in Paris, France

الطارق A Research into Tribal Musical Traditions across the Arab World

2022–ongoing / Performance on May 24, 2024
Research and activation in collaboration with Jad Atoui

Artist and composer Tarek Atoui is known for his collaborative and improvisatory sound performances and installations. Developed from rigorous research on diverse musical histories and cultures, his works encompass self-built instruments and machines, experimental sonic objects, and electronic music. For Atoui, these technologies are catalysts of human interaction and improvisation, through which he expands the experience of sound into multisensorial dimensions and the social sphere. Organizing concerts and workshops is a core aspect of his practice. Atoui studied contemporary and electronic music at the French National Conservatory of Reims. His many projects have been featured in major exhibitions worldwide, such as the 17th Istanbul Biennial (2022), 58th Venice Biennale (2019), and dOCUMENTA 13 (2012).

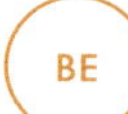

His long-term research and performance project, الطارق (2022–ongoing) focuses on collecting and experimenting with sounds associated with an Arabic musical sensibility known as *tarab*, which describes the emotional thrall and ecstatic state of the listener. Emerging from Atoui's previous research at AMAR Foundation in Lebanon, which houses one of the largest collections of early twentieth-century Arabic music recordings worldwide, الطارق traces the socially defined musical network of circulation. New to this project is Atoui's work with recordings that he has purchased and collected among the tribes and villages situated along a path running from the Atlas Mountains of Northern Africa to the Arabian Gulf and along the nomadic routes of the Tuareg people. Characterized by raw vocals and crossing rhythms, this music resonates in compositions integrating contemporary electronic sounds and field recordings, which are amplified and modified by Atoui's self-programmed computer software and an eclectic collection of instruments.

الطارق goes beyond sound; for the artist the title refers to the "night-comer"—the guest who comes at night seeking knowledge, and also to Venus, the morning star that guided caravan journeys at dawn. The sonic work guides the audience through a variety of locales, from bustling souks to joyous weddings and intimate music salons, reflecting Atoui's extensive research, initially in Morocco and now in Saudi Arabia. The resulting composition is laden with affect and contains rich psychogeographical textures. It also speaks to the shape-shifting nature of musical phenomena, in which the resilience of rural, participatory repertoires interfaces with the shifting, polyglot sounds of urban music to underscore the multifaceted nature of auditory experience.

Documentation of the performance *Al Qabali* at Dream City festival, Tunis, Tunisia, 2023

DIRIYAH CONTEMPORARY ART BIENNALE 2024

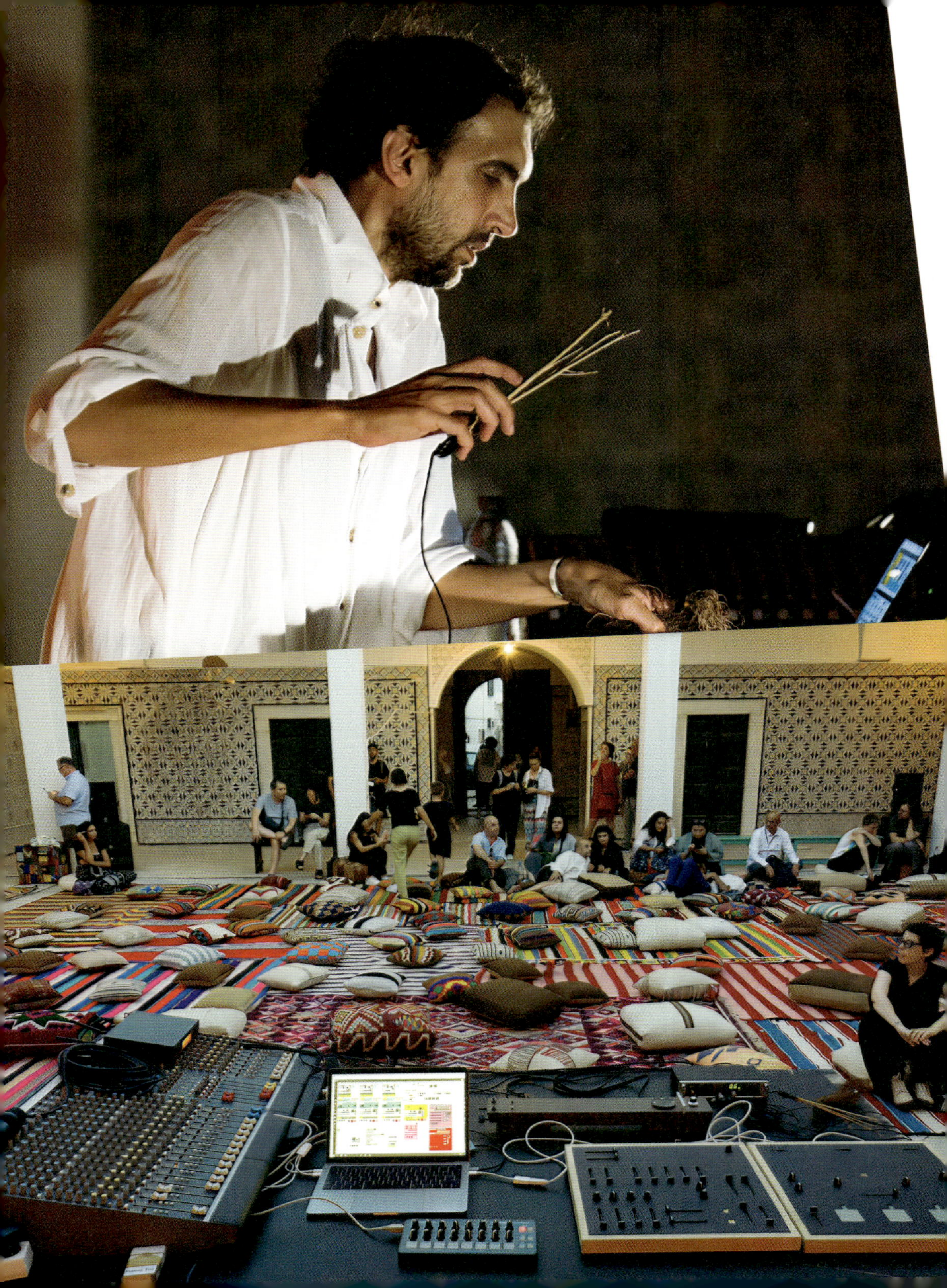

VIKRAM DIVECHA

Born 1977 in Beirut, Lebanon, lives and works in Dubai, United Arab Emirates

Wall Extract (Riyadh)

2024 / Installation and Social Gathering on March 8 and May 11, 2024

Vikram Divecha's practice focuses on "found processes," a term he uses to describe the urban operations he investigates and deploys. Ranging from municipal gardening to demolition, these processes are his realm of intervention. By shifting authorship to collaborators and opening gaps within urban systems, Divecha challenges the nature and modes of artistic production while exploring themes of time, architecture, and migration. His engagements translate into public art, installations, moving images, photography, painting, and drawings. His work has been exhibited regionally and internationally at venues including the United Arab Emirates national pavilion at the 57th Venice Biennale and Sharjah Biennial 13 (both 2017).

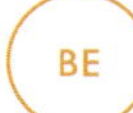

For *Wall Extract (Riyadh)* (2024), Divecha selected a section of wall from a structure in Riyadh that was slated for demolition. Part of *Wall House*, a larger project that began in Abu Dhabi in 2022—for which he envisions collecting hundreds of wall and façade sections from buildings across the region that are to be demolished and stores them in a warehouse-like center—Divecha proposes an urgent "archiving of the present." Serving as starting points for expansive sociocultural mappings of time and place, the wall fragments stand in as bearers of histories—of tenants, infrastructure, materiality, aesthetics, and culture. With its extensive lifeline, how can *Wall Extract (Riyadh)* perform what it has borne witness to? How can this architectural fragment be repurposed into a social object? By incorporating time-based responses involving poetry, cuisine, social relations, and interactions into his work, Divecha turns the artifact *Wall Extract (Riyadh)* into an active participant, transforming urban debris into an agent for conveying an alternative and inclusive cultural history. As the artist points out, "These walls are like tree trunks: they are not made out of concrete and cement, but out of time."

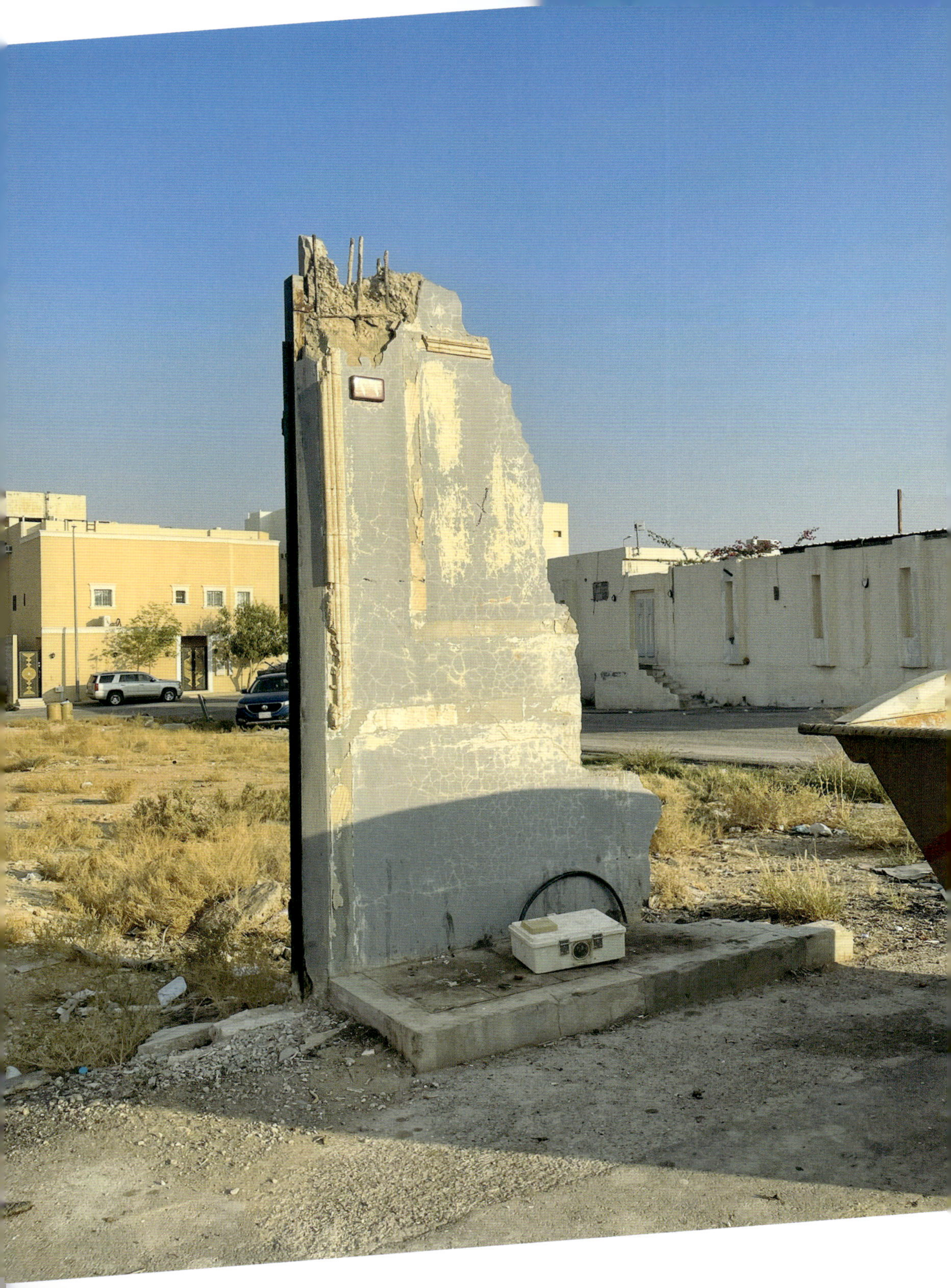

ZARINA MUHAMMAD

Born 1982 in Singapore, where she lives and works

Gentle Ferocities

Night Workshop and Artist Talk on March 23 and 24, 2024

Zarina Muhammad is an artist, educator, and researcher whose practice is situated at the intersection of the ecocultural cosmologies, mythical traditions, belief systems, and historical specters of Southeast Asia. Often involving both human and nonhuman co-authors, Muhammad's works are incarnations of her decade-long research and span the mediums of performance, installation, ritual, sound, moving image, and participatory practice. Her work operates as a mode of cultural translation, revitalizing oral histories and ethnographic literature in polyphonic and discordant ways. Muhammad participated in the Singapore Biennale (2022) and was the winner of the IMPART Art Prize (2022). She was also a finalist of both the Julian Baer Next Generation Art Prize (2021) and Singapore's President's Young Talent Award (2019).

As part of Biennale Encounters, Muhammad's workshop "Gentle Ferocities" is one iteration of her new long-term project on archival and speculative readings of the earth, sky, and sea. Taking place after Iftar during the holy month of Ramadan, it is an invitation to share space, exchange stories, and collectively map out wisdoms and lessons inspired by the various land, sky, and sea creatures from the participants' environments and cultures. Drawing from Southeast Asian mythologies, Muhammad creates a space for discussion and hands-on activities in this workshop, while engaging with vast webs of islands, bodies of water, and spiritual landscapes as well as the interconnected nonhuman and more-than-human ecologies of which we are part.

In the face of pressing urgencies of our times, what can we learn from other living entities? A series of prompts from the artist guide the workshop: "What dispositions and modes of living are we unlearning, retracing, encountering, when we allow our senses to be fully attentive to the smallest creatures, the seasonal rhythms of a landscape, the changing direction of winds, to lifeforms that are ungovernable? What are the ways of being, looking, and leaning in that allow us to give sight and presence to the unobservable, to dark matter, to our own animality, to a gentle ferocity?"

Above: Documentation of the performance *Domesticating Doubt about the Afterlife,* from the exhibition *Stories We Tell to Scare Ourselves With* at Museum of Contemporary Art, Taipei, Taiwan, 2019
Below: Mangrove swamp, Sungei Buloh, Singapore, 2021

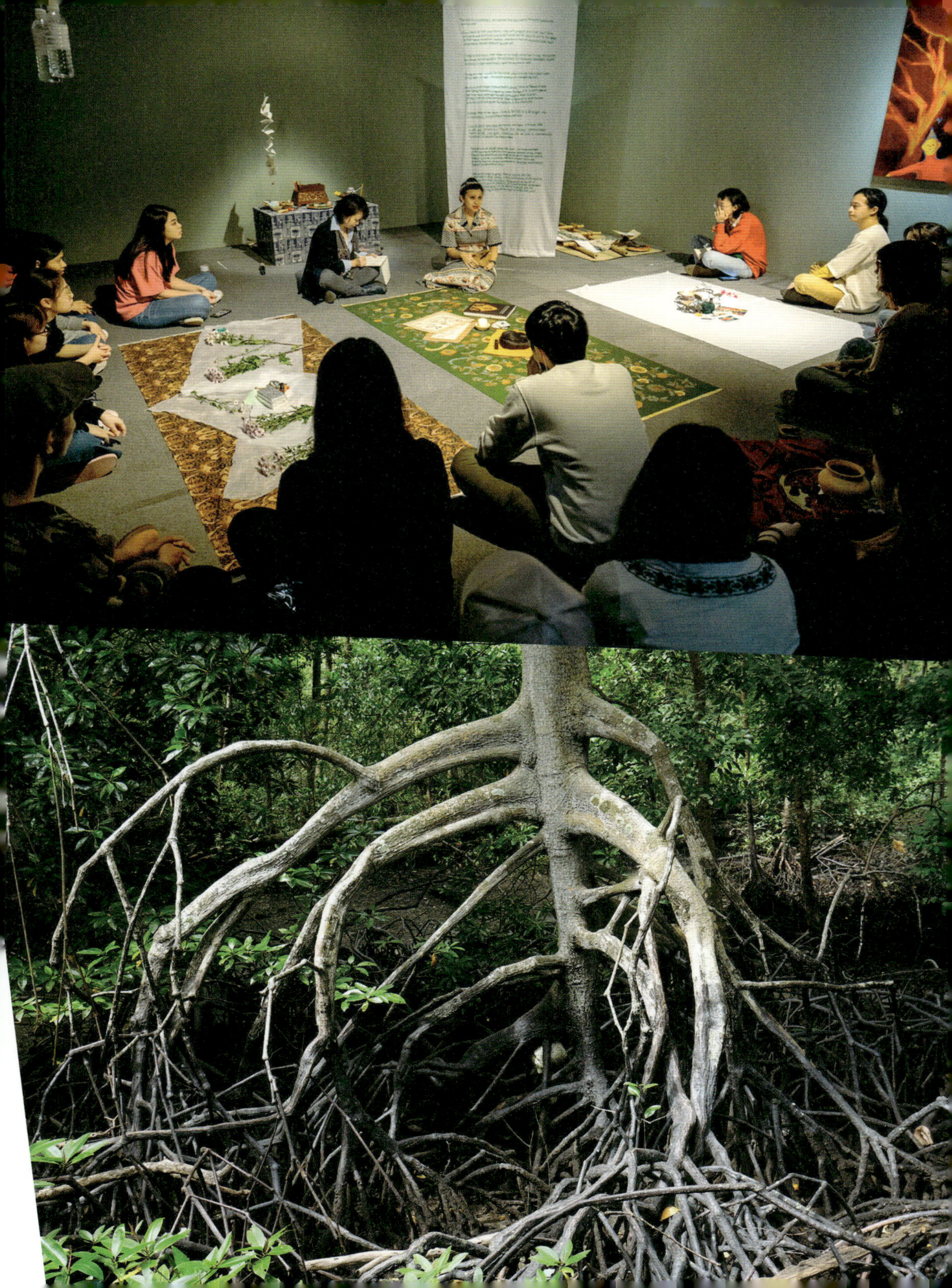

HUSSEIN NASSEREDDINE

Born 1993 in Beirut, Lebanon, lives and works in Beirut and Paris, France

Laughing on the River, Your Eyes Drown in Tears

2023 / Performance on March 2, 2024

Hussein Nassereddine creates installations, videos, and performances that use language and poetry to excavate questions of memory, fragility, and transmittal. A graduate of Ashkal Alwan 2017–18 Home Workspace Program in Beirut, his practice is grounded in a multi-disciplinary approach to image-making. Language is a tool used to create and disrupt. Influenced by the political turmoil and tragedy in Lebanon, Nassereddine uses poetry as a point of departure for accessing people and places that have disappeared. In a practice that seeks to find form for loss, his work becomes a narrative matrix of place, individual experience, and collective stories; processes of erasure are critical to examining absence. Poems written on paper and left exposed to the sun become blanched with time. Materials as varied as steel, natural stone, carbon paper, salt, and concrete all find space in this annotated index of ever-evolving works, along with found footage, digital images, poems written by the artist, original drawings, and videos shot by his mother.

In *Laughing on the River, Your Eyes Drown in Tears* (2023), audiences gather around a lotus-shaped fountain on the ground made of steel and limestone cladding with a water-like surface of painted paper. Before a wall and backdrop covered with wallpaper corresponding to the "water" of the fountain, Nassereddine recites iterations of bygone Arabic poetry, in which poets, according to myth, are transformed by their utterances into shimmering marble. The installation simultaneously suggests a possible reenactment, a plausible fantasy, and an invitation to embark on a journey. His words evoke long desert nights, sea waves swallowing poets' bodies, water turned to silver, ponds like jewels, and rivers of gold. Water becomes the stand-in for loss—for tears gathered into puddles that become large enough to form ponds. Eventually, like history, stories, and memory, these too evaporate, with time. "Nothing remains but the wet voice of the poet, and librarians' records held in dry books, and historians' accounts written on papers flooding with the blue of rivers and springs." The work becomes a verbal, sonic, tactile experience of creating both visual and collective memory around ancient poems that may or may not have existed in the form they are being received.

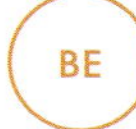

Above: Video still from *Laughing on the River, Your Eyes Drown in Tears*, 2023
Below: Installation view of *A Few Decent Ways to Drown* at Deir Al Kalaa, Lebanon, 2022

تِلكَ الكَلِمَـــــــــــــــات، الِتي تَروي عَطشيَ الغَريب والمَرِيـــــــــــر
Words that could quench my strange and embittered thirst

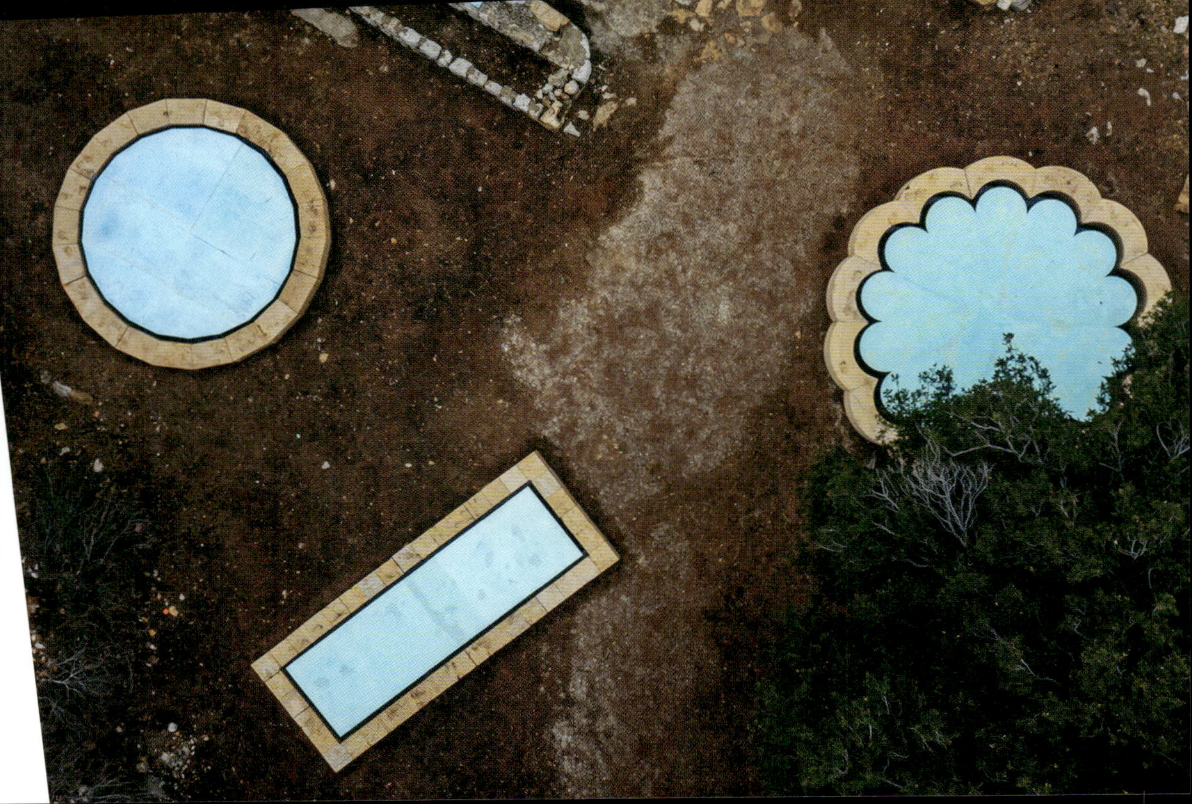

FILWA NAZER

Born 1972 in Swansea, United Kingdom, lives and works in
Jeddah, Saudi Arabia

The Housed Body

Workshop and Artist Talk on April 19–20 and 26–27, 2024

Filwa Nazer is a Saudi artist whose abstract textile works, collages, and drawings merge techniques and materials from the fields of the visual arts, fashion, and architecture. Her explorations of women's lives in the context of Saudi Arabia give visual and spatial form to emotions, personal stories, and collective memories. After graduating from the Marangoni School of Fashion and Design, Milan, Nazer attended classes offered by pioneering Saudi painter Safeya Binzagr, who founded an art gallery, library, and school for other women artists in the early 1990s. Nazer has recently shown her work in a number of major international exhibitions, such as the Middle East Institute, Washington, DC, (2023); the 16th Lyon Biennale (2022); and the Sharjah Art Foundation, UAE (2019).

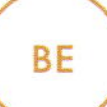

Nazer's practice focuses on textiles, using sewing techniques, hand-stitching and in particular pattern-making, to explore tensions between bodies and the spaces they occupy. Her suspended works, such as *Five Women* (2021), a commission for the 1st Diriyah Contemporary Art Biennale, appear as ghostly inhabited garments, elegantly composed through layers of abstract cross-stitches on calico cotton, muslin, transparent tarlatan, and black tulle. These fabrics are conventionally used in fashion for constructive elements or lining and remain hidden in the final article of clothing. Nazer is also known for her collage works overlaying personal snapshots with tangles of patterned shapes, which visually and conceptually convey stories related to female biographies.

As part of the Biennale Encounters program that allows artists to share their working methodologies, Nazer is conducting two workshops. Each unfolds over the course of two days. One is dedicated to participants from the field of art, design, and fashion interested in experimental and interdisciplinary approaches, while the second workshop is for children. Participants in the workshops are introduced to the pattern-making techniques that define Nazer's process and are encouraged to express their memories, perceptions, and understandings of "home."

Untitled 4, from the series *Topoanalysis*, 2023

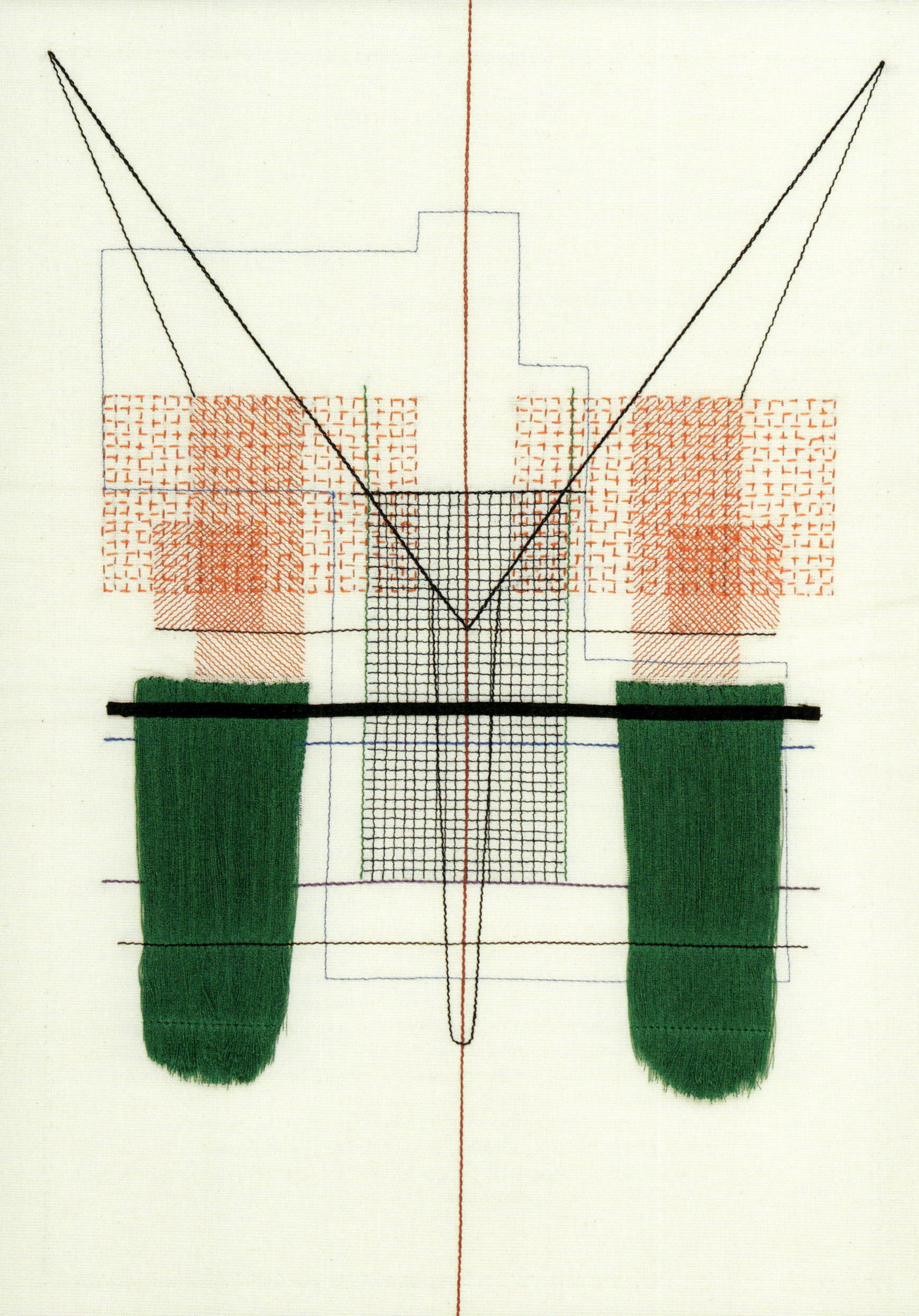

ELIA NURVISTA

Born 1983 in Yogyakarta, Indonesia, where she lives and works

Reading Palm

Workshop and Artist Talk on May 11 and 12, 2024

Elia Nurvista is an artist and curator who explores food as both a medium of artistic practice and a field of research in formats such as workshops, study groups, publications, site-specific works, performance, video, and installations. For Nurvista, food has political, social, and aesthetic implications; its tastes, recipes, and paths of origin not only weave through cultural traditions but also trace the outlines of global inequalities and their geopolitical histories. In 2015 she initiated the interdisciplinary food study group Bakudapan. She is also part of Struggles for Sovereignty, a transnational solidarity platform engaged in struggles for the self-determination of Indigenous people and their access to basic resources: land, water, farming, and food. Nurvista has taken part in major group exhibitions worldwide, including Sharjah Biennial 15 (2023), Dhaka Art Summit (2020), Karachi Biennale (2019), and the 9th Asia Pacific Triennial of Contemporary Art (2018). In 2021 she co-curated Jogja Biennale Equator XVI: *Indonesia with Oceania* (2021) and in 2017 was a nominee for the Visible Award for socially engaged practices.

Her contribution to the Diriyah Contemporary Art Biennale 2024 is part of her ongoing series *Long Hanging Fruits* (2020–present), which explores the cultivation of palm oil in Indonesia. Today the country is the world's largest producer of the ubiquitous vegetable oil, which is made from the fruit of the oil palm, a plant introduced from its native Africa by the Dutch. The mass global consumption of palm oil has not only wrought devastation on Indonesian ecosystems due to the excessive deforestation caused by clearing land for palm oil plantations; it has also created a nationwide dependency on the harmful legacy of colonial plantation economies, which have resulted in land disputes between local communities. In Diriyah, the workshop "Reading Palm" opens up a collective interrogation of the history of palm oil, unfolding through a tasting of palm oil dishes and a group reading of selected chapters from Max Haiven's *Palm Oil: The Grease of Empire* (2022). Consumption takes on literal and allegorical dimensions in Nurvista's workshop. Eating, reading, and digesting together transform palm oil from a symbol of exploitative and industrialized economic cycles originating from the colonial structures of the nineteenth century into a vital ingredient of hospitality, critical exchange, and rethinking patterns of production and consumption.

Above: Palm reading workshop at Künstlerhaus Bethanien, Berlin, Germany, 2023
Below: Open studio at Jan van Eyck Academie, Maastricht, the Netherlands, 2022

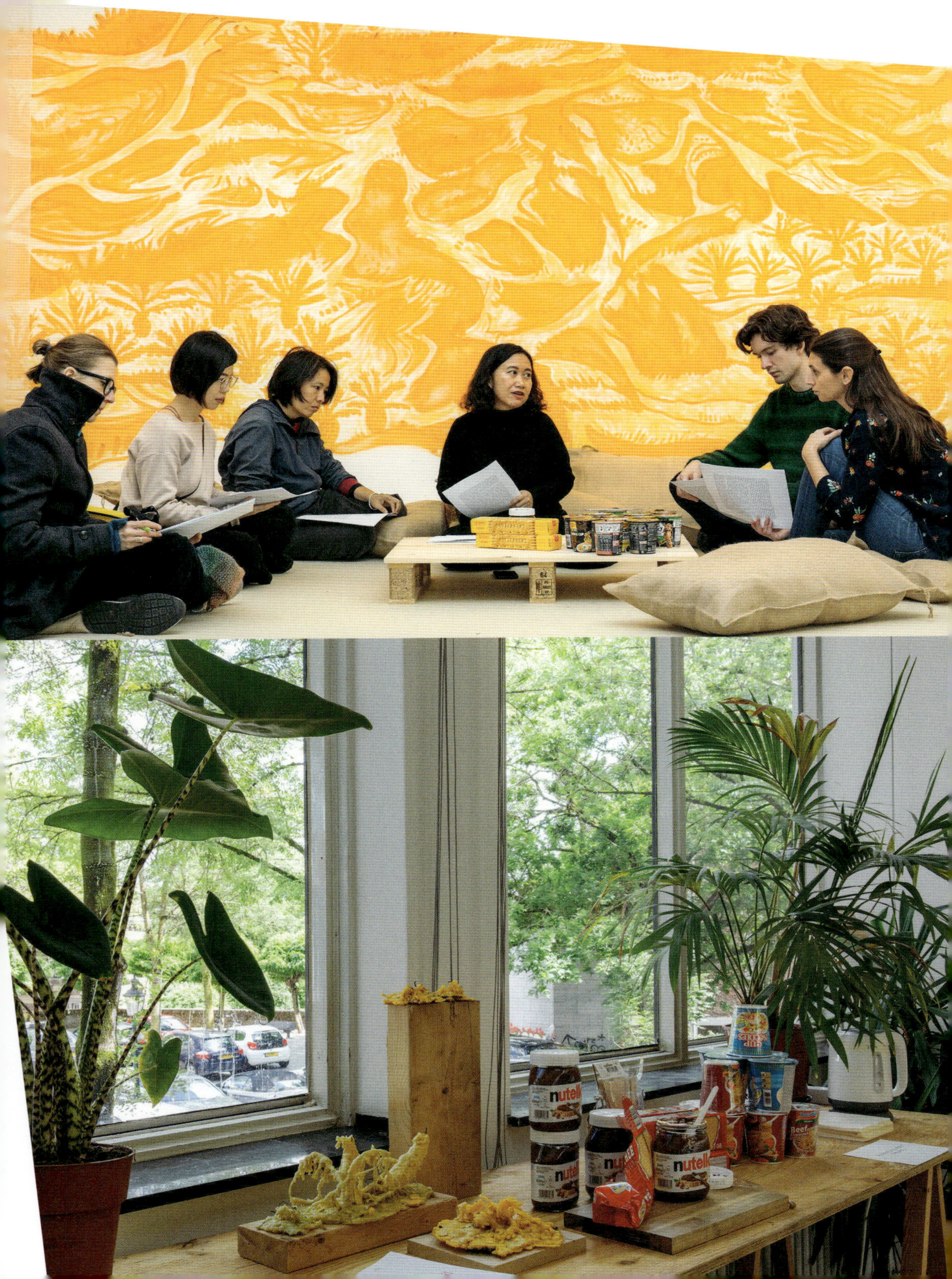

SYN ARCHITECTS

Established 2019 in Riyadh, Saudi Arabia
Sara Alissa born 1990 in Paris, France, lives and works in Riyadh, Saudi Arabia
Nojoud Alsudairi born 1994 in Jeddah, Saudi Arabia, lives and works in Riyadh, Saudi Arabia

Walking Tours
February 20 and 21, March 6 and 7, 2024

syn architects is dedicated to ecologically sensitive architectural design that upholds the material values of innovation, sustainability, and inclusivity. Founded by Saudi Arabian architects Sara Alissa and Nojoud Alsudairi, the practice is grounded in an aesthetic language informed by an awareness of the natural environment and its materials. The practice seeks to reflect and preserve not only the ecology of place but also to engage the inhabitant community in discourse centered around the built and natural landscape. As much a studio as it is an artistic endeavor, the firm's founders lead the research-based Um Slaim Collective, which uses critical investigations of the displacement of the vernacular Najdi architecture of Riyadh to document the disruption of urban ecology. The architects are involved in pioneering work researching and archiving modernist and postmodernist buildings in Saudi Arabia through their sister organization saudiarchitecture.org.

These multifaceted, research-based archival platforms inform and direct the architectural studio, underscoring its concern with ecological and urban continuity. The practice seeks essential, alternative, environmentally specific approaches to both thinking and building, prioritizing user experience and collective accessibility. In their contribution to Saudi Arabia's pavilion at the 18th Venice Architecture Biennale (2023), for example, syn architects drew on a deep knowledge of the natural environment in Saudi Arabia to construct building blocks comprised of soil and crushed stone—a kind of local rammed earth—as well as a prototype set of panels made of woven palm leaves for use in making roofing, shading structures, walls, or screens. Within these contexts of materiality, the practice transforms common ideas of places into site-specific, environmentally dependent buildings and installations, as in their design for the Almasar Mosque (2019) in Riyadh, which was built in part by using repurposed material excavated from the construction site.

syn architects is hosting a series of walking tours for Biennale Encounters, introducing visitors to different parts of Diriyah and central Riyadh, where their studio Um Slaim is located. The walk includes the researchers' stories, personal anecdotes, and reflections on the architecture and social histories of these neighborhoods and is structured to encourage visitor participation and discussion.

BE

Alfotah courtyard house, Um Slaim Collective walk, Alfotah, Riyadh, Saudi Arabia, 2022

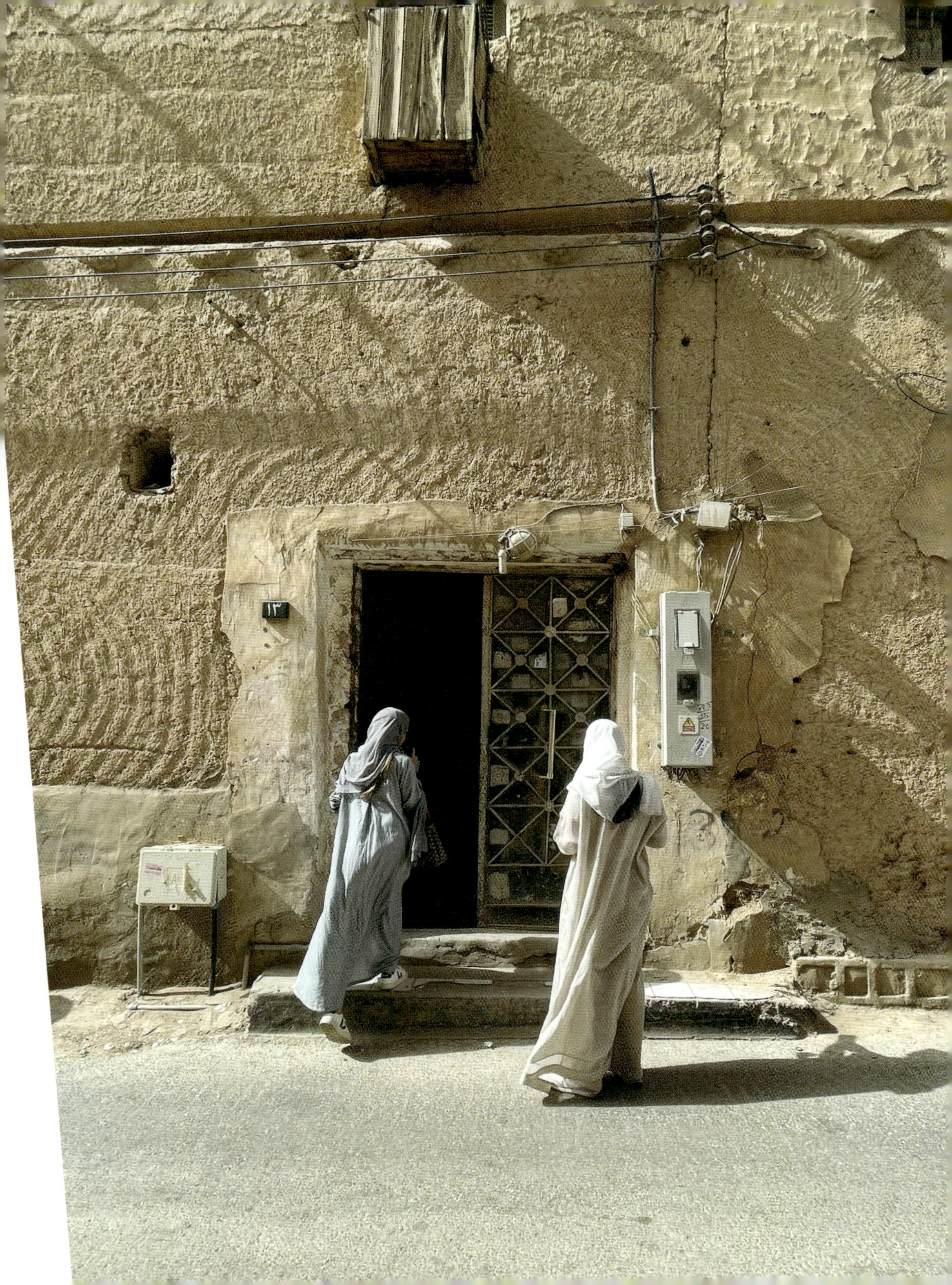

JANA WINDEREN

Born 1965 in Bodø, Norway, lives and works in Innlandet, Norway

Call from the Edge: Under Water

2024 / Concert on March 1, 2024

Jana Winderen works with digital technologies and sound to explore complex and largely inaccessible underwater sonic environments. After studying mathematics, chemistry, and fish ecology at the University of Oslo, she trained as an artist at Goldsmiths, University of London, where she started to work with sound in 1992. In 2011 she was awarded the Golden Nica of the Prix Ars Electronica for Digital Musics & Sound Art. Based on her underwater sound recordings, she makes immersive, site-specific, spatial-audio installations and concerts, which she has exhibited and performed in major institutions and public spaces around the world. In November 2023 she was the first artist-in-residence at CORDAP, Coral Research & Development Accelerator Platform, at the King Abdullah University of Science and Technology (KAUST), Saudi Arabia.

In her new work *Call from the Edge: Under Water* (2024), Winderen draws on her recent multichannel underwater recordings from the edges and interiors of coral reefs in the Red Sea off the coast of Saudi Arabia to create a forty-minute sound performance. The recordings were made during her residency at CORDAP. All across the planet coral reefs are at risk, exposed to warming water, ocean acidification, and dredging, while the creatures living around the coral are impacted by anthropogenic noise. Coral have been around since the time of the dinosaurs, and coral fossils can be found in the vicinity of Diriyah. Trying to bring attention to these biodiverse and important forests of the sea, Winderen urges us to listen to the voices of their inhabitants. In her recordings several species are audible at the same time: fish making grunting, scraping, crackling, and knocking sounds together, forming loud choirs, accompanied by other crustaceans. Such sound environments change depending on the given lunar phase, time of day, and season. This piece continues her investigation into assessing the health of a body of water through sound. It raises the alert on how anthropogenic sound is affecting the ability of underwater animals to communicate, hunt, and orientate themselves in the face of marine environments impacted by the sounds of ships, sonar devices, seismic testing, military activity, leisure boats, and industrial activity both at sea and on land. Winderen's performance serves as an impassioned call to action to preserve the ecological environments that foster oceanic life and allow coral reefs to thrive.

From the CORDAP Artist Residency, KAUST, King Abdullah University of Science and Technology, Thuwal, Saudi Arabia, 2023. Above: Sketches of floats for hydrophone cables and fish likely to be encountered at the coral reefs in the Red Sea / Below: Artist inspecting hydrophones at Rose Reef

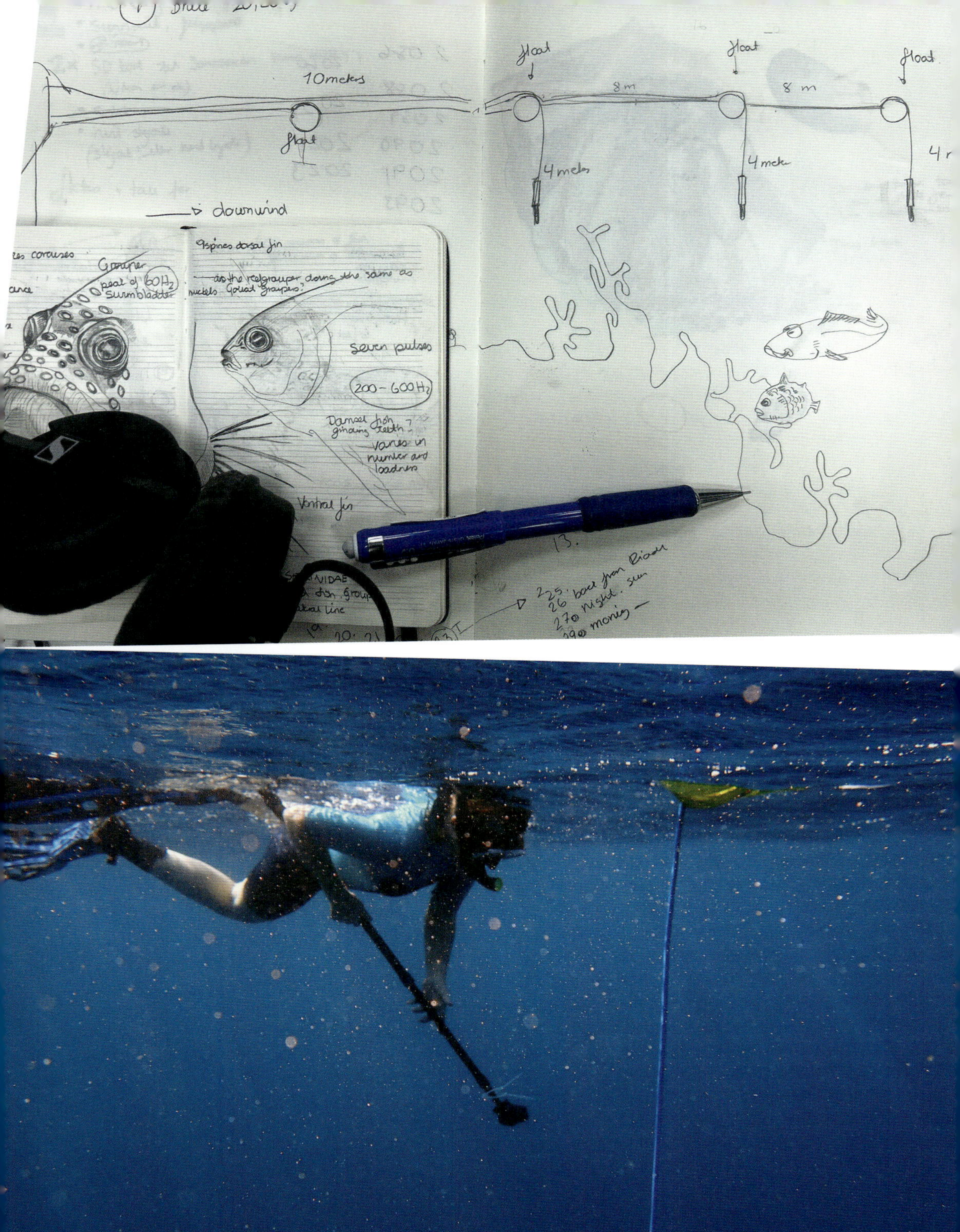

THE LEARNING GARDEN

The Learning Garden is a digital platform for learning with and about
the physical exhibition of *After Rain* and the Biennale Encounters
program of events and performances. Exploring the themes and
questions running throughout the Diriyah Contemporary Art Biennale
2024, the online format acts as a companion to the exhibition and its
programs. It focuses on research-based practices, including a selection
of works commissioned exclusively for the platform as well as content
from artists participating in the Biennale. The latter is harvested for The
Learning Garden in close dialogue with the curatorial team and the
artists. This digital content is often closely related to the works presented
in the exhibition or follows a thread of related investigations.

These supplementary contributions extend the in-person experience
of the Biennale to allow for additional modes of access and return
to the works it includes, expanding its audiences beyond the limits
of physical presence and the dates of the exhibition. It enables the
rigorous creative work of numerous participating artists to be introduced
to a multitude of publics in Saudi Arabia and across the world.

The website architecture and user experience are designed to intuitively
cater to a diversity of users across mobile and web applications,
taking close consideration into questions around accessibility and
ease of use.

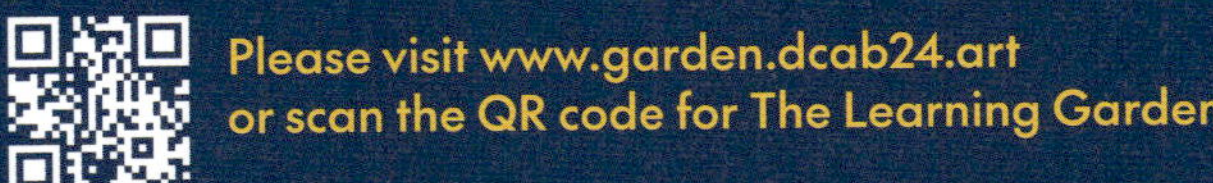

The website incentivizes visitors to craft their own learning journeys through the content on the platform. The site is dynamic and responsive to user's interests and engagement, while allowing the possibility for discovery, refuge, and stillness within a digital media experience.

The research commissioned exclusively for The Learning Garden includes works by Tara Aldughaither & Joe Namy, Circle d'Art des Travailleurs de Plantation Congolese (CATPC), Hiba Ismail, Nidhi Mahajan & Moad Musbahi, Robin Meier Wiratunga, and Feifei Zhou. These durational research-based practices add to the myriad contributions present online, a number of which grow, accrue, and shift over time. The themes explored by the six commissions extend the discourses produced in the Biennale: touching upon translocal sonic histories from across the Indian Ocean; considering digital restitution and collective possibilities of regenerative post-plantation futures; exploring more-than-human perspectives through the vocality and soundscapes of birds from small islands in the Red Sea; listening to experiences of sailors recording and adapting to accelerated changes in climate affecting millennia-old maritime navigation histories; providing an immersion in the acoustic fields of shifting dunes and some of their nonhuman inhabitants; and finally discovering amphibious plant ecologies that enable the reimagining of multispecies coastal futures.

These texts, conversations, microhistories, field notes, workshop manuals, research guides together with the multimedia works are reference materials and germinating seeds, conceived to enable future threads to take root in these fertile grounds of knowledge, memory, and art-making.

TARA ALDUGHAITHER & JOE NAMY

Tara Aldughaither born 1990 in Dhahran, Saudi Arabia, lives and
works in Khobar, Saudi Arabia
Joe Namy born 1978 in Lansing, MI, United States, lives and works
between Beirut, Lebanon, and London, United Kingdom

Rhythms of the Rising Sun
2024

Tara Aldughaither is an artist, curator, and vocalist. In 2020 she founded Sawtasura (meaning "voice of the image"), a community-based reimagination platform focusing on women's musical histories in the Arab Peninsula. The platform has so far launched three physical exhibitions and one digital intervention, as well as amassing a humble collection of original records. Aldughaither is a graduate of the MA Culture, Criticism, and Curation program at Central Saint Martins in London. In addition to her curatorial work with private and public entities, Aldughaither's practice extends into programming, publishing, and performing musical culture as an alternative form of continuing embodied knowledge in collaboration with artists from across the Arab-speaking world and beyond.

Media artist, composer, and educator Joe Namy's practice often addresses identity, memory, and power structures embedded in sound and music. This includes the politics of bass, the color and tones of militarization, the migration patterns of instruments and songs, and the complexities of translation—from one language to another, from drum to dance, and from score to sound. Namy graduated with an MFA from New York University (2010) and has independently studied jazz, Arabic, and heavy metal drumming. His work has been performed, exhibited, screened, and amplified at international venues, biennales, and events across the world.

Rhythms of the Rising Sun (2024) traces migratory rhythmic ecologies from West Asia, the Indian Ocean subcontinent, East Africa, and the Arabian Peninsula. This collaborative research project aims to raise awareness of resonant sound pressures in the region today. It explores how lucid migratory patterns have shaped some of the most prominent rhythms, sounds, and music of the region, and how rhythms have in turn shaped language and ways of life. The project seeks to continue histories of embodied research, through creative methods that are informed by—but not limited to—resituating ethnomusicological collections, social rituals, scoring and notation, sonic mapping, and acoustic archives. The collaborative research work will act as a resource for other musicians and practitioners seeking to engage with these histories through modes of collective listening and performance.

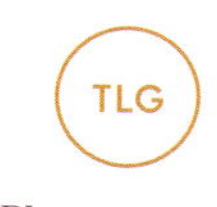

Please scan to
visit the work

Above: Video still, Ismael Dawas Band performing, Manama, Bahrain, 2021
Below: Cassettes from the 1980s and 1990s of female folk artists from the Gulf region

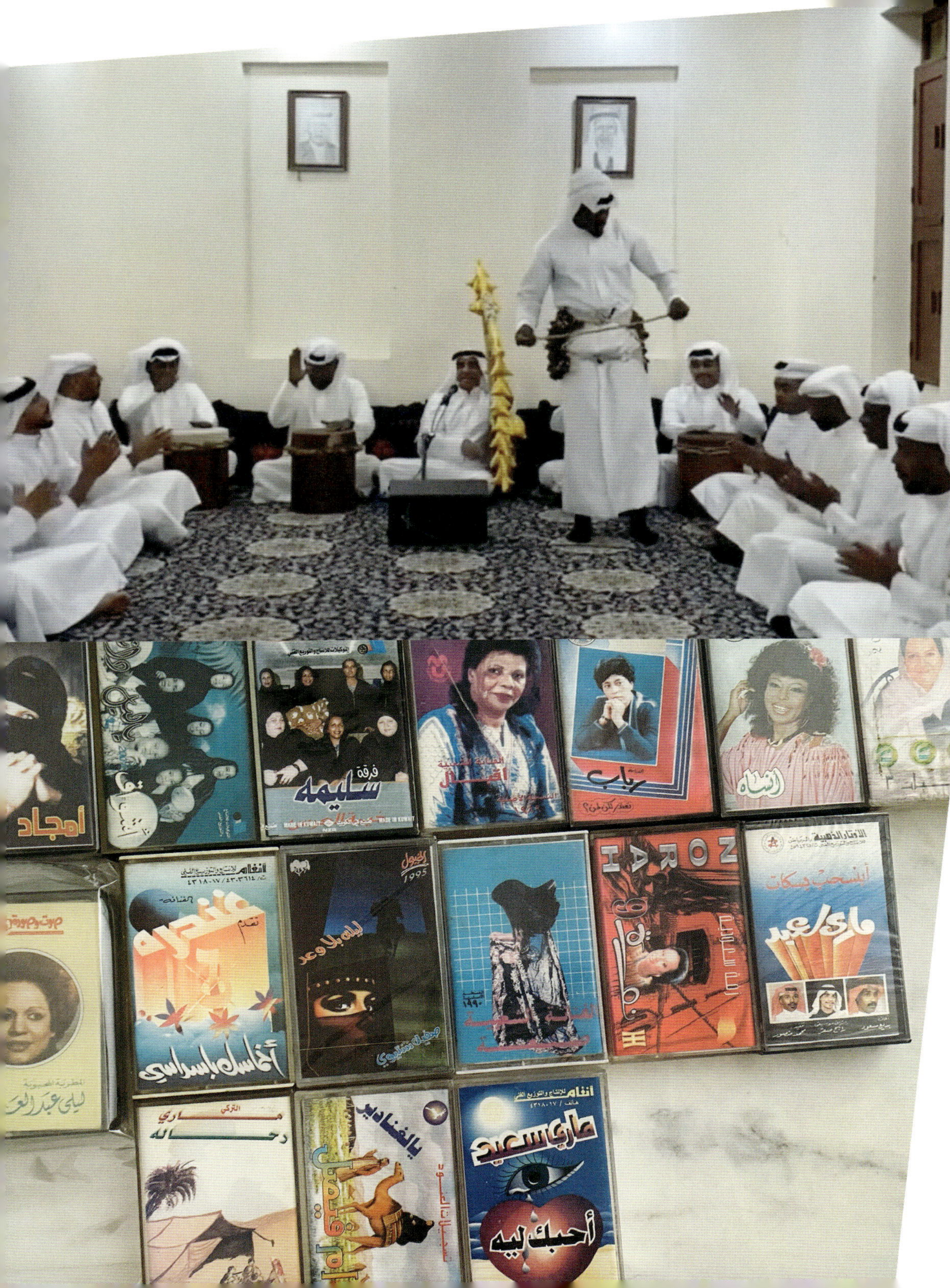

CERCLE D'ART DES TRAVAILLEURS DE PLANTATION CONGOLAISE (CATPC)

Cooperative of plantation workers founded in 2014 and based in Lusanga, Democratic Republic of Congo

Plantations, Museums, and Regenerative Ecologies
2022–ongoing

Since its foundation in 2014, CATPC has been working steadily to use its income from making art to purchase ancestral lands once confiscated by the British company Unilever and its subsidiaries. Two hundred hectares of depleted soil have been reclaimed and recultivated to provide sustenance to the Lusanga community and regrow the surrounding forest. Through a process of sharing and discourse, the collective decides in unison what to produce and how. CATPC defines art as a living force borne of a sacred earth, and art-making is central to the community's attempts to recuperate the knowledge of its ancestral forest lands and its desire to forge more regenerative relationships between art, culture, economy, and ecology. CATPC's works have been exhibited in leading international institutions and will be presented as the official Dutch entry at the Venice Biennale in 2024.

The work *Plantations, Museums, and Regenerative Ecologies* (2022–ongoing) brings together the decade-long collective practice of CATPC in continuing the resistance of the Pende people through the reclamation of land, culture, and "force." For over a century, people on plantations in Congo and elsewhere have been deprived of their culture and forced into unpaid labor. In a radical act of digital restitution, CATPC reclaims a piece of their heritage using funds gained from NFTs (non-fungible tokens) through *Balot NFT*, minted in 2022. The NFT draws on an original sculpture carved in 1931 by the Pende during an uprising against atrocities carried out by the Unilever plantation system and Belgian colonial agents. Depicting the angry spirit of Belgian officer Maximilien Balot, it was created to control his spirit and make him work for the Pende people. A series of short videos share the journey of collective members Matthieu Kasiama and Ced'art Tamasala as they speak to Pende elders, art historians, and academics about the possibility for restitution and lay important ground for the future use of blockchain technology toward regenerative forest ecologies. *Balot NFT* buyers receive a digital rendering of the sculpture. Every purchase helps to directly buy back land, replant the forest, and reintroduce biodiversity, resulting in offsetting carbon emissions and providing autonomy and food security for the community.

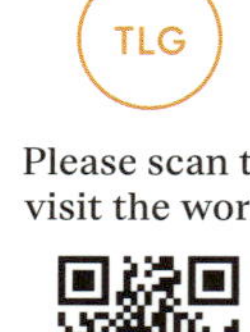

TLG

Please scan to visit the work

Video stills from Renzo Martens, *Plantations and Museums*, 2020 / Above: Ced'art Tamasala drawing Balot in the White Cube / Below: CATPC members (from left): Olele Mulela Mabamba, Irène Kanga, Huguette Kilembi, Jérémie Mabiala, Jean Kawata, Mbuku Kimpala, Ced'art Tamasala, and Matthieu Kasiama

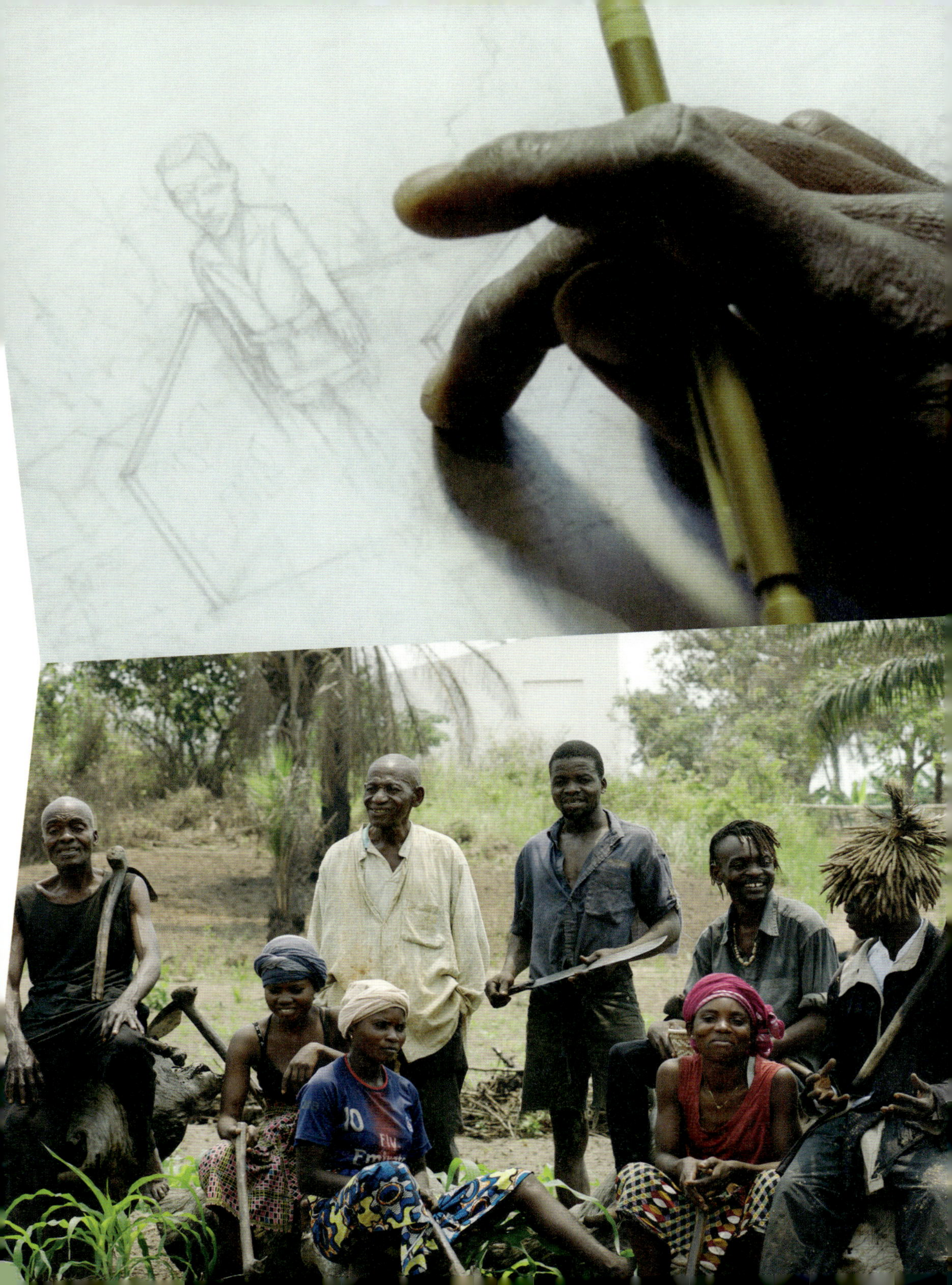

HIBA ISMAIL

Born 1992 in Port Sudan, Sudan, lives and works in West Yorkshire, United Kingdom

Two Islets

2024

Hiba Ismail is a field researcher and artist who works with objects, sound, and video to produce compositions that explore, catalogue, and archive would-be artifacts and object-subjects of natural history. She employs listening as an approach to observing the degrees of intimacy between people, the places we inhabit, and the choreographies of our bodies meeting these geographies as independent bodies. Recent commissions include a sound work for the Red Sea Museum, Jeddah (2024), and *An Ostentatious Paperweight That May or May Not Be the Real Thing* (2021), supported by the Arab Fund for Arts and Culture.

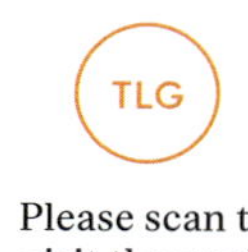

Please scan to visit the work

Two Islets is a body of work that considers the use of indexes and footnotes as a praxis in which ancillary information is reconsidered to carry corporeal weight. Using an ongoing archive of sonic field recordings and images as a starting point to produce a composition, Ismail's practice involves gathering extensive field recordings and images working between the Red Sea and its surrounding areas, resulting in an index of recordings and photographs. The most recent recordings took place on the Suakin Archipelago and multiple locations off the east coast of Sudan. Her work meditates on questions of how the pursuit of knowledge and sovereignty has been infused with dynamics of exclusionary social and national regimes. She seeks to find how art can provide an antidote that positions deep reciprocities in a hostile climate. Ismail reorients the themes of property and extraction away from metaphors of materiality through alternative modes of seeing and listening. Her work is informed by the writing of Édouard Glissant, whose concept of "rhizomatic thought" sees every identity being realized through a relationship with the Other. The process of collecting audio material similarly presents an attempt to understand our relationship to the environment, drawing parallels between contemporary politics, archaeologies, and the natural histories of the earth. Ismail's research work began around the motif of ornithology and the politics of "recording the field" as a postcolonial exercise in subversion. She consolidated the extensive catalogue of archipelago sounds into an audio composition developed in collaboration with sound designer Panos Chountoulidis.

Osprey on nest (*Pandion haliaetus*), Suakin Archipelago, Sudan, 2023

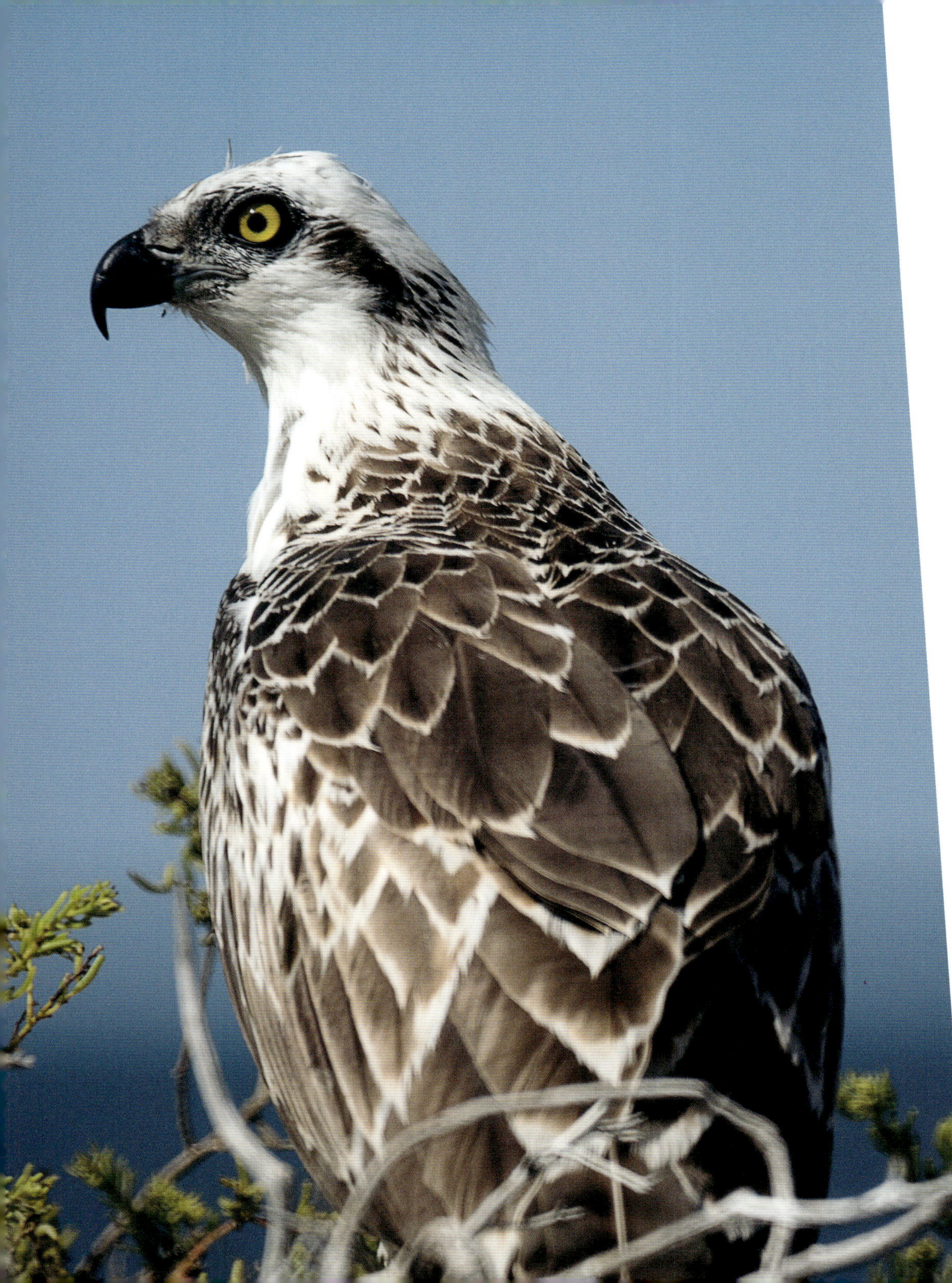

NIDHI MAHAJAN & MOAD MUSBAHI

Nidhi Mahajan born 1984 in Bombay, India, lives and works between
Santa Cruz, CA, United States, and Bombay
Moad Musbahi lives and works on the move

An Excerpt from Kitab Al Marasi: A Composite Navigational Manual for the Indian Ocean

2024

Nidhi Mahajan is an anthropologist whose research examines transregional maritime connections across the Indian Ocean through shipping and trade networks, ports, and their entanglements with state sovereignty. She has a PhD in anthropology from Cornell University and is assistant professor of anthropology at the University of California Santa Cruz. She was recently a Research Fellow at the Africa Institute, Sharjah. Mahajan has developed exhibitions at Fort Jesus Museum in Mombasa, Kenya; Khoj International Artists' Association in New Delhi; and for the 2019 Sharjah Architecture Triennial. Her work has been published in *Comparative Studies of South Asia, Africa, and the Middle East* and *History of the Present*, among other international journals.

Moad Musbahi is an artist, educator, and independent curator whose work as an artist takes the form of collaborative installations, exhibitions, and readings. He holds master's degrees from the Architectural Association and the Royal College of Art in London. He is a doctoral researcher in anthropology at Princeton University and is a visiting lecturer at the Royal College of Art. He has recently presented work at the Kunstverein in Hamburg, Germany (2023); the 18th Venice Architecture Biennale (2023); and the 7th Singapore Biennale (2022). Musbahi currently co-directs the "Taught to Travel" ving program at the Harun Farocki Institut in Berlin in collaboration with RAW Material Company in Dakar.

An Excerpt from Kitab Al Marasi (2024) is a composite navigational manual for the Indian Ocean that draws from the historical cultural practices of local sailors to confront the uncertain future of coastal communities across the Indian Ocean facing extreme climate degradation. These traditional forms of knowledge interweave practices and modes of being from the collective generational memory where sailors on wooden vessels called *dhows* spoke with saints and read the winds, sky, and sea, using methods such as bird sightings or gauging the color of the water to navigate the ocean and predict the weather. Taking this intangible heritage as its starting point, the work creates a repository of Indigenous maritime knowledge that firmly ties the risk of climate change with vernacular forms of knowledge. In bridging the forum of art and cultural work with the space of international heritage and environmental organizations, this research work proposes how the different modalities of display and deployment cast together methods of anthropology, documentation, and Indian Ocean temporalities.

Please scan to visit the work

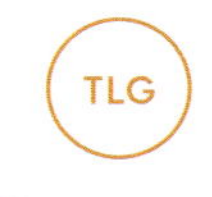

Cyclone Mekunu, 2018. Above: Landing on the coast near Raysut, Southern Oman, May 2019 / Below: Damaged dhow boats awaiting repair, Jam Salaya in the Gulf of Kachchh, India, August 2019

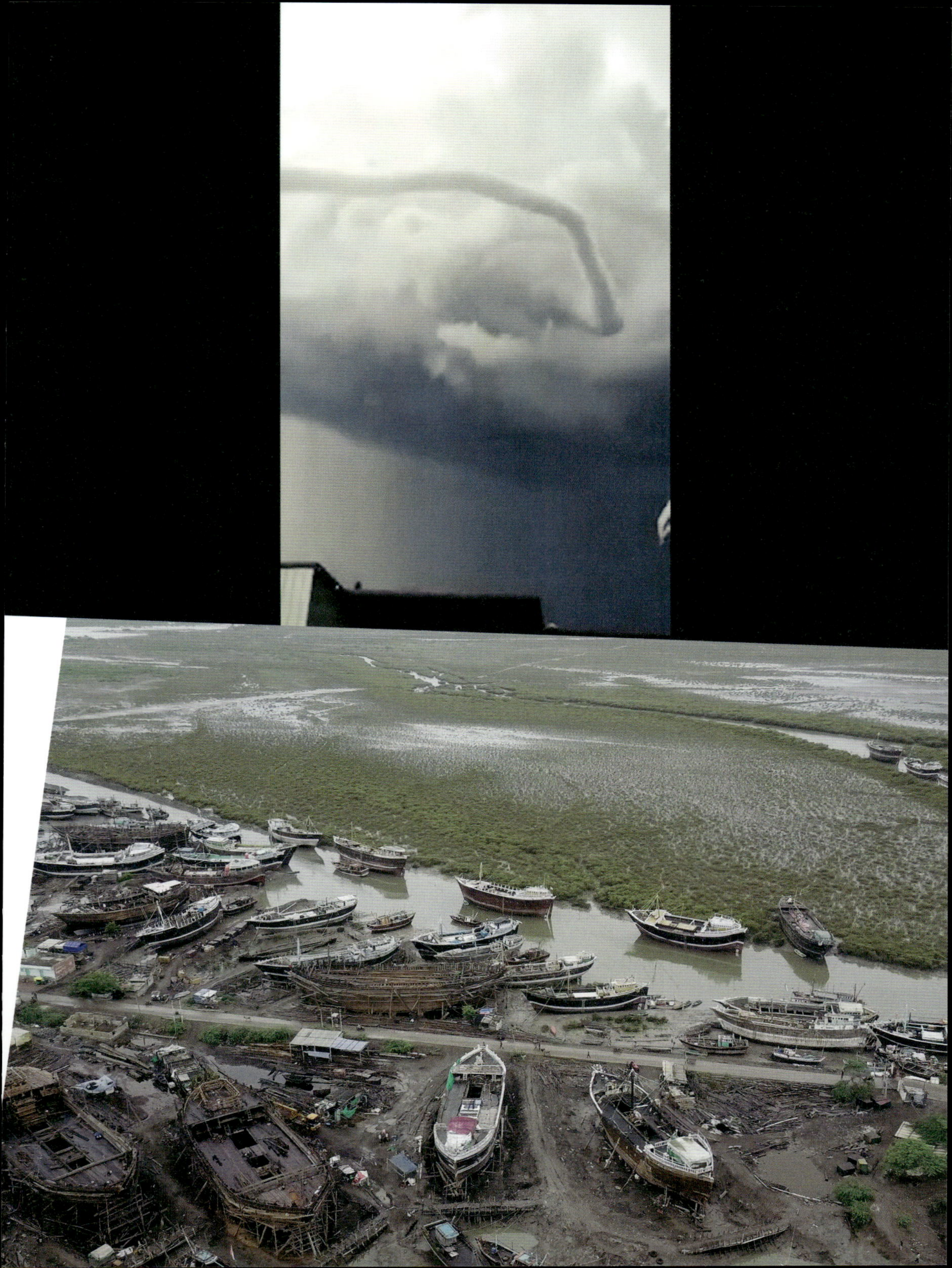

ROBIN MEIER WIRATUNGA

Born 1980 in Zug, Switzerland, lives and works in Paris, France

Waves beneath an ocean of wet air

2024

Artist and composer Robin Meier Wiratunga strives to understand how humans, insects, swarms, and objects think. With a bag of tricks from sound and science, he composes thinking tools made with singing mosquitoes, synchronized fireflies, metronomes, choreographed ants, neural networks, and flute-carrying pigeons. Conducted in close collaboration with specialists and scientific labs, his work blends machine learning with animal intelligence. Arranging human, animal, and nonbiological actors into constellation-like scores, he creates environments and conditions for musical patterns to spontaneously emerge. Meier Wiratunga has a master's degree in cognitive philosophy from EHESS, Paris, France. He has been a music producer at IRCAM / Centre Pompidou since 2006, has taught sound arts at Bern Academy of the Arts in Switzerland since 2021, and has been a fellow of the Istituto Svizzero in Rome since 2018. His projects have been shown at the Palais de Tokyo (2010) and Centre Pompidou (2021) in Paris, the Shanghai Biennale (2016), and Colomboscope in Colombo (2019).

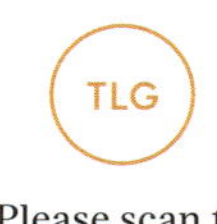
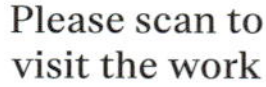

Please scan to visit the work

Waves beneath an ocean of wet air (2024) explores relationships between the desert, its inhabitants, and the gradients of wetness that surround, envelop, and flow within it. The work examines the fluid nature of earth and sand, and how this resonates with the deconstruction of the delineation between water and land as a dominant, colonial fiction. Dunes take shape through repeated patterns of flow that, like musical rhythms, organize particles into undulating waves of stars, parabolas, domes, and other forms, occurring with wind in the desert, water at the bottom of the sea, or ice on the shores of Arctic beaches. As a complex, inhabited ecosystem, the desert is a network of thoughts expressed in rivers of sand and waves of dunes. The chemical composition and shape of each grain of sand speaks of its migration through seabeds, mountains, cities, clouds, and deserts. Meier Wiratunga juxtaposes audio recordings from the Empty Quarters in the Arabian Peninsula—sounds of singing sands, acoustic measurements of dune sediment, and foraging ants from his field work—with submarine recordings from the Indian Ocean, neuroelectric activity of the brain, AI-synthesized vocal sounds, and various other elements to create a generative, polyphonic soundscape, giving a voice to the stories of the desert and weaving a composition with sounds from oceans of varying wetness and its entangled kin.

Centimetric underwater barchan dunes created in a laboratory experiment by Sylvain Courrech du Pont at Université Paris Cité, 2017

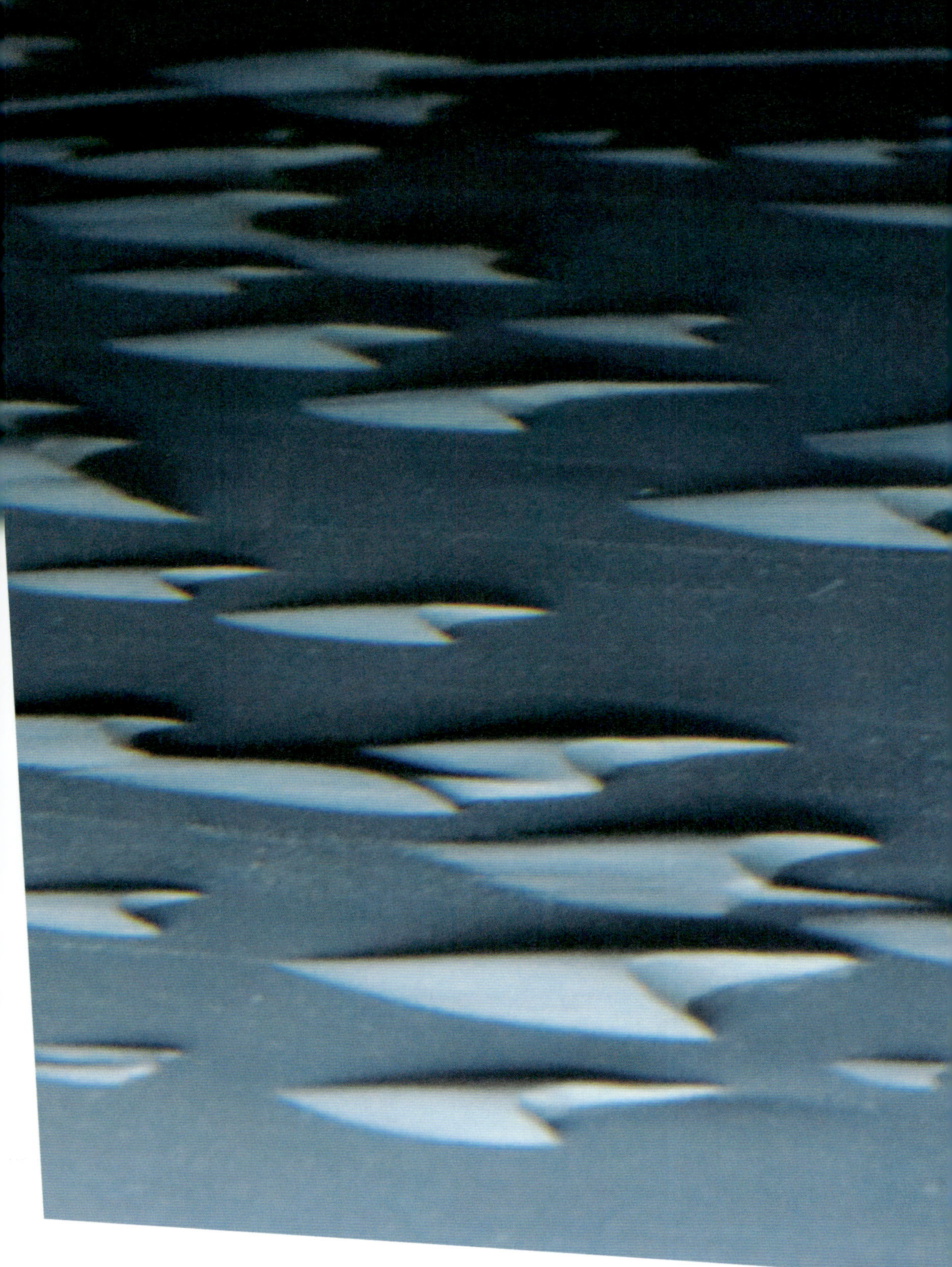

FEIFEI ZHOU

Born 1992 in Jiangsu, China, lives and works between Jiangsu, China, and New York, NY, United States

Before there was land, there were mangroves

2024

Feifei Zhou is an architect, artist, and researcher. Her work explores the cultural and ecological impact of the built and natural environment. Using narrative-based spatial analysis, she collaborates intensively with social scientists to translate empirical observations and scientific research into visual representations that aim to both clarify intricate more-than-human relations and open up new questions. Zhou has a master's degree in architecture from the Royal College of Art, London. She has lectured at international institutions including the Prada Frame: On Forest, the University of Copenhagen, ETH Zurich, Columbia University, the Cooper Union, and Cornell University. As a guest researcher at Aarhus University Research on the Anthropocene (AURA), she co-edited *Feral Atlas: The More-than-Human Anthropocene* (Stanford University Press, 2020). Zhou has published in various international journals and platforms, and her work has been included in international exhibitions and biennials.

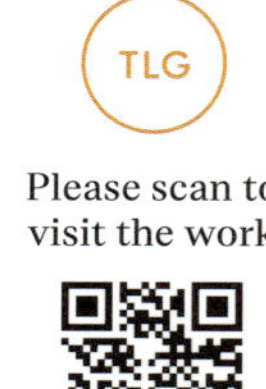

TLG

Please scan to visit the work

Before there was land, there were mangroves (2024) is a long-term, collaborative research undertaking that investigates land reclamation and the intricate ecological, biophysical, and social structures caused by coastal "hardening." Land reclamation is a prevalent phenomenon across coastal regions around the globe. From Singapore and Shanghai to Dammam, miraculous transformations of sparse fishing villages into metropolises are made possible by extensive reclamation that turn porous ocean ecosystems into land. But before there was land, there were mangroves. Mangrove forests exemplify the amphibious coastlines of the Indian Ocean, nurturing a rich range of sea and land creatures including fish, crabs, birds, and shrimp. Critically, their salt-tolerant trunks and roots enable an ever-changing land-water interface, creating a porous environment as a natural barrier for flood protection and tidal impact. While reclaimed land offers opportunities for coastal resettlement and urban development, it does so at the expense of drastically altering and displacing existing ecosystems and multispecies livelihoods. Filled by hard material such as rocks and cement mixed with sand or clay, reclaimed land is often enclosed with concrete for more stability, eliminating porosity and resulting in more severe flooding and biodiversity degradation. These are some of the most pressing battles for coastal communities around the world, pushing us to question and reimagine other kinds of coastal more-than-human relationships.

Above: Feifei Zhou with Zahirah Suhaimi and Jefree Salim, from the series *Shifting Porosities*, 2022 / Below: Feifei Zhou with Kirsten Keller, *Flowing Toxins*, 2020

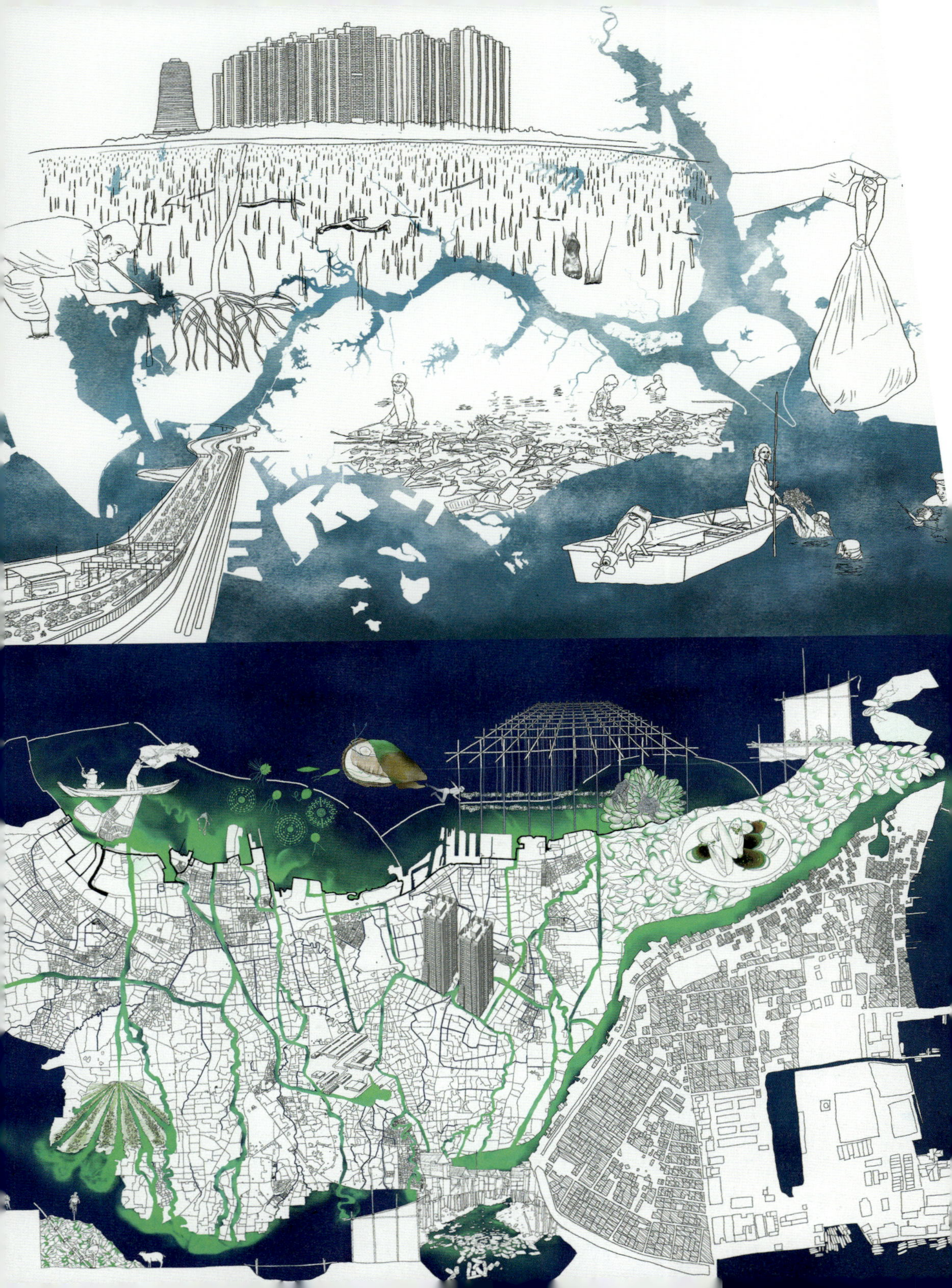

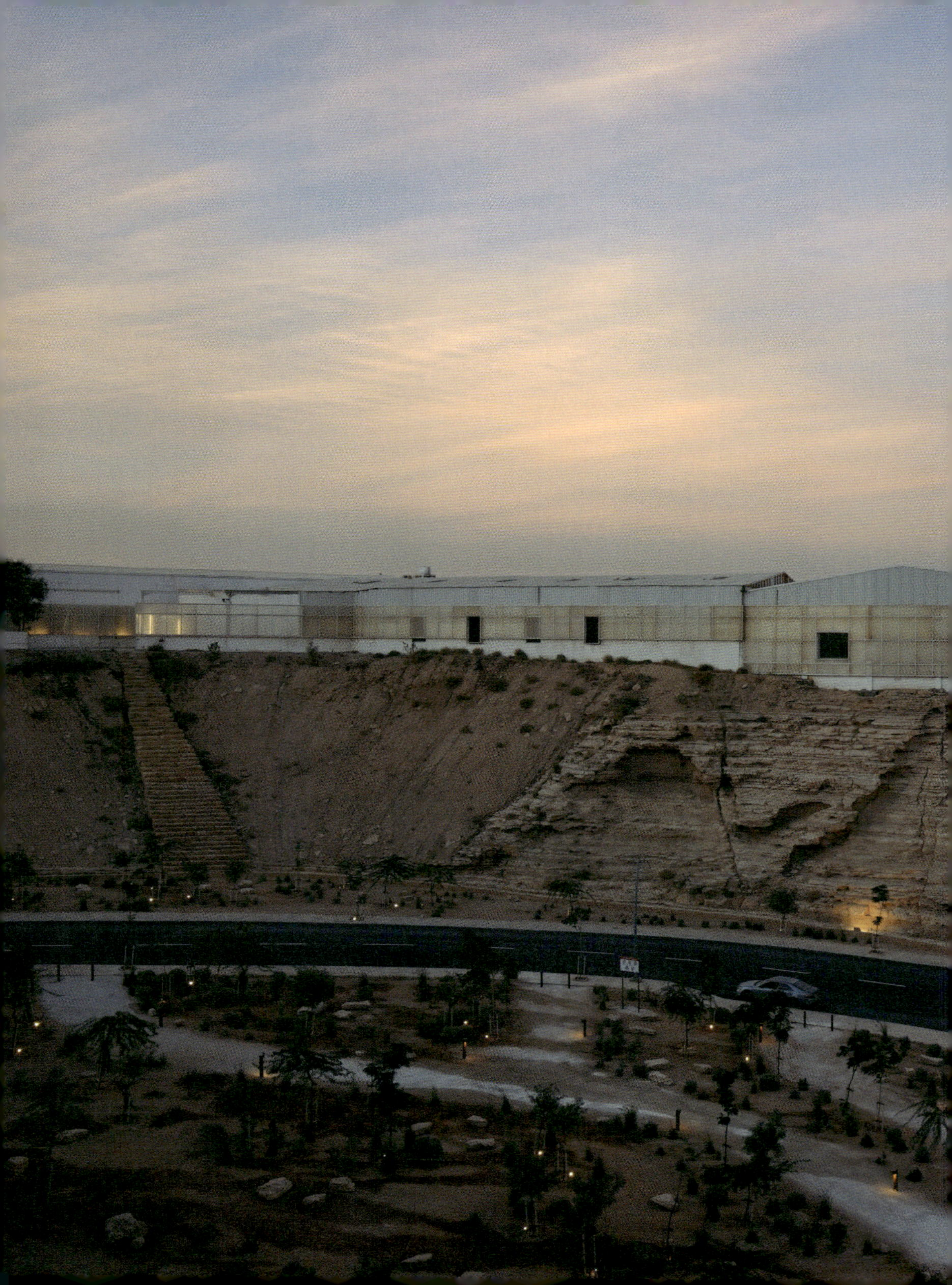

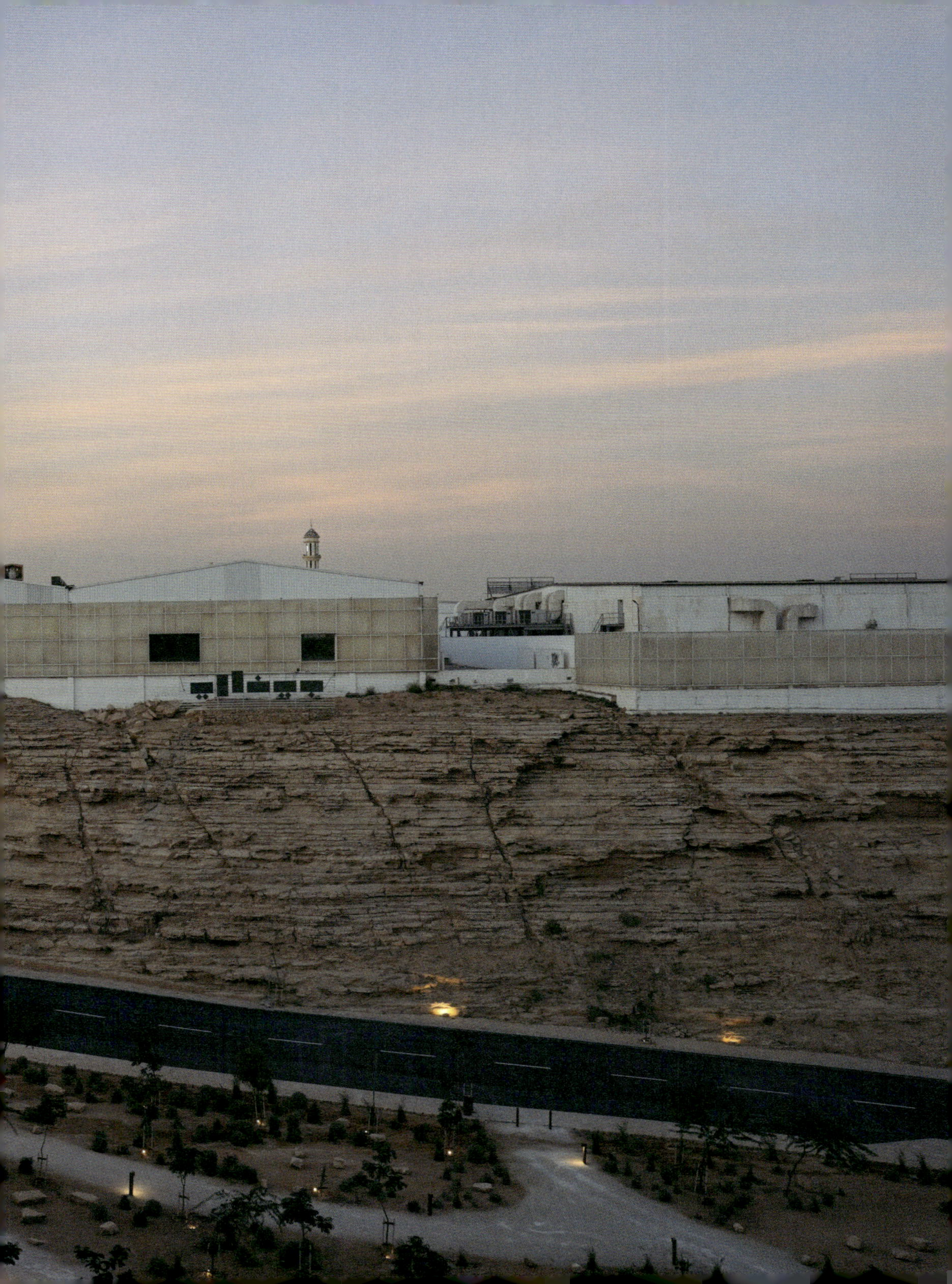

FILM PROGRAM
BLACK BOX EXHIBITION HALL B1

Kheyal
Munem Wasif

2015–19 / Video, black and white, stereo, 23 min 34 sec

Following four characters through neighborhoods of Old Dhaka, the film is an intimate and evocative portrait of the Bangladeshi capital. *Kheyal* (originally derived from the Arabic word for "fiction" or "imagination") is the name of a major form of Hindustani classical music that offers freedom for musical improvisation, often linked to poetry of longing. Part fiction, part documentary, the work amplifies the city's infrastructure and affective textures, pursuing memories kept through all the senses.

Listen to my words
Dana Awartani

2020 / Digital animation, color, sound (recordings of historical poems), 12 min 57 sec

The screen fills with a pattern drawn from ornamental motifs of *jali* and *mashrabiya*, latticed screens for light and air regulation, traditionally used to shield and confine women. Awartani was inspired by Nur Jahan (1577–1645), a Mughal emperor's wife who played a leading role from behind a *jali*. Voices of modern-day Saudi women recite verses from the pre-Islamic era to the twelfth century by Arab poetesses expressing yearning and pride.

18 000 Worlds
Saodat Ismailova

2023 / HD video, sound, color and black and white, 31 min

Drawing from Sufi traditions that suffuse Uzbeki life, this film casts light as the main protagonist. It glances off futuristic atomic-era monuments, burnishes tiled turquoise domes, streams in from a cave ceiling, and appears as resplendent sunrises and sunsets, lime-green auroras, and the moon. There are people, too: wizened and smiling, weaving silk, or plucked from the annals of Soviet military history and Western anthropology through archival footage.

An Invocation to the Earth
Yeo Siew Hua

2020 / HD video, color, sound, 16 min 10 sec

Reviving the Malay folktale of Sang Kancil, a wily mouse-deer who deftly outsmarts its foes, the film intertwines an underdog fable with environmental politics. While Kancil carries her mortal enemy Buaya (crocodile) through the rainforest, Buaya takes long-overdue revenge upon Kancil. A forest fire unites the two protagonists, who flee, while facial-recognition grids of surveillance technology represent the faces and names of murdered ecological defenders from the Philippines.

Forest Mind
Ursula Biemann

2021 / 4K UHD video, sound, 31 min 45 sec

Filmed in Piamonte, Colombia, one home of the Inga people, this video blends the alchemical and biochemical, the scientific and shamanic. A mesmerizing visualization: the digital code of rainforest sound recordings and a biopsy of a seed from the endangered forest are transcoded into a DNA sequence. Neurobiology, quantum biology, ethnobotany, and the anthropology of science share a common paradigm with decentralized vegetal intelligences and cellular states of consciousness.

Aequare: the Future that Never Was
Sammy Baloji

2023 / 4K UHD video, digital projection, single channel, 5.1 sound, 20 min

Combining Belgian propaganda reels from the 1940s and 1950s with present-day footage from the Democratic Republic of the Congo, this video depicts an agricultural research center in colonial and postcolonial times. The brutalities of extractive colonialism morphed seamlessly into economic imperialism—the exploitation of people and environment never ended. Despite the colonizers' attempts "to tame and civilize the land," clearing it for cash crops, the rainforest has grown back.

{if your bait can sing the wild one will come} Like Shadows Through Leaves
The Migrant Ecologies Project

2021 / HD video, 28 min

This film is part of a long-term engagement with Tanglin Halt, one of Singapore's oldest social housing estates, which runs alongside a former railway track. Owned by the Malaysian state until 2011, the track traversed the heart of Singapore for fifty years. In this ten-meter-wide corridor, ornithologists have observed 105 species of birds. The artists traced memories of this contested site, where the once-famous modern housing blocks are slated for demolition.

How to Improve the World / Cải tiến Thế giới
Nguyễn Trinh Thi

2021 / HD video, sound, color and black and white, 46 min

Set in Vietnam's Central Highlands, the film highlights the role of sound and listening in the cultural practices and spiritual beliefs of the Jarai people. The filmmaker asks Ksor Sep, a Jarai shaman, and her own teenage daughter various questions about the role that sound plays for them. Their responses underscore the costs of privileging the visual over the auditory in the hierarchy of senses.

The Great Endeavor
Liam Young

2023 / Video, sound, color, 9 min

Beyond reducing carbon emissions, environmental scientist Holly Jean Buck advocates we "decolonize the atmosphere" by removing greenhouse gases entirely. What if an enormous carbon-capturing infrastructure were built to mineralize carbon dioxide into desert rock or inject it beneath the seabed? What if this were the largest engineering project ever? The video invites us to consider planetary collaboration on a massive and unseen scale, as a hyperrealistic steel structure spins across the endless ocean, attempting to terraform our collapsing planet.

Bitcoin Mining and Field Recordings of Ethnic Minorities
Liu Chuang

2018 / Video, sound, color, 40 min

This monumental essay was inspired by Liu Chuang's observation of a large number of Bitcoin mining sites situated in abandoned dams in rural Western China. Incorporating found and filmed footage and narrated in Muya, a Sino-Tibetan language, the work explores ethnographic, economic, and military histories. Explored is the way revolutionary technologies often claim to counter the concentration of power, while often perpetuating other forms of capitalistic control.

Scheduled screenings on Wednesdays, 7:00 pm:

Fly with Pacha, Into the Aerocene
Tomás Saraceno

2023 / Video, sound, color, 67 min 15 sec

The work is part of an ongoing dialogue with the communities of Salinas Grandes y Laguna de Guayatayoc Basin in Argentina, initiated in 2017. Using archival footage dating from 2006 onwards, it chronicles the record-breaking, fuel-free flight of the Aerocene Pacha hot-air balloon, shown lifting off from the salt flats of the Salinas Grandes, as well as the struggle of local and Indigenous communities against prospective Lithium mining.

BIENNALE ENCOUNTERS SCHEDULE

APRIL 2023

Gathering in Jeddah—Artist Talk in Riyadh
Azra Akšamija, Christine Fenzl, and Armin Linke

Thursday, April 27, 6–8:00 pm (Jeddah)
Islamic Arts Biennale, Public Program Building

Saturday, April 29, 6–8:00 pm (Riyadh)

In Jeddah, Azra Akšamija, Armin Linke, and Christine Fenzl met local artists during the first edition of the Islamic Arts Biennale. In Diriyah, at the first Biennale Encounter, Azra Akšamija shared her long-term engagement with the politics of memory and heritage; Christine Fenzl presented several projects capturing specific communities through the medium of portraiture; and Armin Linke told about his research on infrastructural projects that are changing our landscapes.

JUNE 2023

When We Remember the Music in Our Dreams
Mariah Lookman

Artist Talk, Saturday, June 17, 7–9:00 pm

Mariah Lookman shared her research on the convergence of different knowledge systems, ancient musical instruments, and the role of Turkmen travelers in connecting different regions by their trade routes. The talk previewed her initial ideas for the Diriyah Contemporary Art Biennale 2024 and her interests in traditional Arabic medicinal plants and healing practices spearheaded by women.

Ethics of Dust
Jorge Otero-Pailos

Artist Talk, Sunday, June 18, 7–9:00 pm

Jorge Otero-Pailos introduced his artistic method of experimental preservation, emphasizing his vision of a future for the existing built environment that is centered on mutual care. Presenting his long-term project *The Ethics of Dust*, the artist discussed his process of employing material residues, including atmospheric dust, to reveal hidden meanings and social histories of different monuments around the world.

JULY 2023

What Makes a Neighborhood?
Apolonija Šušteršič, Youssou Diop, and Ahmad Angawi

Artist Talk, Wednesday, July 5, 7–9:00 pm

Artist Apolonija Šušteršič, chef Youssou Diop, and artist Ahmad Angawi shared their engagement with their local communities—a rapidly changing neighborhood in Oslo and the historical district of Al-Balad in Jeddah. Šušteršič and Diop introduced NJOKOBOK, a restaurant and community space in Oslo. Angawi highlighted Zawiya 97 in Jeddah, an initiative committed to local heritage and craftsmanship.

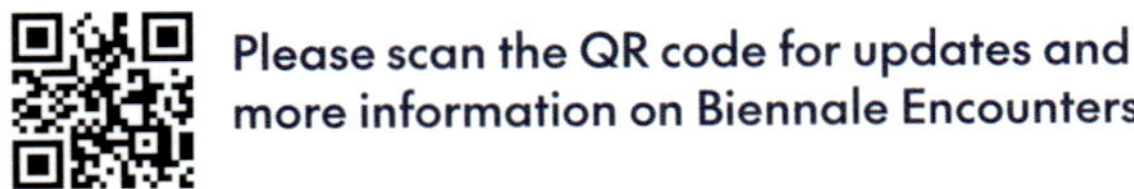

AUGUST 2023

The Embroidery Landscapes
Lucy + Jorge Orta

Workshop, Saturday, August 19, 2–6:00 pm
DBF, Workshop Room

The workshop began with an introduction on native plants in Saudi Arabia provided by Dr. Ahmed Ali Alghamdi, a botanist and consultant at The National Center for Vegetation Development and Combating Desertification. Participants developed a series of embroidery motifs informed by the plants and insects found in Diriyah, Riyadh and other parts of Saudi Arabia. The motifs created by each participant were combined in an imaginary embroidered landscape.

Food-Water-Life
Lucy + Jorge Orta

Artist Talk, Saturday, August 19, 7–9:00 pm

Lucy + Jorge Orta shared their extensive body of work dedicated to core concerns related to the environment, biodiversity, climate change, and migration. The talk also previewed two projects in the Biennale: *70 × 7 The Meal, Act XLVI* (2024), a community dinner that artists have staged in different parts of the world; and *OrtaWater — Purification Factory* (2012), an installation addressing water scarcity.

SEPTEMBER 2023

What Does It Take, What Does It Do to Cook Together?
Britto Arts Trust

Artist Talk and Food Tasting, Saturday, September 2, 7–9:00 pm

Artists Tayeba Begum Lipi and Mahbubur Rahman introduced *Paland and Pakghor (The Kitchen Garden & The Social Kitchen)* (2022), the garden and cooking project central to their contribution to documenta fifteen, which is being presented in a different iteration at the Diriyah Contemporary Art Biennale 2024. Their talk on this project was followed by a live preparation and tasting session involving the popular South Asian snack *fuchka* or *panipuri*.

NJOKOBOK

Food Sharing and Storytelling Session, Saturday September 2, 1–4:00 pm
DBF, Workshop Room

NJOKOBOK invited residents and community members in Diriyah and Riyadh to cook one dish whose story they wished to tell. Participants enjoyed tasting a variety of dishes spanning various regions of Saudi Arabia as well as food of Yemeni, Palestinian, Filipino, Senegalese, and Venezuelan origins reflecting Riyad's diverse fabric of communities.

Desert as Method
Aseel AlYaqoub

Workshop, Saturday, September 16, 4–6:00 pm
DBF, Workshop Room

The workshop addressed representations of the desert from a range of fictional and colonial accounts, cinema, history, art, and architecture. Split into three groups, participants from diverse backgrounds and regions were encouraged to construct new narratives around experiences of the desert as a way of reclaiming the vitality and fullness of this land, to which Saudis share a deep connection.

BIENNALE ENCOUNTERS SCHEDULE

Art Practice as Research
Aseel AlYaqoub

Artist Talk, Saturday, September 16, 7–9:00 pm

Kuwaiti artist, researcher, and writer Aseel AlYaqoub shared insights gained from her research-driven and interdisciplinary practice. AlYaqoub provided practical strategies for navigating complex themes and histories. Through a presentation of some of her projects, she delved into techniques for reading subtle nuances and shifts within specific topics, effective approaches for navigating vast textual resources, and ways to harness the internet as a valuable repository of knowledge.

OCTOBER 2023

How to Remember?
Camille Zakharia

Workshop, Sunday, October 1 to Thursday, October 5, 11:00 am–4:00 pm
DBF, Workshop Room

This five-day intensive workshop explored a typological approach to photography, a systematic and comparative documentation of specific subject matter. Through group fieldwork and critiques, individual participants focused on different subjects, including a tent market, a Sudanese store and spices in the souk, and new buildings in Riyadh.

Camille Zakharia

Artist Talk, Thursday, October 5, 7–9:00 pm

In this talk, Camille Zakharia shared four decades of his photographic practice, which have captured landscapes under transformation, from the coastline of Bahrain to the urban areas of Sharjah, and the war-ravaged buildings of Lebanon.

Strategies for Audience Engagement in Biennales
Gridthiya Gaweewong, John Tain, and Hajnalka Somogyi

Sharing Session, Saturday, October 28, 3–6:00 pm

This session addressed different ways of engaging audiences in perennial large-scale exhibitions and curatorial projects. Looking ahead to the opening of the Diriyah Contemporary Art Biennale 2024, the event was an opportunity for dialogue between this young Biennale in Saudi Arabia and other new initiatives from South and Southeast Asia and Eastern Europe—focusing on audience experience and development.

NOVEMBER 2023

Open Material
Irene Agrivina

Workshop, Friday, November 3, 11:00 am–4:00 pm
DBF, Workshop Room

Soya C(o)u(l)ture, a project initiated in 2014 by the artist and her all-female collective XXLab that creates biomaterial from soy waste using bacteria and tissue culture, served as the basis for the workshop. Participants interested in critical making and DIY processes were guided through a process of turning palm leaves into a biomaterial, a potential alternative clothing material.

Open Hardware
Irene Agrivina

Workshop, Saturday, November 4, 11:00 am–4:00 pm
DBF, Workshop Room

In this workshop, participants were introduced to electronics and the open-source software Arduino, and created DIY audio devices capable of generating sound by touching the surface of leaves. At the end of the workshop, all participants contributed to a collective sound performance with their new audio tools.

Domestic Hacking / Collective Making
Irene Agrivina

Artist Talk, Saturday, November 4, 7–9:00 pm

In this talk, Indonesian artist Irene Agrivina gave an overview of her social and pedagogical practice, which is grounded in critical art-making and design and is committed to the needs of local communities. Her credos are that art, science, and technology should benefit society, and women and girls can spearhead the pathway to sustainable futures.

The Rights of a River
Marjetica Potrč and Jumana Emil Abboud

Workshop, Saturday, November 18 and Sunday, November 19, 11:00 am–4:00 pm
Alzahrani Farm, Diriyah

The environmental, historical, and cultural setting of the Alzahrani Farm inspired the activities of this two-day workshop. Participants engaged in various exercises such as storytelling, role-playing, writing, deep listening, and observation conceived to nourish an understanding of other beings co-existing with us in the living world.

Marjetica Potrč and Jumana Emil Abboud

Artist Talk, Saturday, November 18, 7–9:00 pm

In this joint presentation, artists Marjetica Potrč and Jumana Emil Abboud shared their artistic process and commitment to education and community empowerment. Marjetica Potrč discussed her site-specific projects defined by participatory design and a concern for sustainable solutions. Jumana Emil Abboud introduced her performance-based actions and films, walking, and story-gathering processes that revitalize old narratives and the care of endangered heritage.

Sonic Fieldwork
Jana Winderen with researcher Michelle Nicole-Havlik, KAUST, King Abdullah University of Science and Technology

Artist Talk, Saturday, November 25, 7–9:00 pm

For over three decades, Jana Winderen has been making field recordings in the open ocean that she then collages together into immersive soundscapes. Winderen shared some glimpses of her current research in the Red Sea. The talk was followed by a conversation with KAUST researcher Michelle Nicole-Havlik on the role of bioacoustics in the understanding and conservation of the vulnerable ecosystem of the coral reefs.

Tarek Atoui

Workshop, Sunday, November 26, 2–6:00 pm
DBF, Workshop Room

Tarek Atoui introduced the process behind several of his iconic performance works, such as a long-term engagement with the deaf and people hard of hearing. He also highlighted his current research project, which draws from a diverse collection of musical recordings and traditions along the nomadic routes, tribes, and villages extending from the Atlas Mountains of Northern Africa to the Arabian Gulf.

Tarek Atoui

Artist Talk, Sunday, November 26, 7–9:00 pm

This session explored Tarek Atoui's practice and his long-term commitment to the multifaceted nature of sound, music traditions, and sonic imagination. The artist also offered insights into his research into tribal music traditions from across Morocco and Saudi Arabia.

BIENNALE ENCOUNTERS SCHEDULE

DECEMBER 2023

The Tree of Life
Mona Vătămanu & Florin Tudor

Workshop, Saturday, December 2, 2–6:00 pm
DBF, Workshop Room

This workshop was conceived as an open discussion combined with a drawing activity on the representation and symbolism of plants in the visual arts from an ecological perspective. The starting point was the archaic motif of the "tree of life" and other biomorphic symbols that evoke a preoccupation with immortality, rebirth, regeneration, and afterlife common to many cultures.

Performing History
Mona Vătămanu & Florin Tudor

Artist Talk, Sunday, December 3, 7–9:00 pm

This talk unpacked the artist's engagement with history and the imprints made by past ideologies and twentieth-century modernism on architecture and living environments. The artists introduced their films, installations, textiles, and performative actions that poetically navigate acts of remembrance and erasure, collective memory, and artistic agency.

Brown, Blue, Green, Gray: Urban Rewilding
TAYYŪN

Workshop, Saturday, December 16, 2–6:00 pm
DBF, Workshop Room and Beautiful Garden Nursery

Rewilding is a transformative process of restoring a natural ecosystem to the point of self-sustainability. Workshop participants were introduced to the guiding principles of rewilding interventions that establish complex and dynamic relationships between the soil, water, vegetation, and human-built infrastructure. Combining theory with practice, the workshop included hands-on activities, such as making seed balls and insect hotels, which took place at a local nursery.

TAYYŪN

Artist Talk, Saturday, December 16, 7–9:00 pm

The co-founders of TAYYŪN research studio, Deema Assaf and Yaman Amr, introduced their practice, which is focused on bridging human-made landscapes and native ecologies as well as bringing nature closer to people. Architect Deema Assaf explained the Miyawaki Method, originating from Japan, a planting method that restores forests of native trees ten times faster than natural ecological succession.

FEBRUARY 2024

Zip Zap Circus School
Ângela Ferreira

Activation, Tuesday, February 20, 2:00 pm
Central courtyard

Ângela Ferriera's *Zip Zap Circus School* is a material manifestation of a design for an unrealized school to shelter and provide alternative education for children. Join us to experience these tentlike structures as they are activated by live workshops and performances with local school children, offering a temporary glimpse of the building's original purpose. The activation takes place in collaboration with Mohammad AlFaraj, Nouf Salamah, and Relevé Studio, Riyadh.

The Tree of Life
Mona Vătămanu & Florin Tudor

Activation, Tuesday, February 20, 6–7:00 pm
Exhibition Hall B6

The artists and participants activate their installation through drawing activities and open discussion. Looking at the different expressions of the ancient "tree of life" motif and other biomorphic symbols featured on the carpets and kilims of the work—which largely originate from the Balkans and Central Asia—is the starting point for discussions around climate change, the rights of nature, and the potential of renewal.

Walking Tours
syn architects

Tuesday, February 20, 4:30–6:00 pm
Meeting point: Shamalat

Wednesday, February 21, 3:30–5:00 pm
Meeting point: Um Slaim

syn architects is hosting a series of walking tours, each session of wich is focused on a specific neighborhood and area of research—one in Diriyah and one in central Riyadh, where their studio Um Slaim is located. Each walk includes the researchers' stories, personal anecdotes, and reflections on the architecture and social histories of these neighborhoods. The tours are structured to encourage visitor participation and discussion.

Storytelling Sessions
NJOKOBOK

Tuesday, February 20, Wednesday, February 21, and Friday, February 23, 8–9:00 pm
Terrace 2

NJOKOBOK BAR is activated by a series of storytelling sessions, which draw on the traditional role of the *hakawati,* or "storytellers" in Arabic, who go around coffee shops and souks to engage audiences with their tales. NJOKOBOK has invited different *hakawati*—from the Palestinian, Senegalese, and Indonesian communities in Riyadh—to share stories that are meaningful to their lives and convey their respective cultural traditions.

Super Taus
Taus Makhacheva

Workshop, Saturday, February 24, 11:00 am–1:00 pm
DBF, Workshop Room

This workshop is run by Super Taus, artist Taus Makhacheva's alter-ego, who invites children to imagine ways of being a hero or heroine in everyday life. Children will be encouraged to create their own superhero or superheroine by identifying their powers, tools, and outfits. These choices are then translated into a figurine. At the end of the workshop, each participant shares a story about their superhero or superheroine and can take their hero/heroine puppet home.

This workshop is suitable for children between six and twelve years old. No prior art experience is required. All materials and equipment are provided. Parents or caretakers may accompany children during the workshop.

if your bait can sing the wild one will come
Lucy Davis, founder of The Migrant Ecologies Project

Workshop, Saturday, February 24, 2–6:00 pm
B1 Black Box and Wadi Hanifah

Lucy Davis introduces the collective's film shown in the exhibition and the group's engagement with art and ecology within and beyond Southeast Asia. The workshop includes a walk in Wadi Hanifah guided by the artist and a local ornithologist. The workshop is designed to heighten participants' attentiveness to bird ecologies, offering guided artistic experiments with calls, echoes, and shadows.

MARCH 2024

Call from the Edge: Under Water
Jana Winderen

Concert, Friday, March 1, 9:00 pm
JAX District

In her performance *Call from the Edge: Under Water* (2024), Jana Winderen draws on her recent recordings from the edges and interiors of the coral reefs in the Red Sea off the coast of Saudi Arabia to create a new composition that brings attention to these biodiverse and important forests of the sea. She urges us to listen to the voices of their inhabitants.

Storytelling as a Tool for Inquiry and Renewal
Abdulla Buhijji and Noor Alwan

Workshop, Saturday, March 2, 2–6:00 pm
DBF, Workshop Room

This workshop will foreground folklore and past rituals from the Gulf region as tools for artistic creation, and approach storytelling from the perspective of cultural preservation and acts of togetherness. Participants will be invited to a process of collaborative storytelling where they will create ecological narratives inspired by folklore as a way to observe, record, and map the Anthropocene.

Laughing on the River, Your Eyes Drown in Tears
Hussein Nassereddine

Performance, Saturday March 2, 6:00 pm
Black Box B1

In this performance the audience gathers around a lotus-shaped fountain to listen to Hussein Nassereddine reciting iterations of bygone Arabic poetry, in which poets, according to myth, are transformed into shimmering marble as a result of their utterances.

Walking Tours
syn architects

Wednesday, March 6, 3:30–5:00 pm
Meeting point: Shamalat

Thursday, March 7, 3:30–5:00 pm
Meeting point: Um Slaim

syn architects is hosting a series of walking tours, each session of wich is focused on a specific neighborhood and area of research—one in Diriyah and one in central Riyadh, where their studio Um Slaim is located. Each walk includes the researchers' stories, personal anecdotes, and reflections on the architecture and social histories of these neighborhoods. The tours are structured to encourage visitor participation and discussion.

Wall Extract (Riyadh)
Vikram Divecha

Social Gathering, Friday March 8, 8:00 pm
Location tbc

Divecha has extracted a section of wall from a structure in Riyadh that is slated for demolition. Through conversations, cuisine, and socializing, we gather around the wall, creating new stories, associations, and collective understandings.

Kayīb
Andrius Arutiunian

Sound Performance, Saturday March 9, 8:00 pm
JAX District

Kayīb is a sound performance based on historical songs from the Caucasus region and beyond, the entangled methods of oil and voice extraction, and histories of charlatanism. Through a series of hypnotic and repetitive sonic movements, the performance by Arutiunian unfolds as a complex interplay of multiple illicit voices.

Storytelling Sessions
NJOKOBOK

Friday, March 15, and Friday, March 29,
10:00 pm–12:00 am
Terrace 2

NJOKOBOK BAR is activated by a series of storytelling sessions, which draw on the traditional role of the *hakawati,* or "storytellers" in Arabic, who go around coffee shops and souks to engage audiences with their tales. NJOKOBOK has invited different *hakawati*—from the Palestinian, Senegalese, and Indonesian communities in Riyadh—to share stories that are meaningful to their lives and convey their respective cultural traditions.

Buckets and Waterskins
Rasha Al-Duwaisan

A weekend of poetic interactions with *After Rain*
Friday, March 22, and Saturday, March 23, 10:00 pm
Throughout the exhibition site

Join us for Rasha Al-Duwaisan's commission, juxtaposing historic and contemporary responses to rain in the Arabian Peninsula, combining spoken words, poetry, and sound. This meditative exploration invites us to discover intimate spaces as we move through the exhibition spaces. Alongside Al-Duwaisan's poetic intervention, an open call invites other contributions from writers, artists, and poets who wish to propose a poem, song, or short piece of writing to present in response to the themes of *After Rain*.

Gentle Ferocities
Zarina Muhammad

Night Workshop and Artist Talk, Saturday,
March 23, 10:00 pm–2:00 am and Sunday, March 24,
9:00–11:00 pm
Palan & Pakghor (The Kitchen Garden & The Social Kitchen), Britto Arts Trust

In facing the pressing urgencies of our times, what can we learn from nonhuman beings? How can we observe and give presence to the smallest creatures, gentle ferocities? Drawing from Southeast Asian mythologies, the artist and educator creates a space for discussion and hands-on activities, mapping out wisdoms and lessons about the environment inspired by land, sky, and sea life.

APRIL 2024

The Housed Body
Filwa Nazer

**Workshop, Friday, April 19, 4–6:00 pm, and Saturday, April 20, 11:00 am–6:00 pm (for adults)
Friday, March 26, 4–6:00 pm, and Saturday, March 27, 11:00 am–6:00 pm (for children)
DBF, Workshop Room**

Known for her abstract textile works, collages, and drawings inspired by fashion and architecture, Saudi artist Filwa Nazer's workshops unfold over the course of two days, introducing participants to pattern-making techniques as spatial tools and exploring the theme of "home." One is dedicated to participants from the field of art, design, and fashion. The second workshop is for children.

MAY 2024

Read My Voice
Regina Möller

**Workshop and Artist Talk, Saturday, May 4, 11:00 am–9:00 pm
DBF, Workshop Room**

Introducing the format of the "zine," a form of self-publishing driven by artists and different sub-cultures, the artist guides participants through producing a zine on a chosen topic. The workshop draws from the artist's own zine *regina*—an artwork in the format of women's fashion and lifestyle magazines that question the representation of female identities in mass media.

Reading Palm
Elia Nurvista

**Workshop and Artist Talk, Saturday, May 11, 2–6:00 pm, and Sunday, May 12, 7–9:00 pm
DBF, Workshop Room**

Based on the artist's research project *Long Hanging Fruits* (2022–present) exploring the cultivation of palm oil in Indonesia, the workshop offers a collective interrogation of the history of palm oil, which unfolds through a tasting of palm oil dishes and a group reading. Eating, reading, and digesting together transform palm oil from a symbol of nineteenth-century colonial exploitation into a vital ingredient of hospitality.

Wall Extract (Riyadh)
Vikram Divecha

**Social Gathering, Saturday, May 11, 7:00 pm
Location tbc**

Divecha has extracted a section of wall from a structure in Riyadh that is slated for demolition. Through conversations, cuisine, and socializing, we gather around the wall, creating new stories, associations, and collective understandings.

Gazelle in a Mother's Eye
Jumana Emil Abboud

**Performance, Thursday, May 21, 8:00 pm
Black Box, B1**

In the performance work *Gazelle in a Mother's Eye* (2024), the artist focuses on the landscapes of Saudi Arabia to examine how historic relationships with natural sources, primarily water, have informed the folktales and intangible heritage of the present day. Abboud translates questions around water resources into spoken words, video, movement, sign language, and live drawing to create a context-specific work of both imagination and reenactment.

NJOKOBOK BAR

Storytelling Session, Friday, May 24, 9–11:00 pm
Terrace 2

NJOKOBOK BAR is activated by a series of story-telling sessions, which draw on the traditional role of the *hakawati,* or "storytellers" in Arabic, who go around coffee shops and souks to engage audiences with their tales. NJOKOBOK has invited different *hakawati*—from the Palestinian, Senegalese, and Indonesian communities in Riyadh—to share stories that are meaningful to their lives and convey their respective cultural traditions.

The Tree of Life
Mona Vătămanu & Florin Tudor

Activation, Friday, May 24, 2–3:00 pm
Exhibition Hall B6

The artists' activation of their installation through drawing activities and open discussion is a con-temporary reflection on the enduring relationship between people and plants as expressed in various art forms. The ancient "tree of life" motif and other biomorphic symbols featured on the carpets and kilims of the work are starting points for discussions around climate change, the rights of nature, and the potential of renewal.

الطارق A Research into Tribal Musical Traditions across the Arab World
Tarek Atoui

Performance, Friday, May 24, 10:00 pm

In this solo performance, Tarek Atoui layers sound to create an index of social relationships and networks of musical performance and innovation. The sonic work guides the audience through a variety of locales, from bustling souks to joyous weddings and intimate music salons from throughout Morocco and Saudi Arabia.

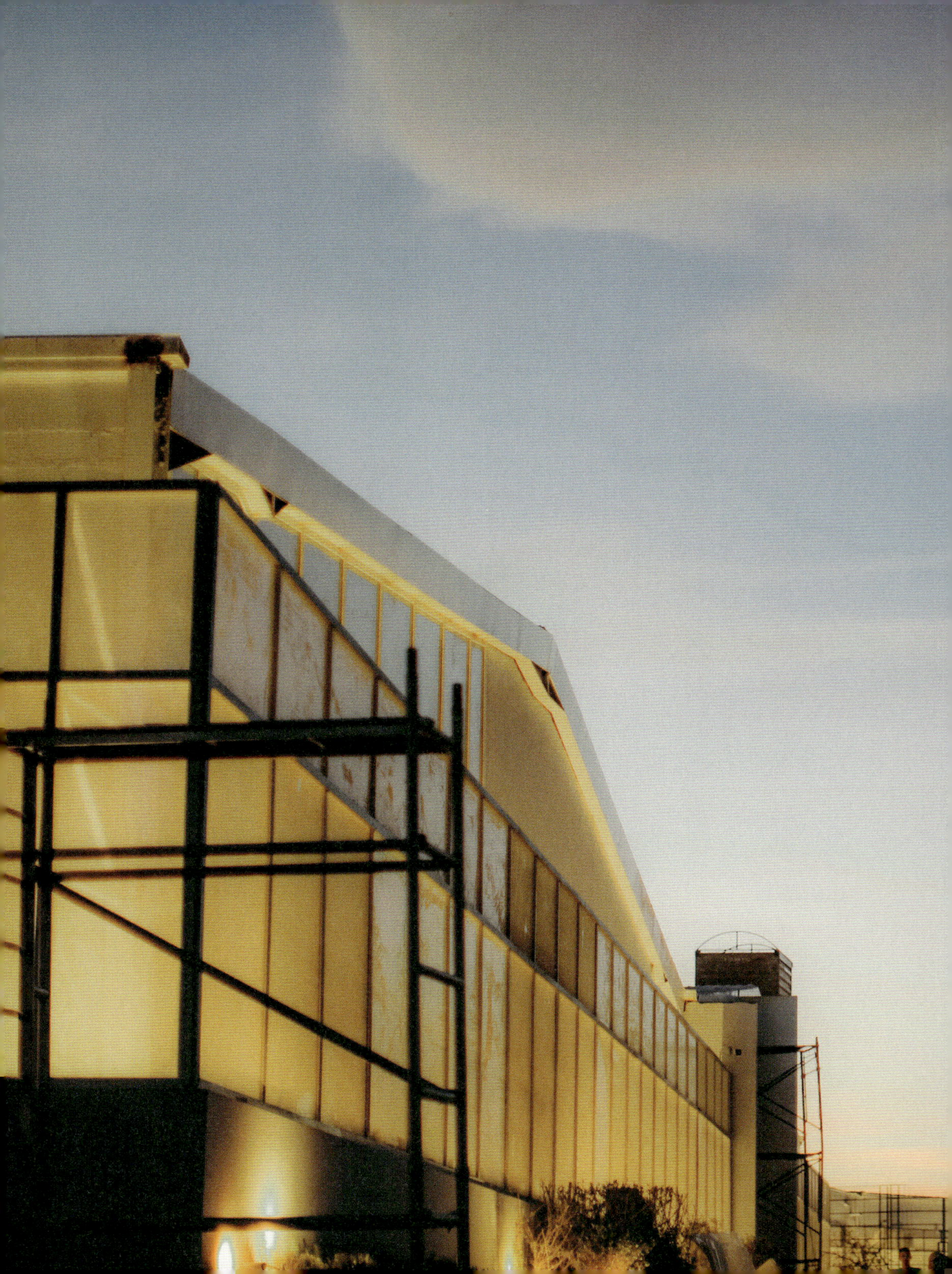

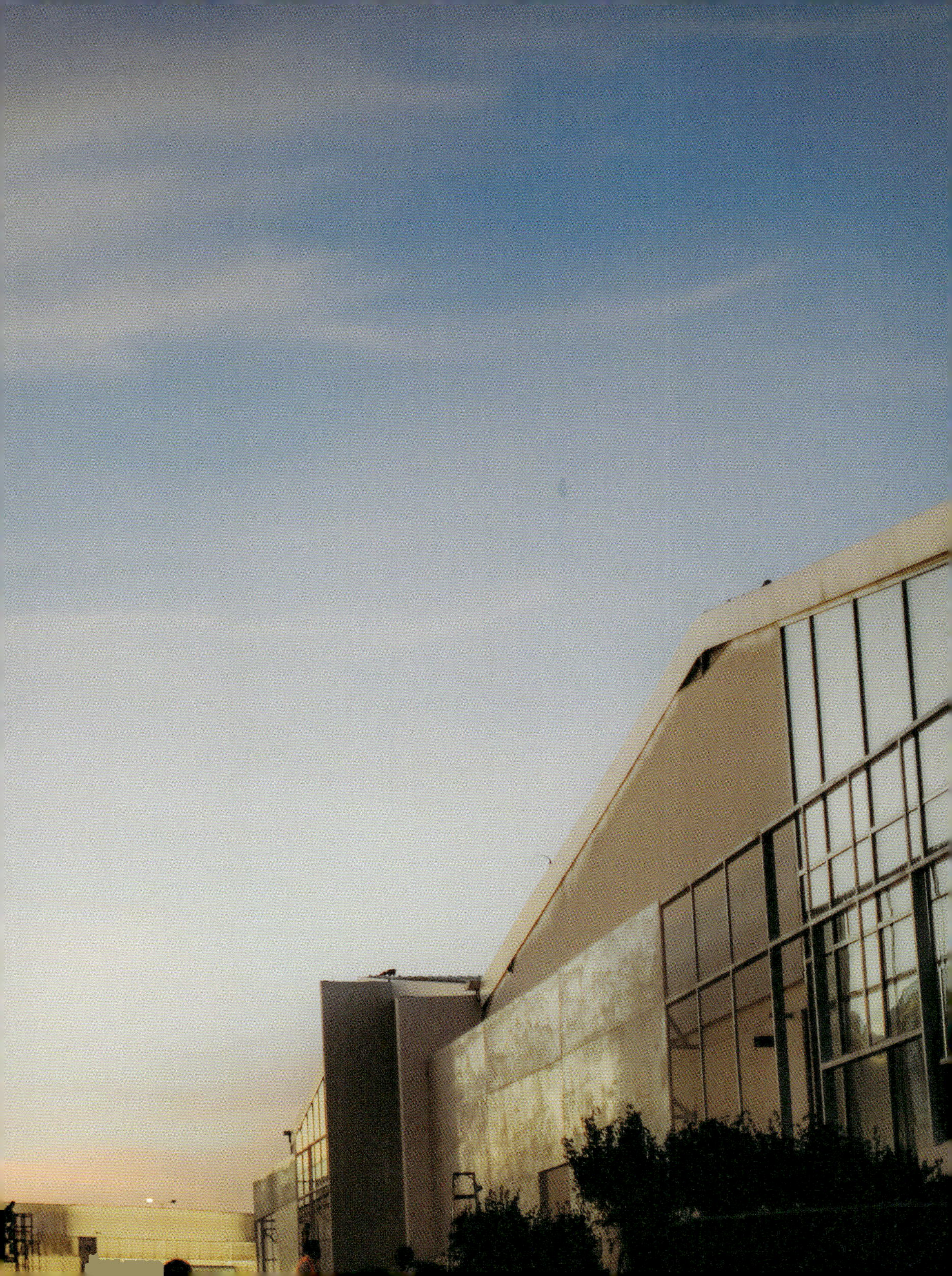

DIRIYAH CONTEMPORARY ART BIENNALE 2024
LIST OF WORKS

Hamra Abbas

Mountain 5, 2023
Lapis lazuli, granite
152.4 × 609.6 cm (ten panels, each
152.4 × 60.96 cm)
Courtesy of Kiran Nadar Museum
of Art, New Delhi

Jumana Emil Abboud

Gazelle in a Mother's Eye, 2024
Multimedia performance,
March 21, 2024
With collaborating performers
Tamara Kalo and Ileana Gonzalez
Pacheco
Biennale Encounters
Courtesy of the artist
Commissioned by the Diriyah
Biennale Foundation for the
Diriyah Contemporary Art
Biennale 2024

The Rights of a River
With Marjetica Potrč
Workshop and Artist Talk,
November 18 and 19, 2023
Biennale Encounters

Sara Abdu

*Now That I've Lost You In My
Dreams Where Do We Meet?*,
2021/2024
Approx. 3500 soap bars,
English and Arabic words
embossed on each bar
3 columns: 260 × ø 170 cm;
200 × ø 130 cm; 180 × ø 120 cm
Courtesy of the artist and
ATHR Gallery
Commissioned by the Diriyah
Biennale Foundation for the
Diriyah Contemporary Art
Biennale 2024

*Now That I've Lost You In My
Dreams Where Do We Meet?*,
2021/2024
Developmental materials
Re/Search

Irene Agrivina

Open Material / Open Hardware
Two workshops,
November 3 and 4, 2023
Biennale Encounters

Domestic Hacking / Collective
Making
Artist Talk, November 4, 2023
Biennale Encounters

Alia Ahmad

Alwasm, 2023
Oil on canvas
430 × 540 cm
Courtesy of the artist
Commissioned by the Diriyah
Biennale Foundation for the
Diriyah Contemporary Art
Biennale 2024

Azra Akšamija

Abundance & Scarcity, 2024
Felt, steel cables, herbal potpourri
Dimensions variable
Created with the Future Heritage
Lab team: Merve Akdoğan,
Lillian Kology, Yi-Ern Samuel Tan,
Nadine Zaza
Courtesy of the artist and Future
Heritage Lab, MIT
Commissioned by the Diriyah
Biennale Foundation for the
Diriyah Contemporary Art
Biennale 2024

Abundance & Scarcity, 2024
Developmental materials, garment
Re/Search

Nabila Al Bassam

Buildings of Southern Arabia, 1993
Mixed media on canvas
160 × 155 cm
Courtesy of Khalid and Sally
Alturki

Buildings of Southern Arabia 1, 1993
Mixed media on canvas
160 × 155 cm
Courtesy of Khalid
and Sally Alturki

The Lighthouse of Saudi, 1999
Mixed media on canvas
82 × 68 cm
Courtesy of the artist
and Arab Heritage Gallery

The Lighthouse of the South, 1999
Mixed media on canvas
82 × 68 cm
Courtesy of the artist
and Arab Heritage Gallery

Untitled, 1999
Mixed Media on canvas
120 × 169.5 cm
Courtesy of the artist
and Arab Heritage Gallery

Untitled, 2020
Mixed media on canvas
212 × 84 cm
Courtesy of the artist
and Arab Heritage Gallery

**Tara Aldughaither
& Joe Namy**

Rhythms of the Rising Sun, 2024
Audiovisual archive and text
The Learning Garden
Courtesy of the artists
Commissioned by the Diriyah
Biennale Foundation for the
Diriyah Contemporary Art
Biennale 2024

Rasha Al-Duwaisan

Buckets and Waterskins, 2024
Poetic interactions with *After Rain*, March 22 and 23, 2024
Biennale Encounters
Courtesy of the artist
Commissioned by the Diriyah Biennale Foundation for the Diriyah Contemporary Art Biennale 2024

Mohammad AlFaraj

The Whispers of Today Are Heard in the Garden of Tomorrow, 2024
Installation and mixed media
Container footprint
1200 × 800 cm

New Palms, 2024
10 sculptures, palm frond, gum arabic, date syrup, resin
Dimensions variable

Fossils of Time II, 2024
17 photographs
Dimensions variable

Love Is to Leave the Gates of Your Garden Ajar, 2024
Acrylic paint on wall
300 × 400 cm

All works courtesy of the artist
Commissioned by the Diriyah Biennale Foundation for the Diriyah Contemporary Art Biennale 2024

Dhali Al Mamoon

Kather Nripati (Wooden Lord), 2021
Five rotating figures, plywood, steel, leather, acrylic, enamel, varnish, electronic turning device
142 × 1000 × 142 cm
Courtesy of the artist
Special thanks to the Samdani Art Foundation, Bangladesh for assistance with shipping

Reem Al Nasser

Blue Windows, 2022
Mixedmedia installation with juniper branches, two welded steel structures, blue paint
Steel structure components: 200 × 300 × 100 cm; 200 × 500 × 100 cm
Courtesy of the artist
Presentation supported by the Diriyah Biennale Foundation for the Diriyah Contemporary Art Biennale 2024

Daniah Alsaleh

A Stone's Palette, 2023–24
Re/Search
Courtesy of the artist
Developed in collaboration with the German Archaeological Institute (DAI) and the Goethe-Institut Riyadh
Commissioned by the Diriyah Biennale Foundation for the Diriyah Contemporary Art Biennale 2024

Abdulrahman Al-Soliman

Palm, Bow, and Fragments, 1990–91
56 drawings from the series
Chinese ink on arch paper
52 × 66.4 cm and 57.9 × 68.4 cm (framed)
Courtesy of the artist
Presentation supported by the Diriyah Biennale Foundation for the Diriyah Contemporary Art Biennale 2024

Aseel AlYaqoub

Desert as Method
Workshop, September 16, 2023
Biennale Encounters

Art Practice as Research
Artist Talk, September 16, 2023
Biennale Encounters

The Secret Lake, 2024
Selection of books, found objects, satellite images
Re/Search
Commissioned by the Diriyah Biennale Foundation for the Diriyah Contemporary Art Biennale 2024

El Anatsui

Detsi, 2008–21
Aluminium and copper wire
Approx. 300 × 800 cm
Courtesy of the artist and Efie Gallery, Dubai

Logoligi Logarithm, 2019
66-part maze of free-hanging curtains made of aluminum and copper wire
Approx. 2100 × 500 × 1000 cm
Courtesy of the artist and Jack Shainman Gallery, New York

Nazgol Ansarinia

Membrane (parts), 2014
Paper, paste, glue
135 × 105 × 4 cm
Courtesy of the artist and Green Art Gallery, Dubai

Membrane (parts), 2014
Paper, paste, glue
129 × 86 × 3 cm
Courtesy of the artist and Green Art Gallery, Dubai

Membrane (parts), 2014
Paper, paste, glue
138 × 105 × 4 cm
Courtesy of the artist and Green Art Gallery, Dubai

Membrane (parts), 2014
Paper, paste, glue
168 × 116 × 8 cm
Courtesy of the artist and Green Art Gallery, Dubai

Article 49, Pillars, 2014
Cast resin and paint
20 × 40 × 40 cm
Edition 2 of 3 + 1 AP
Courtesy of the artist and
Green Art Gallery, Dubai

Article 51, Pillars, 2014
Cast resin and marble powder
62 × 33 × 33 cm
Edition 1 of 3
Courtesy of the artist and
Collection Olivier Georges
Mestelan, France

Article 47, Pillars, 2015
Epoxy resin and paint
65 × 35 × 35 cm
Edition 1 of 3 + 1 AP
Courtesy of the artist and
Green Art Gallery, Dubai

Article 45, Pillars, 2018
Epoxy resin, paint
51 × 40 × 40 cm
AP in edition of 3 + 1 AP
Courtesy of private collection,
Belgium

Rasheed Araeen

People of Karachi, 1955–58
Watercolor, charcoal, pencil,
crayon, and biro on paper
24 paintings, 57 × 43 cm
(each, framed)

Cube as Sculpture, 1966/2020
Aluminum
12 cubes, 61 × 61 × 61 cm (each)

The One that Could Not Float Away,
1970
4 photographs, 63.5 × 63.5 cm (each)

All works courtesy of the artist
and Rossi & Rossi, Hong Kong

Siah Armajani

Chavoshi (Itinerant Chanter), 1956
Ink on paper and cardboard
22.5 × 42 cm and 28.5 × 28.5 cm

Songs #1 and #2, 1957
Watercolor, ink, sealing wax
on paper
57.2 × 62.7 cm

Paria No. 1, 1957
Cardboard, paper, ink, watercolor
on paper
43.2 × 11.4 cm

The Hinge, 1963
Mixed media
30.5 × 30.5 cm

Three Pears, 1966–67
Paint and ink on canvas
Diptych 30 × 60 cm (each panel)

House with a Golden Chimney, 1974
Metal, plastic
17.8 × 46 × 12.7 cm

Seven Rooms of Hospitality #2, 2015
Felt pen and colored pencil on
graph paper
60 × 91.4 cm

Kansas City Bridge No.2, 2016
Balsa wood, bass wood, paint
55.9 × 157.5 × 11.7 cm

All works courtesy of
Rossi & Rossi, Hong Kong

Andrius Arutiunian

Kayīb, 2023
Sound Performance,
March 9, 2024
Biennale Encounters
Courtesy of the artist

Martha Atienza

Equation of State, 2019/2024
24 mangrove plants, automated
winches, basin made of wood,
steel, liner, seawater
Installation containing 3-channel
film (79 min, no sound), single
projection (307 min, no sound)
42 × 409 × 79 cm
Courtesy of the artist and
Silverlens, Manila/New York
Special thanks to King Abdullah
University of Science and
Technology (KAUST), Thuwal
Iteration supported by the
Diriyah Biennale Foundation for
the Diriyah Contemporary Art
Biennale 2024

Tarek Atoui

الطارق *A Research into Tribal Musical
Traditions across the Arab World*,
2022–ongoing
Sonic Fieldwork and Performance,
May 24, 2024
Commissioned by the Diriyah
Biennale Foundation for the
Diriyah Contemporary Art
Biennale 2024

الطارق *A Research into Tribal Musical
Traditions across the Arab World*,
2022–ongoing
Developmental materials
Research and activation in
collaboration with Jad Atoui
Re/Search

Workshop and Artist Talk,
November 26, 2023
Biennale Encounters

Dana Awartani

Come, Let Me Heal Your Wounds,
2020
Hand-embroidered darning
and medicinally dyed silk on
10 wooden stretchers
136 × 477 cm
Commissioned by TBA21
Thyssen-Bornemisza
Art Contemporary
Courtesy of the artist and
TBA21 Thyssen-Bornemisza Art
Contemporary Collection

Listen to my words, 2020
Single-channel digital animation,
color, sound (recordings of
historical poems), 12 min 57 sec
Developed from a multimedia
installation by the same title
realized in 2018
Film Program
Courtesy of the artist
Commissioned by TBA21
Thyssen-Bornemisza Art
Contemporary and produced by
NTU Centre for Contemporary Art
Singapore for st_age

Asma Bahmim

Works from the series *Fantasia*,
2022
Gouache, natural red dye, gum
arabic, 22k gold leaf on handmade
banana paper

by the moon pond
75 × 60 cm (framed)

Code Blue
100 × 65 cm (framed)

Cooperation 1
75 × 60 cm (framed)

Magpie Tawaf
75 × 60 cm (framed)

Neeran the Alopecia
75 × 60 cm (framed)

Red the Fox
75 × 60 cm (framed)

Reflection
50 × 42 cm (framed)

Strong Wings
100 × 50 cm (framed)

Untitled 3
35 × 25 cm (framed)

All works courtesy of the artist
and ATHR Gallery, Jeddah

bahraini-danish

Surface Finds, 2024
Pottery shards, project materials,
documentation
Re/Search
Commissioned by the Diriyah
Biennale Foundation for the
Diriyah Contemporary Art
Biennale 2024

Sammy Baloji

Aequare: the Future that Never Was,
2023
4K UHD video, digital projection,
single channel, 5.1 sound, 20 min
Film Program
Courtesy of the artist

Zarina Bhimji

Yellow Patch, 2011
Single-screen installation,
35 mm film
HD transfer with Dolby 5.1
surround sound, 29 min 43 sec
Courtesy of the artist

Ursula Biemann

Forest Mind, 2021
4K UHD video, sound,
31 min 45 sec
Film Program
Courtesy of the artist

Safeya Binzagr

Turathuna (Our Tradition),
1997–99
22 images and one text panel
from a series of 39 color copper
photogravures:

A Bride from Al Taif
A Diriyah Bride
A Girl from Al Taif
A Najdi Bride
Al Bukhnug
Al Burg'u wa Al Melayah
Al Jamah
Al Shur'ah Al Arabi
Darfat Al Bab
Darra'ah Um Asah
Herob Tribe
Herob Tribe (A Bedouin Woman
from the AlJada'an and
AlJahadilah tribes)
Megna'a wa Luthmat Lulu
*Serwal wa Sedrairiyyah Kum wa
Dayer Mantour*
Thobe Al Naghdah
Thobe Asiri
A Thobe from Al Qatif
Thobe Mokhattam
Thobe Mubadah (Eastern Province)
Thobe Mubadah (Najd Desert,
Northern Periphery, Anzah and
Shammar Tribes)
Turathuna (text panel)
Zabun Mashaber
Zabun wa Thobe Mashaber wa Toug

Printed on "SUMERS" handmade
paper, 200 gr
63 × 52.5 cm (each)
Edition 2/30, signed and
prenumbered by the artist
Courtesy of the Al-Mansouria
Foundation
Presentation supported by the
Diriyah Biennale Foundation for
the Diriyah Contemporary Art
Biennale 2024

Rossella Biscotti

Annalies, 2019
Natural rubber
200 × 100 cm (2 sheets, with relief)

Mei, 2019
Natural rubber, food coloring
240 × 60 cm (2 sheets, with relief)

Princess of Kasiruta, 2019
Natural rubber
230 × 105 cm (with relief) and
210 × 100 cm (plain)

*Sanikem – Nyai Ontosoroh –
Madame Le Boucq*, 2019
Natural rubber, food coloring
350 × 108 cm (with relief)
210 × 100 cm (3 sheets, plain)

Surati, 2019
Natural rubber
240 × 105 (with relief)
and 210 × 100 cm (plain)

Maiko, 2022
Natural rubber
350 × 43 cm (with relief)
and 175 × 43 cm (with relief)

All works edition 3 of 3 + 2AP
and courtesy of the artist
Edition commissioned by the
Diriyah Biennale Foundation for
the Diriyah Contemporary Art
Biennale 2024

Bricklab

*Diriyah Biennale Foundation
Building*, 2024
Architectural model, booklet,
sketches, material samples,
mixed media

Saudi Modern, 2024
Archival material, silicon, wood,
publications, mixed media
Re/Search
Courtesy of the artists
Presentation supported by the
Diriyah Biennale Foundation for
the Diriyah Contemporary Art
Biennale 2024

Britto Arts Trust

Palan & Pakghor (The Kitchen
Garden & The Social Kitchen),
2024
Bamboo, plywood, metal clamps
Approx. 6 × 35 × 10 m
Core Team: Md. Khairul Alam,
Khorshed Alam Alok, Tayeba
Begum Lipi, Mahbubur Rahman,
Shimul Saha, Kazi Sydul Karim Tuso
Artists: Afia Noor, Shimul Datta,
Amir Faisal Ruscho, Aminul
Islam Ashik, Ashim Halder Sagor,
Farhana Ferdausi, Jinnatun Jannat,
Lutfun Nahar, Mahmuda Siddika,
Mehedi Hasan, Mohosin Kabir,
Noman Khan, Sarah Jabin
Craftspeople: Adori Rani Sarkar,
Kalu, Lakkhan, Lata Begum,
Maloti Rani, Masud, Md. Juwel,
Md. Mursalin Polas, Modhu
Chandra
Sarkar, Mohammad Alam Mia,
Mohammad Chunnu Mia,
Mohammad Mansur Mia, Pashan,
Raja, Robiul, Sabur, Sanjay Sarkar
Courtesy of the artists
Special thanks to the Samdani
Art Foundation, Bangladesh, for
assistance with shipping
Commissioned by the Diriyah
Biennale Foundation for the
Diriyah Contemporary Art
Biennale 2024

*What Does It Take, What Does It
Do to Cook Together?*
Artist Talk and Food Tasting,
September 2, 2023

Muhanned Cader

Land and Water, 2024
Collage on Moleskine
accordion book
198 × 13.9 × 8.8 cm
Courtesy of the artist and
Jhaveri Contemporary, Mumbai

**María Magdalena
Campos-Pons**

Works from the series *Liminal
Circularity*, 2021–23

Bench 6 and *Bench 8*, 2021–23
Cast glass
31.75 × 15.88 × 10.15 cm (each)
Courtesy Galerie Barbara Thumm,
Berlin, and Galerie Wendi Norris,
San Francisco

Portrait #2, 2023
Watercolor, ink, gouache, gum
arabic, BFK archival paper
345 × 255 × 7.5 cm (overall)
3 panels, 345 × 85 × 7.5 cm (each)
Courtesy Galerie Barbara Thumm,
Berlin

Untitled, 2023
Watercolor, ink, gouache, gum
arabic, BFK archival paper
345 × 340 × 7,5 cm (overall)
4 panels, 345 × 85 × 7.5 cm (each)
Courtesy Galerie Barbara Thumm,
Berlin

Presentation supported by the
Diriyah Biennale Foundation for
the Diriyah Contemporary Art
Biennale 2024

Cercle d'Art des Travailleurs de Plantation Congolaise

Plantations, Museums, and Regenerative Ecologies,
2022–ongoing
NFT, 6 videos, illustration, text
The Learning Garden
Courtesy of the artists, KOW, Berlin, and Human Activities, Amsterdam
Commissioned by the Diriyah Biennale Foundation for the Diriyah Contemporary Art Biennale 2024

Rachaporn Choochuey

Set the Control for the Heart of the Sun 2.0, 2024
Steel, vinyl-coated polyester screen mesh
420 × 1150 × 1500 cm
Courtesy of all(zone)
Commissioned by the Diriyah Biennale Foundation for the Diriyah Contemporary Art Biennale 2024

Tiffany Chung

Energy Policy vol.166: potential CO2 emissions until 2050 by key fossil fuel and coal extraction projects [each>1 Gt] worldwide, 2023
Embroidery on fabric
140 × 350 cm
Edition 1 (of 2 + 1 AP)
Commissioned by the Diriyah Biennale Foundation for the Diriyah Contemporary Art Biennale 2024

Mapping Global Displacement and Migration: nexus dynamics between conflict & violence and climate disaster [UNHCR, IDMC, EM-DAT: cross-border refugees, asylum-seekers, IDPs and those affected in selected cases >2022<], 2023
Embroidery on fabric
140 × 350 cm
Edition 1 (of 2 + 1 AP)
Supported by the Diriyah Biennale Foundation for the Diriyah Contemporary Art Biennale 2024

All works courtesy of the artist

Ade Darmawan

Tuban, 2019
Installation with distillation laboratory equipment, books, pottery, spices, sea water, leaves, stones, tables
Courtesy of the artist
Furnishing supported by IKEA
Presentation supported by the Diriyah Biennale Foundation for the Diriyah Contemporary Art Biennale 2024

Priyageetha Dia

Mesh: Prelude to Spectre System, 2024
Vinyl print
Dimensions variable
Courtesy of the artist

Spectre System, 2024
Single-channel video, color and sound, 15 min
Courtesy of the artist and Han Nefkens Foundation, Barcelona
Commissioned by Han Nefkens Foundation for the Diriyah Contemporary Art Biennale 2024

Vikram Divecha

Wall Extract (Riyadh), 2024
Various extracted materials, mild steel frame, fiberglass, resin
Dimensions variable

Wall Extract (Riyadh), 2024
Social Gathering
Biennale Encounters
Commissioned by the Diriyah Biennale Foundation for the Diriyah Contemporary Art Biennale 2024

Wall Extract (Riyadh), 2024
Developmental Materials
Re/Search

Ibrahim El-Salahi

Dry Month of the Fast, 1962
Mixed media on Masonite
46 × 61 cm

Untitled, 1962
Oil on canvas
66.2 × 53.5 cm

Fatima, 1968
Oil on canvas
60.5 × 60.5 cm

All works courtesy of Sharjah Art Foundation Collection

Alexander Eriksson Furunes & Sudarshan Khadka Jr.

To Lift Together: Mutual Support and Collective Action, 2024
Documentation of architectural practice
Re/Search
Presentation supported by the Diriyah Biennale Foundation for the Diriyah Contemporary Art Biennale 2024

Alia Farid

In Lieu of What Was, 2019
5 sculptures, fiberglass and
polyester resin
Heb, 255 × 123 × 123 cm
Jarrah, 240 × 130 × 130 cm
Water Bottle, 297 × 100 × 100 cm
Water Tower, 280 × 260 × 260 cm
Zamzamiya, 240 × 160 × 160 cm
Supported by the Diriyah
Biennale Foundation for the
Diriyah Contemporary Art
Biennale 2024

Chibayish, 2022
UHD video, color, sound,
24 min 42 sec
Commissioned by the Whitney
Museum of American Art on the
occasion of Whitney Biennial
2022: *Quiet As It is Kept* curated
by Adrienne Edwards and
David Breslin
Filmed in the southern
marshlands of Iraq with
Riad Samir and Jassim and
Qassim Mohammed

Chibayish, 2023
UHD video, color, sound
15 min 3 sec
Commissioned by The Vega
Foundation and Doha Film
Institute
Filmed in the southern
marshlands of Iraq with Riad and
Fatima Bahrani

All works courtesy of the artist
and Sfeir-Semler Gallery, Beirut /
Hamburg

Christine Fenzl

Women of Riyadh, 2023
13 photographs, archival pigment
prints, framed

Bayan, Al Safarat, Riyadh, 2023
100 × 100 cm

Ghaida, Diriyah, 2023
100 × 100 cm

Ghalia and Fahad, Olaya, Riyadh,
2023
100 × 100 cm

Hind, Al Sulaymaniyah, Riyadh,
2023
100 × 100 cm

*Narmeen and Mustapha, Al
Sulaymaniyah, Riyadh*, 2023
100 × 125 cm

Nejoud, Al Sahafa, Riyadh, 2023
100 × 125 cm

Norah and Joza, Al Andalus, Riyadh,
2023
100 × 125 cm

Raghad, Al Malqa, Riyadh, 2023
100 × 100 cm

Ranya, Al Sahafa, Riyadh, 2023
100 × 125 cm

Rawan, Al Nozha, Riyadh, 2023
100 × 100 cm

Reema, Al Nozha, Riyadh, 2023
100 × 100 cm

Yasser´s Spot, Riyadh, 2023
120 × 150 cm

Zahra, Hitteen, Riyadh, 2023
100 × 100 cm

Courtesy of the artist
Commissioned by the Diriyah
Biennale Foundation for the
Diriyah Contemporary Art
Biennale 2024

Ângela Ferreira

Zip Zap Circus School,
2000–ongoing
Canvas, wood, steel
Semi-circular pavilion,
460 × 350 × 500 cm,
350 cm radius
Semi-circular pavilion,
200 × 50 × 100 cm,
50 cm radius
Quarter-circular pavilion,
730 × 660 × 500 cm, 500 cm radius
Courtesy of the artist and Cristina
Guerra Contemporary Art, Lisbon
Reproduction supported by the
Diriyah Biennale Foundation for
the Diriyah Contemporary Art
Biennale 2024

Activation, February 20, 2024
In collaboration with
Mohammad AlFaraj, Nouf Salamah,
and Relevé Studio, Riyadh
Biennale Encounters

Simryn Gill

Dalam, 2001
260 color photographs,
C-prints, pins
32 × 32 cm (each)
Courtesy of the artist
and 1301PE, Los Angeles;
Jhaveri Contemporary, Mumbai;
Richard Saltoun Gallery, London

Anne Holtrop

Glass to Stone, 2024
Glass, steel
Dimensions 560 × 330 × 200 cm
Courtesy of Anne Holtrop
Commissioned by the Diriyah
Biennale Foundation for the
Diriyah Contemporary Art
Biennale 2024

Glass to Stone, 2024
Developmental materials
Re/Search

Hiba Ismail

Two Islets, 2024
Audio
The Learning Garden
Courtesy of the artist
Commissioned by the Diriyah
Biennale Foundation for the
Diriyah Contemporary Art
Biennale 2024

Saodat Ismailova

18 000 Worlds, 2023
HD video, 31 min
Color and black and white, stereo
Director: Saodat Ismailova
Photography: Carlos Casas,
Saodat Ismailova
Editing, sound: Saodat Ismailova
Archival material:
Eye Filmmuseum, Amsterdam
Film Program
Courtesy of the artist
Realized with the support of
Eye Art and Film Prize

Joan Jonas

Reanimation, 2010/2012/2013
Six videos (color, sound, and
silent) on custom screens within
a prefabricated house structure,
two custom benches (made by
Ed Gavagan) and crystal sculpture,
two wooden theater boxes with
video (color, sound and silent)
Dimensions variable
Soundtrack and voice: Joan Jonas
Sami yoik singing: Ánde Somby
Piano and additional sound
effects: Jason Moran
Courtesy of the artist
Reproduction supported by the
Diriyah Biennale Foundation for
the Diriyah Contemporary Art
Biennale 2024

Susanne Kriemann

Datadust skin of sand, 2024
8 silkscreen prints on cotton
paper, printed with date syrup
and sand
Printed in collaboration with
Fatma Abdulhadi
Text: Lisa Rosendahl
Layout: Isabel Motz
100 × 60 cm each
Re/Search
Courtesy of the artist
Developed in collaboration
with the German Archaeological
Institute (DAI), the Goethe-Institut
Riyadh, and the German Embassy
in Riyadh
Production supported by the
Diriyah Biennale Foundation for
the Diriyah Contemporary Art
Biennale 2024

Liang Shaoji

Lonely Cloud, 2016
Installation with wood, silk,
cocoons, steel pipes
245 × 428 × 114 cm
Courtesy of the artist and
ShanghART Gallery

Armin Linke & Ahmed Mater

Saudi Futurism, 2024
Plywood, plexiglass, prints,
steel profiles
Dimensions variable
Courtesy of the artists
Commissioned by the Diriyah
Biennale Foundation for the
Diriyah Contemporary Art
Biennale 2024

For permission to photograph, the
artists and the Diriyah Biennale
Foundation would like to thank:
Almarai; Aramco; Boutique Group;
King Abdullah University of
Science and Technology (KAUST):
Center for Desert Agriculture /
Coastal and Marine Resources
Core Lab / Visualization Core Lab;
King Abdulaziz Center for
World Culture – Ithra, Dhahran;
King Abdulaziz Foundation for
Research and Archives; NEOM;
The Royal Institute of Traditional
Arts; Saudi Space Agency;
Yamama Cement

Armin Linke

Urban landscape, Riyadh, 2010
21 × 28 cm
Presentation supported by the
Diriyah Biennale Foundation for
the Diriyah Contemporary
Art Biennale 2024

*Riyadh Gate Way, monument,
Riyadh*, 2010
21 × 28 cm
Presentation supported by the
Diriyah Biennale Foundation for
the Diriyah Contemporary
Art Biennale 2024

*Ahmed Mater's artwork in his
studio, Riyadh*, 2023
50 × 60 cm

Aramco, media archive, Dammam,
2023
Triptych 300 × 183 cm (unframed),
each panel 300 × 61 cm

*Frei Otto, Diplomatic Club Heart
Tent, Boutique Group, Riyadh*, 2023
50 × 60 cm

*King Abdulaziz Center for World
Culture (Ithra), library, Dhahran*,
2023
50 × 60 cm

King Abdulaziz Center for World Culture (Ithra), museum, Dhahran, 2023
21 × 28 cm

King Abdulaziz Center for World Culture (Ithra), museum, Dhahran, 2023
Triptych 170 × 183 cm (unframed), each panel 170 × 61 cm

King Abdulaziz Foundation for Research and Archives, Riyadh, 2023
50 × 60 cm

King Abdullah University of Science and Technology (KAUST), Center for Desert Agriculture (CDA), Thuwal, 2023
50 × 60 cm

King Abdullah University of Science and Technology (KAUST), Plant Growth Core Lab, research greenhouse, Thuwal, 2023
50 × 60 cm

King Abdullah University of Science and Technology (KAUST), Supercomputing Core Lab, Thuwal, 2023
50 × 60 cm

King Abdullah University of Science and Technology (KAUST), visualization of rock CT scan, Thuwal, 2023
50 × 60 cm

The National Museum of Saudi Arabia, model of Mecca, urban development, Riyadh, 2023
21 × 28 cm

The National Museum of Saudi Arabia, oil drill bit in showcase, Riyadh, 2023
21 × 28 cm

The National Museum of Saudi Arabia, "Oil from Ancient Life," how oil originates from organic fossils, Riyadh, 2023
21 × 28 cm

NEOM style guidelines for ID, Zero Gravity Urbanism: Principles for a New Livability, NEOM exhibition, Venice, 2023
Triptych 300 × 183 cm (unframed), each panel 300 × 61 cm

NEOM: The Line Experience, exhibition, Riyadh, 2023
50 × 60 cm

The Royal Institute of Traditional Arts (TRITA), Riyadh, 2023
50 × 60 cm

Yamama Cement Factory (Old), view from Manakh King Abdulaziz Park, Riyadh, 2023
50 × 60 cm

Ahmed Mater
Clock Tower (Mecca Time), Mecca, 2015
21 × 28 cm
Presentation supported by the Diriyah Biennale Foundation for the Diriyah Contemporary Art Biennale 2024

Almarai Farm (Al Rabiah Dairy Farm), Riyadh, 2023
21 × 28 cm

Almarai Farm (Al Rabiah Dairy Farm), Riyadh, 2023
21 × 28 cm

Almarai Farm (Al Rabiah Dairy Farm), Riyadh, 2023
50 × 60 cm

Almarai Farm (Al Rabiah Dairy Farm), Riyadh, 2023
250 × 180 cm

Aramco, media archive, Dammam, 2023
21 × 28 cm

Former Saudi Arabian Monetary Agency building, Riyadh, 2023
21 × 28 cm

Former Saudi Arabian Monetary Agency building, Riyadh, 2023
21 × 28 cm

Minoru Yamasaki, Saudi Arabian Monetary Agency Towers (former Saudi Monetary Agency building), Riyadh, 2023
50 × 60 cm

NEOM: The Line Experience, exhibition, Riyadh, 2023
21 × 28 cm

NEOM: The Line Experience, exhibition, Riyadh, 2023
50 × 60 cm

NEOM: The Line Experience, exhibition, Riyadh, 2023
250 × 180 cm

King Abdullah University of Science and Technology (KAUST), Coastal and Marine Resources Core Lab, wet lab experimentation, Thuwal, 2023
50 × 60 cm

King Abdullah University of Science and Technology (KAUST), Visualization Core Lab, 3D interactive immersive rendering of an underwater landscape in the Red Sea, Thuwal, 2023
50 × 60 cm

Yamama Cement Factory (Old), Riyadh, 2023
21 × 28 cm

Yamama Cement Factory (Old), Riyadh, 2023
50 × 60 cm

All works courtesy of the artists
All works from 2023
commissioned by the Diriyah
Biennale Foundation for the
Diriyah Contemporary Art
Biennale 2024

Liu Chuang

*Bitcoin Mining and Field Recordings
of Ethnic Minorities*, 2018
6k (5760 × 1080) video, color, 5.1,
40 min
Film Program
Courtesy of the artist and
Antenna Space
Commissioned for Cosmopolis
#1.5: Enlarged Intelligence with
the support of the Mao Jihong
Arts Foundation

Mariah Lookman

*a Mirage: rivers meet the sea; fresh
and salt waters may intermingle;
an ocean remains distinct, and Poets
have forgotten words for love*, 2024
Installation with water channel,
garden, plants; maps, remedies,
recipes;* sound walk in Arabic
and English, approx. 19 min
Fieldwork guide and translation,
Saudi Arabia: Yahya Ahmed
Haider Abu Talib, Abdul Majeed
al Roudhan
Technical recording, mixing, and
editing: Ali Diwan (Ion Studio)
Sound walk narration:
Hind Alshifa (Arabic), Mariah
Lookman (English)
Design: Ashan Masood
Design and drawing:
Jonathan Edward
Translation into Arabic: Hassina
Warda (interviews), Bisan Saleh
(script, sound walk), Rana Dadi
(foldout)
Courtesy of the artist
Commissioned by the Diriyah
Biennale Foundation for the
Diriyah Contemporary Art
Biennale 2024

*a Mirage: rivers meet the sea; fresh
and salt waters may intermingle;
an ocean remains distinct, and Poets
have forgotten words for love*, 2024
Re/Search

When We Remember the Music in
Our Dreams
Artist Talk, June 17, 2023
Biennale Encounters

*A very special thanks to the spice
and herb specialists in the old
markets of Riyadh for keeping the
knowledge and memories of this
ancient trade alive.

Nidhi Mahajan
& Moad Musbahi

*An excerpt from Kitab Al Marasi:
A Composite Navigational Manual
for the Indian Ocean*, 2024
Mixed-media
The Learning Garden
Courtesy of the artists
Commissioned by the Diriyah
Biennale Foundation for the
Diriyah Contemporary Art
Biennale 2024

Taus Makhacheva

Charivari, 2019
Installation
570 × 1300 × 1300 cm
Architect: Maria Serova
Text: Alexander Snegirev
Costume design: Panika Derevya
Costume production: Margarita
Antonova, Alisa Bunkova, Costume
Studio "Paloma"| Yulia Brikulskaya,
Costume Studio "Ginger Rose"
Sergey Cheltsov, Nadezhda
Danilenko, Panika Derevya, Olga
Kalinina, Anastasia Markova,
Larisa Nikulshina, Anastasia
Rybina, Anna Samsonenko, Alina
Sarancha, Scenic Costume Studio
"M"Art', Alexandra Terekhina,
Anna Vetrova, Denis Yudin

Costume production consultation:
Sofia Egorova, Anastasia Markova
Sound production: Alisa Bunkova,
Marat Ismailov, Karina Salaway
Sound design: Denis Dronov
Sound engineer: Artem Karkach,
Maxim Nikolaev, PicMus Production
Voices: Osama Adda, Abdelrahman
Adhat, Aisha Arabia, Alaa Arabika,
Roga Aya, Yury Brezhnev, Kristina
Chernyavskaya, Lydia Christina,
Nicholas Collet, Lisa Dwan,
Nuha Eltahir, Abdelrahman
Elhout, Michael Geary, Al-terk
Gunwa, Anton Kostochkin, Agnia
Kuznetsova, Baha Lahkham,
Gladston Makhib, Daria Mazur,
Polina Milushkova, Thayer
Mustafa, Hadi Rahma, Susie
Sefton, Ekaterina Shibayeva,
Lubov Tolkalina, Sameh Vohra,
Andrew Winn
Production: Sanan Baghirov,
Kristina Chernyavskaya,
Charles Gohy, Sadagat Isayeva,
Albert Kolambel
Installation production: Good
Support Moscow, Novruz
Mammadov
Research: Vusal Ahmedov, Ulvia
Akhundova, Farah Alakbarli,
Sanan Baghirov, Kristina
Chernyavskaya, Vasilisa Egorova,
Sayara Huseyinli, Asya Sokolova,
Arina Umanskaya
Audio production: Arabic | Ksenia
Ananyeva, Artem Berezin, Igor
Fridenberg, Marat Ismailov,
Temirkan Khanov, Alexander
Lakeev, Eduard Lim, Ivan
Sapozhnikov, Ulyana Tregubenko
Translation: English | Ben McGarr,
Arabic | Inna Alsatkina
Editing: Arabic | Abu Bakr Al Ani
(thelingtwist), Ebrahim Hasan
Language consultation: Arabic |
Inna Alsatkina, Ebrahim Hasan

Special thanks to director of
the Baku National Circus Vagif
Baghir-Zada, circus historian

Radjab Mamedov, director of the
National Archives of the Republic
of Azerbaijan Asger Rasulov,
director of the National Archives
of Photo and Video Documents
of the Republic of Azerbaijan
Vugar Taptygly, gymnast Tamila
Nazirova, clown Lada Sanatskaya,
animal trainers Tofik Akhundov
and Rauf Rasulov, director
of circus shows and concerts
Vladimir Vavilov, archivist Aida
Babazade, poet Leyli Salayeva

Courtesy of the artist and
Private Collection
Commissioned by YARAT
Contemporary Art Space (2019),
production supported by Jameel
Arts Centre (2022) and the Diriyah
Contemporary Art Biennale (2024)
Production of Arabic recording
supported by the Diriyah Biennale
Foundation for the Diriyah
Contemporary Art Biennale 2024

Super Taus
Workshop, February 24, 2024
Biennale Encounters

Robin Meier Wiratunga

Waves beneath an ocean of wet air,
2024
Audio
The Learning Garden
Courtesy of the artist
Commissioned by the Diriyah
Biennale Foundation for the
Diriyah Contemporary Art
Biennale 2024

The Migrant Ecologies Project

*{if your bait can sing the wild one
will come} Like Shadows Through
Leaves*, 2021
1920 × 1080 HD video, 28 min
Film Program

*Railtrack Songmaps multimedia
archive*
*Like Shadows Through Leaves, Book
as a Bird*
Re/Search
Presentation supported by the
Diriyah Biennale Foundation for
the Diriyah Contemporary Art
Biennale 2024

All works courtesy of The Migrant
Ecologies Project (Lucy Davis
in collaboration with Zai Tang,
Kee Ya Ting and Zachary Chan)

if your bait can sing the wild one
will come
Lucy Davis from The Migrant
Ecologies Project
Workshop, February 24, 2024
Biennale Encounters

Małgorzata Mirga-Tas

*Katarzyna Oraczko with her
son Leszek*, from the series
Siukar Manusia, 2022
Textile, acrylic on wooden
stretcher
260 × 270 cm

*Augustyn Gabor with his daughter
Elżbieta*, from the series
Siukar Manusia, 2022
Textile, acrylic on wooden
stretcher
260 × 270 cm

All works courtesy the artist,
Frith Street Gallery, London;
Foksal Gallery Foundation,
Warsaw; and Karma International,
Zurich

Regina Maria Möller

DIE MOTTE (The Moth),
2018/2024
Curtains, porcelain vase,
QR code plates
Concept / Design of all works:
Regina Maria Möller
Curtains: seamstress Petra Korink
(costume designer), Berlin
Porcelain vase: vessel crafted by
One Million (Uli Aigner), Berlin,
painted by Regina Maria Möller
QR codes: animation of the vases
by Inbar Vahab Kranz (motion
designer), Berlin
Photographer of the vases:
Lepkowski Studios, Berlin
Presentation supported by the
Diriyah Biennale Foundation for
the Diriyah Contemporary Art
Biennale 2024

Read My Voice
Workshop and Artist Talk,
May 4, 2024
Biennale Encounters

James Morris

Works from the series *Butabu*,
1999–2000
Archival pigment prints

*Djinguereber Mosque, Timbuktu,
Mali*, 1999
150 × 187 cm

Friday Mosque, Djenne, Mali, 1999
187 × 150 cm

House, Djenne, Mali, 1999
187 × 150 cm

Friday Mosque, Agadez, Niger, 2000
187 × 150 cm

Friday Mosque, Djenne, Mali, 2000
150 × 187 cm

View from the river, Djenne, Mali,
2000
187 × 150 cm

All works courtesy of the artist
Production supported by the
Diriyah Biennale Foundation for
the Diriyah Contemporary Art
Biennale 2024

Butabu
Developmental materials
Re/Search

Tania Mouraud

Initiation Room N°2,
1971/2022/2024
Wood, MDF boards, glossy white
paint, LED band, 4 white speakers,
200-Hz sine wave
830 × 530 × 200 cm

Dream, 2004–ongoing
Printed fabric banner fixed on
aluminum channel frame
4 versions in Arabic, English,
and Urdu
Dimensions variable

All works courtesy
Ceysson & Bénétière
Reproduction supported by the
Diriyah Biennale Foundation for
the Diriyah Contemporary Art
Biennale 2024

Zarina Muhammad

Gentle Ferocities
Night Workshop and Artist Talk,
March 23 and March 24, 2024
Biennale Encounters

Dala Nasser

Mineral Lick, 2019
Mixed discarded fabrics, salt,
and tap water from 25 different
districts across Beirut, Lebanon
800 × 200 cm
Courtesy of the artist

Hind Nasser

Untitled, 1978
Oil on canvas
86 × 88.5 cm

Petra I, 1987
Ink on paper
28.6 × 21 cm

Petra II, 1987
Ink on paper
34.5 × 26 cm

Untitled, 2021
Acrylic on canvas
100 × 100 × 2.5 cm

Untitled, 2021
Acrylic on canvas
100 × 80 × 2.5 cm

All works courtesy of the artist

Hussein Nassereddine

Laughing on the River,
Your Eyes Drown in Tears
Performance, March 2, 2024
with video, sound, 35 min
In Arabic with English subtitles
Biennale Encounters
Courtesy of the artist
Commissioned by Jameel Art
Center, 2023

Filwa Nazer

The Housed Body
Workshops,
April 19–20 and 26–27, 2024
Biennale Encounters

Nguyễn Trinh Thi

How to Improve the World /
Cải tiến Thế giới, 2021
HD video, color and
black and white, sound, 46 min
Film Program
Courtesy of the artist

NJOKOBOK

NJOKOBOK BAR, 2024
Bar furniture, cold pressed juices
from traditional Senegalese
recipes, Senegalese tea, *qahwa*,
storytelling sessions
Furniture produced at
Fellesverstedet, Oslo
Artist assistants: Runa Carlsen,
Linn Lervik, Siv Bugge Vatne,
Klara Suša Večovnik
Commissioned by the Diriyah
Biennale Foundation for the
Diriyah Contemporary Art
Biennale 2024

What Makes a Neighborhood?
Artist Talk by Apolonija Šušteršič
and Youssou Diop with Ahmad
Angawi, July 5, 2023
Biennale Encounters

What Does it Take, What Does
It Do To Cook Together?
Sharing Session, September 9, 2023
Biennale Encounters

Storytelling Sessions at
NJOKOBOK BAR
February 20, 21, and 23,
March 15 and 29, May 24, 2024
Biennale Encounters

Elia Nurvista

Reading Palm
Workshop and Artist Talk, May 11
and 12, 2024
Biennale Encounters

Phi Phi Oanh

A Light Exists in the Spring, 2023
From the series *Palimpsest*
(2013–ongoing)
Lacquerscope composed of recycled medium format projectors,
glass, *son ta* resin, LED spotlights,
aluminum; 8 lacquer slides of
son ta lacquer on laminated glass;
stainless steel, aluminum, iron
stand with acrylic display
Dimensions variable
Courtesy of the artist
Presentation supported by the
Diriyah Biennale Foundation for
the Diriyah Contemporary Art
Biennale 2024

Lucy + Jorge Orta

OrtaWater - Purification Factory,
2012
Factory construction in reclaimed
wood and glass, water purification
system, water tanks, pipes, various
objects, OrtaWater bottles
350 × 150 × 540 cm
Courtesy of the artists

70 × 7 The Meal, Act XLVI, 2024
March 16, 2024
Suhoor meal, long table for 300
Dimensions variable
Courtesy of the artists
Furnishing supported by IKEA
Commissioned by the Diriyah
Biennale Foundation for the
Diriyah Contemporary Art
Biennale 2024

The Embroidery Landscapes
Workshop, August 19, 2023
Biennale Encounters

Food—Water—Life
Artist Talk, August 19, 2023
Biennale Encounters

70 × 7 The Meal, Act XLVI, 2024
Developmental materials
Re/Search

Jorge Otero-Pailos

With contributions by:
Daniah Alsaleh, Bricklab, Ahmed
Mater, HRH Nawaf Bin Ayyaf,
Filwa Nazer, syn architects, Alaa
Tarabzouni & Fahad Al Saud

A Library of Earthen Architectures,
2024
Artifacts of collective memory
and related audio interviews
Dimensions and materials
variable
Courtesy of the artists
Commissioned by the Diriyah
Biennale Foundation for the
Diriyah Contemporary Art
Biennale 2024

Ethics of Dust
Artist Talk, June 18, 2023
Biennale Encounters

Sopheap Pich

Rang Phnom Flower, 2015
Bamboo, rattan, metal wire,
plywood, steel, metal bolts
775 × 415 × 166 cm
Courtesy of Sopheap Pich Studio

Amulet (Hevea Afzelia), 2023
Hand-blown glass, cotton silk rope,
wood, bone
250 × 180 × 30 cm
Courtesy of Cirva, Marseille

Marjetica Potrč

Acre Palafita with Infrastructure,
2024
Wood, palm leaves, energy,
communication infrastructure
650 × 700 × 500 cm
Courtesy of the artist and
Galerie Nordenhake Berlin/
Stockholm/Mexico City
Commissioned by the Diriyah
Biennale Foundation for the
Diriyah Contemporary Art
Biennale 2024

*The Time of Humans on
the Soča River*, 2021/2024
Acrylic paint on wall
350 × 570 cm
Wall drawing from original
drawing *The Time of Humans on
the Soča River*, 2021
Courtesy the artist and Galerie
Nordenhake, Berlin/Stockholm/
Mexico City

The Rights of a River
with Jumana Emil Abboud
Workshop and Artist Talk,
November 18 and 19, 2023
Biennale Encounters

Lala Rukh

Untitled, date unknown
Graphite on carbon paper
12 × 15 cm
Courtesy of Lala Rukh Estate,
Pakistan

Untitled (2), 1983–86
Conté on paper
74 × 56.5 cm
Courtesy of the Lala Rukh Estate
and Grey Noise Gallery, Dubai

Untitled (6), 1983–86
Conté on paper
74 × 56.5 cm
Courtesy of the Lala Rukh Estate
and Grey Noise Gallery, Dubai

Untitled, 2003
Graphite on paper
75.8 × 101.5 cm
Courtesy of Lala Rukh Estate,
Pakistan

Untitled 1, 2 (diptych), 2010
(approximate date)
Graphite on carbon paper
21.5 × 28 cm (each)
Courtesy of the Lala Rukh Estate
and Grey Noise Gallery, Dubai

Presentation supported by the
Diriyah Biennale Foundation for
the Diriyah Contemporary Art
Biennale 2024

Arin Rungjang

Golden Teardrop, 2013
Single-channel video, wood,
iron beams, cast brass
Installation 300 × 500 × 500 cm /
Brass sphere ø 300 cm
Courtesy of the artist and
DC Collection, Thailand
Presentation supported by the
Diriyah Biennale Foundation for
the Diriyah Contemporary Art
Biennale 2024

Tomás Saraceno

*Hybrid dark semi-social Cluster GC
12406 built by: a duet of Cyrtophora
citricola - eight weeks, rotated 180°*,
2019
Spider silk, carbon fiber, glass,
ink, metal
28.6 × 29.1 × 29.1 cm

*An Open Letter for Invertebrate
Rights*, 2020
Spidersilk, paper, pins
Dimensions variable

Fly with Pacha, Into the Aerocene,
2023
Single-channel 2k video,
color/sound
67 min 15 sec

All works courtesy of the artist
and neugerriemschneider, Berlin

Citra Sasmita

*Timur Merah Project XII: Rivers
With No End*, 2023
Wooden pillars, fabric
450 × 1050 × 220 cm
Courtesy of the artist
Commissioned by the Diriyah
Biennale Foundation for the
Diriyah Contemporary Art
Biennale 2024

Seher Shah

Of Dust and Measure (5–9), 2019–21
5 drawings, graphite, ink and
graphite dust on cotton paper
25.4 × 20.3 cm (each)
Courtesy of the artist and
Green Art Gallery, Dubai

Notes from a City Unknown, 2021
Portfolio of 32 screen prints
on paper
30 × 22 cm
Courtesy of the artist and
Green Art Gallery, Dubai

Translation and production of
Arabic booklet supported by the
Diriyah Biennale Foundation for
the Diriyah Contemporary Art
Biennale 2024

Hassan Sharif

A Long Letter, 1979
Photographs and pencil
on mounting board
58 × 41 cm

Light and Dark, 1979
Paper, photographs, ink and
pencil on mounting board
84 × 59.5 cm

Drawing on the Wall, 1982
Photographs and pencil
on mounting board
73.6 × 56.1 cm

Body and Squares, 1983
Photographs, ink, pen and pencil
on paper mounted on cardboard,
pencil
84 × 59.5 cm

Throwing Stones, 1983
Photographs, ink and pen on
paper and pencil on mounting
board
84 × 59.5 cm

Recording Stones, 1983
Photographs and pencil
on mounting board
73.2 × 56.1 cm

Writing, 1983
Photographs, ink on paper and
pencil on mounting board
91 × 66.7 cm

Reading Poem - Four Minutes, 1983
Photographs, ink and pen on
paper and pencil on mounting
board
98 × 73.5 cm

Shadows of Al Loz, 1983
Photographs and pencil
on mounting board
65.9 × 48.6 cm

Jumping No. 2, 1983
Photographs, ink and pencil
on mounting board
73.7 × 56 cm

Sound, 1983
Photographs and pencil
on mounting board
73.5 × 56 cm

Coloured Squares, 1983
Photographs and ink on paper
mounted on cardboard
90.9 × 66.7 cm

Performance is Good, 1984
Photographs, ink on paper and
pencil on mounting board
73.6 × 56 cm

Library, 1984
Photographs, ink on paper and
pencil on mounting board
73.6 × 56.1 cm

All works courtesy of the Estate
of Hassan Sharif and Gallery
Isabelle van den Eynde, Dubai;
Alexander Gray Associates,
New York; gb agency, Paris
Presentation supported by the
Diriyah Biennale Foundation for
the Diriyah Contemporary Art
Biennale 2024

Shooshie Sulaiman

Lore of Equator #2, 2024
Wrapping paper, rubber, canvas,
soil, fruit ink, graphite, charcoal,
kawara pigment, found plastic,
water buffalo horn, wood, rattan,
book, video
Dimensions variable
Courtesy of the artist and
Tomio Koyama Gallery, Japan

syn architects

Walking Tours
February 20 and 21,
March 6 and 7, 2024
Biennale Encounters

Tang Da Wu

*On Tuesday the Delivery Vehicle
Number is ER II, and on Monday
is BG I*, 2022
Paper, glass, steel
650 × 400 × 1180 cm
Courtesy of the artist
Reproduction supported by the
Diriyah Biennale Foundation for
the Diriyah Contemporary Art
Biennale 2024

Paulo Tavares / autonoma

*Trees, Vines, Palms, and Other
Architectural Monuments*, 2017–22
Multimedia installation
Courtesy of Paulo Tavares /
studio autonoma
Originally commissioned by the
Brazilian Public Prosecutor's Office

An Architectural Botany, 2018–22
Multimedia installation developed
in collaboration with botanist
William Balée
Courtesy of Paulo Tavares /
studio autonoma

Presentation supported by the
Diriyah Biennale Foundation for
the Diriyah Contemporary Art
Biennale 2024

TAYYŪN

Insect Hotel, 2024
Wood, steel plate
350 × 30 × 30 cm
Courtesy of the artists
Commissioned by the Diriyah
Biennale Foundation for the
Diriyah Contemporary Art
Biennale 2024

Brown, Blue, Green, Gray:
Urban Rewilding
Workshop and Artist Talk,
December 16, 2023
Biennale Encounters

Sissel Tolaas

IN_side_OUT_edis_NI تربة, 2024
Molecular smell
Commissioned by the Diriyah
Biennale Foundation for the
Diriyah Contemporary Art
Biennale 2024

IN_side_OUT_edis_NI تربة, 2024
Developmental materials
Re/Search

Anaïs Tondeur

Urban Petrichor, 2015–ongoing
72 soil distillates
200 × 160 cm
Protocol developed during a
transdisciplinary residency as
part of Sustainable Cultures
Lab, by COAL and Domaine
Départemental de Chamarande
(2015–16) and during a residency
at Centre Tignous d'Art
contemporain, Montreuil, France
Courtesy of the artist

Urban Petrichor, 2015–ongoing
On the correspondence between
the ground and the sky
Soil distillates, soil fragments,
cartography, video, HDV, color
Re/Search
Presentation supported by the
Diriyah Biennale Foundation for
the Diriyah Contemporary Art
Biennale 2024

Mona Vătămanu
& Florian Tudor

*The Tree of Life / How Do We Read
Signs We Cannot Understand?*, 2023
Installation of kilims and carpets,
euro pallets, trees
800 × 600 cm
Courtesy of the artists, with
the support of Mihai Pop and
Mihaela Lutea collections
Commissioned by Centrul de
Proiecte Timișoara, 2023
Display supported by the Diriyah
Biennale Foundation for the
Diriyah Contemporary Art
Biennale 2024

The Tree of Life / Performing
History
Workshop and Artist Talk,
December 2 and 3, 2023
Biennale Encounters

Activation of *The Tree of Life / How Do We Read Signs We Cannot Understand?*
February 20 and May 24, 2024
Biennale Encounters

Suzann Victor

Strike, 2021
Glass vessels, acrylic strikers, cables, water
750 × 500 cm
Furnishing supported by IKEA
Courtesy of the artist and STPI, Singapore
Edition commissioned by the Diriyah Biennale Foundation for the Diriyah Contemporary Art Biennale 2024

Munem Wasif

Kheyal, 2015–2019
Single channel video, 16:8, black and white, stereo, 23 min 34 sec
Camera: Ferdous Ahmad and Munem Wasif
Sound Design and Music: Saadul Islam
Editing: Sazal Alok and Munem Wasif
Production: Pranabesh Das and Wahed Mahmud
Film Program
Courtesy of the artist

Seeds Shall Set Us Free II, 2016–19
Cyanotypes prints, inkjet prints, archival documents, photographic reproductions of drawings
474 × 137 cm
Courtesy of the artist and Art Jameel Dubai

Ines Weizman

"Of all the gin joints in all the towns in all the world…", 2023
Video, 16 min 30 sec
Printed curtain, booklet
Dimensions variable
Courtesy of the artist
Translation and production of Arabic booklet supported by the Diriyah Biennale Foundation for the Diriyah Contemporary Art Biennale 2024

Jana Winderen

Call from the Edge: Under Water, 2024
Concert, March 1, 2024
Biennale Encounters
Courtesy of the artist
With thanks to CORDAP, Coral Research & Development Accelerator Platform, King Abdullah University of Science and Technology (KAUST), Thuwal
Commissioned by the Diriyah Biennale Foundation for the Diriyah Contemporary Art Biennale 2024

Sonic Fieldwork
Artist Talk, November 25, 2023
Biennale Encounters

Developmental materials
Re/Search

Yang Fudong

Two photographs from the *Blue Kylin* series, 2008
Color inkjet prints
100 × 174.14 cm; 100 × 150 cm

On the Double Dragon Hills, 2012
Multi-channel video, 2-screen, black and white, silent, 25 min 50 sec

All works courtesy of the artist and ShanghART Gallery
Production supported by the Diriyah Biennale Foundation for the Diriyah Contemporary Art Biennale 2024

Yeo Siew Hua

An Invocation to the Earth, 2020
Single-channel HD video, color, sound, 16 min 10 sec
With the support of Akanga Film Asia, NTU Centre for Contemporary Art Singapore, GRYD, and 13 Little Pictures. Coproduced by Singapore International Film Festival and Thyssen-Bornemisza Art Contemporary (TBA21) for st_age Film Program
Courtesy of the artist

Liam Young

The Great Endeavor, 2023
MOV, sound, color, 9 min
Director: Liam Young
Production Design: Liam Young
Producer: Pegah Farahmand
Executive Producer: Partizan
Executive Producers: WaterBear Network: Lisa Cadwallader, Rickey Welch
VFX Supervisor: Alexey Marfin
Original Score: Lyra Pramuk
Costume Designer: Ane Crabtree
Tailor: Hae Min Yun
Matte Painter: Attilio Bonelli
Environment Artists: Andrew Hu, Luis Garcia Grech
Graphics: Neasden Control Center
Science Consultants: Holly Jean Buck, David Goldberg
Impact Producer: WaterBear Network: Jessie Saville
Impact Marketing: Lead WaterBear Network: Jolien Walhof
Presented by: WaterBear Network In Association With Resilient Foundation

With the additional support of:
WaterBear Network National
Gallery of Victoria, Melbourne SCI
Arc, Los Angeles
Film Program

Four costumes designed for the
The Great Endeavor, 2023
Costume Designer: Ane Crabtree

All works courtesy of the artist

Camille Zakharia

Coastal Promenade, 2010
20 photographs, edition 4 of 5
48.3 × 48.3 cm (each)
Printed on Archival Hahnemühle
FineArt Paper
Presentation supported by the
Diriyah Biennale Foundation for
the Diriyah Contemporary Art
Biennale 2024

Al Bar, 2010–16
20 photographs, edition 2 of 5
43.2 × 43.2 cm (each)
Printed on Archival Hahnemühle
FineArt Paper
Presentation supported by the
Diriyah Biennale Foundation for
the Diriyah Contemporary Art
Biennale 2024

The Mountain My Neighbor, 2024
2 books, edition 1 of 3
Printed on Archival Hahnemühle
Rice paper
508 × 76 cm (each)
Commissioned by the Diriyah
Biennale Foundation for the
Diriyah Contemporary Art
Biennale 2024

How to Remember?
Workshop and Artist Talk,
October 1–5, 2023
Biennale Encounters

All works courtesy of the artist

Samia Zaru

Life Is a Woven Carpet, 1995
Mixed media, rope, textiles with
ceramic elements
88 × 138 × 3 cm

Life Is a Woven Carpet, 2001
Mixed media, rope, textiles with
ceramic elements
532 × 280 × 20 cm

All works courtesy of the artist

Feifei Zhou

*Before there was land, there were
mangroves*, 2024
Illustration, animation, text, audio
The Learning Garden
Courtesy of the artist
Commissioned by the Diriyah
Biennale Foundation for the
Diriyah Contemporary Art
Biennale 2024

TEXT CREDITS
ARTISTS TEXTS

Curatorial Team

Amina Diab, Assistant Curator
Reem Al Nasser / p. 154
Mohammad AlFaraj / p. 204
Hind Nasser / p. 130

Rahul Gudipudi, Adjunct Curator
Tara Aldughaither and Joe Namy / p. 254
Cercle d'Art des Travailleurs de
    Plantation Congolaise / p. 256
Hiba Ismail / p. 258
Nidhi Mahajan and Moad Musbahi / p. 260
Robin Meier Wiratunga / p. 262
Paulo Tavares / autonoma / p. 106
Feifei Zhou / p. 264

Wejdan Reda, Co-curator
Nabila Al Bassam / p. 116
Abduhlrahman Al-Soliman / p. 118
Safeya Binzagr / p. 126
Camille Zakharia / p. 110

Anca Rujoiu, Co-curator
Hamra Abbas / p. 140
Irene Agrivina / p. 230
Aseel AlYaqoub / p. 72
Zarina Bhimji / p. 124
Britto Arts Trust / p. 206
Priyageetha Dia / p. 190
Simryn Gill / p. 92
Mariah Lookman / p. 214
Taus Makhacheva / p. 46
The Migrant Ecologies Project / p. 60
Małgorzata Mirga-Tas / p. 96
Filwa Nazer / p. 244
NJOKOBOK / p. 218
Mona Vătămanu & Florin Tudor / p. 198
Suzann Victor / p. 148

Ana Salazar Herrera, Co-curator
Dana Awartani / p. 160
María Magdalena Campos-Pons / p. 44
Rachaporn Choochuey / p. 208
Ade Darmawan / p. 88
Phi Phi Oanh / p. 174
Sopheap Pich / p. 178
Liang Shaoji / p. 170
Shooshie Sulaiman / p. 104
Tang Da Wu / p. 196

Writers and Editorial Team

Angela Ricasio Hoten
Martha Atienza / p. 84
Citra Sasmita / p. 184

Ali Ismail Karimi
Daniah Alsaleh / p. 70
Bricklab / p. 76
Anne Holtrop / p. 212

Ng Mei Jia
Tarek Atoui / p. 236

Sam I-shan
Liu Chuang / p. 58
Nguyễn Trinh Thi / p. 62

Soh Kay Min
Ursula Biemann / p. 54
Tiffany Chung / p. 86
Alexander Eriksson Furunes & Sudar Khadka / p. 78
Zarina Muhammad / p. 240
Elia Nurvista / p. 246
Marjetica Potrč / p. 102
Arin Rungjang / p. 180
Yang Fudong / p. 186

Murtaza Vali
Nazgol Ansarinia / p. 158
Rasheed Araeen / p. 120
Siah Armajani / p. 122
Seher Shah / p. 194

Text on Jorge Otero-Pailos courtesy of the artist.
The texts on all other artists were written by
the editorial team.

IMAGE CREDITS

1 Courtesy Diriyah Biennale Foundation, photo: Hussein Abdullah

2 Courtesy Diriyah Biennale Foundation

12 Courtesy Diriyah Biennale Foundation

18 Courtesy Diriyah Biennale Foundation, photo: Hussein Abdullah

26 Courtesy Diriyah Biennale Foundation, photo: Hussein Abdullah

30 Above: Courtesy Diriyah Biennale Foundation
Below: Photo: Laurian Ghinitoiu

32 Courtesy Diriyah Biennale Foundation, photo: Hussein Abdullah

41 Courtesy Dhali Al Mamoon, photo: Mohammad Zahid Hasan Sufi

43 Courtesy Efie Gallery and Moz Photography

45 Courtesy Galerie Barbara Thumm, Berlin; Gallery Wendi Norris, San Francisco, photo: Barbara Thumm

47 Courtesy Taus Makhacheva; YARAT Contemporary Art Space, photo: Pat Verbruggen

49 Courtesy Ines Weizman

53 Courtesy Sammy Baloji

55 Courtesy Ursula Biemann

57 Courtesy Saodat Ismailova

59 Courtesy Liu Chuang; Antenna Space, Shanghai

61 Courtesy The Migrant Ecologies Project, photo: Kee Ya Ting

63 Courtesy Nguyễn Trinh Thi

65 Courtesy Incantation Films

67 Courtesy Liam Young

71 Courtesy Daniah Alsaleh

73 Photographers unknown

75 Courtesy bahraini—danish

77 Courtesy Bricklab

79 Above: Courtesy Alexander Eriksson Furunes & Sudar Khadka, photo: Alexander Eriksson Furunes
Below: Courtesy Alexander Eriksson Furunes & Sudar Khadka, graphic design: Kirstin Helgadóttir

81 Courtesy Susanne Kriemann

85 Courtesy Martha Atienza

87 Courtesy Tiffany Chung

89 Above: Courtesy Ade Darmawan
Below: Courtesy Ade Darmawan; NTU CCA Singapore

91 Courtesy Christine Fenzl

93 Courtesy Simryn Gill 1301PE, Los Angeles; Jhaveri Contemporary, Mumbai; Richard Saltoun Gallery, London

95 Above: Courtesy Armin Linke
Below: Courtesy Ahmed Mater

97 Courtesy Małgorzata Mirga-Tas; Frith Street Gallery, London; Foksal Gallery Foundation, Warsaw; Karma International, Zurich

99 Courtesy James Morris

101 Courtesy Lucy + Jorge Orta, photo: Justin Yin

103 Courtesy Marjetica Potrč; VISUAL Carlow, Ireland; Galerie Nordenhake Berlin/Stockholm/Mexico, photo: Ros Kavanagh

105 Courtesy Shooshie Sulaiman; Tomio Koyama Gallery, photo: Kenji Takahashi

107 Courtesy Paulo Tavares / autonoma

109 Courtesy Munem Wasif; Project 88, Mumbai

111 Courtesy Camille Zakharia

115 Courtesy Alia Ahmad

117 Courtesy Nabila Al Bassam, photo: Arif Alnomay

119 Courtesy Abdulrahman Al-Soliman, photo: Arif Alnomay

121 Courtesy Rasheed Araeen; Rossi & Rossi; © Rasheed Araeen. All Rights Reserved, DACS 2024

123 Courtesy The Siah Armajani Estate; Rossi & Rossi

125 © Zarina Bhimji. All Rights Reserved, DACS 2024

127 Courtesy Al-Mansouria Foundation, photo: Arif Alnomay

129 Courtesy Sharjah Art Foundation, photo: Danko Stjepanovic; © Ibrahim El-Salahi, courtesy Vigo Gallery. All rights reserved, DACS 2024

131 Courtesy Hind Nasser

133 Courtesy the Estate of Lala Rukh; Grey Noise, Dubai

135 Courtesy the Estate of Hassan Sharif; Gallery Isabelle van den Eynde, Dubai; Alexander Gray Associates, New York; gb agency, Paris

137 Courtesy Samia Zaru, photo: Faris N. Zaru

141 Courtesy Hamra Abbas

143 Above: Courtesy Alia Farid, photo: Diana Pfammatter
Below: Courtesy Alia Farid

145 Courtesy Dala Nasser

147 Above: Courtesy Anaïs Tondeur
Below: Courtesy Eva Dalg

149 Courtesy Suzann Victor; STPI – Creative Workshop & Gallery, Singapore

153 Courtesy Sara Abdu; Athr gallery, photo: Mohammed Eskandrani

155 Above: Courtesy the Visual Arts Commission, photo: Abdul Rahman Alshhri
Below: Courtesy Reem Al Nasser; the Visual Arts Commission, photo: Mohammad Alaskandrani

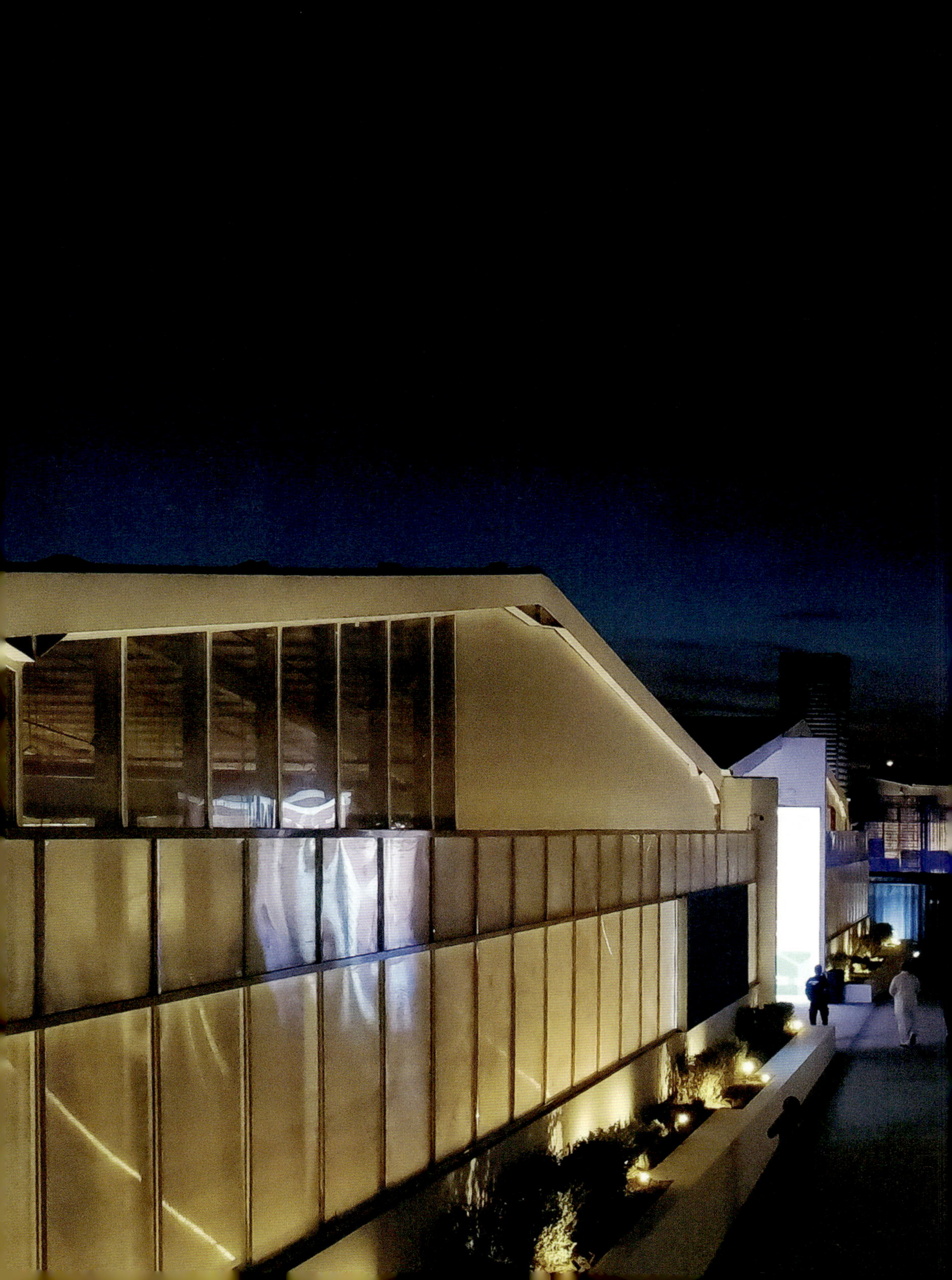

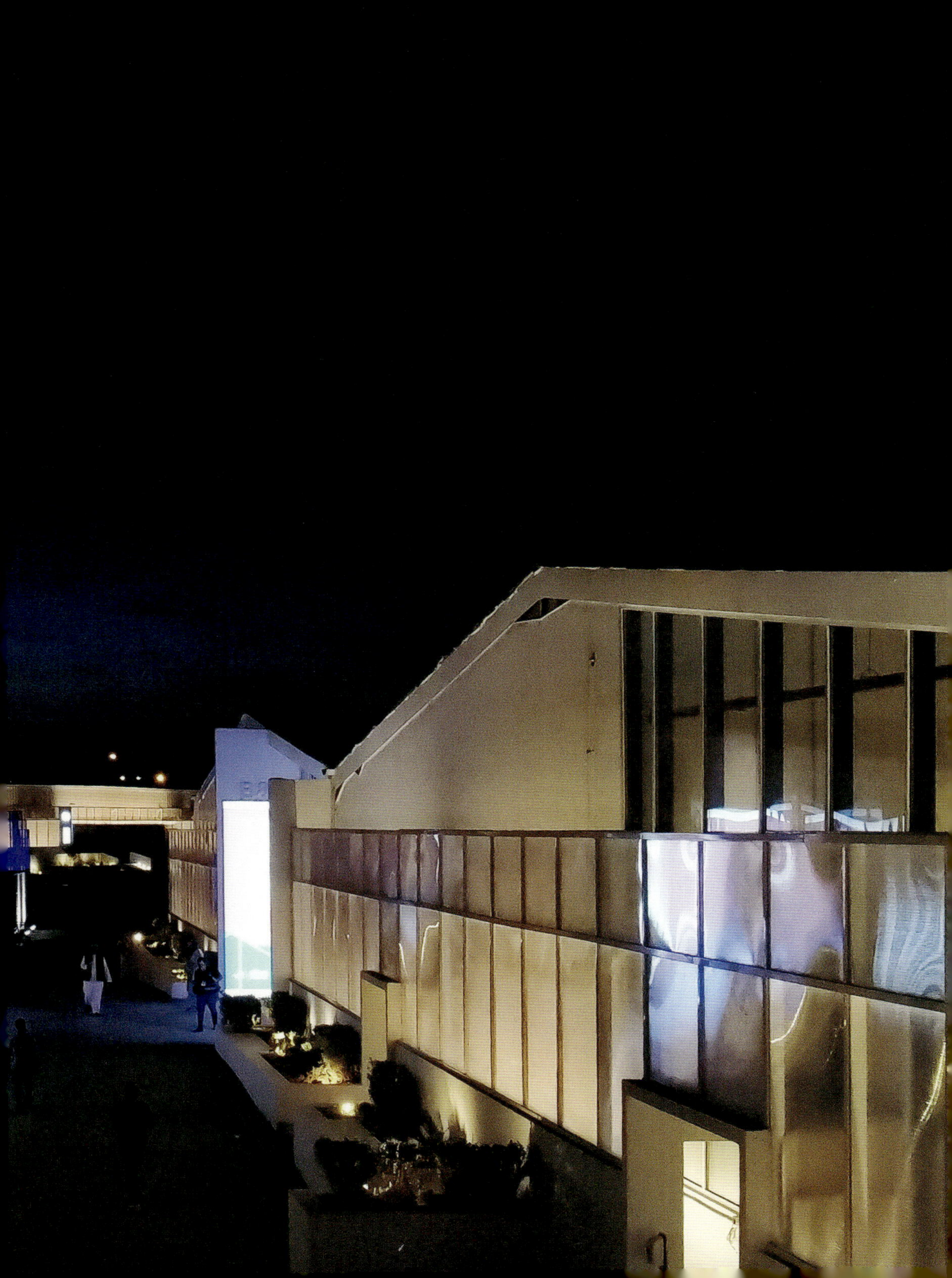

DIRIYAH BIENNALE FOUNDATION

Curatorial Advisory Committee

Rafal Niemojewski, Chair
Sara Binladen
Antonia Carver
Raneem Farsi
Akram Zaatari

Advisor

Alia Al-Senussi

Project Management and Organization

Abdulrahman Al Ghonaim
Sultan Al Idriss
Belal Abdelfattah
Sinad Dado
Tamer Elleisi
Nada Al Muarik

The Saudi Ministry of Culture

Diriyah Biennale Foundation wishes to express its deepest gratitude to the entire Saudi Ministry of Culture and to every department and commission which assisted in realizing this exhibition.

Hala Abuzeid
Muzzafar Ahmed
Beesan AlAjaji
Albara Alauhali
Ayman Abdulgadir
Rola Alghrair
Lamia Alhamad
Abdulrahman Al Dusari
Hamzah Alhamzah
Hala Al Hedeithy
Eisa AlKhalidi
Rasha Al Kerdmimi
Noura Al-Maashouq
Sulaiman Al Mushawah
Asayel Alobathani
Lamia Alrabiah
Abdulrahman Al Rajhi
Asayel Alshammari
Riyam Al Tamimi
Mohammed Alzahrani
Saleh Al Tuwajri
Zeina Amer
Raghda Amin
Abdulrahman Asali
Khaled Baassiri
Mohammed Bay
Abdulaziz Bin Huwaymil
Dareen Bin Mahfood
Abdulrahman Bin Obaid
Hissah BinObaydan
Salma Enani
Abdulmalik Ghazzawi
Hanouf Houthan
Al Johara M. Al Banyan
Karim Maatoug
Jack Persekian
Salwa Samargandi
Ahmad Roboey
Sharif Wafa

AFTER RAIN
DIRIYAH CONTEMPORARY ART BIENNALE 2024

Artistic Director

Ute Meta Bauer

Co-curators

Wejdan Reda
Anca Rujoiu
Rose Lejeune
Ana Salazar Herrera

Adjunct Curator

Rahul Gudipudi

Curatorial Team

Dr. Amina Diab, Assistant Curator
Dian Arumningtyas, Curatorial Assistant
Alanood Alsudairi, Curatorial Assistant

Curatorial Management and Coordination

Snejana Krasteva, Head of Curatorial Programs
Sara Black, Project Manager
Louise Rambaud, Registrar
Yaser Musleh, Project Assistant

Scenography Direction

Laura Miotto, Scenography Design Lead
Savina Nicolini, Scenography Design Lead

Scenography Team

Esther Parn, Senior Designer
Harinisha Tamilselvan, Junior Designer
Aye Aye Hlaing, Junior Designer

Scenography Design Consultancy

Kaveh Dabiri
Natalia Michalowska
Saskia Simon

Lighting Design Direction

Lucas Goy, Lighting Design Lead

Lighting Design Team

Florian Bergera
Melody Beselga
Joelle El Khoury
Anaelle Vincot

Graphic Design Direction

Kai von Rabenau, Graphic Design Lead

English Graphic Design Team

João Pedro Costa
Linda Riedl

Arabic Graphic Design Team

Mohammed Alruways
Abdullah Kenani

The Learning Garden

Leen Ajlan
Nour Annan
Alan Woo

**Produced by the
Diriyah Biennale Foundation**

Editorial Direction

Laura Schleussner, Managing Editor
Ebrahim Hasan, Lead Arabic Editor
Jonas Raam, Image Editor

Editorial Team

Arif Alnomay
Melissa Canbaz
Laura Egerton
Yasmine El Rashidi
Dan Koh
Hashem Reda
Bisan Saleh
Tas Skorupa

Translation Team

Nourah Aldaej
Wael Al Mahdi
Rana Dadi
Nour Sulaiman

Public Program

Ruba AlAmoudi
Yara Aldabbagh
Mohammad Aldandani
Mashael AlNasser
Mashael Al Saie
Ahmad Amer
Khayal Asghar
Ali Chamut
Yousef El Senwar
Jad Hamandi
Nisrine Jaafar
Rawi Kammoun
Masa Milhem Content
Abdullah Saeed
Saeed Saeed
Bayan Saif
Rida Sharaf
Khalil Wanna
Lauren Watson

Sponsorship and Partnerships

Sara Anis
Racha Eldeeb
Shazeen Khan
Lea Khoury
Zena Melki
Rana Sadek

Marketing, Communication, Digital and Public Relations

Hussein Abdullah
Baha Al-Akhras
Khalid AlRayes
Linda Al Shami
Ahmad AlZa'atreh
Khaldoon Aqel
Seif Ariqat
Yasmeen Bakeer
Heba Dasouki
Bernice delos Reyes
Bdour Farhat
Safia Frehat
Andrew Goodhouse
Natalie Habash
Lama Abu Hanieh
Jeremy Higginbotham
Wassef Koleilat
Anne Maier
Sander Manse
Melia Nashat
Dana Owies
Karine Ramadan
Paula Ramírez
Fatima Skeiki
Sultan Suqar
Marie von Ribbentrop
Darine Wehbi

Art Handling

Besim Aksu
Justin Arnheim
Loeva Bersihand
Ronny Cabiles
Barrie Dannik
Robin Eckstein
Eric John Eigner
Andy Herde
Tom Kleverlaan
Marvin Lauer
Alexandre Lefeuvre
Iqbal Muhammad
Peter Macdonald
Walid Rachkidi
Mathieu Renaudineau
Vincent Rischer
Juca Rivera
Mohamed Sadek
Pedro Santa Cruz
Irina Seekamp
Latheef Thazhathu
Andreas Wexel
Olaf Wunsch

Conservation

Stefanie Bruendler
India Carpenter
Phoenix Findlayson-Pugh
Berangere Foucher
Vanessa Griffiths
Lauren Healy
Lisa Herold
Kirsten Hooten
Coralie How Choong
Ffion Howells
Camilla Hughes-Hunt
Zeljana Jurkovic
Erica Oh
Eleonora Pollano
Rebecca Ranieri
Harriet Sharman
Anthi Soulioti
Manuela Torro Silva-Diaz
Federica Traversa
Stella Wilcox

Production Direction and Management

Sabina Beckert
Hassan Bin Arif
Elena Castorina
Dulce Caletti
Giorgia Gobbi
Massimo Fogliati
James Glanville
Kelly King
Marco Lepore
Pietro Meroni
Fabio Pavanetto
Cosy Sagal
Monica Urban
Guido Zanca

Art Production

Jenny Beardshall
Mike Bevan
Federico Dalla Pozza
Roberto Di Pasquale
Federico Elia
Charles Gohy
Afra Rebuscini
Olivia Reid
Gabriela Salhe
Antonio Zanon
Francesco Zanon

Scenography Production

Abdul Abumur
Erubey Acosta
Haroun Barazanchi
Sarah De Fanti
Rajab Gattas
Travis Hayward
Abdulrahman Malallah
Tommaso Piotti
Phillip Schmidt
Romaric Senelas
Sergio Serafica
Roberto Tavella

Events and Operations

Yassal Abdel Hadi
Abdullah Abou Chlieh
Mossa Agoda
Hamza Al-Aqili
Faisal Albissi
Shehab Albitar
Raffaello Alberti
Basil Aldiali
Turki Alghamdi
Abdulmajeed Algothayan
Noujoud Alharbi
Saad Alhayek
Anas Alnadwi
Anastasiia Cherkasova
Talal Gedeon
Chiara Giordano
Valerie Gomes
Mashaal Hossam
Shakeel Khan
Leyla Khuluflu
Howard Lloyd
Charbel Maksoud
Narmin Mammadova
Michael Mangampo
Stevie Manning
Deema Mohamad-Ali
Ayman Mohammed
Abdullah Mosleh
Valeria Pagani
Katrina Pullen
Paulo Quarino
Ali Ramadan
Sara Reda
Alina Rogers
Mai Sabr
Nadeen Said
Timur Shaykhutdinov
Ruby Siwady
Arsida Velija
Valeria Vuzzi

Hospitality and Logistics

Bashayer Abahussain
Walid Abdullah
Razan Al Athamenah
Clare Baarda
Humam Emad
Jessica Ho
Ibrar Khan
Oliver Marriott
Adam MacDonald
Amy Morgan
Roger Parker
Madel Peril
Guy Stevenson
Majell Villafuerte

ACKNOWLEDGEMENTS

The Diriyah Biennale Foundation would like to thank these organizations and institutions, who have assisted in realizing this exhibition.

Almarai
Abdullah Al Yusi

Yamama Cement
Sultan Madkhali

Aramco
Mae Albinali
Nouf AlHarthy
Mohamed Al-Salman
Khalid Al-Zamil

Boutique Group
Fahad AlBjaidi

Diriyah Gate Development Authority (DGDA)
Njoud Alanbari
Abdullah Algoblan
Mishari Almalki
Ghada AlMogren
Abdullah Almuhanna
Abdulaziz Alobaidi
Mohammed Al Sagoor
Tarfa AlSaud
Victor De Laboulaye
Hosam Fatani
Sarah Foryame
Paola Matilde Pesaresi

Alzahrani Farm
Mohammad AlZahrani

Goethe-Institut, Riyadh
Charlotte Hermelink
Katarzyna Wielga-Skolimowska

King Abdulaziz Center for World Culture - Ithra
Farah Abushullaih
Hadeel AlEisa
Noura AlHarby
Kumail Almusaly
Shujoon AlQahtani

King Abdulaziz Foundation for Research and Archives
Turki AlShuwaier, Director General
Sultan Alowadi
Ayman AlHunayhin

King Abdullah City for Science and Technology (KACST)
Muath AlTamimi
Muhammad BaSaif

King Abdullah University for Science and Technology (KAUST)
Hiroko Davis
Carlos M. Duarte
Michelle-Nicole Havlik
Ola Kabli
Lori Moggy
Mohamed Omar
Marika Panagiotou

Misk Art Institute
Nawaf Alharbi
Oliver Farrell

Misk City
Yousef Aldoghtir
Nawaf AlMutairi
Norah AlShalhoub
Maha AlSheikh
Noura AlSwailem
Skye Fisher

NEOM
Ibrahim AlBloushy
Maha AlBulayhi
Haifa AlHarby

National Center for Vegetation Cover Development and Combating Desertification
Ahmed Ali AlGhamdi
Amani AlBlouy
Humeid AlDosary
Abdullah AlSobaihy

Royal Commission of Riyadh City (RCRC)
Raghad AlSubaie
Miguel Blanco-Carrasco

LENDERS

The Royal Institute of Traditional Arts (TRITA)
Dimah AlAjaji
Mashael AlAjmi
Sahar AlDahash
Noor AlMudehim
Sultan AlSalloom

Saudi Ministry of Environment
Hmoud Al Bakri
Douna Saad AlMansour
Yazeed Alshammari

Saudi Space Agency
Faisal AlAngari
Marwan AlJehany

Shamalat
Maha Malluh
Sara Alissa
Nojoud Alsudairi

Wadi Wuthaylan National Park
Turki Alaridi
Zaid Al-Khathlan

The Diriyah Biennale Foundation would like to thank the following institution for supporting the production of the artwork by Priyageetha Dia for the Diriyah Contemporary Art Biennale 2024.

Han Nefkens Foundation, Barcelona
Han Nefkens
Hilde Teerlinck

The Diriyah Biennale Foundation would like to express its deepest gratitude to the artists, collections, museums, and institutions that have generously loaned artwork for this edition of the Diriyah Contemporary Art Biennale.

Al-Mansouria Foundation

Khalid and Sally Alturki

Art Jameel Collection

Centre international de recherche sur le verre et les arts plastiques (CIRVA Marseille)

Collection Olivier Georges Mestelan

DC Collection, Thailand

Estate of Hassan Sharif

Kiran Nadar Museum of Art, New Delhi

Lala Rukh Estate, Pakistan

Mihai Pop and Mihaela Lutea collections

Samdani Art Foundation, Bangladesh

Sharjah Art Foundation Collection

TBA21 Thyssen-Bornemisza Art Contemporary Collection

Our thanks also go to all the private collectors who provided works for the exhibition.

THANKS

Fatma Abdulhadi
Tarek Abou El Fetouh
Sarah Abu Abdallah
Farah Abushullaih
Osama Abu Sitteh
Talal Ahenaki
Tofik Akhundov
Dr. Ali Al-Abdil
Dimah Alajaji
Mashael Alajmi
Leen AlAli
Raghad AlAli
Mohammad Khurshid Alam
Njoud Alanbari
Faisal AlAngari
Fawzia Saleh AlAngari
Turki Alaridi
Maha Alasaker
Kawther Alatiyah
Hmoud AlAttawi
Abdulhamid AlBagshi
Kholoud AlBakr
Mae AlBinali
Fahad AlBjaidi
Ibrahim Al Bloushy
Amani AlBlouy
Maha Albulayhi
Abdullah AlBuraykan
Nourah Aldaej
Sahar Al Dahash
Yousef Aldoghtir
Humeid AlDosary
Hadeel AlEisa
Noor AlFayez
Rawan AlFuraih
Bashaer M. Algethami
Dr. Ahmed Ali Alghamdi
Jaber AlGhamdi
Khalid Al Gharballi
Rola Alghrair
Deema Alghunaim
Haifa Al Harbi
Nawaf AlHarbi
Noura Alharbi
Nouf AlHarthy
Hala Alhedeithy
Dr. Saad AlHowede
Ali AlHowedy
Hissa AlHuthelii
Areej Alizary
Marwan AlJehany

Najla AlKhateeb
Zaid Al-Khathlan
Sultan AlMadkhali
Al-Mansouria Foundation
Naeem Al Masu
Abdullah Al Miteb
Abdulsattar AlMousa
Mohamed Al Mubarak
Kumail Almusaly
Abdullah Al-Mutairi
Nawaf A. AlMutairi
Nermen Al Naimi
Mariam AlNoaimi
Arif Alnomay
Moath Alofi
Sara AlOmran
Jaffar Aloraibi
Saud AlQahtani
Shujoon AlQahtani
Abdullah AlQarni
Nada Al Qasabi
Aziz Alqatami
Faisal Al-Reethi
Mohammed AlResayes
AlRiwaq
Abdul Majeed Al Rodhan
Sultan AlSalloom
Latifah AlSalman
Noura Al Sayeh
Norah Alshalhoub
Abdulmohsen Alshayeb
Maha AlSheikh
Donia Alshetairy
Abdullah AlSobaihy
Alanood Ahmad Alsudairi
Sultan Al-Sudairi
Sultan Ahmad AlSudairi
Noura Alswailem
Muath Altamimi
Raghad Altamimi
Abdullah Al Yusi
Tariq AlZahir
Mohammad AlZahrani
Zena Amer
Ahmed Angawi
Dr. Sami Angawi
Rani Anggraeni
Applied Histories
Yasmin Atassi
Atharna
Aida Babazade

Vagif Baghir-Zada
Hussein Bajabir
Alvin Balilla
Safa Baluchi
Cécile Barrault
Mohammed Basaif
Bashaer, Nayra, captains Abdullah
    and Assam for great times at sea
Mohammad Bashraheli
Mirco Bimbi
Afia Bin Taleb
Darat Safeya Binzagr
Borotia Village
Janke Brands
Olga Bunkova
Umer Butt
Mariel Canote
Runa Carlsen
Gonzalo Carrasco
Haruka Cho
Panos Chountoulidis
Catherine David
Hiroko Davis
Carlos M. Duarte
Clara Dublanc
Bassel El-Husseini
Dania El-Saleh
Stefania Fabris
Reem Fadda
Sumayah Fallatah
Bana Fanous
Fatima Museum of Home
    Decoration and Women's Clothes
Alia Fattouh
Fellesverkstedet, Oslo
Skye Fisher
Issa Freij
Len Garces
Abdulnasser Gharem
Jeannette Gogol
Illeana Gonzalez Pacheco
Melissa Gronlund
Albrecht Gumlich
Luma Hamdan
Hafez Gallery
Qaswra Hafez
Mohammed Hafiz
Abdoulaye Haidara and the
    Senegalese Community
    Association, Riyadh
Issam Hasbini

Salah Hassan
Arnulf Hausleitner
Michelle Nicole Havlik
Charlotte Hermelink
Andrea Hofinger
Mohammad Sazzad Hossain
Roaa Hussein
Riyaz Jafferjee
Jennifer Jurgasch
Kaliganga Arts Institute,
  Bangladesh
Tamara Kalo
Ali Kalthami
Ahmed Karkanawi
Hala Bint Khalid
Samar Khamis
Ammar Khammash
Mona Khashoggi
Khemia'e Studio
Omar Kholeif
Ghada Khonji
Matthieu Kilapi Kasiama
Rasarose (Mai) Kitmungsa
Christina Köhler
Aleksander Komarov
Vito Su Komarov
Kwok Kian-Woon
Oh-Seok Kwon
Linn Lervik
Joseph Liow Chin Yong
Mahfuza Lookman
Polonca Lovšin
Marta Luciani
Wisam Maayah
Fahima Macan-Markar
Sue MacDiarmid
Magdalena Magiera
Studio Mahbub & Lipi
Radjab Mamedov
Mansoojat
Michael Marder
Renzo Martens
Ahmed Mater Studio
Valentina Mintah
Meta Moeng
Ali Moghawi
Sandra Montagner
Yasser Mosleh
Lisa Motz
Asma Mundrawala
Aya Nabih

Mohammad Nadeem
Nani
Tamila Nazirova
Nikolaus Oberhuber
Amarachi Okafor
Nikki Omes
Uchechukwu Onyishi
Mowahhad Othman
Paul Pacifico
Pecharkanda Village
Jack Persekian
Paola Matilde Pesaresi
Phi Studio
Pro QM, Berlin
Puthiajani Village
Fadel Raheem
Maryam Rahman
Asger Rasulov
Rauf Rasulov
Sulafa Rawas
Ibrahim Romman
Lisa Rosendahl
Fabio Rossi
Safat Studios
Leyli Salayeva
Mohammad Salim
Raghad Salman
Nadia Samdani
Rajeeb Samdani
Lada Sanatskaya
Stella Scherer
Simone Sentall
Hamza Serafi
Rotana Shakir
Maisa Shaldan
Abdullah Shalty
Shepherd Studio
Muhannad Shono
Muhammad Zainuddin Fajar Sidik
Nathalie Simoes
Veronika Smirnova
Suha Shoman
Gregor Stemmrich
Abeer Sultan
Marek Szponik
Ibrahim Taleh
Ced'art Tamasala
Vugar Taptygly
Rayhan Uddin
Archaraporn (Pam)
  Vachirasrisuntree

Klara Suša Vačovnik
Sumayya Vally
Bastian Van Manen
Siv Bugge Vatne
Vladimir Vavilov
Artur Weber
Timothy John White
Leah Whitman-Salkin
Katarzyna Wielga-Skolimowska
Ala Younnis
Firas Zaru
Ayman Zedani
Alina Zur

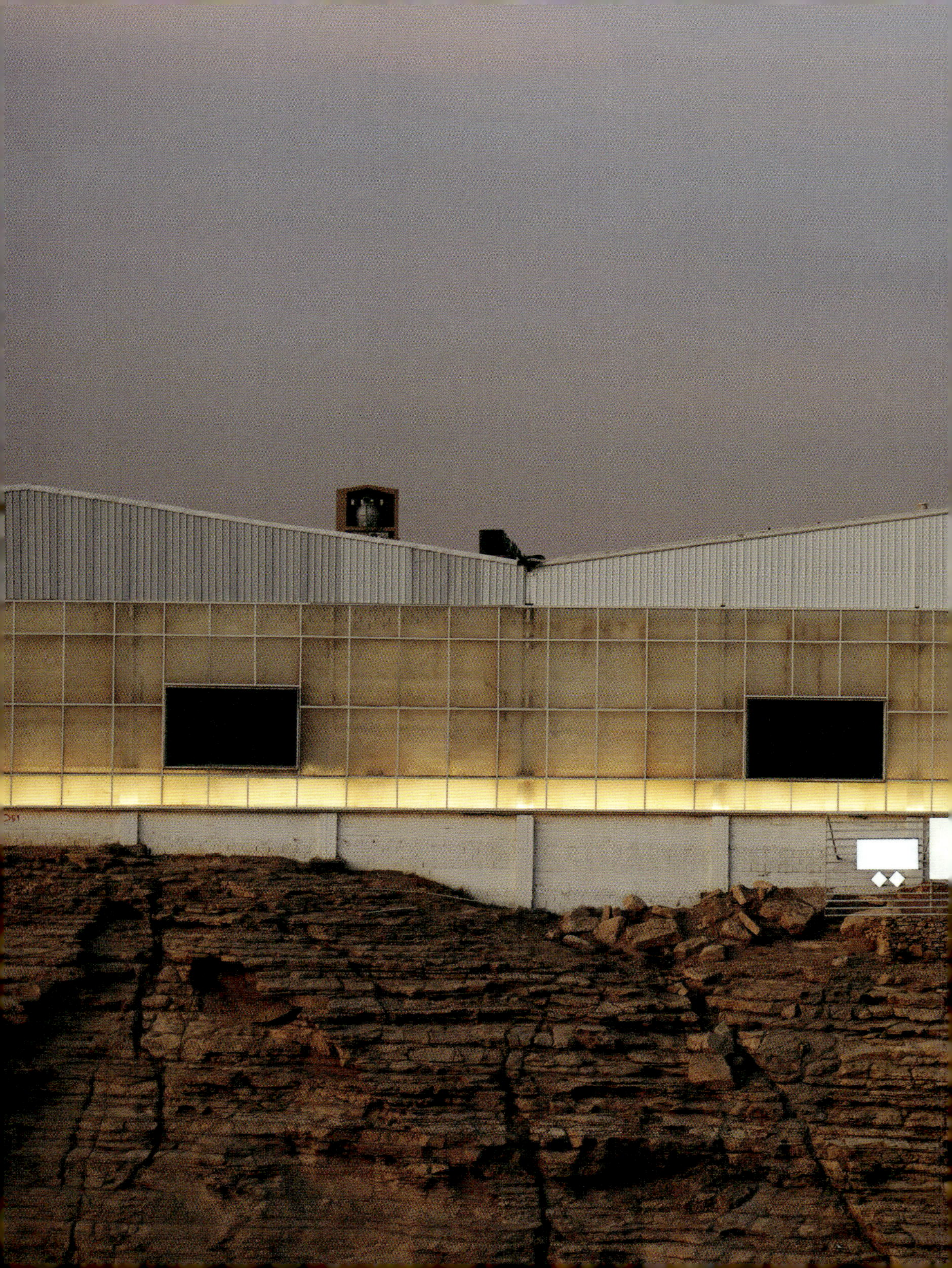

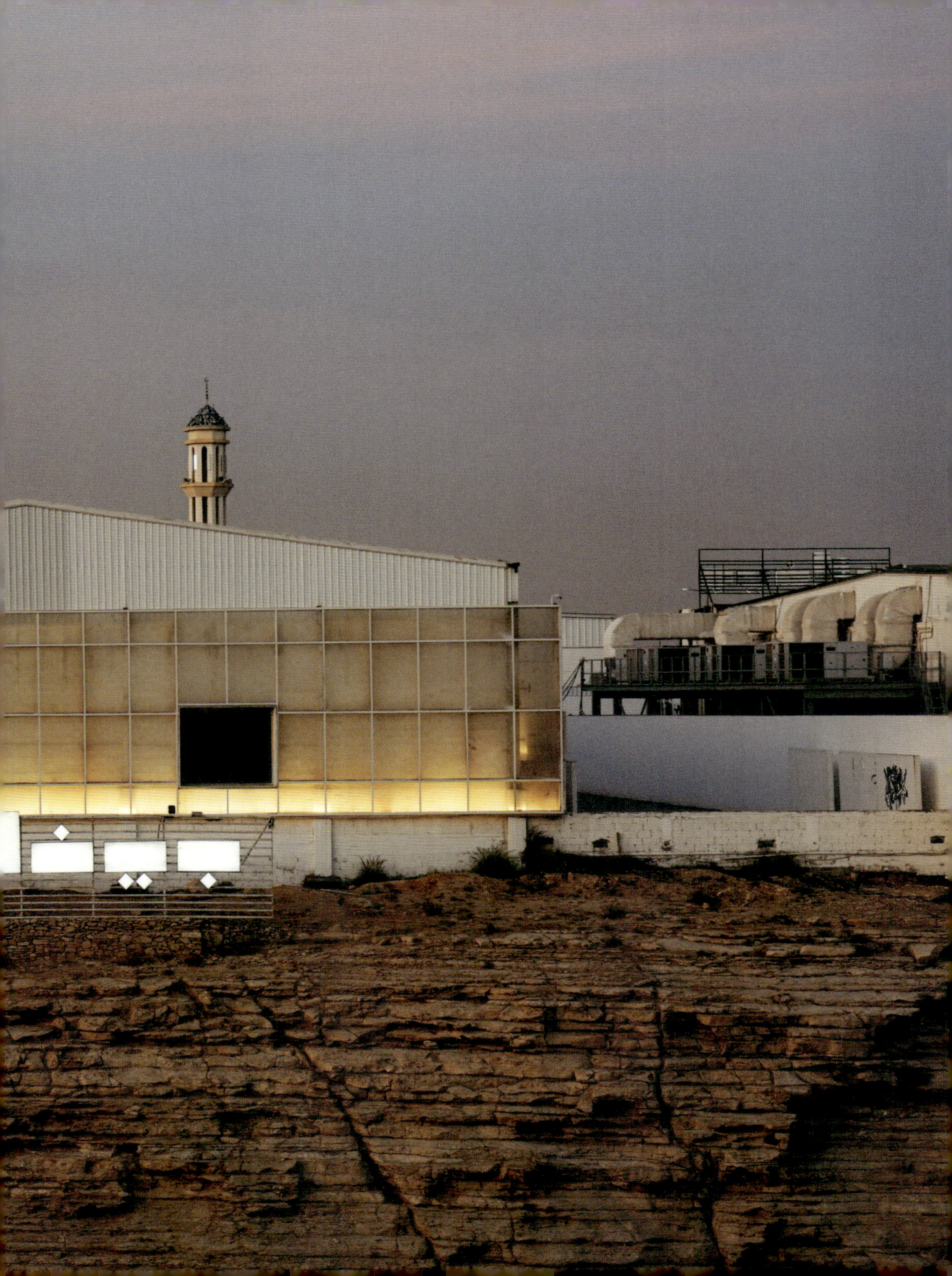

DIRIYAH CONTEMPORARY ART BIENNALE 2024 CURATORIAL TEAM

Ute Meta Bauer
Artistic Director

Ute Meta Bauer (born 1958 in Stuttgart, Germany) is an educator and curator in the field of contemporary art. Since 2013, she has been the Founding Director of NTU Centre for Contemporary Art Singapore and a Professor in the School of Art, Design, and Media at Nanyang Technological University. She currently co-chairs the Master of Arts in Museum Studies and Curatorial Practices and is the Principal Investigator for the three-year research project "Climate Crisis and Cultural Loss."

Bauer has held leadership positions in multiple cultural and academic institutions: as Artistic Director of Künstlerhaus Stuttgart e.V. (1990–94); Professor of Theory, Practice, and Communication of Contemporary Art and Vice Rector of International Affairs at the Academy of Fine Arts Vienna (1996–2006); and Founding Director of the Office for Contemporary Art Norway (2002–05). At the Massachusetts Institute of Technology (MIT), Bauer served as Director of the Visual Art Program (2005–09), as the Founding Director of MIT's program in Art, Culture, and Technology (ACT) (2009–12), and at the Royal College of Art London she was Dean of the School of Fine Art (2012–2013).

Bauer was a co-curator of Documenta11 (2002) on the team of artistic director Okwui Enwezor and served as artistic director for the 3rd Berlin Biennale for Contemporary Art (2004). Together with Paul C. Ha, Director of the MIT List Visual Arts Center, she co-curated the US Pavilion at the 56th Venice Biennale (2015), featuring video and performance pioneer Joan Jonas, for which they received honorary mention for best national pavilion. Most recently she curated the Singapore Pavilion at the 59th Venice Biennale (2022), presenting Shubigi Rao's *Pulp III: A Short Biography of the Banished Book*, and she was a curator of the 17th Istanbul Biennial alongside David Teh and Amar Kanwar (both in 2022).

Bauer has published and co-edited numerous publications in the field of contemporary art including: *The Impossibility of Mapping (Urban Asia)* (World Scientific, 2020); *Culture City. Culture Scape.* (NTU Centre for Contemporary Art Singapore and Mappletree Investments, 2021); *Climates. Habitats. Environments.* (MIT Press and NTU Centre for Contemporary Art Singapore, 2022); the monograph *Joan Jonas: Moving of the Land* (Walther König, 2022); *Pulp III: A Short Biography of the Banished Book* (National Arts Council Singapore, 2023); *Of Haunted Spaces: Cinema, Heterotopias, and China's Hyper-urbanization on the films of Ella Raidel* (NUS Press, 2023); and, co-edited with Dr. Karin Oen and Boon Hui Tan, *SEA: Contemporary Art in Southeast Asia* (Weiss Publications, 2022).

Rose Lejeune
Co-curator

Rose Lejeune (born 1980 in Cheltenham, United Kingdom) is an independent curator based in London. In 2019 she founded Performance Exchange, a United Kingdom–wide program that works with commercial galleries and has established a network of museums to present and acquire performance works. She is also Curator for the Delfina Foundation's Collecting as Practice, which engages with both historical museums and the future of collection development in a global context. Lejeune has worked internationally with organizations including Abu Dhabi Art, LOOP Barcelona, and OÖ Landes-Kultur Linz, and was Program Lead for the British Council's Art Criticism and Curatorial Skills Development program across the GCC. In the UK, Lejeune previously held curatorial positions at Serpentine Gallery and Art on the Underground, among others. Currently, she is finishing a PhD in curating at Goldsmiths College, University of London, focusing on the institutionalization and marketization of performance art.

Wejdan Reda
Co-curator

Wejdan Reda (born 1992 in Jeddah, Saudi Arabia) is the founder of Sahaba, a Saudi-based art consultancy and research hub working with artists, galleries, and public institutions. Co-curator of the 1st Diriyah Contemporary Art Biennale (2021), she also curated *Intimate Dimensions* (2020), a group exhibition exploring the notion of constructed spaces and built environments at Hafez Gallery, Jeddah. In 2020 she was a Curatorial Fellow at Art Jameel, researching public art projects commissioned in Jeddah in the 1970s. She was also co-curator of *Every Second in Between* (2018), a large-scale public art commission by artist

Kyung Hwa Shon in White City, London, United Kingdom. Initially studying architecture, Reda became interested in curating while pursuing her BA in contemporary media practices at Westminster University, London, after which she returned to Saudi Arabia and worked in the Athr Gallery, Jeddah (2015–16). Reda holds an MA in curating contemporary art from the Royal College of Art (2018).

Anca Rujoiu
Co-curator

Anca Rujoiu (born 1984 in Bucharest, Romania) is a curator and editor with more than fourteen years of experience working in contemporary art in Western and Eastern Europe as well as the Asia-Pacific region. She was recently appointed Curator of Exhibitions at Bildmuseet, Umeå University, Sweden (beginning March 2024). She was a member of the founding team of the NTU Centre for Contemporary Art Singapore (2013–18), first as Curator of Exhibitions and later as Head of Publications. In 2019 she was the co-curator of the third edition of the Art Encounters Biennial, Timișoara, Romania. As a member of the curatorial initiative FormContent (2011–13) in London, United Kingdom, she co-initiated the nomadic program *It's Moving from I to It*. More recent curatorial projects include the *Inventory of the Week* (2023), the National Center for Dance Bucharest, and *Solidarity Is a Verb* (2022), Akademie Schloss Solitude in Stuttgart, Germany. Rujoiu is a PhD candidate at Monash University, Melbourne, Australia; her research focuses on institution building, self-organization, and alternative ways of constructing and writing histories.

Ana Salazar Herrera
Co-curator

Ana Salazar Herrera (born 1990 in Paris, France) is an Ecuadorian and Portuguese curator and founder of the Museum for the Displaced (2019–ongoing, mfdisplaced.org). She explores nomadic, polylinguistic, and transcultural subjectivities, proposing inventive questionings of hegemonic geopolitical mappings. Ana was Interim Curator at the Ludwig Forum Aachen (2022–23), and Assistant Curator at NTU Centre for Contemporary Art Singapore (2016–20). She was part of the preselection committee for the 22nd Biennial Sesc_Videobrasil, São Paulo

(2023); Curator-in-residence at Künstlerhaus Schloss Balmoral, Germany (2021–22); a mentee of Project Anywhere (2020–21); and a Shanghai Curators Lab Fellow (2018). She has an MA in curatorial practice from the School of Visual Arts, New York, and a BA in piano from Escola Superior de Música de Lisboa, Portugal. Her writing has appeared in art magazines, exhibition catalogues, and academic journals.

Rahul Gudipudi
Adjunct Curator

Rahul Gudipudi (born 1987 in Jodhpur, India) is Senior Curator at the Center for Art, Research and Alliances (CARA) in New York, United States, where he oversees CARA's programs across exhibitions, publications, and fellowships. He was previously Exhibitions Curator and later Senior Curator at Art Jameel (2019–23), leading on exhibitions and discursive-performative programs at the Jameel Arts Centre in Dubai, United Arab Emirates, and at Hayy Jameel in Jeddah, Saudi Arabia. Previously, he was on the curatorial advisory and editorial boards for The New Alphabet School program (2019–22) at Haus der Kulturen der Welt (HKW) in Berlin, Germany. He is currently on the advisory board of The Story Of, a foundation and transdisciplinary learning platform in Goa, India. He is also a board member of the Anthropocene Commons (www.anthropocene-curriculum.org), a global research and response network organizing education and initiatives on climate change adaptation and collective action.

Amina Diab
Assistant Curator

Amina Diab (born 1990 in Cairo, Egypt) is an art historian and curator based between London and Cairo who specializes in modern and contemporary art of the Middle East. She was associate curator on the first edition of the Islamic Arts Biennale in Jeddah (2023) and worked on an ecolodge art residency project in AlUla. Diab has a master's from the University of Oxford and a PhD from the University of York, in partnership with Tate Modern. She is currently working on her manuscript entitled *A Transnational History of Modern Art in Egypt: Flâneuses et flâneurs des deux mondes*, which uncovers a lost history of Egyptian modernism.

Alanood A. Al-Sudairi
Curatorial Assistant

Alanood A. Al-Sudairi (born 1998 in Glendale, AZ, United States) studied psychology at the University of Arizona in Tucson. She then went on to work at the Women and Gender Resource Center in the same institution. In 2021 she returned to Saudi Arabia to support the international residency program Cortona On The Move run with the Royal Commission for AlUla. In 2022 she joined the Diriyah Biennale Foundation and has since worked on the curatorial teams of both the Islamic Arts Biennale and the Diriyah Contemporary Art Biennale.

Dian Arumningtyas
Curatorial Assistant

Dian Arumningtyas (born 1995 in Bandung, Indonesia) is a researcher and curator who works closely with topics related to cultural mobility, community involvement in artistic instruments, and textual reading through archives and library collections. Her long-term research project dissects how artist-in-residence programs become a cultural strategy driven by the governmental and funders' agendas to develop and revitalize communities. Arumningtyas is interested in the agency of local communities in actively shaping culture. She recently received the Prince Claus Seed Award (2023), and was a fellow of the Ishibashi Foundation/The Japan Foundation Fellowship for Research on Japanese Art (2020).